L.E.L.

L.E.L.

The Lost Life and Scandalous Death of
Letitia Elizabeth Landon
the Celebrated 'Female Byron'

LUCASTA MILLER

Jonathan Cape
London

1 3 5 7 9 10 8 6 4 2

Jonathan Cape, an imprint of Vintage,
20 Vauxhall Bridge Road,
London SW1V 2SA

Jonathan Cape is part of the Penguin Random House group of companies whose
addresses can be found at global.penguinrandomhouse.com.

Copyright © Lucasta Miller 2019

Lucasta Miller has asserted her right to be identified as the author of this Work
in accordance with the Copyright, Designs and Patents Act 1988

First published by Jonathan Cape in 2019

penguin.co.uk/vintage

A CIP catalogue record for this book is available from the British Library

ISBN 9780224079396

Printed and bound in Great Britain by Clays Ltd, Elcograf S.p.A.

For I, O, and O

Forget heroin. Just try giving up irony, the deep-down need to mean two things at once, to be in two places at once, not to be there for the catastrophe of a fixed meaning.

—EDWARD ST AUBYN

Contents

Preface

This book is about a poet who disappeared: about a woman who pursued her career in a blaze of publicity while leading a secret life that eventually destroyed her, and who left a such a legacy of lies and evasion that her true story can only now be told.

Letitia Elizabeth Landon, who published under her initials, L.E.L., was fêted as the female Byron during the 1820s. But after she was found dead in 1838, in West Africa of all places and in suspicious circumstances, the early Victorian publishing industry closed ranks to erase what they had come to see as her shameful history. Her literary reputation declined. She was left on the margins, surrounded by an aura of mystery and occlusion, her work routinely misunderstood.

Over the past couple of decades, she has finally begun to attract more interest. Her work has begun to appear in anthologies of nineteenth-century verse and to be analysed in scholarly articles. She has even begun to feature in a minor way on many university English literature sylla-buses. At the same time, biographical researchers outside the mainstream academy have been collecting increasing documentation. Yet these dis-parate and uncoordinated efforts have still left a haunting vacuum where 'Letitia Landon' ought to be.

The process of uncovering her has proved both troublesome and troubling. Unlike some 'marginal' figures, she was so famous in her lifetime that she is surrounded by a vast wealth of material, including numerous memoirs published by her contemporaries in the aftermath of her death. Such seemingly trustworthy sources, however, frequently turn out to be a tissue of equivocation, half-truths and downright deceit.

Even her own letters can on occasion be shown to tell lies. Often the only way to establish the forensic facts of her life is by recourse to public documents, such as censuses, parish records and wills, though those, too, sometimes contain demonstrable falsehoods.

Most challenging is the problem of interpreting her literary voice, whose unnerving qualities were, as this book will show, the direct result of the fact that it was impossible for her to speak openly. Obsessively circling around her absent 'I', her poetry gives away both more and less than it promises. To those who met her in the flesh she was a shape-shifter, who 'did in truth resemble the disputed colour of the chameleon, changing its hues with the changeful lights around'. Critics lent her others' names as if she had no identity of her own: she was the new Corinne or the English *improvisatrice,* the 'female Byron', or the 'Sappho of a polished age'. Even her friends did not know whether to refer to her as Miss Landon or by her nom de plume L.E.L., using both interchangeably.

What to call 'Landon, or L.E.L.—whate'er thy name', as one contemporary satirist put it, remains a problem. In this book, I have tried to use 'L.E.L.' when referring to her works and 'Letitia' when telling the story of her life. If I do not always stick to that rule, it is because she made the boundary between her different selves so tantalizingly ambiguous.

Prologue

Between eight and nine o'clock on the morning of Monday, October 15, 1838, the body of a thirty-six-year-old Englishwoman, wearing a lightweight dressing gown, was found on the floor of a room in Cape Coast Castle, West Africa. She was the new wife of the British governor, George Maclean, and had arrived there from England only eight weeks previously.

Cape Coast Castle was the largest trading fort on the western coast of Africa: a stark white complex bristling with cannon, perched on the edge of the Atlantic Ocean in what is now Ghana. During the eighteenth century, it had been the 'grand emporium' of the British slave trade. Countless captives had been held in its underground dungeons before being shipped to the Americas, while slave dealers did business in its precincts. Following the Abolition Act of 1807, the castle had remained under British command, its dungeons repurposed for housing local 'prisoners'.

A soldier in a sentry box stood at the entrance to the governor's quarters, which were decorated in the European style: prints on the walls, a shining mahogany dining table, impressive table silver. The room in which the body was found, painted a deep blue, featured a toilet table and the deceased's own portable desk, one of those small wooden boxes, typical of the period, that opened to form a sloping writing surface.

Deaths from disease among Europeans in what was then known as the 'white man's grave' were not uncommon. Indeed, the fatality rate was so great that the local Methodist missionary was having difficulty recruiting volunteers. But this death was different. In the woman's hand was a small empty bottle. Her eyes were open and abnormally dilated.

The last person to see the governor's wife alive was her maid, Emily Bailey, who had travelled out with her from England. She later testified that she had found Mrs Maclean 'well' when she went in to see her earlier that morning. On her return half an hour later, however, Emily Bailey had had difficulty opening the door. It had been blocked by her mistress's body.

Soon after Mrs Bailey raised the alarm, the castle surgeon arrived. He attempted to revive the patient, but in vain. Garbled news soon spread to the nearby hills. Brodie Cruickshank, a young Scottish merchants' agent, arrived at the fort within the hour, mistakenly supposing that it was the governor himself who had perished. In his memoir *Eighteen Years on the Gold Coast of Africa*, he later recalled his shock on entering the room where Mrs Maclean's body had been laid out on a bed. He had dined with the Macleans only the evening before, when she had appeared to be in 'perfect health'. The governor himself was in the room. He had slid down into a chair and was silently staring into space, his face 'crushed'.

Later that very day, an inquest was held at the castle, the jury hastily convened from among the local merchant community. No autopsy was performed, but the empty bottle was produced in evidence and its label carefully transcribed: 'Acid Hydrocianicum Delatum, Pharm. Lond. 1836, Medium Dose Five Minims, being about one-third the strength of that in former use, prepared by Scheele's proof.' The deceased was said to have been in the habit of using the contents, prussic acid in everyday parlance, for medicinal reasons, and to have taken too much by mistake. A verdict of accidental death was recorded.

After the inquest, the corpse was hastily interred under the parade ground. During the burial, a tropical shower burst from the sky in such torrents that a tarpaulin had to be erected over the gravediggers. By the time the final paving stone was replaced it had grown dark. The workmen finished the job by torchlight.

West Africa was so remote from England that it was not until the morning of January 1, 1839, that a discreet death notice appeared in *The Times:*

At Cape Coast Castle, Africa, on Monday, the 15th of October last, suddenly, Mrs. L.E. Maclean, wife of George Maclean Esq., Governor of Cape Coast Castle.

But after the evening *Courier* revealed the woman's maiden name later that day, the story became headline news. She was one of the most famous writers in England: Letitia Elizabeth Landon, better known by her initials, 'L.E.L.'

The Tangled Web

Although she remains little heard of today outside specialist circles, L.E.L. was a 'legendary figure' in her own time. According to a critic writing in 1841, her name was 'so identified with the literature of the day, that not to know anything of it is scarcely possible'. Elizabeth Barrett (who later added Browning to her name following her marriage) believed her unrivalled among women poets for her '*raw* bare powers'. In America, Edgar Allan Poe thought her 'genius' so self-evident that it was 'almost unnecessary to speak' of it. In Europe, she was admired by Goethe's family, Heinrich Heine, and the influential Parisian *Revue des deux mondes*. Closer to home, her poetry was devoured by the young Brontës in provincial Yorkshire.

L.E.L. was, however, the voice of a lost literary generation. Her career, which spanned the 1820s and 1830s, coincided exactly with the 'strange pause', as the historian G. M. Young called it, between the Romantics and the Victorians. Modern scholars are still unsure exactly what happened during this troublesome transition phase between the deaths of Keats, Shelley, and Byron and the rise of Dickens. Referred to as 'an embarrassment to the historian of English literature' and an 'indeterminate borderland', it resists periodization, and has never been dignified with a name. However, it should probably be called the 'post-Byronic' era, since the fallout from Byron's celebrity cult had such a profound impact on the writing of the day. Following his death in 1824, every hack wanted his—or her—own cult of personality. Yet the labile, often ironized voices writers created in response remain hard to interpret, their tone difficult for the modern reader to pin down. None is harder to read than that of the inscrutable L.E.L.

No one knew who she was when she first began to publish under her mysterious initials in the early 1820s. But in 1824 she emerged in public as the star author of a new best seller, *The Improvisatrice*. A skilful improviser of her own image, she soon became a celebrity, her portrait exhibited at the Royal Academy, her presence a fixture on the London social scene.

If she was the female Byron, 'female' was the operative word. She was the 'poetess' par excellence in a period in which, unusually in literary history, women dominated the genre. The eighteenth-century cult of sensibility, regarded by some modern cultural historians as the *fons et origo* of English Romanticism, had already produced some notable female poets, including Charlotte Smith and Mary Robinson, Letitia Landon's literary foremothers. Following the untimely deaths of Keats, Shelley and Byron, the 'poetess' became culturally supreme. Not just in England, but in France, Germany, Russia and America, a new generation of women Romantics staked their careers on the supposition that their gender made them more sensitive and intuitive than men, and thus more poetical.

All the poetesses made capital out of the emotions, but Landon's work struck its own peculiar chord. Her main English rival, Felicia Hemans, focused on the 'domestic affections' and the moral value of altruism and empathy. But Letitia Landon's favourite topic was thwarted romantic love. 'I have sung passionate songs of beating hearts,' she wrote, summing up her feminine sensibility in the slogan 'the fallen leaf, the faded flower, the broken heart, and the early grave'. In the view of Germaine Greer, writing in 1995, 'No female poet before L.E.L. had ever written of women's passion as she did. It was not like the love plaints of men, but the fierce, impotent, inward-turning tumult of a woman's heart, the agony of a creature unable to speak or act, forced to wreak her vengeance on herself.' The passion in the work was always unrequited, always doomed, and invariably expressed in the first person. Whether the 'I' of the poetry reflected Letitia Landon's own true feelings remains to this day the ultimate crux of her legacy.

Later nineteenth-century women poets, such as Emily Dickinson, Emily Brontë and Christina Rossetti, dressed like nuns and shunned society. But L.E.L. danced until the early hours and favoured risqué décolletages in pink satin, scarlet cashmere or black velvet. Contemporaries were startled by the contrast between the emotional extremism of her poetry and her society persona as a sardonic, glittering wit, a Dorothy Parker *avant la lettre*.

Behind the scenes she was an indefatigable worker, preternaturally productive in her bid to fill the public's emotional void with her literary lamentations. Her oeuvre is so vast that it is yet to be fully catalogued. By the time she died at thirty-six, she had published six stand-alone poetry collections, three novels and a book of short stories, plus at least ten further poetry collections in the then fashionable format of the 'annual'. That, however, made up only a portion of an output that also included reams of occasional verses, prose fictions and critical writings, plus an unknown number of unsigned reviews. A tragedy and a further novel were published posthumously.

No writer of Letitia Landon's generation achieved wider currency in terms of sheer word count or name recognition. Given her lifetime fame, her subsequent disappearance from standard literary histories, even if only as a name, remains a conundrum. But that is not the only puzzle surrounding her. From the moment her death was announced in early 1839, it was clouded by an aura of mystery and mistrust, which grew and mutated as the story spread.

Some early reports erroneously stated that she had died in Africa of a tropical disease, including the story that appeared on the front page of the Brontës' local paper, the *Leeds Mercury*, on January 5, 1839, under the capitalized banner 'DEATH OF LEL'. However, the provincial press was slow off the mark. News of the prussic acid bottle was already in circulation, thanks in the first instance to Cape Coast's resident minister, the Reverend Thomas Freeman, who had sent an on-the-spot account to the Methodist paper *The Watchman*. It was only because Freeman feared that news of yet another European casualty would put off potential missionaries that he wanted it on record that Letitia Landon's death was 'not occasioned by any sickness peculiar to this climate (her general health having been very good from the day she landed until yesterday morning, when she was found dead in her room, lying close to the door, having in her hand a bottle which had contained prussic acid, a portion of which she had taken, . . . the remainder being spilt on the floor).' In that parenthesis, the minister caused a sensation.

The verdict of accidental death failed to convince. On January 10, *The Times* put into print the obvious inference that had been doing the rounds for the best part of a week: that the 'poor lady' must have been so 'very wretched' that she had 'destroyed herself'. However, Letitia Landon's friends disagreed. They could, they said, find nothing in her cheerful and healthful letters home to indicate that she had been suicidal. Her correspondence from Africa showed her praising the delicious pineapples and making plans for future publications. The letter found on her writing desk on the very morning she died was upbeat in tone. 'I must say, in itself, the place is infinitely superior to all I ever dreamed of,' she told her correspondent, Marie Fagan. 'The castle is a fine building—the rooms excellent. I do not suffer from heat; insects there are few, or none; and I am in excellent health.'

Suspicions yet darker than suicide were already taking shape. As early as January 3, the *Morning Post* first floated the possibility that L.E.L. might have been murdered. Distrust was further aroused when her London doctor went into print to question how she could have had access to so dangerous a substance as prussic acid: there had been none in the travelling medical chest he had supplied. The hurried inquest and absence of an autopsy further aroused suspicion. Some surmised that Mrs Maclean had in fact been killed by some unnamed indigenous poison, in whose mysteries the natives were said to be adept.

Declaring it to be the duty of the press to penetrate into the 'remotest and darkest nooks of colonial dependency', the *Weekly True Sun* alleged that there was indeed a person at Cape Coast 'towards whom suspicion might naturally point': an African woman. It revealed 'that according to the rude, unchristian, and of course, not legal, customs of the country, the Governor of Cape Coast Castle had a half-caste domestic partner who shared his battlemented state'. While he was away in England, 'wooing and winning the English poetess', this shadowy woman had allegedly 'remained, unaware of his proceedings, in the Castle, awaiting his return'. In her veins ran the 'hot blood of Africa'.

Fuelled by the doctor's assertion that Landon had no prussic acid in her possession, rumours were soon rife that Maclean's jealous African consort had done away with her English rival. Cape Coast Castle took on gothic dimensions in the popular imagination. It was, according to the *Mirror of Literature* on January 26, a 'strange and dismal place', a 'dreary abode', a 'fatal spot'.

'All manner of outrageous reports were circulated and eagerly believed,' recalled Brodie Cruickshank. 'It was . . . told, from mouth to mouth, that there was a dark secluded portion of the castle, to which Mrs

THE CASTLE IN WHICH "L E L" DIED.

'Cape Coast Castle—that dreary abode, the strange and dismal place of sojourn, and the fatal spot wherein that gifted being, "L.E.L.," closed her valuable life': The *Mirror of Literature* reports on Letitia Landon's death in January 1839.

Maclean was never admitted; and the imagination was allowed to people this abode with shapes of infamy.' The purported scenario prefigured that of *Jane Eyre* (1847), with its madwoman in the attic, the Creole Bertha Mason, another hot-blooded first wife from the tropics.

Some asked whether Governor Maclean himself had connived with his African consort to do away with his new bride. Such were the suspicions of the dead woman's own brother, the Reverend Whittington

Landon, who wrote privately to the Colonial Office demanding a murder inquiry. It was never pursued. The reason given by officials in a tardy response was that the relevant documents had been lost.

On February 4, from his home in Chelsea, not far from where Letitia Landon had lived before her marriage, Thomas Carlyle passed on the latest gossip to his brother in Scotland:

> What newspapers do you see? Great talk has been here in certain circles about the death of L.E.L. by Prussic acid. It is generally suspected there was some foul play in it and not a mere mistake. At any rate, the poor creature is now heavy and asleep for ever[.] Her Pictures in the Printshops nor no gabble of tongues will now touch her any more.

His combined image of word-of-mouth whisperings and mass-produced prints perfectly summed up the texture of Letitia Landon's fame. Few poets have ever commented so acutely on their own dissemination. 'I lived / Only in others' breath,' wrote L.E.L. in the voice of one of her many fictional alter egos.

In the anarchic print culture of the 1820s and 1830s, information and misinformation mixed and separated as promiscuously as on the web today. Even before her death, rumour had replicated around L.E.L. like a virus. Before she married George Maclean, she had spent most of her career living in a rented room above a girls' school. But the respectability of her spinster lodgings had not prevented her romantic poetry from provoking a welter of salacious speculation about her private life. Aspersions were cast on her virtue, and several men were named as her supposed lovers.

Writing about passion in a female voice was a risky business for any nineteenth-century woman, as Charlotte Brontë later discovered when she published *Jane Eyre* and was suspected by the London literati of being the mistress of Thackeray, whom she had never met. In her late poem 'Gossipping' [*sic*], L.E.L. hit back at the rumourmongers:

> *These are the spiders of society;*
> *They weave their petty webs of lies and sneers,*
> *And lie themselves in ambush for the spoil.*

Her death gave the spiders something new to spin. As far away as India, tongues were gabbling. On June 15, 1839, more than five months after the story broke, Emily Eden, sister of the governor-general, wrote home from Simla, demanding an update. 'We have been a long time without letters, and nobody knows when we shall have any again,' she complained. 'There are several stories left *hanging* on something which ought to have been cleared up a long time ago, and never will be now—poor L.E.L.'s death! We have heard twice from you since the first account, and it never appeared whether Maclean was a "brute of a husband" or she, poor thing! very easily excited . . . we never could find the end of that story.' But the end of the story was a long way off.

Meanwhile, an official biography was commissioned from a journalist, Samuel Laman Blanchard, who had known Letitia Landon since the mid-1820s and was also a friend of the up-and-coming Charles Dickens. His aim, he said, was to 'elucidat[e] all that was mysterious in her fate'. When his *Life and Literary Remains of L.E.L.* was published in 1841, anyone looking for lurid sensation would have been disappointed, however. He dismissed the rumours about her love life as mere malicious gossip, and put her death down to prosaic natural causes, tentatively diagnosing a bursting ear abscess.

Some readers professed themselves satisfied. 'After fully examining the evidence relating to this tragedy, the author arrives at the conclusion that her death was natural and instigated neither by her own sorrows nor by the jealousy of others,' wrote Edgar Allan Poe in *Graham's Magazine*. However, few in London were so convinced. 'There is a mystery somewhere. Indeed, everywhere over the book we are perplexed in the extreme,' complained Elizabeth Barrett. Not only the story of Letitia Landon's death, but that of her life, seemed only half-told.

Soon afterward, L.E.L. suffered a second death: that of her reputation. In 1858, the printing plates for her one-time best seller, *The Improvisatrice*, were melted down. By the end of the nineteenth century her poems had ceased to appear even in anthologies. Yet she continued to lead a half-life on the sidelines of literary history as an unsolved case.

'Do you know the story of L.E.L.?—the poetess who committed suicide, as some say; but others feel sure was murdered?' wrote Virginia Woolf to Lytton Strachey in September 1927, keen to tell him that she had just commissioned a book on the subject for the Hogarth Press from their mutual friend Doris Enfield. When it came out in 1928, Enfield's

L.E.L.: A Mystery of the Thirties, did little to rehabilitate its subject's literary reputation. Looking down on Letitia Landon with Bloomsbury hauteur, Enfield saw her as a 'sexually ignorant' fantasist who had unwittingly opened herself up to lubricious gossip by publishing her naïve romantic effusions, and had gone on to commit suicide after marrying because the reality of sex failed to live up to her flowery imaginings.

Yet Enfield left so many ends untied that the case remained open. In the 1940s, one critic picked up on contemporary reports that Letitia Landon had suffered from unexplained blackouts, and concluded that she had died of epilepsy, not prussic acid. More recently, the heart condition Stokes-Adams syndrome has been proposed as the cause of the mysterious fainting fits and also of her death.

In the light of the contradictory and inconclusive evidence, it is hardly surprising that the current edition of the *Oxford Dictionary of National Biography* concludes, open-endedly, that Letitia Landon's death is unlikely ever to be satisfactorily explained. However, a more recently discovered aspect of her personal history—too new and untried to have made it into the latest *DNB* article of 2004—has the potential to illuminate the enigma of her life, her work and her death.

It first emerged on the fringes as long ago as 2000, when a man named Michael Gorman, of Antipodean heritage but then living in Japan, came forward claiming to be a direct descendant of Letitia Landon. On the face of it, that seemed unlikely. Her union with George Maclean had produced no children; she had died only four months after their wedding. The then critical consensus was that she had been a 'virgin' until her marriage: a woman who 'knew only that she had never yielded to another's passion' when she composed her poetry with its 'painfully vivid narcissistic fantasies'. Letitia Landon's contemporary memoirists, including her biographer Blanchard, had all united in asserting that 'slander more utterly groundless never was propagated'. Feminist critics of the 1990s as a result dismissed the gossip about her love life as a clear example of patriarchal prejudice: the smearing of a woman simply because she had dared to step outside her proper sphere by publishing at all.

However, Gorman's claim was confirmed after he was put in touch, via the internet, with an American researcher, Cynthia Lawford, who managed to find the baptismal records for two of the children, Ella and Laura; their brother Fred was not christened. Since then, a wealth of family correspondence has emerged confirming the three children's existence.

Lawford had hit on the first significant clue to unlocking what had been referred to as the so-called mystery of L.E.L. since at least the 1850s. But it left many questions unanswered, and its wider cultural and historical ramifications were not fully recognized. With its scene ranging from the publishing offices and salons of literary London to the murky world of corrupt business in West Africa, Letitia Landon's true story turns out to offer unique access into the 'strange pause' between the age of Byron and that of the Brontës, an era dominated by unregulated capitalism, rapid media expansion and commercial celebrity culture. Without L.E.L., we cannot fully map the contours of nineteenth-century literature. She is the missing link, one of those 'morbid symptoms' that, according to Antonio Gramsci, appear in moments of historical transition.

CHAPTER 2

The Three Magical Letters

Letitia Landon's story ends with the brute fact of a body against a door, but it does not begin with her physical birth. This is the biography not just of a woman but of an imaginary persona, an image, a poetic brand. It first came into being in late 1821, when fugitive poems signed with the enigmatic initials 'L.E.L.' began appearing in a magazine called the *Literary Gazette*.

A decade later, the novelist and future politician Edward Bulwer[*]—who had by then become a friend of the real-life Letitia Landon—recalled the excitement generated by the mystery poet among his fellow undergraduates at Cambridge:

> We were young and at college . . . and there was always in the reading room of the Union a rush every Saturday afternoon for the Literary Gazette; and an impatient anxiety to hasten at once to that corner of the sheet which contained the three magical letters 'L.E.L.' All of us praised the verse, and all of us guessed at the author.

The fact that the students only had to wait until 'Saturday' for the next poem was in itself a novelty. In a world of quarterlies, the *Gazette* was cutting edge: the first cultural periodical to come out weekly, speeding up the traditional publishing cycle. From the start, L.E.L.'s persona

---

* Edward Bulwer changed his surname to Bulwer-Lytton in 1844 following his mother's death.

was bound up with the means of its dissemination; the medium and the message were inextricably entwined.

Readers clutched at clues as to L.E.L.'s identity as, week by week, more poems appeared. Internal evidence suggested that she was young and female. The initials even sounded like the echo of a girl's name. Glimmerings of an absent woman's form shimmered through the disembodied page.

Three months on, the editor of the *Gazette* printed a tribute poem from an admirer, 'To L.E.L., on his or her Poetic Sketches in the Literary Gazette.' The author, Bernard Barton, was happy to sign his work, but declared himself content for L.E.L.'s identity, and even gender, to remain veiled:

> *I know not who, or what thou art;*
> *Nor do I seek to know thee,*
> *While thou, performing thus thy part,*
> *Such banquets canst bestow me.*
>
> *Then be, as long as thou shalt list,*
> *My viewless, nameless Melodist.*

However, the editor added a footnote that confirmed what many readers already hoped and suspected: that L.E.L. was 'a lady yet in her teens'. Interest surged in the Cambridge Union. As Bulwer recalled, 'We soon learned it was a female and our admiration was doubled, and our conjectures tripled.'

The fact that she was 'a female' cannot alone explain the excitement. Readers of 1822 were used to women poets. Spearheading the older generation was the dramatist Joanna Baillie, widely regarded as a modern Shakespeare. More recently, Felicia Hemans had made her name with *Poems of the Domestic Affections,* and with *The Sceptic,* which made the case for religious faith, attacking Byron's moral character en route.

However, L.E.L.'s poetry had such a 'stamp of originality' that 'it was impossible to trace in the character of her imagination and the peculiarities of her style, any resemblance to those qualities which had gained distinction for other gifted women,' according to her 1841 biographer Laman Blanchard. He neglected to explain exactly what made her work so different.

L.E.L.'s appeal to young male readers of 1822 would be inexplicable were one only to read her posthumous critics, who generally dismissed her as a saccharine lady sentimentalist. 'In all the work of L.E.L. there is no observation, no insight, no power of analysis; to the end her phantasies remain those of a schoolgirl,' wrote Doris Enfield witheringly in 1928. During the twentieth century, L.E.L. was relegated to a feminine backwater as a minor poetess who wrote bland verses about flowers and birds. She was certainly never mentioned in the company of red-blooded male Romantics such as Keats, Shelley and Byron. However, when she first began to publish in the early 1820s, contemporaries saw her as following directly in their footsteps. Rebel Shelley had fallen like a comet. Would L.E.L., one critic asked, be the 'moon of our darkness' in his wake?

L.E.L.'s twentieth-century critics were hampered by the fact that her early, most daring work was published in the ephemeral format of a magazine column and thus escaped their notice. In fact, her first fans regarded her as edgy, dangerous, and (if it is not anachronistic to use such a term) cool. Yet even from the start her rebel allure was not to be found on the surface. Her poetry worked via buried allusions, half-quotations and hinted insinuations. It took its meaning, sometimes ironically, from the contemporary web in which it was enmeshed, and from the implicit connections that her audience was silently invited to make.

Later critics looked for eternal verities in L.E.L.'s poetry. Finding it wanting, they dismissed it as superficial and naïve. The real Letitia Landon had no faith in eternal verities. Knowingly mired in her own moment, she was less a winsome sentimentalist than a proto-postmodern. As one of her most perceptive contemporary critics put it, her true subject was not romance but 'all is vanity': what happens in a world emptied of intrinsic value.

Absence was the heart of L.E.L.'s aesthetic. It is no coincidence that two of her favourite formats were the 'song' without music and the 'poetical illustration' of a painting that her readers could not see. L.E.L. made meaning radically unstable. Epistemologically she was a sceptic, who believed that 'no one sees things exactly as they are, but as varied and modified by their own method of viewing'. She vested her identity in the eye of the beholder, and yet constructed herself as a moving target. She was indeed moonlike, always waxing and waning.

Words were mere counters in her sophisticated linguistic game. 'All things are symbols,' she later wrote, questioning the existence of any accessible reality behind the web of language. The postmodern concept of intertextuality could have been invented for her. Her flowers and birds were never just flowers and birds. They always gestured towards something else.

In the early 1820s, that something else usually meant the unmentionable topics of sex and suicide. Letitia Landon's self-invention as L.E.L. can only be understood in its historical micro-context. The persona she created in 1821 was a product of the culture wars that were gripping the reading nation that year, as what we now call Romanticism came under increasing attack from the moral majority.

The first two decades of the nineteenth century—the lead-up to L.E.L.'s creation—had seen poetry enjoying a cultural capital not dissimilar to that of pop music in the 1960s. Dubbed 'metromania' by *Blackwood's Magazine,* the craze for metrical composition was seen at every level of creative endeavour, from advertisements for the face cream Gowland's Lotion ('Eruptive humours fly before its power, / Pimples and freckles die within the hour') to the abstruse abstractions of Shelley. As L.E.L., Letitia Landon would combine the wily marketing tactics of the former with the wayward genius of the latter.

The poetry boom achieved its first spike in 1810, when Walter Scott's verse romance, *The Lady of the Lake,* sold twenty-five thousand copies in the first eight months. Two years later, it reached new heights when Byron burst onto the scene with the first instalment of *Childe Harold's Pilgrimage.* It sold out in three days and went through five editions in 1812 alone. The success of Scott and Byron was rooted in their manipulation of new poetic methods, which engaged the emotional complicity of their audience, techniques L.E.L. would expand and refine.

By flooding the text with floating emotions and nonspecific subjectivity, Scott invited readers to project their own feelings onto his poetry, and to come away believing that he understood their own inner lives better than they did themselves. Byron took the method further by relocating the centre of interest in the poet himself, inventing a brooding hero who was generally supposed to be a self-portrait. Readers were no longer simply projecting their own emotional experiences onto the work. Each imagined that he—or more often she, as is attested by the many fan letters he received from women—could alone understand Byron. His work hinted darkly at nameless crimes that made the public imagination run riot.

As Byromania burgeoned, his private life became the stuff of theatre, with high society agog at his tempestuous amour with Lady Caroline Lamb, and then fascinated when he married the puritanical Annabella Milbanke. Such gossip fuelled the commercial poetry boom. In 1816, Byron's Irish friend Thomas Moore secured an exorbitant £3,000 for his orientalist fantasia *Lalla Rookh*. But that year, Byron's celebrity turned to notoriety when he split from his recently married wife and fled to the Continent, amid rumours he had committed incest with his half sister. In the wake of the scandal, a rift opened up between the mainstream and the counterculture.

Byron cemented his new outsider status by throwing in his lot with Percy Bysshe Shelley, then a little-known figure on the fringes. A champion of free love, atheism and revolution, the upper-class renegade Shelley had succeeded in shocking even the anarchist philosopher William Godwin, godfather of the 1790s radical movement. Having cultivated his support, not least by offering the cash-strapped guru helpful loans, Shelley horrified him by eloping with his fifteen-year-old daughter, Mary. Not to be outdone, Mary's stepsister Claire inveigled herself into Byron's bed.

Together, the rebel cohort sought a 'paradise of exiles', as Shelley called it, first in Switzerland, and then in Italy. Abroad, at bay, and out to shock, Byron grew ever more provocative with his sexual and political satire *Don Juan,* which was published in instalments. Its political liberalism and sexual libertarianism generated outrage back in England. Hostility increased towards 'the Godwinian colony, that play "the Bacchanal beside the Tuscan sea"'.

Anxiety that permissiveness would undermine the nation's stability had been brewing for a long time. In the wake of the French Revolution of 1789, many believed that unless the lid was kept on human passions, violence and anarchy would result. In 1802, the Society for the Suppression of Vice was set up in England to police public morals. Even Shakespeare came to seem in need of expurgation. Bowdler obliged in 1807.

British victory over the French at Waterloo was followed by an economic crisis that only intensified fears of insurrection at home. In the Peterloo Massacre of August 1819, the army was ordered to attack a crowd of democracy demonstrators. The climate of political repression was matched by increasing sexual squeamishness. By October 1819, even the exiled Byron was feeling constrained. 'I had such projects for the Don— but the *Cant* is so much stronger than *Cunt*—now a days,—that the benefit of experience in a man who had well weighed the worth of both monosyllables—must be lost to despairing posterity,' he complained.

'Cant', a term much bandied about during the 1820s, is a key concept for understanding Letitia Landon. It is etymologically derived from the Latin *cantare,* to sing, and one theory of its ancient origins points to lackadaisical monks going through the motions, chanting Latin services without understanding or caring what the words meant. In the nineteenth century it was usually used pejoratively to signify hypocrisy or affected moralism covering unpalatable truths. Yet 'cant' also had the sense, as in 'thieves' cant', of an underground jargon designed to exclude outsiders. The 'songs' L.E.L. sang—she rarely used the word 'poem'—played on the idea of secret messages that only the initiate could understand.

The six months leading up to L.E.L.'s first appearance in the *Literary Gazette* saw Byron and Shelley under increasing attack. In March 1821, the poet laureate Robert Southey, once a youthful revolutionary but now a conservative, struck out at their 'lascivious' works. He saw them as elevating a libertine lifestyle into a philosophy that struck at the heart of civil society and its building block, the family. In his view, they were 'men of diseased hearts and depraved imaginations, who, forming a system of opinions to suit their own unhappy course of conduct, have rebelled against the holiest ordinances of human society, and . . . labour to make others as miserable as themselves by infecting them with a moral virus that eats into the soul!' He called them 'the Satanic school'.

Southey intended the label as a throwaway insult. But it was adopted by youthful rebels as a badge of pride. 'Satanic mania' raged among 'young gentlemen without neckcloths', who swaggered around 'playing the Corsair and boasting that they were villains', their open-necked shirts a tribal statement of rebellion. It was among them that L.E.L. found her first fans.

The moral panic intensified in May 1821, with the appearance of a pirated edition of Shelley's poem *Queen Mab,* a mystical paean to free love, which eventually led to the imprisonment of its publisher after a successful prosecution by the Society for the Suppression of Vice. Then, in July, Shelley struck back with *Adonais,* an elegy for the 'Cockney' poet Keats, who had died in February in Rome. Shelley accused the

Percy Bysshe Shelley, painted by Amelia Curran
in 1819. The open-necked shirt was a symbol of
youthful rebellion.

conservative press of having hounded Keats to death by mocking his
sensual, pagan, antiestablishment poetry as vulgar and uneducated.

Editorially, the *Literary Gazette* paid lip service to the values of the
Society for the Suppression of Vice. Its review of *Queen Mab,* published
in May 1821, expressed 'sorrow, indignation and loathing' at the 'abominable and infamous contagion' being spread by Shelley, in whom 'one
of the darkest of fiends' had 'clothed himself in a human body'. Shelley
was, the paper could reveal, a 'debaucher' who had thrust 'an unfortunate wife and mother into ruin, prostitution, guilt and suicide'. This was
one of the first references in print to Shelley's first wife, Harriet, whom
he had left for Mary Godwin, and who had indeed gone on to drown
herself in 1816.

It was only as a warning, thundered the *Gazette,* that it felt duty-
bound to 'lay before our readers the examples of his poetry'. Such a
preamble allowed the editor to quote large chunks from the offending

THE LITERARY GAZETTE,

AND

Journal of Belles Lettres, Arts, Sciences, etc.

| No. 226. | SATURDAY, MAY 19, 1821. | PRICE 1s. |

REVIEW OF NEW BOOKS.

Queen Mab. By Percy Bysshe Shelley. London, 1821. 8vo. pp. 182.

The mixture of sorrow, indignation, and loathing, with which this volume has overwhelmed us, will, we fear, deprive us of the power of expressing our sentiments upon it, in the manner best suited to the subject itself, and to the effect which we wish our criticism to have upon society. Our desire is to do justice to the writer's genius, and upon his principles; not to deny his powers, while we deplore their perversion; and above all, when we lay before our readers the examples of his poetry, to warn them against the abominable and infamous contagion with which in the sequel he poisons these splendid effusions. We have doubted whether we ought to notice this book at all; and if our silence could have prevented its being disseminated, no allusion to it should ever have stained the *Literary Gazette*. But the activity of the vile portion of the press, is too great to permit this hope*, and on weighing every consideration presented to our minds, we have come to the conclusion to lay, as far as we are able, the bane and antidote before the public. *Queen Mab* has long been in limited private circulation, as a duodecimo; and the first two or three cantos, under the title of The Demon of the World, were reprinted at the end of a poem called Alastor; as was also the principal note against Christianity in a detached pamphlet. Though the hellish ingredients, therefore, are now for the first time brought together into one cauldron, they have, like those of the evil beings in Macbeth, previously disgusted the world in forms of separate obsceneness.

We have spoken of Shelley's genius, and it is undoubtedly of a high order; but when we look at the purposes to which it is directed, and contemplate the infernal character of all its effects, our souls revolt with tenfold horror at the energy it exhibits, and we feel as if one of the darkest of the fiends had been clothed with a human body, to enable him to gratify his enmity against the human race, and as if the supernatural atrocity of his hate were only heightened by his power to do injury. So strongly has this impression dwelt upon our minds, that we absolutely asked a friend who had seen this individual, to describe him to us—as if a cloven foot, or horn, or flames from the mouth, must have marked the external appearance

* As this is a book of so blasphemous a nature, as to have no claim to the protection of copyright; it may be published by Scoundrels at all prices, to destroy the moral feeling of every class of the community. In the present instance the author has not, we imagine, been consulted.

of so bitter an enemy to mankind. We were almost disappointed to learn that the author was only a tall, boyish looking man, with eyes of unearthly brightness, and a countenance of the wildest cast: that he strode about with a hurried and impatient gait, and that a perturbed spirit seemed to preside over all his movements. It is not then in his outward semblance but in his inner man, that the explicit demon is seen; and it is a frightful supposition, that his own life may have been a fearful commentary upon his principles †—principles, which in the balance of law and justice, happily deprived him of the superintendance of his infants, while they plunged an unfortunate wife and mother into ruin, prostitution, guilt, and suicide.

Such, alas! are the inevitable consequences of the fatal precepts enforced in this publication, which spares not one grace, one good, one ornament, nor one blessing, that can ameliorate our lot on earth; which wages exterminating war against all that can refine, delight or improve human kind; which ridicules every thing that can contribute to our happiness here, and boldly tries to crush every hope that could point to our happiness hereafter.

As we shall, however, have to say something of these matters in detail, we shall now turn to the review of *Queen Mab*.

The rythm is of that sort which Mr. Southey employed so forcibly in his Thalaba, and other poems; and it is no mean praise to observe, that in his use of it, Mr. Shelley is not inferior to his distinguished predecessor. The first Canto opens with great beauty, in the same way as Thalaba.

> How wonderful is Death,
> Death and his brother Sleep!
> One, pale as yonder waning moon
> With lips of lurid blue;
> The other, rosy as the morn
> When throned on ocean's wave
> It blushes o'er the world:
> Yet both so passing wonderful!

Hath then the gloomy Power
Whose reign is in the tainted sepulchres
Seized on her sinless soul?
Must then that peerless form
Which love and admiration cannot view
Without a beating heart, those azure veins

† We are aware, that ordinary criticism has little or nothing to do with the personal conduct of authors; but when the most horrible doctrines are promulgated with appalling force, it is the duty of every man to expose, in every way, the abominations to which they irresistibly drive their odious professors. We declare against receiving our social impulses from a destroyer of every social virtue; our moral creed, from an incestuous wretch; or our religion, from an atheist, who denied God, and reviled the purest institutes of human philosophy and divine ordination, did such a demon exist.

Which steal like streams along a field of snow,
That lovely outline, which is fair
As breathing marble, perish?
Must putrefaction's breath
Leave nothing of this heavenly sight
But loathsomeness and ruin?
Spare nothing but a gloomy theme,
On which the lightest heart might moralize?
Or is it only a sweet slumber
Stealing o'er sensation,
Which the breath of roseate morning
Chaseth into darkness?
Will Ianthe wake again,
And give that faithful bosom joy
Whose sleepless spirit waits to catch
Light, life, and rapture from her smile?
Her dewy eyes are closed,
And on their lids, whose texture fine
Scarce hides the dark blue orbs beneath;
The baby Sleep is pillowed:
Her golden tresses shade
The bosom's stainless pride,
Curling like tendrils of the parasite
Around a marble column.
Hark! whence that rushing sound?
'Tis like the wondrous strain
That round a lonely ruin swells,
Which, wandering on the echoing shore,
The enthusiast hears at evening;
'Tis softer than the west wind's sigh;
'Tis wilder than the unmeasured notes
Of that strange lyre whose strings
The genii of the breezes sweep:
Those lines of rainbow light
Are like the moon-beams when they fall
Through some cathedral window, but the teints
Are such as may not find
Comparison on earth.

Behold the chariot of the Fairy Queen!
Celestial coursers paw the unyielding air;
Their filmy pennons at her word they furl,
And stop obedient to the reins of light:
These the Queen of Spells drew in,
She spread a charm around the spot,
And leaning graceful from the ethereal car,
Long did she gaze, and silently,
Upon the slumbering maid.

Oh! not the visioned poet in his dreams,
When silvery clouds float through the wildered brain,
When every sigh, of lovely, wild, and grand,
Astonishes, enraptures, elevates,
When fancy, at a glance, combines
The wondrous and the beautiful,—
So bright, so fair, so wild a shape
Hath ever yet beheld,
As that which reined the coursers of the air,
And poured the magic of her gaze
Upon the maiden's sleep.

The broad and yellow moon
Shone dimly through her form—
That form of faultless symmetry;
The pearly and pellucid car
Moved not the moonlight's line:
'Twas not an earthly pageant:
Those who had looked upon the sight,
Passing all human glory,
Saw not the yellow moon,

text in a lead review spread over eleven columns—thus giving readers the forbidden content they craved.

The *Gazette*'s review of *Adonais,* published on December 8, continued in the same vein, although the lower-middle-class Keats was treated more patronizingly than the upper-class rebel Shelley. Keats was dismissed as a 'foolish young man' who had written some indecent verses in the hope of making some cash, and had caught cold and died because he refused to wear that 'anti-poetical . . . encumbrance', a neckcloth.

Some readers probably took the *Gazette*'s editorial cant at face value. But after L.E.L. began to appear in the autumn of 1821, others could see that its new poetess was furtively spreading the virus. In a discreet homage to Shelley's lament, and to Keats himself, she offered a 'Requiem' to an unnamed, outcast poet, whose 'daystar was even in dawning o'ercast'. On January 19, 1822, she again lamented the loss of her Keatsian 'bright star', quoting from his now famous sonnet. A week later, she continued the theme with a threnody for an unnamed poet driven to death by the 'cold mockery' of critics. It was written in a style so unmistakably Keatsian that aficionados could not have failed to recognize it as such:

John Keats on his deathbed, 1821, drawn in
Rome by his friend Joseph Severn. L.E.L.'s
poetry column surreptitiously channelled Keats's
influence, while the *Gazette*'s editorials outwardly
mocked him as a 'foolish young man'.

Sweet Poesy!
How witching is thy power upon the heart;
Enchantment that doth bind our senses up
In one unutterable influence.

By admitting that her own 'influences' could not outwardly be
'uttered', L.E.L.—whose initials had their own echo of 'hell'—was slyly
positioning herself as the first female poet of the Satanic school.

L.E.L. could mimic Keats's style, but she was, to use his phrase, a
'cameleon [*sic*] poet' whose 'poetical Character' had 'no character' and
'no self' and was 'every thing and nothing'. Her voice changed with the
wind like an Aeolian lyre, Shelley's image for the poet. Her first *Gazette*
contribution to hint that she was young and female was a series of 'Six
Songs' that offered such a baffling range of subject positions that readers
were left in a state of heightened uncertainty.

The opening lyric was written in the Byronic style. In it, the speaker
altruistically offered to share life's burdens with her beloved, but the final
lines were suspiciously open-ended:

I shall not shrink, or fear to share
The darkest fate if it be thine!

It was up to the reader to decide which sins L.E.L. was prepared to commit for love. Anything from adultery to a suicide pact was possible.

A further lyric was a love spell purportedly written in the voice of a
simple young girl innocently yearning for a romantic relationship, her
supposed sexual purity symbolized by a wreath of white roses:

Oh! come to my slumber
Sweet dreams of my love,
I have hung the charm'd wreath
My soft pillow above.

The roses are linked
In a chain pure and white;
And the rose-leaves are wet
With the dew drops of night.

Readers of Keats would, however, have recognized in the verses an allusion to his unabashedly sensual 'The Eve of St Agnes', which was regarded as 'unfit for ladies,' since the heroine's dreams become a reality when a flesh-and-blood lover enters her room and brings her to orgasm in her sleep.

L.E.L.'s next poem was provocatively titled 'Truth', as if inviting readers to search out its true meaning. It spoke a language of flowers and birds that only the wilfully blind could have failed to spot as sexual metaphors. L.E.L. imagined spending the night on a 'leafy couch' in an island paradise with a lover while the 'bulbul' sang their serenade.

The pastoral-erotic style was borrowed from the Italianate 'Della Cruscan' school of English poetry. Fingered by *Blackwood's Magazine* in 1821 as the common ancestor of Keats, Shelley and Byron, it had initially flourished in the 1790s in the hands of the scandalous actress/courtesan turned poet Mary Robinson, among others. Thomas Moore's early Della Cruscan collection, *The Poetical Works of the Late Thomas Little Esq.*, was considered so obscene by Coleridge that, he exclaimed, 'my heart sickens, at the very thought of seeing such books in the hands of a child of mine.'

Blackwood's called the original Della Cruscans merely 'foolish and profligate', but claimed, in a frenzy of manufactured outrage, that the new generation was offering 'fiend like insult to feeling moral ties and Christian principle' and courting 'reprobate popularity by raising the banner to all the vicious of the community'. L.E.L.'s Della Cruscan detour ended on a note of jeering bathos which suggested that she was already sexually jaded:

> *I thought thus of the flowers, the moon*
> *The faery isle for you and me;*
> *And then I thought how very soon*
> *How very tired we would be.*

Her last 'Song' in the series was a jangling joke about marrying for money:

> *He must be rich whom I could love,*
> *His fortune clear must be,*
> *Whether in land or in the funds,*
> *'Tis all the same to me.*

It could have been taken as safe comedy in the Jane Austen mould, a dig at husband-hunting girls. But with its near-blasphemous title, 'Matrimonial Creed', it was also a Shelleyan attack on the institution of marriage as legal prostitution.

Traditionally, L.E.L. has been ranked with Felicia Hemans as a sentimental proponent of emotional sincerity as a conventional moral force. However, her twisted early lyrics have much more in common with those written by her great German contemporary Heinrich Heine at the same date, described by a recent critic as a 'combination of willed *naïveté,* extravagant sentiment, and jeering irony' that 'suggest a persona in which the self has thinned out to a kind of linguistic diagram, a raggle-taggle bunch of clichés strung together by a self-consciousness that can neither accept nor exclude them.'

Heine, whom Letitia Landon later met in Paris, created his famously equivocal voice in response to the post-Napoleonic repression of the Metternich regime. He used poetic ambivalence, and the overt topic of romantic love, to register covert political resistance. The idea of the radical libertine, a commonplace of the eighteenth century, went underground after the end of the Napoleonic Wars. All over Europe, the 1820s and 1830s saw the avant-garde retreat from public life. Artists relocated their disappointed revolutionary instincts in the world of the private, rebel emotions, from Stendhal's cold, clinical analysis of love's psychopathology in *De l'amour,* to the virulent bittersweet of Schubert's *Winterreise,* to the ironies of Pushkin's *Eugene Onegin.*

L.E.L. shared her male contemporaries' refusenik embrace of the discourse of romantic love. But because of her gender, she was placed in a much more complex and compromised situation. The slipperiness of her poetic identity, in terms of style, voice and viewpoint, reflected an fundamental reality: that as a woman, her subjectivity and autonomy were under constant threat.

Although the British poetic counterculture was politically liberal, Byron and Shelley had cordoned off poetry as a male-only genre. The women they attracted were undoubtedly sexually daring. But if they published, they did so in the lesser medium of prose, as in Mary Shelley's *Frankenstein* (1818) and Caroline Lamb's kiss-and-tell attack on her former lover Byron, *Glenarvon* (1816). The Satanic poetess was a contradiction in terms.

L.E.L. attempted to square the circle by giving a voice—or indeed voices—to the Satanic muse. She soon buried the sardonic abrasions of 'Six Songs' and shifted grammatically from the first to the third person. Next up was a series of narrative 'poetic sketches', which showcased, but did not embody, a lineup of tragic, lovelorn heroines drowning in an operatic welter of conspicuously 'feminine' emotion: a 'Maniac' gurning like some-latter day Ophelia for her lost Keatsian 'bright star'; a Byronic corsair's discarded mistress, whose shade haunts a sexually symbolic cavern; a jilted princess who dons male attire to stalk her fickle lover, as Lady Caroline Lamb had done in real life after Byron forsook her.

L.E.L.'s heroines did not all 'die virgins', as was assumed in the 1990s. They were in fact typically portrayed bemoaning their 'sweet ruin' at the hands of some Satanic seducer, like the 'woman wailing for her demon lover' in Coleridge's 'Kubla Khan'. If Byron was commonly dubbed a fallen angel, L.E.L. embraced the proverbial figure of the 'fallen woman' as his doppelgänger and covert competitor.

In doing so, she identified herself with a specifically female tradition: that of the legendary Greek poetess Sappho, who was literally a fallen woman, as she was said to have thrown herself to her death from a cliff into the sea as a result of her unhappy love affair with the ferryman Phaon. (Although now associated with lesbian love, Sappho was then primarily regarded as an emblem of heterosexual passion.)

The scandalous actress Mary Robinson, who had died in 1800, had been called the 'English Sappho' after publishing her sonnet sequence *Sappho and Phaon* in 1796. L.E.L. was clearly suing for the title herself. But rather than focusing on Sappho's private love agonies, as would have been the convention, she portrayed the Greek poetess performing before a massed crowd in a stadium:

> *She leant upon her harp, and thousands looked*
> *On her in love and wonder—thousands knelt*
> *And worshipp'd in her presence—burning tears,*
> *And words that died in utterance, and a pause*
> *Of breathless agitated eagerness,*
> *First gave the full heart's homage: then came forth*
> *A shout that rose to heaven, and the hills.*

This unusual gesture was a subliminal invitation to readers to project the magic of fame onto the unseen L.E.L. herself. The syntactical ambiguity as to whose tears, whose shout we are witnessing—Sappho's or the crowd's—exposes her perception of literary identity not as a fixed entity but as a co-creation between the poet's imagination and the reader's fantasy.

L.E.L. often borrowed gothic motifs. In one grisly yet perfectly symmetrical lyric, slimy earthworms slither among discoloured bones. But her true debt to gothic was the way in which she transposed its techniques of reader manipulation to the new phenomenon of the weekly poetry column. Long before Dickens discovered the formula for serial fiction, she worked out how to keep her readers reading: by keeping them in a heightened state of permanent arousal like the 'bold lover' on Keats's Grecian urn, who can 'never, never . . . kiss,' though 'winning near the goal'. The desire to penetrate her subtexts became a metaphor for sex itself.

The ultimate question that reverberated around the Cambridge Union was more salacious than Bulwer let on in retrospect: Was the real woman behind the veil a virgin, or was she a devotee of Shelley's fatal free love cult? The issue became a topic of euphemistic dispute in the columns of the *Gazette* itself. The anonymous 'A.H.R.' asserted that she must be writing from sexual experience: 'Truly it has been thine to feel love's power on thee.' But another contributor, 'W.L.R.,' was convinced that she was still pure and unsullied: 'Long may the sorrows of thy song / Be in thy guileless heart unknown.'

Those who chose to read L.E.L. as an innocent sentimentalist included Bernard Barton, whose tribute poem prompted the editor to reveal to readers that she was a lady yet in her teens in 1822. In real life, Barton was a 'sober Quaker' who worked in a provincial bank. In a previous *Gazette* contribution he had championed Felicia Hemans for her Christian spirituality, attacking the male Satanics for failing to support 'religion's cause'. However, even Barton admitted that he was turning a blind eye on purpose: 'nor do I wish to know thee.'

Some readers no doubt genuinely believed that the lady yet in her teens was employing erotic literary conventions without understanding their import. The *Edinburgh Review* had, after all, decried Thomas Moore's Della Cruscan poetry as more dangerous than downright old-fashioned 'obscenity', because it did not 'excite the suspicion of the modest,' and therefore failed 'to become the object of precaution to those who watch over the morals of the young and inexperienced'. After her death, Letitia

Landon's memoirist Emma Roberts claimed, in a roundabout, delicate fashion, that the young poetess had been blind to the sexual implications of her own verse:

[T]he wonderful precocity of her intellect rendered it scarcely possible for those readers, beyond the then narrow circle of her acquaintance, to imagine that her poems were the production of a girl who had not yet left off her pinafores, and whose only notion of a lover was embodied in a knight wearing the brightest armour and the whitest of plumes.

However, the poetry L.E.L. published in the early 1820s reveals how knowingly she teased her audience. She presented a split perspective on her imagined self:

> *There were two Portraits: one was of a Girl*
> *Just blushing into woman; it was not*
> *A face of perfect beauty, but it had*
> *A most bewildering smile,—there was a glance*
> *Of such arch playfulness and innocence.*

The face in the second picture is 'wasted'. The girl has been 'wrecked by love's treachery'. Her 'young flower' has been 'crushed'. It was up to the reader to decide which image best suited the nameless melodist.

L.E.L.'s perspective segued between external and internal, but she was always most tantalizing when writing in the first person. Nearly forty of the poems she published in the *Gazette* begin with the word 'I'. She experimented with a new form, the dramatic monologue, usually assumed to have been developed later in the nineteenth century by Tennyson and Browning. With all narrative context removed, all that was left was a voice.

One was a study in erotic abjection that invited readers to eavesdrop on the inner turmoil of a nameless young woman in the grip of uncontrollable emotions: the 'throbs' of desire like some disease, the obsessive overinterpretation of the love object's 'looks and words', the endless feverish 'circling' of her thoughts. A variation on Faust's Gretchen, the speaker was a girl on a self-appointed trajectory towards seduction and a suicide's 'unhallow'd grave'.

'[C]oncealment preys on me,' she confesses. Yet the poem, contrari-
wise, bares all, forcing the reader into a voyeuristic position. Full of rep-
etitions and panting parentheses, the nearly sixty lines of blank verse flow
so unstoppably that they are barely verse at all:

> *I must turn from this idol: I am kneeling*
> *With vows and homage only made for heaven;*
> *I must turn from this idol. I have been*
> *Like to a child who plays with poisoned arrows,*
> *And then is wounded by them. I have yielded,*
> *Foolishly, fondly yielded, to the love*
> *Which is a curse and sickness to me now.*
> *I am as one who sleeps beneath the power*
> *Of some wild dream; hopes, fears, and burning throbs*
> *Of strange delight, dizzy anxieties,*
> *And looks and words dwelt upon overmuch,*
> *Fill up my feverish circle of existence.*

'I would bring order to my troubled thoughts; / Like autumn leaves
scattered by driving gales, / They wander round,' says the voice. But the
very point of the poem is its studied portrayal of uncontrol. Whoever
wrote it had as elastic a facility with blank verse as the great Regency
actor John Kemble, who was famous for being able to converse in iambic
pentameters as naturally as in ordinary speech.

L.E.L.'s best poems, however, were her achingly plangent first-person
love lyrics. They invited readers to suppose that the author was genuinely
experiencing her own tragic romance, in real time: that she had given her
heart—and by implication her virtue—to some mystery man, who failed
to return her feelings. A title such as 'Extracts from my pocket book'
suggested true-life, diaristic confession. Her pellucid love plaints were
mini-masterpieces of distilled emotional pain. But, like horoscopes, they
were open-ended enough to be applied to the private romantic travails of
any reader. Her 'I' was elastic, an empty space to be filled.

The following example, plucked at random, was published in the
Gazette on May 31, 1823:

> *Farewell, farewell! Then both are free,—*
> *At least we both renounce our chain;*

And love's most precious boon will be
Never to feel the like again.

There is no gift beneath the sky,
No fairy charm, no siren lure,
Would tempt me yet again to try
What love once taught me to endure.

Its burning hopes, its icy fears,
Its heartlessness, its sick despair;
The mingled pains of many years
Crowd into its one hour of care!

I blame you not,—you could not tell
That love to such a heart as mine
Was life or death, was heaven or hell;
How could you judge my heart by thine.

Each pulse throbs to recall again
What once it was my lot to feel;
I have flung off my weary chain,
The scar it left I may not heal.

Anyone who had ever experienced romantic disappointment could identify with the sentiments, while those who knew Byron's work were also invited to congratulate themselves on identifying an allusion to his lyric 'The chain I gave' from *The Corsair*. L.E.L., though, took the metaphor of love as a chain binding two people to a much more visceral level than he had: *her* chain had chafed in such a way as to create a bodily wound.

The plain monosyllables of the final line—'The scar it left I may not heal'—belied their seething suggestiveness, created with extraordinary economy of means. The scar would have been read by salacious contemporaries as a metaphor for loss of virginity, but that's only the start of the semantic slippage. She could have written, more straightforwardly, 'the scar it left may never heal,' but L.E.L. chooses a first-person pronoun and the transitive form of the verb 'to heal', making the 'may not' seem less a conditional than a prohibition. As a result, she subliminally conjures up the idea that the speaker is unable to stop herself from picking at her 'scar'. Compulsive self-harm shades into compulsive masturbation as she throbs to re-create, solo, what she once experienced with her lover.

Masochistic pain and narcissistic self-destruction were central to L.E.L.'s poetic self-image. She had long been as 'half in love with easeful Death' as Keats in his 'Ode to a Nightingale' of 1819. After Shelley drowned himself and his companions in 1822 off the coast of Italy, after recklessly refusing to trim the sails of his yacht in the face of a coming storm, Romanticism as we now call it was increasingly defined as a death cult.

By May 1823, L.E.L.'s wreath, which had hung so pure and white over the maiden's bed in her 'Song' of 1821, had become her funeral wreath, and at the same time her poet's laurel crown, a composite leitmotif fusing sex, fame and death:

> *Twine not those red roses for me,—*
> *Darker and sadder my wreath must be . . .*
> *The blighted leaf and the cankered stem*
> *Are what should form my diadem.*

She greeted the new year, 1824, in suicidal tones, as if aching to join Keats and Shelley: 'A deep, a lone, a silent grave / Is all I ask, dark Year, of thee.'

Yet far from planning her own death, the real Letitia Landon was aiming for greater literary success. So far, she had managed to establish herself as a minor cult figure via her *Gazette* column. But in the summer of 1824, at the age of nearly twenty-two, she burst onto the wider scene with her best-selling book *The Improvisatrice*. Following its publication, she revealed herself in society for the first time. Few concluded from the title the extent to which she was improvising her own identity.

Literary London queued up for a sighting of the new girl genius, including many who had never followed her column. Curious callers started arriving at her home in Sloane Street, where she was living with her grandmother. She was said to be an orphan.

The callers were bemused by what they found. There was seemingly nothing in common between the love plaints of 'L.E.L.' and the 'restless little girl, in a pink gingham frock' who met their eyes. When the novelist Anna Maria Hall turned up, she was astonished to find her 'frolicking from subject to subject with the playfulness of a spoiled child'. The tragic poetess

> had been making a cap for her grandmother, and would insist on the old lady's putting it on, that I might see 'how pretty it was'. To this, 'grandmamma' (Mrs Bishop) objected. She 'couldn't', and she 'wouldn't' try it on; how could Laetitia be so silly? And then the author . . . put the great be-flowered, be-ribboned thing on her own dainty little head with a grave look . . . and folding her pretty little hands over her pink frock made . . . a curtsey, skipping backwards into the bedroom.

Another visitor, Rosina Wheeler, who also called at 131 Sloane Street 'in hot haste', some time later, recalled finding the infant phenomenon somewhat more provocatively attired:

> I was surprised, and somewhat scandalised, when I first saw her; for though only 2 p.m., she had her neck and arms bare, a very short, but elaborately flounced white dress, and a flower in her hair.

Two sorts of females wore short, ankle-revealing skirts: schoolgirls and courtesans. Letitia Landon was as ambiguous in her person as in her poetry.

These two vignettes were written long after the event and were coloured by the writers' subsequent relations with Letitia Landon. While Anna Maria remained protective, Rosina turned against her. A comparatively confused on-the-spot testimony, written on August 24, 1824, is perhaps more instructive. It comes from a letter written by Mary Howitt, a young married Quakeress who later made her name as a children's author.

Mrs Howitt had not yet seen L.E.L. for herself. But she was so fascinated by the gossip she had heard that she could not resist passing it on. The new young poetess baffled and mesmerized onlookers as her fame spread like wildfire through the literary community. According to Mrs Howitt, Letitia Landon had caused a stir at a recent party that she had attended with her patron, William Jerdan, the editor of the *Literary Gazette*:

She is, I understand, rather short, but interesting-looking, a most thoughtless girl in company, doing strangely extravagant things; for instance making a wreath of flowers, then rushing with it into a grave and numerous party, and placing it on her patron's head. . . . However, she is but a girl of twenty, a genius, and she must be excused.

L.E.L.'s dumb show with the wreath was in reality more calculated than 'thoughtless'. At one level, it was a coded expression of her allegiance to the forbidden poetic counterculture: Keats and Leigh Hunt had similarly crowned one another with wreaths in 1817, as recorded in Keats's poems 'On Receiving a Laurel Crown from Leigh Hunt' and 'To the Ladies Who Saw Me Crown'd'. More daringly, it was also a public offer of sexual availability from the young poetess to her patron, William Jerdan, the editor of the *Gazette*, who was a married man twenty years her senior. Anyone conversant with her use of the floral wreath as a literary symbol could have known that.

Mary Howitt chose not to read the signs. She assumed that the infant phenomenon was the editor's ward. In fact the 'restless little girl' had been sleeping with him for some time. The previous year, she had given birth to his baby. She would go on to have two more children by him during the course of their long liaison.

CHAPTER 3

Keeping Up Appearances

Letitia Landon's affair with her Svengali is the key to understanding her life. The equivocal way in which she played on her backstage sexual 'secret' is also the key to understanding much of her poetry. Yet these crucial aspects of her career were so successfully buried after her death that posterity was left in the dark, unable to make sense of the clues she left.

By the time she died, the Regency culture of what was called *demi-connaissance,* or half-knowledge, through which high society tacitly condoned illicit sexual relationships, had hardened into the full-blown denial of Victorian bourgeois hypocrisy. Her contemporary memoirists did all they could to draw a veil over her shameful history.

Even her early life, before she became L.E.L., was sanitized in retrospect. As with almost every aspect of her existence, her childhood and family background can be reconstructed only by patchworking a range of sources. Her memoirists cannot be relied on straightforwardly, although they often let slip comments that only make sense in the light of recent revelations about her suppressed sexual history. Public records, bald and unemotive as they are, are telling. Widening the net to include contemporary commentary, not directly referencing Letitia Landon but tangentially connected to her or those who knew her, builds the jigsaw puzzle further.

In his 1841 *Life and Literary Remains of L.E.L.,* Laman Blanchard traced Letitia's family back four generations, and drew on her brother's vivid memories to create a heartwarming picture of a happy childhood in a well-to-do home. His comments have been taken at face value to date, but he in fact suppressed the more rackety elements of her Regency upbringing because they had so inexorably led to her dangerous life choices.

As Blanchard rehearsed in ponderous detail, Letitia was descended on her father's side from the landed gentry. She was also related to a plethora of respectable clergymen, including her great-grandfather, her grandfather, two of her uncles and her brother. The most successful was her illustrious paternal uncle Whittington Landon, who became dean of Exeter, provost of Worcester College, Oxford, and, for a time, vice chancellor of Oxford University. Another uncle, James, pursued a quieter career as a Yorkshire vicar.

By emphasizing these connections, Blanchard strove to make Letitia look beyond reproach, both socially and morally. The true situation was more ambiguous. Letitia's great-grandfather had only gone in the church as a desperate career move after his father, Sir William Landon, lost the Herefordshire family seat as a result of unwisely investing in the South Sea Bubble in the early eighteenth century. Despite their loss of property, the family retained control over the local living, so there was little choice for the next generation but to take Holy Orders if they were to maintain caste and garner a guaranteed middle-class income. Even Letitia's high-flying uncle Whittington was more worldly than godly. In 1829, he was attacked in the press for his lack of interest in the 'spiritual welfare' of his nominal flock in Bow parish, Devon, and for raking in £1,000 per annum for the rectorship, despite the fact that he never turned up and paid his deputy a pittance.

Letitia's father, John (c. 1756–1824), grew up in Herefordshire, the eldest son of a country clergyman. He must have been less academic than his brothers, as he was sent to sea, rather than university, in his youth. One of the voyages he made was to Africa, where his famous daughter later died. However, his naval career came to an end in 1794 when his sponsor, Admiral Bowyer, apparently a distant relative, retired after being wounded in a naval battle during the French revolutionary wars.

Only exceptional talent could trump family connections in the navy. John clearly did not have it. By then in his late thirties, he found himself out of a job. Luckily, his well-connected brother managed to find him a civilian position in London with an army agency, Adair and Co. The firm had offices just off fashionable Pall Mall, soon to be the site of the capital's first gas street lighting, installed in 1807, and its first department store, Harding and Howell, established in 1809.

Despite the misleading job title, army agents needed wheeler-dealer financial skills, not prowess on the battlefield. The agencies were quasi-banks, firms that managed military finances, which were at that time outsourced to the private sector. One of the agencies' functions was to negotiate the purchase of supplies on behalf of the War Office, which deposited funds with them for that purpose. They were also the middle-men responsible for brokering the sale of officers' commissions.

While the more traditional navy depended on quasi-feudal family connections, military rank depended on purchasing power. Socially somewhat anomalous, the agent's role suited a 'gentleman' without private means, since a patina of class was helpful for schmoozing privileged young bucks keen to buy their way into regiments. Jane Austen's brother Henry also became an army agent, after an early stint as a soldier, before going on, in his case, to run a civilian bank. Both he and John Landon eventually went bust following the financial crash of 1816. Letitia's father's ruin would be the making of L.E.L.

During the Napoleonic Wars, however, business was good for army agents. John was soon promoted to a partnership at Adair and Co., which was by then doing so well that it almost ran itself. Following his promotion, he felt financially confident enough to marry. The wedding took place at St Luke's, Chelsea, on June 15, 1797.

Although John was not a young bridegroom, neither was his new wife, Catherine Jane Bishop, in her first flush by the standards of Regency marriage market. At twenty-five, she had almost reached the age at which Jane Austen's Anne Elliot in *Persuasion* assumes she will never find a partner. How the couple met is nowhere divulged.

Letitia's biographer Blanchard remains tight-lipped about her mother. All he tells us is that she was of Welsh extraction, in contrast to the care he lavishes on her paternal heritage. Since the Landons' ancestral Herefordshire was on the Welsh border, some long-standing local connection may have played a role. More likely, the couple first hooked up in London, perhaps encountering one another at some ticketed event, the Regency equivalent of online dating. By the early Victorian age, the notion of paying to procure personal introductions had become infra dig, with *Punch* inveighing against the fictional 'Mr and Mrs Spangle Lacquer,' at whose house 'you will always be certain to meet . . . a great many persons . . . to whom you can assign no fixed position in society, having generally met them in places where distinction was acquired by paying for it.' The previous generation was less squeamish. In Austen's *Northanger Abbey,* Catherine Morland and Henry Tilney meet after buying tickets to the Assembly Rooms in Bath.

Memoirists less discreet than Blanchard hint that Catherine Jane Bishop's background was less comme il faut than John Landon's, which might explain why she had not previously succeeded in hooking a husband. In a novel based on Letitia's life, published by her friend Anna Maria Hall in the 1850s, Catherine is fictionalized as a woman who 'had been elevated by her marriage, and regarded those who knew her in her days of obscurity as if they were prepared to do her an injury'. Every fragment of independent evidence supports this.

Catherine was the daughter of a 'Mrs' Letitia Bishop, but no marriage certificate or Mr Bishop can be found. Evidently illegitimate, she remained so cagey about her origins that, as an impoverished old lady living in a rented room in Chelsea, she gave conflicting information about her place of birth in the 1841 and 1851 censuses. In the former, she took the path of least resistance, simply ticking the box for same as current parish. Her mask appears to slip in the second, in which she reveals that she had been born in France, though she was a British subject. Perhaps Letitia Bishop crossed the Channel back in the 1770s to give birth discreetly to Catherine out of wedlock.

These details matter, because Letitia Landon's poetic persona was based on the idea that social status, and identity itself, were fictional constructs. In L.E.L.'s universe, masquerade is the ultimate human condition, both life's greatest opportunity and its inevitable tragedy. The self beneath the mask, if it exists at all, is no more than an amorphous 'mass':

> *Oh, what am I, and what are they?*
> *Masquers but striving to deceive*
> *Themselves and others; and believe*
> *It is enough, if none should know*
> *The covered mass of care below.*

Public records point to the conclusion that Letitia's maternal grandmother was not from the same class as the educated Landons. Her will, made in 1829, is signed with an 'X'. Her mark bears no sign of shakiness to suggest that infirmity was the reason. Evidently, she never learned to write, although that did not necessarily mean she was unable to read.

Nevertheless, she had enough of a private income to enable her to live 'genteelly' in Sloane Street. She was clearly some sort of superannuated kept woman. William Jerdan later expressed a vague idea that Mrs Bishop herself was the natural daughter of a nobleman. He may have shifted the stain of illegitimacy back a generation to spare the feelings of Catherine, who was still alive when he published his autobiography.

Whoever Catherine's father was, he was wealthy enough to provide for his daughter. She brought to her marriage '£14,000, her horse and her groom'. While not plutocratic, that was a substantial sum, which would have yielded a comfortable upper-middle-class income of £700 a year, even without John's salary from the army agency. For comparison, Jane Austen's Mr Elton in *Emma* is proud to catch Augusta Hawkins, who has £10,000, while in *Pride and Prejudice* a Miss Grey with the same sum attracts the fortune-hunting Wickham. Emma Wodehouse and Georgiana Darcy are in a different league with £30,000 apiece.

Like their fictional counterparts in Anna Maria Hall's 1857 novel *A Woman's Story*, John Landon and Catherine Bishop appear to have contracted a 'late marriage of convenience'. She traded her fortune for his respectable name. Certainly, their union, which ultimately ended in separation, did not inspire Letitia with a sentimental view of matrimony. She later described it as 'a treaty in which every concession is duly weighed'.

Material comfort was not in question when John and Catherine moved into their first home, 25 Hans Place, in 1797. It was a new-built terraced house in a pleasant garden square in the then burgeoning London suburb known as Brompton. It was there, near the site of today's Harrod's, that Letitia, their first child, was born in 1802. She went on to spend almost her entire life in the same area, much of it in the same street.

Although L.E.L.'s poetry dealt in roses and lilies and songbirds, Letitia Landon was incorrigibly metropolitan. On a visit to the real countryside in 1826, the only emotion she confessed to feeling was aroused by the provincial shops, which made her 'sentimentally recal [*sic*] the glories of Bond-street'. In one of her funniest short stories, 'Grasmere Lake,' a Londoner relocates to the Wordsworth country in the hope of finding poetic inspiration, but becomes afflicted by ennui. In an effort to enliven things, he plots to persuade a few idealistic young poets to come and commit suicide in his front garden.

The fast-growing metropolis in which Letitia Landon made her career terrified the Scotsman Thomas Carlyle. He thought it was 'like the heart of all the universe; and the flood of human effort rolls out of it and into it with a violence that almost appals one's very sense. The people are situated here like plants in a hot house, to which the quiet influences of sky and earth are never in their unadulterated state admitted.' But Letitia, herself a hothouse plant, thrived on the city's febrile anonymity. London was, for her, 'my country, city of the soul'.

Brompton was a paradigm of the frenetic urbanization that changed the face of London during the late eighteenth and early nineteenth centuries. Residential terraces, built by speculators, sprang up among market gardens in what had previously been countryside. Hans Place itself was scarcely finished when the new Mr and Mrs Landon first moved in; they may have been the very first occupants of number 25.

The neighbourhood provided the perfect cover for anyone, such as Catherine, keen to disguise less than genteel origins. It was so recently developed that no one there had long-standing local roots. In 1807, Robert Southey complained that social and geographical mobility were making it so difficult to 'place' people that 'there never was an age or any country so favourable to the success of imposture, as this very age and this very England'.

Although it had a leafy *rus in urbe* feel, Regency Brompton was far from suburban in attitude. Aspirational middle-class residents—including Henry Austen, who moved between various different addresses in the neighbourhood, including 23 Hans Place—were attracted by its genteel comforts, but equally drawn to its edge of boho-bourgeois glamour. The area was popular with stage celebrities, such as the opera stars Mrs Billington and Angelica Catalani. The actress Mrs Jordan later set up house in Brompton after her long-standing and highly publicized affair with the future William IV broke down.

Letitia's maternal grandmother's one recorded social connection is intriguing. Mrs Bishop was an old friend of the fabled Shakespearean actress Sarah Siddons, whose daughter Sally, Catherine's contemporary, embroidered the first cap ever placed on baby Letitia's head. As Mrs Siddons and Mrs Bishop were both of Welsh extraction, their acquaintance might have gone back a long way. It is even possible that Letitia's maternal grandmother was a minor actress herself in her youth. A single 'Mrs Bishop' is recorded as having performed in London theatres in the 1770s, in bit parts and out of season—when Letitia's grandmother, who was eighty-two when she died in 1832, would have been in her twenties—though that may be a false lead.

Certainly, the performative poetic voice Letitia later created was rooted in a thespian sensibility. She regarded her public role as a writer as being similar to that of the actress. In later life, she confessed to the dramatist James Planché that she 'would give all the reputation I have gained, or am ever likely to gain, by writing books, for one great triumph on the stage; the spontaneous thunder of applause of a mixed multitude of utter strangers, uninfluenced by any feelings but those excited at the moment, is an acknowledgment surpassing, in my opinion, any other description of approbation'.

Actresses emerged in the late eighteenth century as the original modern celebrities, but their position in society remained doubtful long into the nineteenth. Letitia's grandmother's friend Mrs Siddons was worshipped as a great artist. Yet even she felt she had to be hyperprotective of her image as a virtuous woman, despite the fact that she was genuinely (if problematically) married, unlike many who adopted the title 'Mrs'.

In the late 1790s, Siddons made friends with the famous firebrand feminist writer Mary Wollstonecraft, but unceremoniously dropped her when it became public knowledge that the latter had given birth to a baby out of wedlock by the American adventurer Gilbert Imlay. Siddons had been more than happy to turn a blind eye to any irregularity as long as Wollstonecraft kept up appearances by calling herself 'Mrs Imlay'. It was only when Wollstonecraft married the radical philosopher William Godwin—thus making it plain that she had not been legally married before to the father of her child—that the actress rejected her.

Mrs. Siddons was fearful of contaminating her own reputation by being seen to consort with a known fallen woman. Whatever a woman did in private, her reputation was defined by her public sexual status and that of her associates. 'Love, love is all a woman's fame,' Letitia later wrote as L.E.L. Her doubling of the word 'love' encoded the contorted double standards of the culture in which she was raised. She grew up to test and shape them to the limit.

As a child, Letitia was raised in a comfortable, polite, bourgeois world recognizable from Jane Austen's fiction, complete with clergyman uncles, amateur theatricals and feminine accomplishments. Yet an undertow of insecurity pervaded her milieu from the start. Even the suburban square where she was born was less respectable than it appeared on the surface.

The history of Hans Place offers a microcosm of the tensions in Regency literary culture, which later fed into the voice of L.E.L. Genteel Jane Austen stayed there twice, in 1814 and 1815, after her banker brother Henry took up residence at number 23 following his wife's death. Yet in 1815 lodgings in Hans Place were also chosen by the rebel runaways Shelley and Mary Godwin as a suitably anonymous location for the birth of their first—illegitimate and short-lived—child. In 1816, it was also from Hans Place lodgings that Shelley's abandoned wife, Harriet, walked out to drown herself in the lake in Hyde Park, pregnant with another man's baby.

The Landons were no longer in Hans Place at the time Jane Austen and Shelley stayed there, but they retained deep local connections and were soon back in Brompton. The family undoubtedly had acquaintances in common with Henry Austen, and the teenage Letitia may have heard local gossip about rebel Shelley and his women.

As children, Letitia and her younger brother, Whittington, two years her junior, were well provided for. There was a 'magnificent rocking-horse' in their nursery. However, their socially ambitious mother appears to have been less interested in hands-on childcare than in gossiping with her friends about 'Mrs Siddons and the French fashions'. During the week, Letitia was often farmed out to her grandmother, Mrs Bishop, who lived in nearby Sloane Street.

On Sundays, the children were frequently left at home alone while their mother went out visiting. The servant who was supposed to mind them often went out for the day, locking them in. No older than five and seven at the time, they used, Letitia later recalled, 'to sit at the open parlour-window, to catch the smell of the one-o'clock dinners that went past from the bakehouse, well knowing that no dinner awaited us'. In her posthumously published novel *Lady Anna Granard, or keeping up appearances,* Letitia caricatured her mother as a monstrous social climber who abandons her daughters to go to a prestigious house party, and refuses to return even when one of the girls falls dangerously ill and the maid absconds with the silver.

Where John Landon was on Sundays is not recorded, but it is unlikely he was with his wife. Sometime in Letitia's childhood, he acquired a 'fancy farm' in Barnet just north of London, where he could play at being a landed squire. Its elegant and commodious former cowsheds and dairies survive today as the headquarters of Mill Hill Golf Club, paying testimony to its former glory as a luxury status symbol. Long after Marie Antoinette was guillotined, the English upper classes regarded dairy farming as an elite hobby. The exquisite dairy at Lord Mansfield's North London seat, Kenwood House, just a few miles from John Landon's farm, can still be visited to this day.

The farm provided John with a gentlemanly leisure activity. It also gave him an excuse to spend time away from home, which may have been a boon as the Landon marriage appears to have become troubled early on. In Anna Maria Hall's novelization, *A Woman's Story*, the parents quarrel constantly. Their daughter is used as a go-between, made to lie to her father on her mother's behalf about the latter's extravagant spending. In the light of L.E.L.'s subsequent canniness at playing off different factions among her readership and in the world of literary politics, that rings true.

In such an environment, Letitia grew up attention-starved and precociously driven. She learned to read early. Although it would have been the norm in middle-class households for her mother to teach her, she had to rely on a kindly neighbour, who scattered alphabet tiles on the floor and gave her a treat whenever she picked the right letter. Letitia never failed to 'display' her reward when she got home. She was less interested in the treats—which she instantly handed over to her little brother—than in impressing Catherine.

At the age of five, Letitia was sent to a fashionable girls' school. It was located seconds from the family home at 22 Hans Place. She later returned there in adulthood to lodge in the attic, a symptom of her life-long yearning for stability.

The school's prestigious alumnae included the aristocratic future Lady Caroline Lamb. In his early Victorian biography, Blanchard made it sound like a model of calm Victorian propriety, but Regency girls' schools had a reputation for being more permissive than prim, as seen in Edward Francis Burney's satirical cartoon (see plates). The atmosphere at 22 Hans Place was in reality febrile, with a high turnover of privileged

MISS LANDON'S RESIDENCE AT HANS PLACE.

Letitia's childhood school at 22 Hans Place, located only a few doors
down from her family's home at number 25. As an adult she returned
to Hans Place to live in an attic room above the school.

but insecure students. Lady Caroline stayed less than a year after being
sent there at ten in 1795 because her family could not control her, even
with laudanum, the Ritalin of the day.

The couple in charge were a French émigré, Dominique St Quentin,
who styled himself *comte,* and his English wife, Anne. They had previously run Jane Austen's old school at Reading, but had had to give it up
due to Monsieur's gaming debts. They had arrived at Hans Place with a
former pupil, Frances Arabella Rowden, in tow. She took on the bulk of
the teaching, while Madame St Quentin sat in the parlour in a stupor.

Frances Rowden proved an inspirational schoolmistress. A published
poet herself, she focused her curriculum on literature and drama. She
took pupils on theatre trips and organized them in amateur theatricals,
as 'stage-struck', to use a Regency coinage, as the characters in *Mansfield*

Park. Henry Austen, whose interest in amateur theatricals is often cited as a source for that novel, may thus have found something more in common with Frances, when he moved in next door in 1814, beyond her connection with his sister's old school.

Prior to her teaching Letitia, Miss Rowden's pupils had included the writer Mary Russell Mitford (1787–1855). According to the latter's letters, Miss Rowden was involved in an illicit *amitié* with her boss and quondam teacher Monsieur St Quentin. The ménage à trois went on for many years. After the St Quentins finally gave up the Hans Place establishment sometime after 1816, Miss Rowden followed them in hot pursuit to Paris. There among her pupils was the future actress Fanny Kemble, Mrs. Siddons's niece, who was amused to find a portrait of her uncle John Kemble in pride of place on the teacher's wall. Miss Rowden finally succeeded in marrying the *comte* after his wife died in the 1820s.

In his mealy-mouthed 1841 biography of L.E.L., Blanchard did not mention the St Quentins, only Miss Rowden, who, he erroneously stated, kept the school. However, he admitted in a footnote that Miss Rowden afterwards became Madame St Quentin, indicating that he knew of the scandal but chose not to publicize it. It was politic not to draw attention to the less than decorous aspects of Letitia's early education. Miss Rowden's affair paralleled that between Letitia and her *Literary Gazette* Svengali rather too closely.

Blanchard stated that Letitia was only taught by Miss Rowden between the ages of five and seven, when the Landons moved out of London for a time. However, Letitia's early published poetry shows Rowden's literary influence so plainly that it is likely they kept in touch. L.E.L.'s later 'amorous and botanical' mode was a more daring variant on Rowden's early work *A Poetical Introduction to the Study of Botany,* a sentimental verse treatise on flowers influenced by the works of Erasmus Darwin, which personified plants to describe natural reproduction.

In *The Pleasures of Friendship,* published in 1810, Miss Rowden went on to offer a coy hymn to a mystery beloved mentor, whom Mary Russell Mitford immediately identified as St Quentin. Rowden delicately distanced herself from the 'grosser' aspects of human intimacy in her preface, declaring, 'If the introduction of the passion of Love should be deemed incompatible with the chaster feelings of the mind, let it be understood that by love is only meant those delicate movements of the soul.' The critics were not so convinced. '[W]e do not agree with her in thinking that *Friendship* inspired the Maid of Corinth with the idea of tracing her lover's likeness on the wall,' went one arch review.

It is unlikely that Letitia between the ages of five and seven could have been consciously aware of the sexual tensions in the school. But even that experience could have habituated her to the idea that adult reality included a mysterious hinterland, a harbinger of her later poetic double dealings. Certainly the love triangle became her narrative trope of choice, and the erotic hint her stock-in-trade.

As a child, Letitia was twitchy, insecure, and determined to grasp attention at all costs. She hated to walk in line with the other girls on school outings. On one occasion she slipped away, ran off home, and burst into the nursery. Outraged to find her little brother sitting astride the rocking horse, she threw a tambourine at him with such force that he fell off and was hurt.

It is a testimony to her charisma that she not only made her mark as the school rebel but simultaneously became its prize pupil. When she left at seven, she was presented with the top award: a dress embroidered by Miss Rowden's own hand. It must have been some accolade, as Mary Russell Mitford recalled the teacher as a scatty seamstress who was always leaving her sewing things around. Blanchard recorded straight-faced that the dress was thenceforth known in the family as Letitia's 'robe of grace'. That pseudo-evangelical phrase was more likely a sarcastic Mary Craw-fordism of Mrs Landon's.

Letitia received her prize from the hands of none other than Lady Caroline Lamb, who returned to the school as a young married woman to present the awards. Although Lady Caroline was yet to disgrace herself with Byron, the irony was not lost retrospectively on Letitia's memoirist Katherine Thomson. 'How little could Lady Caroline have imagined that the future L.E.L.'s was among those smiling eager faces, or that in that very room was to be decided her tragical fate,' she opined darkly.

In 1809, the upwardly mobile Landons moved out of London to a more prestigious new house in Hertfordshire, Trevor Park, a minor Jacobean mansion with a grand oak staircase, set in substantial grounds, since demolished. It even had a romantic history that might have appealed to the already rebellious young Letitia: the Jacobean princess Arabella Stuart was briefly held captive there in the early seventeenth century after eloping without the king's consent.

At that time, it was fashionable for businessmen to relocate out of the city to bucolic residences within easy reach of their offices. The brewing magnate Walker Grey, for example, commissioned a grandiose neo-classical villa at Southgate from John Nash (now an upmarket mental hospital). From Trevor Park, John Landon could commute to his office in Pall Mall, and to his 'toy' farm, on horseback.

He may have been attempting to restore the fallen fortunes of the Landons, who had lost their country seat a century before in the South Sea Bubble. More likely, as William Jerdan later inferred, he was trying to keep up with his old boss at the army agency, Alexander Adair, by then retired. That rings true when one discovers that Adair already had a Jacobean mansion, Flixton Hall in Suffolk.

In the 1790s, utopian radicals wanted to believe that all men were equal on the inside. In the wake of the French Revolution, social mobility increased, but the outside turned out to be what mattered. Competitive conspicuous consumption proved to be more of a leveler than liberty, equality and fraternity. Social status became ever more tied to what you bought.

According to the arriviste dandy Beau Brummel, personal status depended on the right cravat, as long as it was correctly tied and bleached into perfect whiteness by a team of expensive laundresses. His own cravat gave him the confidence first to cultivate his 'fat friend' the prince regent and then to insult him. In 1824, William Thomson complained in his *An Inquiry into the Principles of the Distribution of Wealth Most Conducive to Human Happiness,* 'Who is not alarmed at the every day increasing tendency . . . to the ostentation of excessive wealth on the part of the few?' According to the more cynical commentator Edward Gibbon Wakefield, 'respectability has various meanings in England: with some it means to keep a carriage, with others a gig.' For Jane Austen's Mrs Elton in *Emma,* it meant a barouche-landau.

John Landon was entering a race that he could never win. Trevor Park was a mere manor house compared to Flixton. Surviving photographs of the latter, which was demolished in 1953, show that it was a massive Jacobean jewel. In Adair's day, it was a stately home filled with old masters, including a Rubens. In 1821, shortly after John Landon had been ruined, Flixton was featured in an envy-inducing book on the gentlemen's seats of England.

Alexander Adair's engraved portrait shows him lolling in a landscape with an entitled mien. Known for his extravagance, he was a very rich man, whose tax records reveal an income in 1800 alone of £14,000, as much as Catherine Landon's marriage portion. However, his main wealth did not come from the army agency, on which John Landon relied, but from ancestral estates in Ireland.

Despite the loosening of class boundaries, entrenched privilege still won out. Letitia grew up bitterly aware of the inequality of opportunity in her society. As she put it in 1837, the 'child of the rich'—a boy, obviously—is cosseted from birth, heir to educational advantage and crucial social networks as much as to inherited wealth:

> Eton or Westminster, Oxford or Cambridge, have garnered for his sake the wisdom of centuries; he is launched into public life, and there are friends and connexions on either hand, as stepping stones in his way. He arrives at old age: the arm chair is ready and the old port has been long in the cellars of his country-house to share its strength with its master.

John Landon did not retain his country house long enough for the port in his cellars to age. Indeed, he did not even own it. Trevor Park was leased. The portraits on the walls—Letitia never forgot one stately lady in a ruff—gave the impression of old money. But they were of someone else's ancestors. Nor could John afford to maintain the grand new property. Letitia later recalled Trevor Park as a 'large, old, and, somewhat dilapidated place' where 'only part of the grounds were kept up in their original high order'.

In 1836, two years before she died, Letitia recorded her memories of her childhood at Trevor Park in a fictionalized first-person sketch titled 'The History of a Child'. Her biographer Blanchard went on to dismiss it as pure invention, bearing as much relation to reality 'as phantasies do to facts'. However, Letitia herself privately told another friend at the time she wrote it that it was literally autobiographical, and it contains numerous corroborative details about Trevor Park.

If Blanchard was at pains to dismiss its real-life basis, it was because he was desperate to dispel the idea that there could have been any 'original melancholy' in Letitia's nature that might ultimately have led her to suicide. The little girl in the sketch is not just unhappy but plainly disturbed. Blanchard chose instead to rely on Letitia's brother Whittington's light-hearted recollections. Even those, however, reveal a dysfunctional childhood beneath the positive spin.

Letitia's relationship with her brother remained symbiotically close into adulthood, although he turned out a wastrel and a drain on her resources, despite attending Oxford and taking Holy Orders. Their interdependence was cemented in childhood through a bizarre system of vicarious discipline instituted at Trevor Park. When one sibling was naughty, the other was punished by being locked in a closet. The porous identity boundaries on which L.E.L.'s poetic persona later relied were rooted in childhood experience.

In the recollections he passed to Blanchard, Whittington professed to find the punishment system funny. But it seemed so cruel and unusual to the children's nursemaid at the time that she used to push sweets under the door to succour the sufferer within. When Letitia was incarcerated, she used to save the sweets to give to Whittington on her release. Perhaps she did not quite realize that she was thus inciting him to further acts of naughtiness and visits to the closet for herself. On the other hand, she might even have sought the closet as a welcome release from the tensions of daily life in the Landon family.

The confusing atmosphere at Trevor Park certainly led Letitia to retreat into escapism. She used to walk up and down in the garden talking to herself, holding out her 'measuring stick' (presumably a ruler) as a weapon or magic wand to ward off intruders. If anyone approached, she would tell them not to speak to her because she had such a delightful thought in her head.

Schooled in poetry by Miss Rowden, Letitia soon gave her metrical form to her imaginings. She used, she later recalled, to 'lie awake half the night, reciting my verses aloud', and was only too pleased if she could get her mother to listen to them. Her prize dress must have been awarded for recitation rather than writing, as her preternatural capacity to memorize verse was a response to a disability unusual in someone destined for a literary career. Although she was a precocious reader, she had extreme difficulty learning to write. However hard she tried, the letters came out looking like 'pothooks'.

She was probably left-handed and forced to write with her right hand. However, her dyspraxia was treated as naughtiness in the family, leading to frequent cupboard punishments for Whittington. Even in adulthood, her script never achieved the elegance admired in the nineteenth century. As a professional poet, Letitia always relied on an amanuensis to correct her manuscripts before they were sent to the printer, first her Svengali Jerdan, and later, after their relationship broke down, her brother.

As a result, L.E.L.'s literary imagination was essentially aural. She habitually composed verse by ear in the first instance, writing it down afterward. Her poetry often only comes to life when read out loud, her seemingly naïve sentimentalism exposing its bitter and cynical depths when voiced.

Like the sensualists Keats and later Swinburne, L.E.L. was often accused by her detractors of putting sound ahead of sense. Because she was female, her supposed errors of prosody were put down to ignorance. Yet there is rarely a moment in her poetry when the disjunction between metrical rhythm and meaning is random. In, for example, her early 'Song' about the girl who places a white rose wreath above her bed to conjure a vision of her lover, L.E.L. makes the metrical emphasis fall inappropriately on the insignificant particle 'for', rather than on 'him', the object of the girl's devotions:

> *Let sleep bring the image*
> *Of him far away—*
> *It is worth all the tears*
> *I shed for him by day.*

The point is to create a first-person speaker so narcissistically caught up in the incantatory rhythms of her own love spell that the identity of 'him' is incidental to the fantasy.

According to Whittington, little Letitia was helped in her handwriting endeavours by a shadowy old gentleman, but even he gave up in the end, dismissing her with a kiss and telling her that her 'dear little fingers' were too straight. Who he was, and what he was doing hanging around the household, is not explained. Perhaps Mrs Landon, who had married for prudence rather than passion, was one of those 'fine ladies' who 'were going to the devil now-a-days that way,' as Fanny Price's forthright father puts it in *Mansfield Park*.

Letitia's memoirist Katherine Thomson later attested to Catherine's warm nature and noted that one could tell from the expression in her eyes whence her daughter's talents came. Only in the light of our new

knowledge about Letitia's own sexual behaviour does the insinuating subtext come to life. After the move to Trevor Park, Catherine gave birth to
another baby, Elizabeth Jane. Letitia and Whittington never regarded this
new sister as any more than an irritation at best. The extremity of their
negative reaction goes so far beyond normal sibling jealousy as to make
one wonder whether they suspected that she was not John Landon's child.

An anonymous short story called 'The Boudoir', published in *The
Keepsake* for 1831, prefigures Henry James's *What Maisie Knew* in its picture of a puzzled, knowing little girl trying to make sense of the adult
world. Her naïve question 'what is a boudoir?' elicits embarrassed mum-
blings from her governess. It transpires that the boudoir is the room
in which her mother receives her lover, sometimes in the presence of
the child herself. Unsurprisingly, given its risqué content, the story is
unsigned, but it was probably written by Letitia, who contributed three
signed pieces to the same volume and admitted in 1837 that her 'contributions to various periodicals—whether tales, poetry, or criticism—
amount to far more than my published volumes.'

After the move to Trevor Park, Letitia, like the girl in the story, was
taught at home by a governess: her cousin Elizabeth Landon, who came
to live with the family. Aged around eighteen when she arrived, she must
have been a poor relation on John's side. However, she was comman-
deered into becoming Catherine's right-hand woman. Even after the
family broke up, the two ladies continued to live together, in reduced
circumstances, through the 1841 and 1851 censuses.

Catherine, who gloried in her trophy acquaintance with Mrs Siddons, created an atmosphere in which poetic feats were prized. Letitia
was sometimes ushered into the drawing room to recite for her parents,
and possibly their guests, who may on occasion have included Sarah Siddons herself. Even John, who was more interested in his farm, became
caught up in the family metromania. When Whittington asked him
for three shillings, he offered him half that amount, but only if the boy
would learn a long ballad by heart. Whittington refused, but Letitia
learned all thirty verses instead, recited them perfectly, and was rewarded
with a paternal kiss and the full three shillings. She immediately handed
the coins over to her brother and went on, with extraordinary patience,
to teach him the ballad line by line.

L.E.L.'s poetess heroines always have to pay for their superior talent
by abjection to the men they love. Yet Letitia also learned to use poetry

as a source of underhand power. She refused to play with Whittington unless he agreed to listen to her recite the battle scene from Scott's *The Lady of the Lake*. She knew the entire text by heart. It is six cantos long and came out when she was eight.

In other moods, she and Whittington were partners in crime, running wild in the grounds with their bows and arrows in war games of Spartans. She was the better shot. On one occasion they annoyed the gardener so much that he deposited them on the top of a high yew hedge from which they could not get down. Letitia suggested they should punish the unfortunate man by making him a *'public character'*. She was brought up to believe that social humiliation was the worst possible fate, but as L.E.L, she would transform herself into a scandalous 'public character' herself.

Part rebel tomboy, part feminine people-pleaser, Letitia was conflicted in her gender identification. She idolized her father, whom she rarely saw, waiting patiently at the gate for the sound of his horse's hooves when he was expected home, and listening rapt to his seafarer's tales. Her favourite books in childhood featured lone male adventurers: *Robinson Crusoe*, Captain Cook's *Voyages, The Travels of Sylvester Tramper Through the Interior of South Africa*. Increasingly isolated after Whittington was sent to boarding school at Merchant Taylors', she used to play out her lonely Crusoe fantasies on an island in the pond at the bottom of the garden, reached by a fallen tree, with the family dog as her Man Friday.

Yet her favourite book of all, a present from her father, featured a female protagonist whose very life depended on her storytelling prowess: *The Arabian Nights*. Its power over her was such that she could never forget the odour of its leather binding. As L.E.L., she would become the Scheherazade of her generation, destined to please the public while risking social death.

Things were different in the schoolroom. Although Catherine was not an involved mother, she expected results. Her fictional counterpart in *A Woman's Story* wants her daughter to excel 'just to outshine' other girls. She spends every penny she can on her education, instilling in her a 'panting for admiration' and a 'love of display,' reluctant to suppose that her own child should turn out to be anything but 'A STAR'. The fact, recorded by Blanchard, that Letitia was taught the piano by Miss Bisset confirms that in real life no expense was spared.

Catherine Bisset was a renowned virtuoso who made her London debut in 1811.

The Regency culture of feminine accomplishments could be ruthlessly competitive and demanding. 'Talk of education! What course of Eton and Oxford equals the mental fatigues of an accomplished young lady?' opines a character in Letitia's novel *Romance and Reality*. Although the underlying purpose was to make girls attractive in the marriage market, accomplishments became an end in themselves, a form of parental conspicuous consumption and a symbol of social aspiration.

Letitia was brought up during an era of academic hothousing, a joint result of Rousseau's theories, which stressed the innate ability of children, and a new emphasis on 'talent', fuelled by the relaxing of old hierarchies. Her near contemporary John Stuart Mill (born 1806) was taught Greek at the age of three. Dickens later struck out at the pressure put on children in *David Copperfield,* whose protagonist endures misery-filled maths lessons at the hands of Mr Murdstone.

The fact that girls were not being educated for jobs or university did not reduce the pressure on them. Although the female curriculum focused on displayable skills, girls were encouraged to be as aggressively driven as boys, but with the additional burden of having to appear modest and self-deprecating at the same time. The results could be damaging.

In 1829, Robert Southey expressed disquiet at female hothousing in an article on the American poet Lucretia Davidson, who died at sixteen from what would now be called anorexia. Letitia, who was later marketed as an 'infant genius', was educated to emulate female prodigies. As a teenager, she devoured the posthumous works of Elizabeth Smith, a literary and linguistic wunderkind who died young.

Letitia's governess piously told Blanchard that her pupil had always been a compliant marvel. However, Whittington's memories are somewhat different. He recalled that his sister used to fling her books around in a rage, and was then made to perform the ritual of kneeling to beg God for forgiveness. Humiliation later became a key ploy in L.E.L.'s poetic erotics, her portrayals of masochism sometimes startlingly literal. In *Romance and Reality,* a discarded mistress is shown kneeling in an act of self-flagellation, a flail in her hand, drops of blood on the floor.

Letitia looked back on the schoolroom as a place of pain and degradation. Punishments included boxes on the ears, bread and water, and the dunce's cap. The regime also featured 'stocks and dumbbells' and 'backboards and collars,' devices designed to perfect the Regency girl's body along with her mind. The lovely arms Jane Austen's Mary Crawford displays to Edmund Bertram in *Mansfield Park,* when she plays the harp in an effort to seduce him, were no doubt toned with dumbbells. Stocks were fitted on the hands to straighten them. Due to her dyspraxia, Letitia probably received, on a minor level, attentions comparable to the painful truss Byron was forced to wear in a vain attempt to cure his clubfoot.

As a result, Letitia became crippled with performance anxiety, even in tasks she should have found easy, such as memorizing the multiplication table. Despite her prodigious memory for verse, she often found herself so anxious that she was unable to repeat the schoolroom lesson that she had in fact learned by heart, leading to further punishments, which she had to bear alone after Whittington was sent to boarding school and the vicarious system collapsed.

Moreover, the emphasis on physical perfection added to her chronic self-consciousness. In her 'History of a Child' she recalls how mortified she was to overhear the servants describing her as plain when she was being dressed up for a children's party. Although she later invited readers to imagine L.E.L. as a classic beauty, the unvarnished reality was less rosy. She was short and dumpy, and her face failed to fit conventional standards. As her friend Anna Maria Hall put it, she was 'certainly not beautiful—perhaps she can scarcely be described as handsome . . . her features were not regular.'

An eyewitness anatomization of her looks in Blanchard's 1841 biography isolates some features for praise: her 'dark silken hair'; her long eyelashes that cast a shadow under her 'grey, well-formed and beautifully set' eyes; her eyebrows, 'perfect in arch and form'; and her ears, which were apparently 'of peculiar beauty'. Her small stature is depicted as 'sylph-like', but there is a hint of bathos in the statement that her figure 'would have been of perfect symmetry were it not that her shoulders were rather high', More worrying is the assertion that 'the underjaw projected a little beyond the upper.'

From this, one could conclude uncharitably that Letitia had a Neanderthal look: a low forehead, a protuberant jaw, and a squat neck. Some hint of those characteristics is found in certain of the extant portraits of her. One unflattering posthumous engraving, published by Colburn in

1839, gives her such a short neck as to render her dwarfish. Visual evidence from her many portraits—even allowing for idealization—suggests that her chin was marked, but not that she had a grotesque Habsburg jaw.

Nevertheless, it is clear that when she later conquered society, her attractiveness was a performance, an act of will. As Anna Maria Hall put it, it was her 'EXPRESSION' that seduced onlookers, her features constantly in motion. 'It was strange to watch . . . the many shades of varied feeling which passed across her countenance even in an hour,' says an anonymous source.

As a child, it was only when reciting verse, or retreating into lonely literary fantasy, that Letitia felt able to escape the humiliation of being herself.

In the Romantic period, artistic creativity was often believed to result from childhood trauma. In his *Confessions,* Rousseau traced the roots of his own genius to the sexually charged whippings he had received from a pretty child-minder in infancy. In a poem published in 1826, L.E.L. ascribed Byron's genius, in a similar vein, to some unmentionable early betrayal, which left him unable to form stable adult relationships but fed his poetic drive. She was probably alluding to gossip that he had been sexually and physically abused by his nurse May Gray, as was indeed the case.

In her 'History of a Child', Letitia portrayed her own Ur-betrayal as her abandonment by her nursemaid, presumably the kindly woman whom Whittington described pushing the sweets under the cupboard door. She described being so emotionally starved that she used to push her little brother off the nurse's knee, demanding that she love 'me, and only me'. The nurse promised she would stay with her for ever, but was secretly planning to leave the household to marry a sailor, as Letitia learned by eavesdropping on the servants. The discovery that she had been deceived made her feel 'worthless'. On the morning of the nurse's departure, she crept out of the house to intercept her in the drive, cling-ing, kicking and screaming.

With the coach waiting, the woman tried to soothe her by cajoling, but finally lost patience and shook her off as a 'tiresome' child. Letitia went cold. Politely wishing her former ally good morning, she ran off, threw herself down on the grass, and decided never to expose herself to the humiliations of intimacy again. This single incident cannot in reality have led to Letitia's loss of trust, but the nurse's betrayal provided a useful symbol in retrospect. As she put it, 'childhood . . . images forth our after life.'

Letitia came to realize that outward compliance was the only route to survival. At seventeen, after her first poetry had been accepted for publication, she wrote a thank-you letter to the governess who had hit and humiliated her. 'It has always been my most earnest wish to do something that might prove your time had not been altogether lost,' she wrote. 'To excel is to show my grateful affection to you.'

By adolescence, Letitia's literary tastes had moved on. No longer attracted to lone wolf Robinson Crusoe types, she turned to romantic fiction. Her governess later primly told Blanchard that she had forbade her charge to read novels on moral grounds. However, Letitia's own account of the books she enjoyed as a teenager shows that she lapped up the sensibility fiction of Charlotte Smith and Mary Robinson, and the gothic of Ann Radcliffe (though she thought the latter's heroines too pure). She read Jane Austen too, but found the novelist's worldview frustratingly polite and controlled, dismissing Mr Darcy as a wooden cutout. Only the melancholy of *Persuasion* appealed.

According to Whittington, the young Letitia also worked her way through Cooke's Library, a hundred-strong series of popular novels. The titles turn out to have included earthy eighteenth-century works by Fielding and Richardson, written before the age of Bowdler, as well as Hugh Kelly's soft-porn *Memoirs of a Magdalen* (1767), a *Fanny Hill* spin-off, republished by Cooke in 1795.

Girls' reading was a site of controversy in the Regency. The moralist Hannah More saw female addiction to romantic novels as equivalent to heavy drinking among young men. By exciting girls with imaginary vistas of forbidden passion, they paved the way for the 'surrender of virtue'. Letitia's own 'fall' when it came was in some respects a textbook example.

Letitia's literary preference was, however, for poetry, in which taste she had been schooled by Miss Rowden. 'Happily for her, the pure high toned works of Walter Scott were the reading of the day. Well does every parent judge who has them in his library,' wrote her memoirist Katherine Thomson at the height of the Victorian cult of domesticity in 1861, expressing relief that the young Letitia's reading had been 'free from the poisonous casuistry of Shelley' and 'devoid of the passionate gloom of Byron'. That beggars belief, given the numerous allusions to Shelley and Byron found in the poetry Letitia published before she was twenty. Although Letitia is unlikely to have read Shelley before she came into the orbit of the *Literary Gazette* in 1820, she could hardly have avoided the ubiquitous Byron, the superstar of her youth. Even after the separation scandal, his works were widely read by respectable young ladies. Letitia's contemporary Harriet Beecher Stowe, the daughter of a puritanical American pastor, read *The Corsair* with her aunt as a child. In Letitia's *Romance and Reality*, the heroine reads it with her governess. Charlotte Brontë later read *Don Juan* as an adolescent, although she advised her schoolfriend Ellen Nussey to avoid it.

Girls were fed a diet of double standards. In a letter of 1822, Letitia pointed out the odd juxtapositions that appeared in young ladies' albums, where racy passages from Moore or Byron rubbed shoulders with sententious extracts from sermons. The mixed message was endemic in the culture of her day. She went on to transform it into her poetic calling card.

In 1816, the year Letitia turned fourteen, her father's finances began to suffer as a result of the nationwide economic crisis that succeeded the Napoleonic Wars. Though not yet ruined, he was forced to give up his farm and Trevor Park, and moved his family back to London. Blanchard says that they lived briefly in Fulham, but within a year they were back in Brompton.

Their new home was not so grand as Trevor Park, but it was still more than a step up from the terrace where they had started out. A substantial detached house with a large garden and paddock, it was described by a contemporary estate agent as a '[r]emarkably neat and retired VILLA, most delightfully situated . . . modern brick-built House . . . 9 bed chambers, 2 dressing-rooms, a handsome drawing-room, breakfast and dining-room, kitchen, larders, store room, wash-house, and cellaring; double coach-house, six-stall stable, cow-house and piggeries, pleasure grounds, productive kitchen garden.'

Now that they were back within a stone's throw of her old school at 22 Hans Place, it is likely that Letitia returned to Miss Rowden for extra lessons, even if there was no more money for expensive outside tutors. Catherine was also concerned about the teenage Letitia's pudgy physique. In *Romance and Reality*, young ladies do 'calisthenic exercises'

MISS LANDON'S RESIDENCE AT OLD BROMPTON.

Brompton Villa was 'most delightfully situated,' according to a contemporary estate agent. William Jerdan's cottage backed onto the garden and he used to ogle the teenage Letitia from his window when she went out to exercise.

to improve their figures. Letitia was made to run around the garden bowling a hoop. She registered her resistance by holding a book in the other hand so she could read as she ran.

Adjacent to the garden of Brompton Villa was a narrow passage called Love Lane. On the other side was a row of smaller houses. In one of them, Rose Cottage, lived William Jerdan, the editor of the *Literary Gazette*, with his wife, Frances, and their young family. He took to watching the girl from his window as she ran around with her hoop and her book. As he later recalled, he was enthralled by the sight of her 'plump' body and 'exuberance of form'.

Exactly what happened in the Landon family between 1816 and 1820 is shadowy. Blanchard skates over their financial embarrassments as quickly as he can. Anna Maria Hall's novel *A Woman's Story* offers parallels, but the extent to which she fictionalizes is uncertain. In the novel, the father, a City banker, at first shores himself up with loans, while his wife receives visitors in yellow satin and jewels in a pathetic attempt to keep up appearances. They struggle on for another three years, but eventually face total ruin. The wife leaves the husband, disgusted at his failure and the loss of her own capital. He ends up in debtors' prison.

After 1816, John Landon perhaps attempted new business ventures, but may have simply eaten into Catherine's capital. His wife was certainly left with little money of her own. By 1820, he could hold out no longer. He left the family and ran off to evade his creditors. When he died in 1824, he was living in the parish of Yarpole, in the Landons' ancestral Herefordshire, where his high-achieving brother held the living in absentia.

Bankruptcy was common in the roller-coaster economy of the period. In Lady Blessington's 1823 short story 'The Auction', we are guided through the house of a once opulent bankrupt to inspect the books, paintings, musical instruments and furniture now on offer to the highest bidder. The narrator imagines the impact on the daughters of the house, 'delicate looking females driven from their home, stripped at once of all the elegancies of life, and sent to brave a world, the hardships of which they are now for the first time to learn'.

Whittington's education was safe, guaranteed by his Landon uncle, who soon received him into Worcester College, Oxford. But the marriage prospects for his sister had evaporated. It was with John Landon off the scene, and the prospect of eviction looming, that the first move was made towards attempting to establish Letitia in a literary career, probably engineered by her mother but put into motion by her governess.

Her poetic precocity had previously been viewed as an ornament. Now it offered some hope of remuneration. As Letitia herself later put it, the 'embarrassed state of my father's circumstances . . . led to a thousand projects for their amelioration—among others, literature seemed the resource.'

Despite the reputational risks of stepping into the public sphere, talented women from genteel backgrounds often did so when pressed by financial need. Letitia's former piano teacher Miss Bisset was the daughter of an intellectual clergyman, Edmund Burke's biographer. She turned professional, even appearing on the Paris stage, when the family hit hard times.* Mary Russell Mitford, similarly, became a professional writer when her father's gaming debts spiralled out of control. The poetess Felicia Hemans turned to her pen for her bread when her marriage broke down, leaving her with small children to support. Apart from governessing, regarded as a grim fate by Jane Fairfax in *Emma,* writing was almost the only possible employment option for an educated woman.

On February 13, 1820, the editor of the *Literary Gazette* received an unexpected note from Letitia's governess. Enclosing a poetry manuscript, it went as follows:

Miss Landon, though not having the pleasure of personally knowing Mr Jerdan, from the very great politeness the family have at all times received, ventures to intrude the enclosed lines. They are written by a young friend, for whom Miss Landon feels most anxious solicitude. If Mr Jerdan will, therefore, give his candid opinion whether he considers any taste or genius is expressed, or, on the contrary, if he should only call it a waste of time from which no benefit can arise. Miss L. feels the liberty she is taking; trusts Mr Jerdan will believe it is an obligation never to be forgotten.

* According to the *Oxford Dictionary of National Biography,* Catherine Bisset's father, Robert, kept an academy in Brompton's Sloane Street in the early 1800s, which is presumably how the Landons found her.

CHAPTER 4

The Songbird and the Trainer

William Jerdan is scantly mentioned by Letitia Landon's contemporary memoirists, but he was one of the most flamboyant and ubiquitous figures in the publishing industry of the first half of the nineteenth century. If he has been ignored by literary history until recently, it is because the Victorians brushed him under the carpet, owing to his reputation for dubious ethics and his scandalous affair with his protégée.

Carlyle called him the 'satyr-cannibal Literary Gazetteer,' and determined to keep as far away from him as possible. His shameless libertinism rendered him a joke figure in the eyes of Nathaniel Hawthorne, who found him 'drunken and rowdyish on the edge of the grave' in the 1850s. But Jerdan had appealing energy, as well as an enormous appetite for alcohol and a reputation for having 'seduced innumerable women'.

In his heyday, Jerdan's ebullient glee was infectious. According to one contemporary, many 'liked and regarded without respecting' him. More to the point, he oversaw the transformation of the *Literary Gazette* into a powerhouse whose reviews were capable of making or breaking a book. As S. C. Hall recalled in the 1870s, 'It would be difficult now to comprehend the immense power of *The Literary Gazette* for a period of time extending over the years between 1820 and 1840. A laudatory review there was almost sure to sell an edition of a book, and an author's praise was established when he had obtained the praise of that journal.'

Like the Landons, Jerdan was an incomer to Brompton, having been born in Kelso, Scotland, in 1782. His father, a small landowner, ensured that he received a good grammar school education, while he was 'pampered and petted' in childhood by his 'mammy' and his equally adoring aunt 'Mammy Nan'. Jerdan makes his own spoiled self-indulgence a running theme of his autobiography, a rambling four-volume affair published in the 1850s. He remained as forgiving of himself as his doting mother had been.

His chutzpah was apparent early. In his teens he made his way to London to pummel his way into the office of the prime minister's public secretary, where he presented a cipher of his own invention for use in secret government documents. He was turned away, but his confidence—some called it his 'indomitable effrontery'—remained undimmed. His interest in ciphers and secret messages would later resurface in the coded erotic poetry of L.E.L.

After an uncertain early start, including an abortive apprenticeship in an Edinburgh lawyer's office, he returned to London to make his living by his pen. One of his first jobs was on a magazine catering to the hotel industry, an indication of the new commercial opportunities opening up in journalism. Like many young writers—including, later, Dickens—he briefly served as a parliamentary reporter. He was present in the lobby of the House when the prime minister Spencer Perceval was assassinated in 1812. Jerdan himself wrested the gun from the assailant and did not stint in publicizing his own role. He briefly edited *The Sun* and secured the patronage of the powerful Tory politician George Canning, who went on to stand godfather to one of his sons.

Jerdan's big break came in 1817, when he took on the editorship of the *Literary Gazette,* which had recently been founded by Henry Colburn, one of the most ruthless businessmen in publishing. Along with another publisher, Thomas Longman, Jerdan also became a third shareholder. He would remain at the helm until the 1850s.

Colburn initially founded the *Gazette* because he realized that it was in the interests of a book publisher to own a magazine, since it could offer a source of endless free publicity in an era when reviews were conventionally unsigned. Having exploited the Byron moment by publishing *The Vampyre* by Byron's doctor, Polidori, without the author's consent, and Caroline Lamb's kiss-and-tell novel *Glenarvon,* he became known as the father of 'puffery', a concept that incorporated the modern 'hype' but was surrounded with a seamier penumbra of corruption and insider trading. By 1830, puffery's dark arts were so endemic and considered such a blight that Thomas Babbington Macaulay complained that 'no artifice by which notoriety can be obtained is thought too abject'.

Throughout his career, Jerdan was accused of being a 'puppet of certain booksellers' who 'dispensed praise or blame at their bidding, and, it may be feared, "for a consideration."' The book publishers to whom he was most frequently said to be in hock were his own fellow shareholders in the *Gazette,* especially Colburn. His undoubted literary enthusiasm was combined with a wheeler-dealer mentality, though, as we shall see, he was less competent in the latter than he believed himself to be.

A surviving early letter of his to the publisher William Blackwood, written in 1819, is indicative of his attitudes. Acting as agent for the poet 'Barry Cornwall' (Bryan Waller Proctor), he solicits a good review for Cornwall's new book in *Blackwood's Magazine,* offering to repay the favour, either in kind—that is, with positive coverage of Blackwood's books in the *Gazette*—or 'in any other . . . manner,' presumably cash payment:

A friend of mine in whose literary fame I take a sensible interest is about to publish a small volume under the assumed name of B. Cornwall. . . . [A]s I greatly admire my friend's poetical genius I trust my recommendation will awaken a kindred feeling in you, in which case you will favour him with an early and kindly Review. By doing so you will confer an obligation on me which I shall be happy to requite, in any other or the same manner.

Notably, Jerdan clothes his negotiations in the vocabulary of sensibility: 'friend . . . sensible . . . kindred feeling . . . kindly.' The emotionalism of L.E.L.'s poetry would also cloak its market function, which was to seduce readers and build the *Gazette*'s circulation.

From the start, the *Gazette* was conceived as a commercial enterprise. As the first cultural weekly in a world of quarterlies and monthlies, its unique selling point was that it was able to provide up-to-the minute coverage of the latest books, plays, and exhibitions. On the advice of his patron George Canning, Jerdan steered clear of political commentary. An apolitical press was in the interests of the ruling elite at a time of instability, but it also made publishing sense. The revolutionary 1790s had seen a boom in radical pamphleteering, but by 1817, the war-weary public was looking for entertainment. The expanding middle class was, moreover, increasingly defining itself through cultural aspiration.

In the early days, the *Gazette*'s target demographic was the youth market, as is shown by the inclusion of university news in its pages, an

intuitively canny move on Jerdan's part at a time when the nation's average age was falling, due to the population boom that caused Malthus
such anxiety. In addition to privileged undergraduates, the *Gazette*'s
young target audience included 'sallow clerks' too poor for university,
who were equally caught up in the Byronic moment; 'even our footmen
compose tragedies,' complained *Blackwood's*. A surviving unpublished
letter to Jerdan from one such anonymous reader asks for guidance on
library provision in London on behalf of young men who had 'betaken
themselves to literature'.

In the age of 'metromania', many readers had a special investment
in a literary magazine because they saw themselves as potential poets. In
contrast to the Olympian pose of the *Quarterly Review*, Jerdan strove to
build a close rapport with his audience. His innovations included a readers' column and a 'By Correspondents' poetry section for amateurs. It
was there that Letitia's first poem appeared in print, on March 11, 1820,
signed with the single initial 'L'.

The creation of 'L.E.L.' was still some eighteen months away, but
Jerdan's interest had been piqued as soon as he received the manuscript
from her governess. He later affected to believe that the governess herself
was the true author, prompting Letitia to perform more and more poetic
feats to prove her worth. In reality, he must have instantly suspected that
the 'young friend' responsible was the plump pubescent he had secretly
ogled from his window. Mrs Landon had previously told him in passing
that her daughter was 'addicted' to writing poetry.

Nevertheless, the poem submitted by the governess jarred with Jerdan's preconceptions. It seemed to him too sophisticated to be the work
of a young girl who had on occasion played with his own children in the
lane between their houses. Grandly titled 'Rome', it showed off a knowledge of classical history. Written in heavy anapests, to sound like the beat
of a funeral drum, it began:

> *Oh! how thou art changed, thou proud daughter of fame,*
> *Since that hour of ripe glory when empire was thine,*
> *When earth's purple rulers, kings, quailed at thy name,*
> *And thy Capitol worshipped as Liberty's shrine.*

But it was not the second-hand classical learning, nor the distinctive meter (in fact derived from Byron's *Hebrew Melodies*), that made

Jerdan sit up. It was the poem's incendiary political message. To submit a threnody for republican liberty, some mere six months after the Peterloo Massacre, was a daring choice for a genteel young lady about whom the editor so far knew little save that she lived in a mansion far superior to his own cottage. Perhaps he already hoped that a girl so keen on political freedom would be equally open to the idea of free love—which would explain why he published 'Rome', despite Canning's strictures.

The revolutionary despair encoded in 'Rome' is indeed surprising. The Landons were so unimpeachably 'Church and King' that the epitaph on Letitia's great-grandfather's grave lauded his determination to support the establishment by routing dissenters. However, the upwardly mobile Catherine was said to have loved the republican French nation even during the Napoleonic Wars, perhaps inspired by Napoleon himself, the ultimate parvenu, as well as by her own French heritage. Liberalism had been so fashionable in the 1790s that even the heir to the throne had been painted by George Stubbs in relaxed anti-aristocratic attire. After Waterloo, English liberals continued to register dissent through republican symbols. Hazlitt had a statuette of Napoleon; Keats had a Napoleon snuffbox.

Competing discourses of liberty mixed and separated. Rather as the idea of sexual liberation in the 1960s was seen by some to mean *Playboy* and by others to mean feminism, liberty could encompass everything from the moral high ground of Mary Wollstonecraft to the depravity of the Marquis de Sade, from slavery apologists campaigning under the banner of free trade to proto-socialists demanding equal rights. No one was better attuned to the power of the mixed message than Letitia. Her voice was already so compromised by her circumstances that it could only thrive on uncertainty and ambiguity.

L.E.L.'s late novel *Ethel Churchill*, published the year before her death, features an unlikely friendship between two contrasting characters: a politically idealistic but doomed young poet, and a cynical actress who cheerfully exploits her wealthy lovers. Even in childhood, Letitia herself exhibited a split personality, swinging between the 'Spartan' rebel and the manipulative people-pleaser. At eighteen, she was a bold political dissenter, but also fully fledged in the coquetry and guile that Wollstonecraft regarded as the bane of socially constructed femininity.

After the shock tactics of 'Rome', Letitia's next submission to Jerdan could not have been more ladylike or refined. It was a slight lyric on the purity of the Michaelmas daisy in which she coyly paraded her own innocence. In fact, she was gearing up for a mutual seduction that had more in common with the erotic brinkmanship of *Les liaisons dangereuses* than with Wollstonecraft's ideal of love as an equal, open and sincere partnership.

In August, Letitia's mother wrote to Jerdan, soliciting a further publishing opportunity for her daughter. Catherine's unpublished note, preserved among Jerdan's papers in the Bodleian, is dated from 138 Sloane Street, indicating that the eviction from the big Brompton house had already taken place. Its language suggests that she was desperate for Jerdan's patronage, although not herself highly educated:

> Should the favour Mrs Landon requests be admissible, or not, she trusts Mr Jerdan will pardon, the very great liberty she is taking; a friend of Mrs Landons [*sic*] wishes much to see a triffle [*sic*] of Letitia's in the Gazette of the next or the following Saturday. The kindness her family have experienced from Mr and Mrs Jerdan will not be obliterated from the mind of Mrs Landon, it will give her much pleasure to hear they are all well.

Catherine's warm reference to Mrs Jerdan shows that the neighbours were by now socializing *en famille*, which they had not done when the Landons were living in their mansion with John there as head of the family. The constipated formality of the prose makes her social anxiety only too plain. The former mistress of Trevor Park was by now so sunk that she was forced to employ another aspect of the discourse of liberty: that of taking a liberty with a superior.

Catherine was still too embarrassed to admit that she had any longer-term pecuniary motive in pushing her daughter forward, ascribing her desire to see Letitia's work in print to wanting to please 'a friend'. There may have been an element of truth in that, as by now the socially conscious Catherine had little else to show off about. Even the exaggerated etiquette by which she referred to herself in the third person underlined the pressures on her status and identity.

Letitia's 'triffle' was duly published in the *Gazette* on August 5. The poem was a tasteless squib about a nouveau riche 'West Indian dandy' and his sly black valet, probably intended to be regarded as a slave. In it, she took a detached view of the power relations in which she was herself already immersed. We can see her laughing, beneath Catherine's radar, at the values of conspicuous consumption that had contributed to the Landon family's ruin.

Although superficially at odds with the romantic tones she later adopted, the 'triffle' reveals that the young Letitia was already rehearsing the ideas that she subsequently fed, underhand, into her self-construction as 'L.E.L.': mirroring; splitting; doublespeak; the notion of identity both as a costume put on and as vested in the eye of the beholder. The humour turns on verbal slippage, and on an ironic inversion of power.

The wealthy plantation owner struts in front of the glass in his new suit and tight stays, inviting admiration for his 'Bond Street' chic from his 'Negro', who fawningly tells him he looks like a 'lion'. But the would-be dandy is so out of touch that he fails to register that 'lion' is the on-trend slang word for a celebrity socialite. Taking his valet literally, he questions how the latter could know what such an animal looked like, assuming that he could never have seen such an exotic beast (itself an irony given the African heritage of West Indian slaves).

Pretending to be as stupid as his 'massa' thinks he is, the valet insists in pidgin that he knows exactly what a lion looks like, but goes on, sarcastically, to describe a long-eared donkey, claiming he can see one right there. His master turns to the window to look out into the street. The final line deploys a crude pun on 'ass', as he looks back over his shoulder to see his own backside reflected in the mirror (one recalls Mary Crawford's crude pun on rears and vices in the navy, which continues to astound readers of *Mansfield Park*).

Letitia later became a literary 'lion' herself in London society, but retained the perspective of the outwardly sycophantic but secretly snickering 'Negro'. Under the silken surfaces of her poetic sentimentalism, she always configured human relationships in terms of brutal power dynamics. The final irony in the squib's mesh was that, in his literalness, the 'massa' is unwittingly right in exposing human pride in 'lion' status as a base animal instinct.

Parallels between the position of women and that of slaves were frequently drawn by radicals in the 1790s. In her *Vindication of the Rights of Woman,* Mary Wollstonecraft complained that patriarchy had duped women into putting on 'silken fetters', manipulating them 'into endurance, and even love of slavery.' L.E.L.'s iconic poetess figures were often romantically portrayed as slave-girl singers in exotic harems. But Letitia was a generation younger than Wollstonecraft, and had no faith in feminist idealism. 'I do not dwell,' she wrote in 1823, 'amid the days / Utopia may have known.'

Letitia's next submission to Jerdan marked a watershed. It told the story of a girl abandoned by a lover 'careless of the passion which / He had awakened into wretchedness.' For the first time, she used a floral metaphor to indicate loss of virginity: 'But love is like the rose, so many ills / Assail it in the bud.' Neither her mother nor her governess questioned the poem's propriety. However, it sent Jerdan just the message he wanted to hear.

Letitia was now dispatched out of London to stay with friends or relatives in Bristol at what must have been a trying time. There, she began working on a more ambitious project: her first book. Its centrepiece was a narrative poem in two cantos, *The Fate of Adelaide*, written in the same meter as Miss Rowden's *Pleasures of Friendship*, and devised as a concoction of sub-Scott medievalism with a Byronic love triangle at its centre. Letitia privately had few illusions about the passions she depicted. 'I wished to pourtray [*sic*] a gentle soft character and to paint in her the most delicate love,' she archly told her governess. 'I fear her dying of it is a little romantic; yet what was I to do as her death must terminate it?'

However, she was desperate for Jerdan to recognize her talents. When she sent him Canto One, her covering letter flattered his sense of power. 'I am too well aware of my many defects, and the high advantages of your opinion, not to anxiously avail myself of your permission to submit it to your inspection,' she wrote submissively. She also slipped a seductive message into the text of the poem, in which she addressed him as the anonymous 'belov'd Inspirer of thy youthful minstrel's dream,' just as Miss Rowden had namelessly hymned her mentor in *The Pleasures of Friendship*.

Canto Two was then dispatched. It included an even more flattering declaration of fealty from poetess to patron. Letitia informed Jerdan that her ambition was unstoppable. She wanted to rank among the 'bards of Greece'. But she could not do it without her male muse: 'It is . . . my cherish'd prize, / To breath one song not quite unworthy thee.' Miss Rowden's tribute to Monsieur St Quentin paled by comparison.

The Landon women waited on tenterhooks for Jerdan's answer. It did not come. Catherine wrote to him anxiously on November 4 on her daughter's behalf: 'Need I say how anxious she is for your opinion?' she wrote. 'I trust you will not think her arrogant, as I believe you are aware of her reasons for wishing to publish.' This was Mrs Landon's first explicit allusion to their reduced circumstances, which would in fact have been obvious to the editor from the moment they moved out of their big house. By openly admitting the weakness of their position, Catherine was effectively placing herself—and her daughter—in Jerdan's hands.

Catherine wrote again to Jerdan in increasing desperation. She was anxious not to be 'troublesome', but without his encouragement her daughter had 'no resolution to go on'. She had asked the revered Mrs Siddons to accept the honour of a dedication, but the actress was not pre-pared to put her name to Letitia's volume unless Jerdan wrote a testimo-nial. The friendship was evidently less important to the status-conscious actress than it was to the imperilled Mrs Landon.

Letitia's depressed state when Jerdan did not reply was replaced by a manic high when he finally did, expressing his approval of her work. 'How happy I am!' she wrote to her mother. '[I]t so surpasses my expecta-tions, convinced as I am that a kind of curse hangs over us all, it seemed too delightful to happen to one of the Cahets.' (The Cahets were not, as has been suggested, a long-lost branch of Letitia's mysterious maternal family, but a fabled race of goitered outcasts supposed to inhabit the cut-off mountainous regions of Europe, alluded to by Letitia herself in her 1831 novel *Romance and Reality*, where she refers to 'the frightful goitres which so disfigure the inhabitants of the Valais'. She was making a joke of her financially disgraced family's pariah status.)

After these letters, the on-the-spot trail goes dead until the publica-tion of *The Fate of Adelaide* just over six months later, in July 1821. No poems of Letitia's appear in the *Gazette* for more than a year. No relevant correspondence is extant.

Jerdan's autobiography, however, waxes lyrical on this lost year. He reveals that during that period he took Letitia on as his pupil to prepare her for a literary career. 'From day to day and hour to hour,' he recalled, 'it was mine to facilitate her studies, to shape her objects, to regulate her taste, to direct her genius.' During the course of the lessons, he also endeavoured, as he somewhat quaintly put it, 'to cultivate the divine organisation of her being'.

Jerdan lavished Letitia with the attention she had always craved but rarely received. On a single day, he took her to visit St Paul's Cathedral, which she had never seen before, then on to a private performance by

the celebrated comedian Charles Mathews, ending up at a literary dinner party given by the publisher Thomas Longman, where Letitia may
have been the only female guest. Mathews was famous for his stage show,
'Stories', in which he proved himself a chameleonic master of the quick
change, adopting new identities at speed. Letitia's own talents for masquerade may have been encouraged by witnessing him in action.

Catherine Landon did not chaperone her daughter on these cultural
jaunts. She must have turned a blind eye to Jerdan's grooming, only too
delighted that he was prepared to put in so much time and effort.

Jerdan attempted to interest Longman in *The Fate of Adelaide,* but
to no avail. The publisher was not prepared to take a risk on a young
unknown, no doubt surmising that Jerdan's enthusiasm for his protégée
was not purely literary. In the end, the book was taken on by John Warren of Bond Street, who agreed to publish it but only at the author's
expense. Letitia's grandmother Mrs. Bishop found the money, and Mrs
Siddons was finally persuaded to accept the dedication.

The Fate of Adelaide was finally published in July 1821 with the
author's full name, Letitia Elizabeth Landon, on the title page. Jerdan did
his best to puff it with a glowing review in the *Gazette,* adding as a pro-
viso that the young neophyte needed to work harder—presumably under
his tutelage—to fulfil her potential. However, the book failed to find an
audience. ' 'Twas my first,' Letitia later told an admirer, 'perhaps you will
be so very good as to read it; I believe no one else has.' Certainly, no one
made the connection when, only a few weeks later, the first poems signed
'L.E.L.' began appearing in the *Gazette.*

Letitia had signed her dedicatory epistle to Mrs Siddons with her
initials. It was probably on seeing them there that Jerdan first formulated
the plan to use 'L.E.L.' as an alias: the sonorous palindrome with its
Satanic hint of 'hell,' its echo of the French for 'she' evoking the eternal
feminine, and, as Laman Blanchard later pointed out in a comic poem,
its parallel with the somewhat less romantic 'L.S.D.': pounds, shillings
and pence.

Jerdan had learned that in literary marketing, as in seduction, the
oblique method could be more effective than the overt appeal. In exploiting the idea of the unseen author, he was following recent trends. Walter
Scott had hidden his identity from the public when financial pressures
inspired him to turn from poetry to the less prestigious but roaring trade

of fiction. Although not consciously intended as a marketing ploy, publishing his *Waverley* novels anonymously earned him the title the 'Great Unknown' and created a mystery that boosted sales. By the time he was definitively unmasked in 1821, he had become the most successful novelist of the day.

L.E.L., who was only semi-anonymous, offered Byronic added value, since her poetry revolved around the poet's unseen 'I'. Her adoption of the initials in September 1821 led to her promotion from the amateurs' column to the prestigious 'Original Poetry' slot. It also opened the poetic floodgates. Verse after verse began to pour forth on a near-weekly basis.

'Throughout the year 1822, L.E.L. was as full of song as the nightingale in May; and excited a very general enthusiasm by [her] Sapphic warmth,' Jerdan later put it. Behind the scenes, the new alter ego may have intensified the physical encounters between poetess and patron, as if L.E.L. could do things Letitia could not have done, although we cannot know exactly when they first slept together.

In his autobiography, Jerdan stated that the 'mystery of L.E.L.' could only be unlocked by a hidden master key, without which 'critics and biographers' would 'guess, and speculate, and expatiate for ever' but make 'nothing of their reveries'. The secret, he claimed, was that all her poetry had been inspired by her passion for himself, which he overtly depicted as Platonic 'grateful and devoted attachment' on her part, in spite of his insinuating use of sensual vocabulary elsewhere.

Now that we know they had three children together, his portrayal of their relationship as an innocent one-way crush sounds laughable. But Jerdan was not wholly inventing it when he said that Letitia's early poetry was personally addressed to him. Some of it demonstrably was.

Letitia's sketch on Sappho, for example, published in the *Gazette* on May 4, 1822, interpolated a new backstory whose private significance could only have been evident to Jerdan, as her wider readership had no idea of her real-life situation. Making Sappho's legendary beloved Phaon a mere stand-in, she gave the Greek poetess a more important, unnamed first love: her poetry tutor.

As L.E.L. depicted it, the young Sappho looked up to him with all

Youth's deep and passionate idolatry:
Love was her heart's sole universe—he was to her

Hope, Genius, Energy, the God
Her inmost spirit worshipped.

Whether or not the verse expressed Letitia's unvarnished feelings for her real-life mentor is less certain. The very fact that she could step back far enough to portray her devotion to him as 'idolatry' suggests she could already see his feet of clay. However, she was caught in a cycle of seduction. She had to flatter Jerdan, week after week, to ensure he would keep publishing her poetry.

Letitia Landon's great paradox is that the clues she left about her private life are not to be found in diaries or letters but in her most public utterances, her poetry. The relationship between the latter's emotional content and her private, subjective feelings is the hardest aspect of her legacy to unravel. She brings into focus one of the knottiest philosophical problems in criticism: that of authorial intentionality.

Even in her own time, L.E.L.'s emotional sincerity or otherwise was regarded as the crux of her literary identity. Was her love poetry 'true to the very life'? Or were her 'passions' mere 'pasteboard'? Jerdan claimed that the emotions in the poetry were genuine, but Blanchard went out of his way 'to impress on the reader's mind the fact, that there was not the remotest connection or affinity, not indeed a colour of resemblance, between her every-day life or habitual feelings and the shapes they were made to assume in her poetry.'

The uncomfortable reality is that both Jerdan and Blanchard told a version of the truth. Across her career, Letitia's poems turn out to be demonstrably full of buried references to her real-life situations. Yet they do not provide the straight 'emotional honesty' of unimpeded access into her naked feelings. Her work was, rather, less expressive than performative, less existential than instrumental. Indeed, her project of poetic sentimentalization was a textbook reflection of Schiller's theory, outlined in his seminal 1796 essay *Über naïve und sentimentalische Dichtung*. According to Schiller, the corrupt complexities of the modern world meant that art could no longer directly express authentic feeling. Instead it had to translate banal experience into idealized formulae.

Letitia's own accounts of the process of composition suggest that, far from writing to express her feelings, she wrote to prevent herself from having to feel them. Poetic composition provided her with a druglike escape. 'Poetry always carries me out of myself,' she explained. 'It is the most subtle and interesting of pleasures, but, like all pleasures, it is dearly bought; it is always succeeded by extreme depression of spirits, and an overpowering sense of bodily fatigue'. While focused on the task, 'the whole frame trembles with eagerness'. When it is over, there is 'no strength left to bear life's other emotions'.

In Keats's 'Ode to a Nightingale,' the poet experiences a dissociated state under the influence of 'some dull opiate' and is then returned to his 'sole self'. Letitia's self was never sole. She was always putting on another mask.

In her Sappho poem of 1822, Letitia used the simile of a bird to depict the poetess's relation to her mentor:

> *. . . she was unto him*
> *As a young bird, whose early flight he trained,*
> *Whose first wild songs were sweet, for he had taught*
> *Those songs.*

In their personal mythology, she was the songbird and Jerdan her trainer. His favourite line of hers was 'We love the bird we taught to sing.'

The bird image was a standard Romantic topos, used by Keats in his 'Ode to a Nightingale', and by Shelley, who compared the poet to 'a nightingale, who sits in darkness, and sings to cheer its own solitude with sweet sounds; his auditors are as men entranced by the melody of an unseen musician, who feel that they are moved and softened, yet know not whence or why'. When used by a female poet, which it sometimes was, the metaphor's ugly subtext was foregrounded.

In classical mythology, Philomel was turned into a nightingale after being raped by Tereus, who cut out her tongue to prevent her accusing him, as is hinted at in the 'purple-stained mouth' of Keats's ode. Once a bird, Philomel would forever sing a beautiful song. Her fate was that its meaning—the history of the rape—would never be understood by human listeners.

In making the import of L.E.L.'s 'songs' purposefully obscure, Letitia was using the Philomel myth, hinting at her own 'fall', yet burying the truth about the backstage sexual transactions that lay behind her public voice. There is no evidence that Jerdan forced himself on her with physical violence, as Tereus did on Philomel, but their relationship was unequal. He was a middle-aged man with the patriarchal power of patronage; she was a teenager desperate for affirmation.

Jerdan frequently took the credit for L.E.L.'s creativity, but the dynamic between them was much more complex than, say, the one-way trajectory that exists between the fictional Trilby and Svengali in George du Maurier's classic 1894 novel. Trilby is an uneducated singer whose extraordinary performances are unlocked when her master hypnotizes her into a trance; on waking, she can recall nothing. L.E.L.'s poetry often alludes to the myth of the unconscious artist but suggests that she was always conscious: both of the power play in which she was involved and at the multiple levels at which her own consciousness was operating.

Letitia had an uncanny ability to split off the unspoken, embattled aspects of herself and symbolize them through the surrogate of L.E.L. With her brain caught up in her own technical skill at performing the role of the lovelorn woman, she was insulated from feeling, yet able to access and project the conflicts inherent in her actual situation. Her poetry invites us to see and not see, but the most intriguing aspect of her sensibility is her self-voyeurism. She was performing for her trainer, and for the readers of the *Gazette*, but she was her own audience too, as, with a mix of disinhibition and cold calculation, she projected her 'cave-locked' psyche into dissociated poetic formulae.

In the following extract, for example, published in the *Gazette* in March 1825, she put a fateful, phallic engraving tool into her teacher's hand while conjuring an image of herself in a traumatized, incantatory dream state:

> *And you took my young heart,*
> *And what did you grave there,*
> *But a deep and deadly lesson*
> *Its first and last despair . . .*
> *And my tears shall be as streams*
> *Cave-locked beneath the earth*
> *Of whose flowing no one dreams.*

As so often, the theatrical artifice with which she plays the submissive role in the poetry contains its own hint of buried irony. In reality, it was always Letitia's lines that would be 'graved' (or printed) in the next issue of the *Gazette*. As she produced poem after poem, the contrast with the editor's own lack of creativity was obvious. Her work frequently invoked the Pygmalion myth, but she was Jerdan's Pygmalion as much as he was hers, as she transformed him over and over again, with semi-mocking excess, into the idol for whom her abject heroines hungered.

Jerdan harnessed Letitia's extraordinary drive to the full. In May 1822, he put her to the test. On their way back from a joint trip into town, they passed St George's Hospital at Hyde Park Corner, whereupon he challenged her to produce an extempore poem on the subject.

The power loom had transformed the textile industry. Horse-drawn transport had become so effective that it was shrinking distances more astonishingly than the coming of the railways later would. Since 1814, new technology meant that *The Times* was now being printed at 1,100 sheets per hour. The editor was clearly hoping for similar advances in poetic productivity.

Letitia did not disappoint. As Jerdan recalled, 'Dinner passed, and within an hour the ladies were joined at tea, by which time a most touching poem of seventy-four lines was completed on the given theme.' The resulting composition, published in the *Gazette* on May 27, 1822, was indeed an extraordinary feat of extemporization. However, the word 'touching' does not quite describe its queasy aesthetic.

Conjuring the modern city as a place of morbid decay, the poem captures the fall of Romanticism into decadence, embodying the diseased 'mawkishness' Keats embraces in his preface to *Endymion*. L.E.L. imagines herself stepping from a crowded London street into a ward for the dying. Three anonymous patients capture her attention: a soldier, whose mangled body is gashed with scars; a seduced girl who had 'loved, / Trusted and been betrayed,' the victim, perhaps, of an offstage suicide attempt or botched abortion; and a consumptive Keatsian poet, 'too visionary for this world,' en route to an atheist's defiant death. The sufferings of all three heroic outcasts are aestheticized, and thus politically neutralized. With her 'marble brow,' the girl has become a beautiful, passive work of art.

The poem's perverse sentimentalization of violence, pain and degradation contrasts oddly with the cozy bourgeois scenario in which it was composed: a middle-class party with ladies drinking tea. It puts one in mind of Heine's ironic lyric 'At the Tea Table' ('Am Teetisch'), first published in 1822, in which a group of respectable ladies and gentlemen euphemistically discuss the sordid risks of love, including sexually transmitted disease, while politely pretending they are not. When a *Fräulein* innocently expresses incomprehension at their drift, it is left up to the reader to decide if she is feigning.

Such it was with Letitia, whose original audience, perhaps including her own mother and governess, could never decide quite how knowing she was. There is a cognitive dissonance at play in 'St George's Hospital, Hyde-Park Corner,' where the dying poet's 'fallen state' is simultaneously 'mark[ed]' and 'unheeded.' For Letitia, the adrenaline rush of composing under pressure was intensified by the thrill of hiding in plain sight at Mrs Jerdan's tea table.

William Jerdan was a family man but also a libertine. In the absence of John Landon, not just Letitia but her brother was drawn into his saturnalian orbit. Although Whittington went up to Oxford in March 1823 to read for the Church, he too, it transpires, was taken under Jerdan's wing.

Neither sibling had a good relationship with Catherine. Both in John's absence transferred their allegiance to their new father figure, encouraged by his generosity with alcohol. L.E.L.'s early poetry contains a surprising number of drinking songs, and several references to beautiful young girls disinhibited by wine. One of Whittington's few published works is a free-form essay on the drinking habits of the Bacchanalian, 'Elixir Vitae.' It appears next to a piece by Jerdan on 'The Last Bottle' in a macabre volume, *Death's Doings* (1827).

That volume's slippery tone and sick humour are typical of the age of cant. Showcasing the pleasures that lead humans to their graves, it poses as a series of morality tales, but leaves the reader in little doubt that dangerous pleasures are worth the hazards. After the Napoleonic Wars, a devil-may-care hedonism permeated culture all over Europe. The 'wine, women, and song' of Schubert's circle—the 'sex, drugs, and rock and roll' of the day—was born of despair, not cheery optimism. Letitia's feminine contribution to Dagley's volume sentimentalizes death as the ultimate risk of sex for a woman.

In contrast to the depressed Catherine, Jerdan offered excitement at a time when the Landon family was in disarray. He not only flattered Letitia's embryonic talent and printed her work, but introduced her into the inner circle of the literary avant-garde. Letitia's one extant letter from

1822 is addressed to a previously unidentified Mr Richards. He must in fact have been Thomas Richards, who had been at school with Keats. His brother Charles, another schoolfellow, had published Keats's first book, *Poems* of 1817.

This was access to bona fide 'Cockney' culture, as it was then known. The term later became identified with working-class East Enders, but in Keats's day it referenced the bohemian subculture of London's suburbs. Letitia gushingly told Richards how gratified she felt that he had compared her style to Keats's, telling him how much she admired *Lamia* and *Endymion*. She also informed him jokily that she was no more 'rationalised or reformé' than when last they met, apparently boasting about how liberated she was. In the early days, she positively flaunted her affair with Jerdan among literary men. Her lack of discretion later came back to haunt her.

Cockney society certainly accommodated a few liberated women who pursued love for its own sake out of wedlock, such as the mysterious Isabella Jones, with whom Keats had an affair before he fell in love with Fanny Brawne. Isabella's surviving correspondence is written in a style almost identical to that of Letitia's letter to Richards, combining poetical enthusiasm with Mary Crawford wit.

Mrs Jones was, however, in her thirties, evidently separated from her husband, and possessed of a private income that allowed her to live alone in comfortable lodgings, which she furnished with a statue of Napoleon and an Aeolian lyre, emblems of radical chic. She lavished her toyboy Keats with presents, but also confused him with her coquettish mixed messages, frequent disappearances and enigmatic origins. Even so independent a woman as Mrs Jones felt she had to erect a smokescreen.

As a cash-strapped minor, Letitia was in a far more perilous position. Out of feminine modesty, she declined Richards's request that she inscribe a memorial volume of Keats's 1817 poems with a tribute of her own. She must have been afraid of appearing too pushy. The volume still exists, but the tributes are all by male keepers of the flame. Although Cockneys were politically liberal, they had long since dispensed with Wollstonecraftian ideas of gender equality. 'I have an utter aversion to Bluestockings. I do not care a fig for any woman that knows even what an author means,' wrote William Hazlitt in 1821.

Letitia registered her resistance to her situation by playing her hyperfeminine role with over-the-top extravagance. Her stylized poetic theatrics were comparable to the virtuoso operatic performances of the great bel canto sopranos she admired, such as Henriette Sontag and Giuditta Pasta (her memoirist Emma Roberts, in a somewhat unfortunate turn of phrase, described how Letitia used to 'kneel down in the front of the box . . . as she gave her whole soul to Pasta'). Sontag she regarded as having the 'finest natural organ modulated by first rate science', but she preferred those singers, like Pasta, who took technical risks in pursuit of creating emotional effects.

Mutually complicit in the performativity of L.E.L., Letitia and Jerdan shared a love of the theatre in all its forms, benefiting from the Gazette's endless supply of complimentary reviewers' tickets. However, his tastes were more lowbrow than hers. He had a particular penchant for female freak shows, such as the Sicilian fairy, only nineteen and a half inches tall. He caused a stir at the exhibition when he picked the fairy up and kissed her, expressing amusement when she wiped her diminutive cheek in disgust. In 1822, the Gazette also covered the exhibition in Bond Street of Tono Maria, the scarified 'Venus of South America'. She had 100 scars, one for each act of adultery. It was said that her tribe would allow 104 such acts, but would kill her when she got to 105.

If Jerdan was the showman, Letitia was his female freak, the 'infant genius' from whom sexually suggestive poetry poured in such abundance. How many adulterous scars ('The scar it left I may not heal') would she be able to sustain before her own tribe turned on her?

The relationship between female freaks and their impresarios was notoriously problematic. After the South African 'Hottentot Venus', Sarah Baartman, was exhibited in London in 1810, anxious abolitionists protested and attempted to liberate her through the courts. They had to retreat after she testified that she was acting of her own free will and was being paid for her appearances. How 'free' she really was remains a disturbing historical condundrum. Letitia was English, white and edu- cated, but her frequent allusions to female poets as harem slaves suggest that, as a disillusioned liberal, she conceived her own situation as less than free.

Letitia's mother had tacitly encouraged her to flirt with Jerdan at the start. She turned a blind eye as long as there were no physical conse- quences. But when the inevitable occurred, and Letitia became pregnant, Catherine could not cope.

Memoirists refer obliquely to a mysterious froideur arising between mother and daughter. Elizabeth Barrett complained on reading Blanchard's biography that there was only one letter from Letitia to her mother and that it was oddly cold. In a letter to Bulwer, Katherine Thomson privately admitted that Mrs Landon blamed Mr Jerdan for the rift. The real cause was almost certainly Letitia's pregnancy. On discovering it, Catherine, who was already ashamed of her own illegitimacy, threw her daughter out.

Letitia never forgave her mother, although she later supported her financially. Her poem *The Zenana,* published in the 1830s, features the honour killing of an Indian princess, who creeps out of the harem for a tryst with her lover. As she 'runs over the grass, half-woman half child', we can almost see Letitia exercising in the garden with her hoop. The heroine's mother cannot forgive her dishonoured daughter. She demands that she commit ritual suicide, and stands over her as she drinks 'the death cup'.

Real life was less luridly melodramatic. Rather than swallowing poison, Letitia was taken in by her grandmother Mrs Bishop, whose own sexual history made her more tolerant than her socially anxious daughter. Mrs Bishop appears to have smiled on Jerdan and to have facilitated the continuance of the affair. When she died, she left him her gold watch as a memento. Her estate went to Letitia but Catherine was left nothing.

Exactly when Letitia became pregnant can only be dated by piecing together disparate clues. We know from the baptismal record that this first baby was christened at St James's Church, Paddington, on April 4, 1824. Her parents presented themselves as 'Laetitia and William Stuart', using Jerdan's mother's maiden name as an alias. They called their daughter Ella, after their other joint creation, 'L.E.L.'

As there was no legal requirement to register births at the time, there

Ella's baptismal record. Her surname, 'Stuart', was Jerdan's mother's maiden name. He habitually adopted that alias in public records relating to his illegitimate offspring.

is no record of exactly when Ella was born. According to family tradition among her descendants, her birthday was on December 31. But her age was registered as eighty-seven when she died in Melbourne, Australia, on July 10, 1910, suggesting that she must have been born in an earlier month in 1823.

As Anna Maria Hall put it in her novel about L.E.L., *A Woman's Story*, 'clouded births are seldom correctly dated'. Numerous clues conspire to indicate that Ella was actually born in September 1823. That date was in fact alleged in a scurrilous press report of 1826, in which Letitia was said to have given birth in 'Canterbury of all places', to where Jerdan had allegedly conveyed her for that purpose. It is corroborated by an unlikely source: a surviving letter from Letitia to the 'sober Quaker' Bernard Barton, written in September 1823, and dated from Mrs Bishop's home at 131 Sloane Street, where Letitia was later to be found receiving callers.

On the surface, the letter is all polite platitude. Letitia apologizes to Barton for having been so slow in responding to his last letter of April 15, explaining that she has been unwell. 'For the first two or three months after your last letter writing was equally painful and fatiguing,' she explained; 'then as you will perceive from the date we moved into another house, where we are hardly . . . settled even now.' The unspecified ill health was in all likelihood her pregnancy and its attendant stresses, the move the result of the row with her mother.

Following the Landon women's eviction from Grove House in 1820, Catherine wrote to Jerdan from 138 Sloane Street. This was presumably where Mrs Bishop, recorded as a long-term Sloane Street resident, was then living. Catherine came encumbered with two daughters and the governess. That Letitia was sent off to Bristol suggests how cramped the lodgings were for them all.

However, after the row, 138 was given up. Letitia and her grandmother appear to have taken new lodgings together a few doors down at 131, while Catherine and her younger daughter, Elizabeth Jane, moved to Halkin Street a little to the east of Sloane Street, probably with the governess in tow. At least that is the address on the burial record for Elizabeth Jane, who died of consumption, aged fourteen, in September 1825. Letitia's split with her mother must have been total until then. She later recalled her shock at her sister's emaciated appearance on her deathbed, as she had not seen her for so long.

In her letter to Barton, Letitia mentions in passing that she has only just returned from a stay at the seaside, though 'few things are to my taste more tiresome than a sea excursion, mine was to Ramsgate, of all dull places surely the most dull.' The visit was undoubtedly more interesting than she let on. Ramsgate is near Canterbury, where Letitia was later alleged to have given birth. It was just the place to convalesce. The poem L.E.L. published in the *Gazette* the day before Ella's christening records what sounds like a significant seaside visit:

> *Do you recall one autumn night,*
> *We stood by the sea-side,*
> *And marked a little vessel tost*
> *Upon the foaming tide?*

Letitia's letter to Barton is bland and smooth. However, the unusual seal she used to close it tells another story. Pressed into the wax is the image of an all-seeing eye. It was a private joke at the myopic Barton's expense.

A birth in September 1823 would have meant that Letitia's pregnancy would have become apparent the previous spring. She was clearly too 'ill' to respond to Barton's letter of April 15. Her poetry in the *Gazette* shows an unusual departure that month. Normally, her heroines die of love. But the 'dramatic scene' she published on April 12, 1823, features a fallen woman who lives on to give birth to a 'child / Of sorrow and of shame'. The piece is loosely inspired by *Lover's Vows,* the racy play featured in Jane Austen's *Mansfield Park,* which involves a transgressive affair between a young woman and a tutor.

In May, by which time Letitia's pregnancy would have been a fait accompli, she published her most flamboyantly morbid poem to date: the love-hate lyric 'Twine not red roses for me'. The poetess announces that she will die 'for love', and in doing so wreak her revenge on her lover, leaving him 'drooping' like a fallen tree over her grave, his potency sapped. Suicide was the clichéd response to the dishonour of an illegitimate pregnancy, as demonstrated in real life by Harriet Shelley. Letitia made her surrogate, L.E.L., threaten suicide, so that she would not have to do so herself.

Letitia's pregnancy came at an inconvenient moment in her career.

She had been contributing week after week to the *Gazette* for over a year, but the 'mystery poetess' strategy could not hold out indefinitely. Jerdan could not count on L.E.L.'s readership remaining 'for ever panting', like the lovers on Keats's Grecian urn. She would have to raise her game by publishing a book and appearing in person.

The Improvisatrice, which launched her to stardom in June 1824, was in fact written 'a year' before she saw the proof sheets, that is, in the spring of 1823. Her pregnancy is the only possible explanation for the delay in publication. The infant genius could hardly be launched on society as a literary lion with a swelling belly.

The enforced delay scuppered some extravagant publicity plans. It is likely that the launch of *The Improvisatrice* was originally intended to coincide with the unveiling at the Royal Academy summer exhibition of 1823 of a new picture called *L'Improvisatrice* by Henry William Pickersgill (1782–1875), depicting a sultry female minstrel playing the lute in Italian peasant dress (see plates).

Pickersgill was one of the most skilful and prolific portraitists of his generation, with a sideline in exotic genre images of female subjects, such as *The Oriental Nosegay*, featuring a melancholy harem beauty (made the subject of a 'poetical illustration' by L.E.L., 1825). Frequently puffed in the *Gazette* during the 1820s, Pickersgill later made two 'fancy portraits' of Letitia herself, each in a different theatrical costume. His *L'Improvisatrice*, now in a private collection, is almost certainly an earlier variant on that theme, possibly the unspecified early Pickersgill portrait of Letitia that Blanchard refers to as having been made in '1822 or 1823': the first glimpse of her.

A work on the cusp between portraiture and genre painting, it is as much a fantasy as a realistic portrayal of an individual, and exactly how an artist would have portrayed an imaginary female Byron in 1823. The ethnic costume echoes Byron's portrait in Albanian dress by Thomas Phillips, already iconic by that time, while the full-profile pose recalls Richard Westall's equally celebrated portrait of Byron. Despite her ethnic attire, the sitter is not quite a peasant. Instead of the traditional Italian folded headscarf, she is wearing a turban: the liberal female intellectual's headgear of choice, popularized by Madame de Staël. A few dark ringlets—artificially curled?—escape from the scarlet cloth she has wrapped nonchalantly around her head. This is in fact a masquerade costume, owing as much to London stylishness as to indigenous Italian traditions. A fashion plate from *Ackermann's Repository* of 1819 shows a lady playing the guitar in a similarly shaped headdress.

The postponement of Letitia's launch must have been irritating to Pickersgill if he had counted on joint publicity. But he must have been mollified by the fact that *L'Improvisatrice* was instantly sold in exhibition—to a *Gazette* contact, the second Marquess of Landsdowne, who may have been the illegitimate half brother of Henry Colburn.

Letitia may already have suspected she was pregnant by the time she was sitting for Pickersgill and, contemporaneously, writing the long title poem for *The Improvisatrice*. She completed it in 'less than five weeks'. Her manic drive always intensified with her pregnancies, as if a book would make up for the baby she would have to give away. But her increased productivity was also a response to the fear that Jerdan might abandon her if she did not offer him further feats of poetic prowess.

His eye was already wandering, probably in reaction to his mistress's inconvenient pregnancy. In 1823, he began to showcase the work of another teenage poetess in the *Gazette,* Louisa Costello. Louisa chose the irritatingly egotistical initials 'M.E.' under which to publish her romantic effusions. On October 4, 1823, not long after Letitia had given birth to Ella, 'M.E.' and 'L.E.L.' rubbed shoulders in the Original Poetry column, both with love lyrics of unrequited torment. However, Letitia clearly succeeded in roping Jerdan in. Louisa Costello's contributions to the *Gazette* dried up and Jerdan joined his young mistress at Ella's christening in April.

There is no evidence that Letitia ever saw Ella again. The baby must have been farmed out to foster care, as often happened with illegitimate children, who were frequently referred to euphemistically as 'orphans'. However, family letters show that Jerdan was in touch with Ella in later life. As an old man of 'eighty-four and upward', he sent his 'dearest Ella' an inscribed copy of his recently published autobiography.

Despite her dubious origins, Ella grew up to defy the odds. In adulthood, she earned her living as a governess, before emigrating to Australia in 1852, when she was twenty-five. She married the ship's captain, James Gregson, whom she met on the voyage out, and went on to bring up five children while running a girls' school in Melbourne. She enjoyed riding to hounds but was said by her children to have had particularly strict Victorian standards of morality.

Writing to Ella on the eve of her departure, Jerdan wished her a 'prosperous and happy journey into the distant world to which she is now going', expressing the hope that 'the new generation in the next few years may lead to many acceptable recognitions when I am in the grave.' Ella's Australian family, however, later recalled that she had left for the colonies with her father's voice 'ringing in her ears that she would never be welcomed back'.

CHAPTER 5

Fame

From her first printed poem, 'Rome', onward, the rhyming words 'fame' and 'shame' recur again and again in Letitia's work. Her career was a tightrope act between the two. A hint of scandal could boost celebrity and sales. Too much could kill them. With the publication of *The Improvisatrice* in June 1824, both the potential rewards and the potential risks increased.

The title poem drew on recent literary trends to fashion a Frankenstein's monster of a best seller. It was written in the first-person voice of an unnamed Italian Renaissance poetess, or 'Improvisatrice', who is fêted by audiences of adoring Florentines but unhappy in love. Readers who had recognized Byron in Childe Harold were primed to identify the character with the writer. As the title implied, Letitia was improvising the new identity glimpsed in the Pickersgill picture of 1823.

The real-life Italian tradition of the poetic improviser went back to the Renaissance, and enjoyed a revival in the late eighteenth and early nineteenth centuries. The male *improvvisatore* or female *improvvisatrice* (the word has a double 'v' in Italian) occupied an ambiguous space between the performing and creative arts. Their oral riffs, sometimes on themes sprung on them by audience members, were usually accompanied by music on the lute or guitar. Some were low-life buskers on the street. Others were high-class salon artistes, who impressed with the erudite literary allusions they could weave into their acts. The most celebrated could sell out theatres. In 1778, the virtuoso *improvvisatrice* Corilla Olimpica was crowned poet laureate at a special ceremony at the Capitol in Rome, although the accolade was not without controversy, given her gender, her actress status, and her reputation for taking lovers.

During the Romantic period, the phenomenon attracted wide-spread international interest. Wilhelm Müller—the poet of Schubert's *Winterreise*—compared himself to an *improvvisatore*. So did Hans Christian Andersen, whose first successful book was the teasingly semi-autobiographical *The Improvisatore, or Life in Italy* (1835). Mary Shelley, who witnessed the phenomenon in Italy, thought that the improvisers channelled divine inspiration. Byron was equally fascinated to hear the celebrated exponent Tommaso Sgricci perform in Milan in 1816, but, in contrast, cynically set him down as a poseur.

England was already in the grip of improvising fever by the time Letitia leveraged it for her bestseller. Thomas Lovell Beddoes had published his *The Improvisatore* (a poem in 'three fyttes') in 1820. Around the same time, the Italian émigrés Ugo Foscolo and Gabriele Rossetti

Corilla Olimpica, the most famous *improvvisatrice* of them all. She was crowned poet laureate at the Capitol and later inspired Madame de Staël's bestseller *Corinne.*

(father of the painter Dante Gabriel and the poet Christina) began giving lectures in London on the Italian literary imagination. In March 1823, probably just before Letitia began writing *The Improvisatrice,* the *Literary Gazette* reported on a polyglot 'Dutch improvisator', who could 'pour forth a torrent of original ideas and images clothed in the most beautiful poetic diction' at a moment's notice in a range of languages. It was another challenge, like the test Jerdan had set her the previous year.

The female *improvvisatrice* had special iconic status in women's literature, owing to *Corinne,* the international bestseller published in 1807 by Europe's premier female intellectual, Germaine de Staël. Its eponymous heroine was loosely inspired by the real-life Corilla Olimpica, who had been born Maria Madalena Morelli in 1727, the daughter of a violinist. Although the historical Corilla was recently described by a modern historian as a 'court poet, show-woman, adventuress', de Staël reworked her as a heroine of sensibility. Her Corinne is an idealized conduit for truth and nature. Her unforced genius raises her to artistic heights, and leads to her being crowned poet laureate at the Capitol. But her emotional authenticity leads her into fatal conflict with oppressive societal norms. She dies of a broken heart after her aristocratic English lover rejects her for a conventional woman from his own class.

Many nineteenth-century women writers adopted Corinne as a symbolic figure embodying the conflict between their private and public roles. Some saw her as a feminist martyr. Others slotted her into a more conservative worldview. In Felicia Hemans's treatment of the story, Corinne laments her genius as a curse because it has made her miss out on woman's noble destiny: the domestic bliss of hearth and home, marriage and children.

Letitia took the bare bones of her plot from *Corinne.* Her unnamed Improvisatrice was also a poetess-genius destined to die of a broken heart when she discovers her lover is betrothed to another woman. Female readers were given the option of investing the work with their own emotional conflicts, and with de Staël's high seriousness and liberal politics. But Letitia, who had been a rebellious tomboy in childhood, borrowed from male writers too.

She blatantly stole her frame-style structure from Thomas Moore's commercial hit *Lalla Rookh,* about a male minstrel performing at the court of an Indian princess, all glittering surfaces, the literary equivalent of the Brighton Pavilion. She aped Moore's descriptive bravura in

Europe's foremost female intellectual, Germaine
de Staël, author and turban trendsetter.

her highly wrought depiction of the exotic Florentine palace inhabited
by her heroine, with its tinkling fountains, its overpowering odour of
flowers, and its marble floors cool to the touch of the naked foot.

She also channelled Keats's earthier sensualism, pushing the boundaries of taste yet further than she had hitherto dared. In 'The Eve of St.
Agnes' the hero plays a 'ditty' on the heroine's 'hollow lute'. L.E.L. borrowed the erotic metaphor, but made her female protagonist play on her
own lute, a scene depicted in literal terms by Pickersgill in his 1823 painting *L'Improvisatrice*. Metaphorically, the lines reinforced Byron's contention that Keats's poetry was 'a sort of mental masturbation':

> *My hand kept wandering on my lute,*
> *In music, but unconsciously*

My pulses throbbed, my heart beat high,
A flush of dizzy ecstasy
Crimsoned my cheek.

The key word was 'unconsciously'. Letitia was not unconscious of what she was doing, but she was determined to see how far she could push the wilful blindness of her audience. It was she who, dangerously, flirted with her own destruction.

One probable source for *The Improvisatrice* is a clever novel published anonymously in London in 1820, *Andrew of Padua, the Improvisatore*. It riffs from start to finish on ideas of artifice, role-play, performance and deception. The narrator, Furbo (Italian for 'crafty'), meets an old man claiming to be the renowned *improvvisatore* Andrew of Padua. 'Andrew' recounts the history of his glorious stage career and puts the secret of his success down to the sincerity of his performances, his unveiling of the 'peculiarities of my own individual character'. But he is eventually revealed as an impostor. In reality he is not a celebrated artiste but a nobody. The irony is that he has so successfully improvised an entire life story that he is indeed a great artist. 'Softly, softly,' he concludes, 'do not call it falsehood, fiction is the term, and if it has amused you as well as if it had been all true, what signifies the little stratagem that I have played.'

Letitia was playing her own stratagem. The very roughness around the edges of her verse was designed to make her seem like an untutored genius. If she wrote a clunky line, she left it in because it added to the effect. But her *naiveté* was *faux*.

By now she had put in so many hours of practice that she was in reality a master craftsman. In taking on the first-person voice of the unnamed Improvisatrice, she embodied the double paradox of performed authenticity and authentic performance. She was a young poetess playing the role of a young poetess. In doing so, she exposed femininity itself as masquerade.

In *The Improvisatrice*, L.E.L.'s poetic idealization of female abjection reached new levels of excess, designed to titillate her readers, but also perhaps a tangential comment on the power relations between the sexes in her society. The poems within the poem, supposedly performed by the Improvisatrice herself, included a glamourized portrayal of Hindu suttee and a visceral depiction of a girl injured by running barefoot through briars ('blood was on her small snow feet'). Yet the hero of the poem, Lorenzo, is presented as effeminate and oddly limp despite his clichéd pulchritude: a mere adjunct to the ego of the heroine, a tool in her masochistic self-drama.

In real life, Letitia was dependent on the editorial power of a middle-aged, married man. By adopting a theatrically submissive role in her poetry, she could make out—to herself—that their imbalanced relationship was her choice. At the same time, she could privately humiliate her middle-aged Svengali for his failure to live up to Lorenzo's ideal youth and beauty. In one scene she makes her imagined hero and heroine visit an art gallery together, just as she and Jerdan frequently did in real life.

The Improvisatrice has too often been read straight and found wanting, dismissed as 'rubbishy sentimentality' as late as 1998 by a male scholar of the Romantics. That is a mistake. It is in fact sophisticated high camp.

Humming birds or A Dandy Trio, by George Cruikshank, 1820. The fashion for improvised performing was associated with what we would now call 'camp'. It is embodied by three effete young men in this imagined satire by the great cartoonist. While a limp-wristed singer warbles to the sound of his friend's lute, a figure at the back admires himself in the glass.

Indeed, the artifice, excess, and sexual ambiguity of what we now call 'camp' was part and parcel of the early-nineteenth-century improvising tradition. Tommaso Sgricci was notorious for his flamboyant homosexuality. Thomas Lovell Beddoes was also homosexual, yet so uncomfortable in repressive English society that he ended up exiling himself to Europe, where he eventually committed suicide.

Letitia's theatrics as L.E.L. were rooted in her compromised subjectivity in a society that rendered the fallen woman null and void, just as it marginalized the homosexual. In many ways her career as a literary lion pre-echoes that of Oscar Wilde. Neither could openly admit their sexual status in public, but both flirted dangerously with exposure in their pursuit of literary celebrity. There's a hint of queerness to L.E.L.'s performative literary sensibility, echoed in a satirical cartoon of 1820 by Cruikshank, which features two effete young men on a sofa in a drawing room, one singing, the other playing the lute, while a third admires himself in the mirror.

On July 2, 1824, Jerdan rose to new heights of puffery in his review of *The Improvisatrice*. Like all reviews at the time, it was of course unsigned. The superstar Byron's death in April, he announced, had left a vacancy. Only L.E.L. could fill it. 'As far as our poetical taste and critical judgment enable us to form an opinion,' the showman concluded with an exorbitant flourish, 'we can adduce no instance, ancient or modern, of similar talent or excellence.'

The hype worked in a way that L.E.L.'s regular poetic contributions to the *Gazette* had not. *Ackermann's Repository* commended her 'extraordinary poetic talents' with as much enthusiasm as it praised French fashions. *The Gentleman's Magazine* applauded the 'young Lady just out of her teens' for her 'vivid imagination, felicity of diction, vigorous condensation of language, and passionate intensity of sentiment'. Only the *New Monthly Magazine* discreetly but admiringly alluded to Letitia's erotic subtexts: 'There is . . . scarcely an image which is not connected with the heart by some fine and secret association.'

The first impression of *The Improvisatrice* sold out in a day. A second edition was issued in September, and a third before the year was out. During 1825 the book was reprinted three more times. Nor was its success limited to the home market. Its first outing received a three-column front-page review in the Parisian *Globe*, followed by a second adulatory article a year later, and it was also published in America.

While Letitia's poetry sentimentalized neglected genius, her own career demonstrates how deeply she had internalized her mother's social ambitions. In August, the address of 'Miss Letitia Elizabeth Landon' was leaked to *Blackwood's Magazine* in an attempt to solicit invitations with the aim of establishing her as a literary lion. The so-called review barely touched on the literary qualities of *The Improvisatrice* but offered directions as to how to get to 131 Sloane Street from Hyde Park Gate.

The invitations clearly started coming immediately, as Mary Howitt's gossipy letter about the new girl genius was written on August 24. Previously, Letitia's literary contacts appear to have been exclusively men. Only now do we find her taken up by literary hostesses. Given her private situation, this was no mean achievement. No respectable lady would consort with a known fallen woman.

Letitia's first 'patroness' was the veteran writer Anne Isabella Spence, who 'in those days of leo-hunting was proud to be the first to present to a select circle . . . the veritable L.E.L., fresh caught for their amusement.' An ageing hangover from the days of the eighteenth-century bluestocking, she wore a turban in the manner of Madame de Staël (or at least an approximation of one in gauze and wire) to indicate her literary status and liberal principles. She welcomed the new 'English Corinne' into her salon, held regularly in her shabby rooms on the top floor of a tall house in Little Quebec Street, Mayfair.

Miss Spence's existing 'lions' included her near neighbour Lady Caroline Lamb, who used to turn up in an ermine cloak she called her catskin. By then an addled addict, separated from her husband and living under the watchful eye of expensive hired carers, Lady Caroline had been shunned by high society following her indiscreet affair with Byron. Although Miss Spence was not out of the top drawer, Caroline's desperate family was only too relieved that their black sheep had found a hostess willing to accommodate her. Caroline would soon be dead, aged only forty-two.

Miss Spence was adamant that she invited Lady Caroline on account of her 'litr'y abilities', not her rank. In reality, Caroline's title was a protecting factor in the eyes of social inferiors, given her notoriety. Her antics with Byron were well known, largely because she herself had done so much to publicize them.

Letitia was as little constrained by sexual morality as Caroline, from whose hands she had received her school prize at seven. But while Miss

Letitia's first 'patroness,' Miss Spence, sporting an approximation of a turban in the manner of Madame de Staël.

Spence was indulgent towards the noble lady's peccadilloes, she would have balked had it been common knowledge that the infant phenomenon L.E.L. was the mother of an illegitimate baby. When rumours belatedly began to circulate, Letitia rightly complained that her lack of 'rank' and 'opulence' rendered her vulnerable.

Attitudes toward fallen women were hardening. After Shelley's death in 1822, his wife, Mary, felt able to return to England from Italy only because their union had been ultimately regularized by marriage. It was an advantage to her that their sole surviving child was born in wedlock. In contrast, her unmarried stepsister Claire Clairmont—who had given birth to Byron's short-lived daughter Allegra and probably to another baby by Shelley—stayed away. Fearing pariah status at home, she wandered in exile through Europe, taking governess jobs as far afield as

Russia to make ends meet. In middle age she looked sourly back on her relationships with Byron and Shelley, concluding that sexual liberation only benefited male libertines.

Letitia soon became a fixture in the salon of Miss Spence, and in that of another ageing, beturbanned bluestocking, Miss Benger, who also took her up. The literary hangers-on she met there were intrigued by the striking contrast between the tragic melancholy of L.E.L.'s poetry and Miss Landon's vivacity in company. As one later put it, 'the instant L.E.L. was known, the circle around her became disenchanted. She pleaded guilty to no sentiment; she abjured the idea of writing from her own feelings. She was so lively, so girlish . . . so full of pleasantry, so ready with her shafts of mind, that one felt half-angry with her for being so blithe and real.'

Few were in fact so confident that her social persona was indeed her 'real' self. 'Witty and conversant as she was,' recalled William Howitt, 'you had the feeling that she was playing an assumed part.' No one could be sure which was the true face and which the mask.

There seemed to be two of her. As ever, Letitia was culturally on trend. The dyadic relationship between 'Miss Landon' and 'L.E.L.' embodied the newfangled concept of the doppelgänger, recently introduced to English readers via R. P. Gillies's translation of E. T. A. Hoffmann's tale, published the same month as *The Improvisatrice*.

The frisson of uncertainty generated by her contrasting selves was the key to her charisma, which affected some who met her like a 'stroke of electricity, throbbing and exciting'. She created cognitive dissonance. Simultaneously alien and strangely familiar, she was 'uncanny' in the Freudian sense: a real-life, textbook exemplar of the return of the repressed. What was repressed in Letitia's case was the tawdry truth about her sex life, which could never be openly mentioned in polite society.

In her progress through literary London, Letitia cannily played the blithe Miss Landon off the traumatized L.E.L., exploiting society's willing blindness, and especially the reluctance of ladies to 'see' that they were paying court to a strumpet. Being lied to as a child had made her feel worthless. Now she would get her own back by entangling Miss Spence, Miss Benger, et al. in her net. In 'the society of her own sex', Letitia 'was very careful how to steer her way.' She took particular pains to cultivate a dour headmaster's widow 'who had such a plethora of character and respectability that she had enough to spare for all Babylon.'

Her new friends included three young women her own age who prized their own respectability and later became her most assiduous and protective memoirists: the recently married Mrs Katherine Thomson and Mrs Anna Maria Hall, and the spinsterish Miss Emma Roberts. Although all three later established minor literary careers of their own, they were impressed by Letitia's larger fame and magnetism when they first met her. After her death, they asserted to a woman that their dear L.E.L. had always been sexually virtuous. Quite how much they privately guessed about her situation at the start, and at what point they realized the full truth, is the great conundrum of these 'friendships'. But it is safe to say that Letitia's capacity for intimacy was compromised by her backstage secret from the start.

Letitia costumed herself for the round of literary parties in keeping with her role as infant genius. She 'drest upon an idea', adopting an extravagantly boho style, with flowers in her hair in the middle of the day. Playing up to her image as an ingenue, she was apparently unaware that her skimpy gown was always falling off her shoulder. Women could put this down to her unselfconscious, childlike innocence. Men could read it as they chose.

With men, she worked her 'arch playfulness' to the limits of acceptability. When one moony young gentleman asked her what was on her mind, she replied with an 'air of merry scorn' that her head was filled with nothing but the latest fashions:

'Oh, I have been puzzling my brain to invent a new sleeve; pray, how do you like it?'
'You never think of such a thing as love, you who have written so [much] poetry upon it?'
'Oh! That is all professional, you know!'

Describing herself as a professional at love could have been taken as tantamount to declaring she was a prostitute.

Letitia's reference to a 'sleeve' was fashion-forward. In March 1824, *Ackermann's Repository* hymned the delights of a double sleeve with a 'short sleeve made very full and confined to the arm by a band' attached to a 'half sleeve' formed of 'a row of cornets as a sort of trimming, which sticks out in such a manner as to remind one of the quills of a porcupine.' By the mid-1820s, the 'natural' aesthetic of the revolutionary period, with its clinging dresses and liberated tresses, was being superseded by the artifice of the dandy era. Letitia herself would soon be abandoning her boho Cockney style in favour of the exigencies of high fashion, as waists tightened, skirts became stiff triangles, sleeves ballooned, and hair was looped up (often with the addition of false hairpieces) into increasingly bizarre variants of the 'Apollo knot'.

Like her contemporary Hans Christian Andersen, she understood the psychology of the emperor's new clothes, and indeed the literal value of clothes themselves in image terms. Her ever-changing costumes dominate her extant portraits, which also show that her coiffure too underwent repeated and often extreme transformations, though a surviving lock of her dark hair reveals that it was indeed naturally 'silken', fine and flyaway. In the early 1820s, she adopted the informal girlish style known as *à l'enfant*, in a concerted attempt to play the ingenue: loose ringlets framing the face. In Letitia's 1831 novel *Romance and Reality*, a Miss Martin calculatedly affects simplicity as 'by a crop curled in the neck *à l'enfant*'. Around 1826 she had her hair 'cut short to curl' (leading, she complained, to the 'martyrdom of curls'). She subsequently adopted extravagant versions of the Apollo knot, and then, as more demure early Victorian styles came into view, smoothed it down under a hairband. Such efforts occasioned complaints about bad hair days, as Letitia could not afford an expensive coiffeur.

Her social skills, however, were second to none, tested to the utmost once she made her salon debut. Trusting no one, she developed a relentless capacity for flattery, as was later spittingly recalled by another young woman she met at Miss Spence's: the Irish beauty Rosina Wheeler, who became her boon companion for a time. Aware how important it was to secure allies in her perilous position, Letitia sought to win Rosina over by endlessly praising her looks. She addressed her as 'carissima' or 'ma belle Rose' in a play of assumed intimacy that rivals the affectation of Jane Austen's Mrs Elton in *Emma* with her 'caro sposo'. Chameleon-like as ever, Letitia chatted to Rosina in the vernacular of the bright young things of the 1820s, who were as addicted to superlatives as those of the 1920s. A century apart, both generations embraced hedonism and heartless gaiety as a response to having been brought up in the shadow of war.

Rosina's mother, Anna Doyle Wheeler (c. 1780–1848), had escaped from an abusive marriage, contracted in Ireland when she was only fifteen, to become a radical feminist and socialist at a time when such ideas were increasingly relegated to the lunatic fringe. Her worldlier daughter, in contrast, was out to party rather than to protest. The penniless Rosina, her face her only fortune, was keen to secure herself through marriage. Letitia advised her on matters of courtship. 'Marry ma charmante rose, and your London season will be the wonder of the morning post,' she told her winningly on November 30, 1825.

Rosina's fiancé, whom she met chez Miss Spence, was none other than Edward Bulwer, who had been such a keen reader of L.E.L. as an undergraduate. A would-be mini-Byron himself, he had published a volume of verse while still at Cambridge and had followed yet more closely in his hero's footsteps by briefly serving as the raddled Caroline Lamb's toyboy. He became ensorcelled by the gorgeous Rosina, whom he married (against his mother's wishes) in 1827.

Letitia did not reveal much about her real situation to her new friends. In 1826, Bulwer told a correspondent that L.E.L. was 'only eighteen' (she was by then twenty-four) and 'a Dean's daughter, or something of that sort' (it was her uncle who was the dean of Exeter). She had clearly exaggerated both her youth and her social credentials in an effort to make herself more appealing, a sign of how insecure she must have felt.

Bulwer went on to become a best-selling novelist, a member of Parliament from 1831, and subsequently a cabinet minister. By 1834, however, following infidelities on both sides, his marriage had begun to dissolve into the most vitriolic and public separation since the Byrons'. Bulwer remained loyal to Letitia for life, but Rosina turned against her around the time their marriage collapsed, going on to allege in an angry private memorandum that Letitia was Bulwer's 'cast-off' mistress.

Given Rosina's florid paranoia—she later accused her estranged husband of committing sodomy with Disraeli to get into the cabinet—that cannot be taken too seriously. What *is* clear from the on-the-spot sources is that during the 1820s Letitia and Jerdan used both Bulwers as pawns in their own game of hearts, and as a cover for their affair. 'Mr Jerdan says . . . he thinks it too bad and too exorbitant of you to be both the beauty and the wit,' Letitia told Rosina in a letter full of frisky badinage in 1825, in which she thanks Rosina for sending a delightful epigram and caricature of Jerdan. Jerdan was obviously looking over Letitia's shoulder as she wrote, titillated by the idea of employing his young lover as a conduit through which to flirt with her best friend.

Bulwer himself was relaxed, he told Jerdan, about 'witnessing the usual flirtation which takes place between you and Mrs Bulwer when ever . . . you meet.' But outsiders were shocked by the attentions Letitia openly paid to Rosina's husband. When the recently married Bulwers gave a country house party, a fellow guest noted with distaste how outrageously Miss Landon flirted with the host. The same guest also recorded, as an apparent afterthought, that William Jerdan happened to be staying overnight too, unaware of the implications.

Rosina was not wrong to spot that there was a private understanding between her husband and Letitia. However, the intimacy that subsisted between them was that between a man of the world and a fallen woman whose situation, though unspoken, he could acknowledge in a way that no lady could have done. Rosina, who was hardly unworldly, must have had more of an inkling about Letitia's relationship with Jerdan than she later claimed to have had. Yet in line with the rules of *demi-connaissance,* Letitia did not openly confide in her *carissima.*

By 1825 Letitia's social rise was such that she was receiving some rather grand invitations. 'I have been quite a round of dinner parties, very pleasant to myself but very indescribable,' she told Rosina archly. As ambivalent towards conspicuous consumption as she had been when she satirized the West Indian dandy, she noted that 'at one the table was so covered with gold plate that I began to look somewhat anxiously for a dish that had something in it.'

By now, Letitia was also a hostess herself, though her own rather more down-at-heel salon was held at her grandmother's Sloane Street apartment. According to her memoirist Katherine Thomson, 'Nothing could be more lively than these little social meetings and nothing more unexceptionable.'

The gatherings, at which Jerdan was a frequent presence, were undoubtedly more riotous than Mrs Thomson let on. They certainly included dancing, which must have been sweatily close in the confines of a flat so small that the living room opened directly onto the bedroom. In one surviving early letter, Letitia invited fellow *Gazette* writer Alexander Alaric Watts to an impromptu 'quadrille' party.

Letitia's celebrity profile was given a fillip in April 1825 when her portrait was exhibited at the Royal Academy. Like *L'Improvisatrice* of 1823, it was painted by H. W. Pickersgill. In an effort to maximize publicity, the earlier image was borrowed back from its buyer, the Marquess of Lansdowne, and exhibited simultaneously in the Royal Academy's spillover gallery at the British Institution (the rule was that no picture could be

Inconveniences in Quadrille Dancing by George Cruikshank. Letitita hosted quadrille parties in her grandmother's cramped apartment.

exhibited twice in the main venue). Visitors that year were thus presented with a bona fide portrait of Miss Landon in one gallery, and a staged image of a fantasy *improvvisatrice* in another. Nothing could better illustrate the diffusion of self that Letitia's public image entailed.

The 1825 portrait, known from the engraving made for Jerdan's autobiography in the 1850s, is innocuous-looking to the modern eye (see plates). To knowing contemporaries, however, it encoded Letitia's ambiguous identity. Those who invested in Letitia's purity were scandalized. The critic for the *European Magazine* complained that Pickersgill had 'made a modest and retiring young lady a virago-looking Amazonian in a Spanish hat, which unquestionably the improvisatrice never wore.'

The portrait shows Letitia wearing her hair in the innocent *à l'enfant* style. She is, however, also sporting faux-historical slashed sleeves and the objectionable flamboyant feathered hat. The hair said 'infant genius', but the costume suggested a female Don Juan. It mimicked that worn by the racy actress Madame Vestris when she appeared *en travestie* in the title role in the recent vaudeville hit *Giovanni in London* (see plates).

Letitia is also smiling enough for her teeth to be visible. As Colin Jones has shown in *The Smile Revolution,* such details had a wealth of hidden meaning. Only actresses smiled in portraits. In Pickersgill's many portraits of respectable high-society ladies, the sitters' mouths are closed. 'When she was in the first flush of her fame, Pickersgill made her the subject of one of his most perfect pictures—as a picture, but I never thought it like; it was too womanly, too self-confident for L.E.L.,' Anna Maria Hall later complained, objecting to it as too sexualized.

The exhibition of the portrait was designed to usher in Letitia's next work, *The Troubadour,* published that summer, a mere year after *The Improvisatrice.* Written in the third person, the new book showed a marked retreat from L.E.L.'s earlier erotic confessionalism. Afraid that she had gone too far in risking her reputation, Letitia was attempting to improvise a fresh identity.

The new book had an autobiographical postscript in which she played up the image of herself as an innocent little girl. Writing in a style so childlike as to be almost doggerel, she recalled the success of *The Improvisatrice,* including a politic note of modest thanks to the reviewers who had applauded it: 'Scarce possible it seem'd to be / That such praise could be meant for me.' She then went on to reveal that the triumph of *The Improvisatrice* had been overshadowed by personal tragedy, recording her sorrow at the death of her father, which had indeed taken place in November 1824:

> *My page is wet with bitter tears,—*
> *I cannot but think of those years*
> *When happiness and I would wait*
> *On summer evenings by the gate . . .*
> *Then run for the first kiss, and word,—*
> *An unkind one I never heard.*
> *But these are pleasant memories,*
> *And later years have none like these:*
> *They came with griefs, and pains, and cares,*
> *All that the heart breaks while it bears.*

John Landon—for whom Letitia had in reality been accustomed to wait at the gate of Trevor Park in childhood—appears to have been an affectionate father, for all his improvidence. Letitia had been genuinely fond of him. However, L.E.L. had by now taken over her life so entirely, disrupting the norms of private and public, that she exploited her recent bereavement to gain the sympathy of wavering readers.

In fact, her innocent-seeming filial tribute was designed to keep her identity in suspension. It reinforced the idea that all her first-person work was literally autobiographical, thus promoting the suspicion that her previous love confessions had been equally authentic. *The Troubadour* was blatantly dedicated to William Jerdan, thanking him for his 'surveillance'.

Jerdan responded with a typically effusive review in the *Literary Gazette*. As ever, he puffed his protégée shamelessly, claiming she was 'endowed by nature with talents so far above the general lot as to be justly entitled to present admiration and future immortality'. As if fearing that the new note of filial piety might cancel out L.E.L.'s hard-won image of sexual allure, he reminded readers that she was a 'gifted individual who commands all the range of human passions'. He also recommended that she must undertake 'severer studies' if she wants to 'attain . . . the greatest name in the annals of . . . imaginative female literature, whether of ancient or modern times'. L.E.L.'s literary Pygmalion was still there in the wings, urging her on.

Elsewhere, *The Troubadour* was well reviewed. The *New Monthly Magazine* pronounced it 'beautiful and graceful'. *The Times* called L.E.L. 'no common writer' and praised her 'extraordinary facility and power of expression'. The *Examiner* pointed to her 'exquisite finish'.

However, a backlash was forming. The *Examiner* also quoted a passage in *The Troubadour* about a fictional poet damaged by empty praise. 'Take the hint, Mr Jerdane [*sic*] and be more discriminative and less magnificent in future, especially when a work has benefited from your own surveillance,' it concluded personally.

The *Westminster Review* went further in a considered article on L.E.L.'s oeuvre, which drew attention to her sexual subtexts, 'sickly thoughts clothed in glittering language that draws the eye off from their real character'. Though acknowledging her 'poetical talent', it advised her 'to avoid the subject of love' in future, and, especially, 'not to be elated by the praise or guided by the . . . critical judgement of the *Literary Gazette*'. It was a warning to disentangle herself from Jerdan.

William Jerdan, meanwhile, was a man visibly on the rise. In 1825, he moved his family into a house every bit as prestigious as the mansion from which the Landons had been evicted in 1820. His new home, Grove House, sometimes known as Brompton Grove, was situated on the Brompton Road, a stone's throw from where he had first seen Letitia with her hoop. It had a thirty-two-by-eighteen-foot drawing room, housed in an extension built by an earlier occupant in honor of a visit by the prince regent.

Jerdan was tickled by the fact that his immediate predecessor as householder was the anti-slavery campaigner William Wilberforce, who had been instrumental in founding the Society for the Suppression of Vice. Wilberforce had, surprisingly, left behind a cellar of fine wines. In his autobiography, Jerdan confessed that he loved 'ostensible wealth' and all life's luxuries. He spared no expense in furnishing his new home. The kitchen cooker alone cost £100.

While Letitia was establishing her small-scale female salon at 131 Sloane Street, Jerdan set about making Grove House the engine room of his ambitions. One contemporary recorded that 'his house was ever open to the leading literary men, artists, dramatic authors and actors of the day'. He sent out invitations to the great and the good, the famous and the influential, although the extent to which they were accepted is debatable. He was widely rumoured to be in the habit of running a wheelbarrow round the gravel in front of the house to give the impression of 'carriage visitors'.

The enthusiasm with which Jerdan boasts about his Grove House days in his autobiography suggests that he was just as vocal in his own praise at the time. It is perhaps not surprising, then, that he aroused envy among strugglers in the literary trade. Few knew that Jerdan had paid for Grove House and its extravagant furnishings by running up a massive £4,000 debt.

The financial crisis of 1816, which ruined John Landon, was not an isolated incident. The roller-coaster economy dipped again in 1824–25. The world of literature was no more protected than any other business. By 1825, the publishing boom of the early 1820s was becoming an unsustainable bubble.

In March 1826, the *Sunday Times* was prompted to defend the industry against charges of fiscal irresponsibility, in terms that suggest crisis mode:

We are happy to be enabled to state that the grounds of our defence of the Booksellers generally, against the calumny of a Daily Paper, were perfectly correct; and that although one or two have by over-speculation (circumstances which happen among the members of all trades, without calling down on the trade generally a sweeping denunciation), not only embarrassed their own concerns, but disarranged for a time those of indisputably solvent houses, the great body of the trade have gallantly weathered the storm, and come into port with flying colours. They have with great prudence, for the present suspended the amount of publication, by which for several years (a pretty ground of charge, forsooth on the part of any member of the community of letters, unless it be some disappointed Grubean) they stimulated talented rivalry, and patronized authors with a liberality unprecedented.

In an insecure environment, the *Gazette* seemed to be aggressively determined to expand its market share at the expense of others. Jerdan seemed to be benefiting. An anonymous flyer sent to publishing houses in January 1825 accused him of corruption. Illustrated with an image of a chamber pot, it was a spoof prospectus for '*The Literary Jordan*', satirically promoting it as 'the best receptacle' for the 'effusions' of the 'literary body'. It alleged that there was an unhealthy relationship between advertising and editorial at the *Literary Gazette,* and that Jerdan would accept any article or poem as long as it was submitted 'accompanied by the expected gratuity of a one pound note'. He was said to dispense positive reviews on the same principle, and damnation to those who did not comply. A pointed reference to the 'effusions' of 'literary ladies' was a harbinger of what was to come.

Backstage, Letitia had not been spending all her time making frilly caps for her grandmother and attending gold-plated dinners. By 1825 she had become so involved in the day-to-day running of the *Gazette* that Jerdan later described her in his autobiography as his effective coeditor, although her role was never formally acknowledged. She was widely known in the industry to be the author of many of the *Gazette*'s anonymous reviews and to spare none of her vitriol. In this, she exceeded even the coeditor's requirements. In one extant note she admits to Jerdan that she now sees the error of 'butting' (i.e., of making reviewees the butt of her attacks) and promises to be 'so positive' in the future.

According to Blanchard, it was those writers who had suffered at Letitia's hands, and those who envied her success, who now began to spread negative rumours about her morals. 'What malignity begins,' he opined disingenuously in his 1841 life, 'ignorant, idle, even sometimes well-meaning gossip, finishes. Those who professed to know nothing about her, aided by their silly curiosity the insidious objects of those who might falsely pretend to know.'

Blanchard retrospectively attributed the rumours to Letitia's over-exuberant social manner, which he put down to her naiveté: 'Unfortunately, the very unguardedness of her innocence served to arm even the feeblest malice with powerful stings; the openness of her nature, and the frankness of her manners, furnished the silly or ill-natured with abundant materials for gossip.'

As is now clear, Letitia was no ingenue. But Blanchard was perhaps right to suppose that she underestimated the viper's nest into which she had been thrust by becoming a 'public character'. With respectable married ladies from Mrs Howitt to Mrs Hall closing their eyes to her 'fallen state', she was living in a bubble. She later depicted the psychological experience of celebrity as treacherously cocooning:

> And I,—I felt immortal, for my brain
> Was drunk and mad with the first draught of fame.

However, female fame inevitably brought with it the risk of female shame. In aiming at Sappho's glory, Letitia had flown too high.

CHAPTER 6

Shame

In his 1841 biography, Laman Blanchard could barely bring himself to mention the rumours that now began to spread about Letitia, leaving their contents unspecified and alluding to them with 'a reluctance which will at least ensure brevity'. His oblique account makes them sound like vague whispers in corners. So it comes as a surprise to discover that the gossip was not only convincing and circumstantial, but printed in the recently founded *Sunday Times*.

On March 5, 1826, that newspaper published a report under the headline 'Sapphics and Erotics', which resolved the equivocations of 'L.E.L.' into a storyline of explosive simplicity. It revealed that there was one person for whom the voyeur fantasies of the poetess's readers had indeed become a reality: the Jerdans' charwoman. She had spied on the adulterous couple in flagrante through a slit in the study blinds at Grove House and gone on to sell her story.

Neither party was overtly named, but the identities of the 'well-known English Sappho' and the 'literary man' were obvious to anyone in London publishing circles. The article went on to allege that Letitia had given birth to a baby in September 1823, although it misreported Ella's sex, calling the child a 'young Terpander' after the male Greek poet. It also gave a lively account of the matrimonial fracas that, according to the charwoman, had occurred in the house of Jerdan after she informed her mistress of what she had seen. The story ran as follows:

A well-known English Sappho, and like her Greek prototype famous for the amorous glow of her fancy, has just been detected in a *faux pas* with a literary man, the father of several children.

SAPPHICS AND EROTICS.

A well-known English Sappho, and like her Greek prototype famous for the amorous glow of her fancy, has just been
detected in a *faux pas* with a literary man, the father of several
children. The discovery happened when the *placens*, or rather
' *complacens uxor*,' and brats were sent off *a l'ordinaire* last September to the waterside, and was effected by means of a charwoman, who *did* for the family. (Indeed, she *did*; but we
much wonder how *literatuli* and blues can employ such marplot
reviewers.) Observing, that as often as the youthful Sappho
arrived at the embowered recess of Love and the Muses, the
blinds on the ground-floor *study* were *pulled down*, and the
shutters *pulled up*; and wondering how *books* could be read in
the dark, this female busybody stationed herself so ingeniously
on one of the Uplands of the Suburban Parnassus as to see the
whole poetical mystery, by which ' hearts throb with hearts,'
and ' souls with souls unite.' This she expounded to the wife,
whose face immediately exhibited an ' intensity of *blue*,' sufficient to have made any one a first-rate *blue stocking*; ' fair was
foul and foul was fair :' chaos was come again : and every link
of the chain of Platonic friendship was broken for ever. Other
truths then came out, from which it appeared that the ' virgin gentleness, the orphan muse' had honored her *Benedict* (though not
Benedictus) Phaon with a young chubby Terpander, or son of a
lyre, two years before, and at Canterbury of all places, whither
the gay deceiver cantered with her (so he gave out) on his way
to Margate, for the purpose of seeing his better half and seven
fractions, like a good spouse, back to London.

The *Sunday Times* exposé, 'Sapphics and Erotics.'

The discovery happened when the *placens,* or rather '*complacens
uxor,*' and brats were sent off *à l'ordinaire* last September to the
waterside, and was effected by means of a charwoman, who *did*
for the family. (Indeed she did; but we much wonder how *literatuli* and blues can employ such marplot *reviewers.*) Observing,
that as often as the youthful Sappho arrived at the embowered
recess of Love and the Muses, the blinds on the ground-floor
study were *pulled down,* and the shutters *pulled up;* and wondering how *books* could be read in *the dark,* this female busybody stationed herself so ingeniously on one of the Uplands of
the Suburban Parnassus as to see the whole poetical mystery, by
which 'hearts throb with hearts' and 'souls with souls unite.' This
she expounded to the wife, whose face immediately exhibited
an 'intensity of *blue,*' sufficient to have made anyone a first-rate
blue-stocking: 'fair was foul and foul was fair': chaos was come
again: and every link in the chain of Platonic friendship was
broken for ever. Other truths then came out, from which it
appeared that the 'virgin gentleness, the orphan muse' had honoured her . . . Phaon with a chubby young Terpander, or son of

a *lyre,* two years before, and at Canterbury of all places, whither the gay deceiver cantered with her (so he gave out) on his way to Margate, for the purpose of seeing his better half and seven fractions, like a good spouse, back to London.

Oral gossip was one thing, but factual revelations in the public prints were quite another, a shibboleth exploited by the blackmailing courtesan Harriette Wilson in her salacious kiss-and-tell memoirs of 1825. In Jane Austen's *Mansfield Park* (1814), Maria Rushworth becomes a social pariah when details of her adultery with Henry Crawford are published in a gossip column, courtesy of her mother-in-law's maid. According to Henry's sister Mary, the affair could have been 'hushed up' and continued ad infinitum had not Maria given the maid the power of exposure by her careless talk. Fanny Price and Edmund Bertram are horrified to discover that, in Mary's view, Maria's only mistake is to have been found out.

Today, the charwoman could have used her phone to take a photograph through the gap in the study blinds, but no such ocular proof was possible in 1826. The story could be denied. That is what Letitia did next.

She tactically chose to issue her rebuttal through a private rather than a public channel, in a letter to her friend Mrs Thomson, a doctor's wife who was known, according to Blanchard, for her high sense of moral rectitude. Undoubtedly composed with a wider audience in mind than its named recipient, the letter was printed in Blanchard's 1841 biography as proof of Letitia's innocence, and subsequently taken at face value by later commentators.

Letitia couched her self-defence in the shape of a formal apologia for the professional woman writer. As such, her letter is a rhetorical tour de force. But though it spoke many truths about the struggles facing female authors in the 1820s, it was also of necessity a masterpiece of dissimulation.

She began by proclaiming her commitment to her craft in the face of the male-dominated press, which had built her up and was now gleefully knocking her down:

I must begin with the only subject—the only thing in the world I really feel an interest in—my writings. It is not vanity when I say, their success is their fault. When my Improvvisatrice [*sic*] came out, nobody discovered what is now alleged against it. I did not take up a review, a magazine, a newspaper but if it named my book it was to praise 'the delicacy,' 'the grace,' 'the purity of feminine feeling' it displayed. . . . But success is an offence not to be forgiven. To every petty author, whose works have scarce made his name valuable as an autograph, or whose unsold editions load his bookseller's shelves—I am a subject of envy—and what is envy but a name for hatred?

She then went on to throw the ball back into her critics' court, claiming that only the dirty-minded could find anything indecent in her work: 'With regard to the immoral or improper tendency of my productions, I can only say that it is not my fault if there are minds which, like negroes, cast a dark shadow on a mirror, however clear and pure in itself.' Behind her casually racist simile lurked the West Indian dandy's slave, smirking in the glass behind his self-lionizing master as he pretends to simple-minded innocence.

'You must forgive this,' Letitia continued, rising to an emotional peroration. 'I do not often speak of my own works, and I may say this is the first time I have ever done so boastingly; but I must be allowed to place the opinions of the many in opposition to the envious and illiberal cavillings of the few.' Only then, as if in a postscript, did she come to the point.

'As to the *report* you named,' she wrote in allusion to the *Sunday Times*, 'I know not which is greatest—the absurdity or the malice.' She admitted she was 'very much indebted to the gentleman, for much of kindness', refusing even to name Jerdan, but only in a professional sense as her agent and editor. 'But it is not on this ground,' she went on, 'that I express my surprise at so cruel a calumny, but actually on that of our slight intercourse. . . . He is in the habit of frequently calling on his way into town, and unless it is on a Sunday afternoon, which is almost his only leisure time for looking over letters, manuscripts, etc., five or ten minutes is the usual time of his visit.'

By some sleight of hand, Letitia managed to present as negligible what sounds like rather frequent contact. Jerdan came to see her at 131 Sloane Street on a near-daily basis on his way to work. In addition he spent his Sunday afternoons with her—plenty of time in which to conduct an affair while her sympathetic grandmother made herself scarce.

The letter is all the more intriguing because its recipient, Katherine Thomson, was not just any respectable doctor's wife, but the wife of Letitia's own doctor, Anthony Todd Thomson. With a fashionable practice in Sloane Street, he had attended her since her 'girlish days' and was her 'constant medical friend and advisor'.

It beggars belief that Letitia could have hidden her pregnancy from her own doctor. Dr Thomson certainly had obstetric experience. In 1810 he delivered the future novelist Elizabeth Gaskell, whose aunt was his first wife. He was also, quite literally, in Jerdan's pay. Since January 1824 he had been the *Gazette*'s regular medical columnist. The column was initiated shortly after Ella's birth in the last quarter of 1823, perhaps as a quid pro quo for discreet medical attentions to the editor's mistress during her first pregnancy.

In her 1837 novel *Ethel Churchill*, Letitia compared the personal physician to a confessor priest. How much she openly confided in her friend

Dr. Anthony Todd Thomson, Letitia's
personal physician

Katherine, Dr Thomson's much younger second wife, is more debatable. In the era of *demi-connaissance,* respectable ladies had to distance themselves from fallen women, even to the extent of pretending not to notice their swelling pregnancies. Letitia's letter was self-defensive, but it may have also been designed to protect Mrs Thomson from overt knowledge that might have impacted on the latter's reputation.

Letitia was certainly careful to put Mrs Thomson in her debt. She flattered her to the hilt in the spring of 1826 when her first book, a biography of Henry VIII, came out: 'Already I see you a regular lioness. "Have you got Mrs Thomson's autograph? I am sure you will be at my party when I tell you Mrs Thomson is to be there—she is the great historianess, a most charming delightful woman."' Letitia was no doubt responsible for the glowing review of Mrs Thomson's book that then appeared in the *Gazette* in May 1826. Later that year, the *Gazette* also published a blistering attack on a book entitled *On Hypocrisy,* which attempted to expose and excoriate the double standards of the day. The reviewer—probably Letitia herself—mocked the author for his determination to call a spade a spade. She herself was dependent on hypocrisy for her social survival.

However, Letitia signed off her letter to Mrs Thomson with a sentence that spoke more truth than it openly confided: 'No one knows but myself what I have had to contend with; but this is what I have no right to trouble you with.' At the time she wrote this, in June 1826, she almost certainly had more to hide than even the *Sunday Times* had alleged.

So much obfuscation surrounds this period of Letitia's life that documentation is hard to come by. Yet what clues survive point to the probability that by March 5, when the *Sunday Times* exposé was published, she was pregnant for a second time. By June, when she penned her letter to Mrs Thomson, she was either about to give birth or had just done so.

That Ella had a brother, Fred, who shared her parents and her surname Stuart, is not in doubt. An undated letter from Fred to his 'dear sister' Ella, written in adulthood, survives. Yet his date of birth is yet more clouded since he has no extant baptismal record. When Ella was christened, Letitia was still the nameless melodist. By 1826 she was a literary lion whose private life was being raked over by the press. It would have been prudent to keep any new 'child of shame' out of public records.

On October 7, 1826, *The Wasp,* a short-lived satirical periodical, claimed that the previously sylphlike Letitia had 'in the course of a few months acquired so perceptible a degree of *embonpoint*, as to induce her kind friend Jerdan to recommend a change of air, lest her health and strength should be affected. She followed his advice, and strange to say, such was the effect of even two months' absence from Brompton, that she was returned as *thin* and poetical as ever!' A week later, *The Wasp* went on, charging 'L.E.L. (alias Letitia Languish)' with having 'written a sentimental elegy on the *Swellings of Jordan*. She pleaded that *the flood had gone off;* but the plea was overruled; and she was ordered into the country to gather *fruit,* and to *deliver* an account thereof on her return.'

During 1826, Letitia is indeed on record as having spent much time out of London. She paid two long visits to Aberford, the Yorkshire home of her uncle the Reverend James Landon, the less successful brother of the dean of Exeter. The first stay occurred around Christmas and New Year of 1825–26, the second between July and October. But the rest of her movements that year are hard to trace, to the extent that it seems that a move is afoot to cover her tracks.

It is not clear where Letitia was in 'June' when she wrote to Mrs Thomson. She was probably out of town giving birth to Fred. Her next letter to Mrs Thomson was written in July from Aberford, where she had evidently only just arrived, as she described her coach journey. She apologized to Mrs Thomson for not having called on her in London before departing for Yorkshire: 'I had intended, my dear Mrs Thomson taking my chance of spending Monday evening with you, but my cousin's return home with me, and the beneficial effect of leaving everything to the last, prevented my going out.'

Clearly, Letitia had been away from home somewhere else with her 'cousin' before returning to London to pack hurriedly and set off for Aberford. The cousin she mentions can only have been her former governess Elizabeth Landon, who had initially pushed her in Jerdan's direction, and was now, it seems likely, dealing with its consequences by taking Letitia away for her confinement.

The attack of *The Wasp* at the beginning of October resulted in Letitia's staying out of town longer than she had intended. Instead of going straight home from Aberford, in October she travelled from there to Biggleswade in Bedfordshire, where she remained until the end of the year, apparently staying with a local 'Mr Ashwell', whom she mentions as having driven her to the high road to pick up the London coach when she finally returned to Brompton in December. As the name Ashwell does not reappear in her correspondence, he may simply have provided her with paid lodgings.

Letitia's son Fred Stuart is the most enigmatic of her children. As with Ella, it is not known how he was brought up, but a hint exists in the 1841 census. It lists an 'Alfred Stewart', aged fifteen (i.e., born c. 1826), as pupil at a boarding school in Uxbridge, then a village just outside London. In his autobiography, Jerdan mentions that one of his schoolboy acquaintances was an English lad who had come to Scotland under the care of a tutor who was the former headmaster of a school in Uxbridge. Jerdan may have remembered the place when looking for somewhere to send his natural son by L.E.L.

Whether or not the 'Alfred Stewart' of the 1841 census was in fact Fred Stuart, it is all too likely that Letitia's son would have been sent to boarding school. Anyone who has read *David Copperfield* or *Jane Eyre* will shiver at the thought of such pre-Victorian establishments. Some, chillingly, boasted 'no holidays' in contemporary newspaper advertisements, an obvious advantage to parents keen to get inconvenient offspring out of the way.

When Fred grew up, Jerdan 'exported' him to the West Indies, as he also did with one of his legitimate sons, the latter of whom died in Jamaica. In the 1850s, the increasingly indiscreet editor told his neighbour Francis Bennoch that Fred was 'going on prosperously in Trinidad and his sister Ella so well married in Melbourne as to be able to send him £50 to clear off early settling scores'. Fred's one surviving letter, written to Ella, offers a less rosy picture. He describes himself as 'penniless and homeless' and suffering from 'bad West Indian fever'. In Trinidad, he apparently tried to pursue journalism, but unsuccessfully. He seems to have married and had a child, since a Victorian photograph survives in the family archive of a pitifully sickly-looking little girl named 'Emily Ella Stuart', taken in a Port of Spain studio. After that, Fred and his emaciated little daughter disappear from the historical record.

Since the triumphant high point of the spring of 1825, when her portrait was exhibited at the Royal Academy, Letitia had undergone a series of traumatic experiences. In September 1825, she had seen her sister on her deathbed, and had been forced to reestablish contact with her mother for the first time since their estrangement. That same month, her lover's wife had been apprised of the affair by the charwoman, causing a marital row, with whatever consequences for Letitia that involved. Soon afterward she discovered she was pregnant again.

Then in March came the blow of the *Sunday Times*. It was followed by a private tragedy in the Jerdan family that would inevitably have impacted Letitia's relationship with her lover. On April 25, William and Frances's youngest daughter, Georgiana, died, aged sixteen months. Their devastation is suggested by the unusually full death notice Jerdan inserted in the press, and by the fact that it was one of the very few family events he referred to in his autobiography. We can only surmise what Jerdan felt about Letitia's pregnancy in the light of losing a beloved legitimate child. The same goes for Letitia's feelings about his public expressions of grief for Georgiana, when her own baby would have to be given up.

Mrs Jerdan, meanwhile, had little choice other than to be complaisant until humiliated by the charwoman into putting on a display of anger. Even after that, Letitia appears to have been accepted as a part of the family setup. When Dickens's future father-in-law George Hogarth wrote to Jerdan in 1829, 'with a delightful recollection of the great kindness we received from you when in London', he particularly asked to be remembered to 'Miss Landon'.

However, Jerdan's 1831 short story 'The Sleepless Woman' points to marital tensions. An exercise in ludicrous light gothic, it features a tormented young baron who drowns himself in a lake to escape the permanently open eyes of his wife. It is, the author boasts, an 'ingenious allegory': 'if a jealous wife can't drive a man out of his mind and into a lake, we do not know what can!'

Astonishingly, through all this, the literary partnership between Letitia and Jerdan carried on as if nothing had happened. While no longer contributing at the extraordinary rate of 1822–24, Letitia continued to write plaintive love lyrics for the *Gazette,* marked by her characteristic combination of emotional acuity and narrative vagueness. Some of the poems invited dangerous interpretations from readers now primed more than ever by the *Sunday Times* to find personal import in the thwarted love scenarios imaged in her verse.

It was not until just after *The Wasp* fired its first sally on October 7 that her contributions to the *Gazette* finally dried up, not to resume again until the start of 1827. By coincidence, L.E.L.'s last poem of 1826 was published on the very same date, October 14, as *The Wasp's* second assault, with its satiric reference to 'Letitia Languish' gathering 'fruit.' Her poem included a fruit image that was perhaps too embarrassingly apropos even for her and Jerdan:

> *Leaves grow green to fall,*
> *Flowers grow fair to fade,*
> *Fruits grow ripe to rot—*
> *All but for passing made.*

Katherine Thomson later claimed that Jerdan considered bringing a libel action against the *Sunday Times*. This is unlikely given the facts. It would have been as self-defeating as Oscar Wilde's action against the Marquess of Queensberry later in the century. It was not until December 30, 1826, that the editor finally responded to the allegations, on the back page of the *Gazette:*

> When we can find nothing better to entertain readers with, and not till then, will we notice the contemptible writers who (we are told and in a few instances have seen) find a constant exercise for their eminent talents in attacking the *Literary Gazette*. Should they ever succeed in attracting any public attention by their lively and entertaining malignity, we shall begin to think it time to change our plan, and contribute our share to the general fund of intelligence, instruction, and improvement by devoting our columns to interesting personal squabbles and abuse of distinguished contemporaries, instead of the dull subjects of literature, science and art.

In the same issue, he gave front-page prominence to a review of a new book called *A Treatise on the Law of Libel and Slander* that dismissed lawyers as pests and made the case for free comment. It was a disingenuous attempt to make it look as though it was the editor's principled devotion to press freedom that lay behind his failure to sue, not the inconvenient truth that the facts were against him.

In contrast to her real-life situation, Letitia's letters to her female friends written that summer sparkle with brittle wit. It is as if there is no communication at all between the manic Miss Landon and the melancholic L.E.L., for whom fruits rot and flowers fade. After the serious and considered self-apologia she wrote to Katherine Thomson in June, her epistolary tone returned to high-spirited archness.

In July, having just arrived at her uncle's in Aberford, she joked to Mrs Thomson that the strangers she met in the coach had not 'the slightest idea of my original sin, no thought of my taint of blue'—as if bluestocking intellectualism, not a sexual fall, were the only shocking thing about her. Her letters from Aberford to Rosina Wheeler and Emma Roberts are positively bubbly, although at times the comedy seems forced.

In August, for example, she made a laboured pun on ants/aunts in a letter to Rosina:

> We have past divers rural days, dining in woods &c. to my taste more picturesque than pleasant, while a chair or a table are to [be] had, I shall infinitely prefer them in their rosewood or mahogany shapes, to making a chair of a stump, a table of my knees and par consequence a table of my frock, much as I like my relations, I prefer taking my dinner with any than my *ants*.

But she was on form when she transformed a minor eye infection and a bonnet disaster into a major drama:

> A heavy misfortune befell me the other day—one of those misfortunes which really do affect my feelings. I was ruralizing, was caught in violent rain, and my bonnet, my best bonnet, new trimmed, was utterly hopelessly spoilt; and what was worse, my beauty, if I have any; for I caught cold, and had a great gathering in my left eye, which besides being very painful gave me a most pugilistic appearance. I arranged a black silk handkerchief as well as I could over the poulticed side, but, alas! it did not at all resemble

> —'*the mask which shades*
> *The face of young Arabian maids,*
> *A mask which leaves the one eye free*
> *To do its best in witchery.*'

The image of the mask (a quotation from Thomas Moore) refracted Letitia's own façade: the lightness of tone she had to adopt in the face of public humiliation; the denial of her children's existence; the pose of modesty overlying sexual realities. Before cranking up her satirical mode, Letitia made a brief, bitter allusion to the 'utter cold worldliness' of London society, where 'disinterested friendship' did not exist. Her only acknowledgement of any emotional life of her own, in a letter to Katherine Thomson, was a parenthetical reference to 'feelings (if I have any)'.

On August 19, the *Gazette* ran L.E.L.'s most cynical lyric to date, 'The World as It Is'. The speaker responds to the coldness of her lover by embracing a disconnected and purely exchange-driven view of human relations:

> *Why should I shed a single tear,*
> *When none is shed for me?*
> *Or sigh amid a careless crowd,*
> *Where sighs should never be?*
>
> *Why should I love? a fair exchange*
> *Is all my love will give:*
> *As I am loved, 'tis fair for that*
> *An equal love should give.*

Acknowledging that 'Utopia's days' are over, L.E.L. cleaves to the 'modern creed', which she expresses in a sardonic cliché: 'when out of sight / Best to be out of mind'. The 'careless laugh and mocking eye' are her only defences.

Letitia's own mask was firmly in place when she declared in a letter to Emma Roberts in December, 'if such a novelty as a lover should ever fall to my share, I should not be able to help bribing the bellman to make it generally known.' Given her situation, her bravado astounds.

A clue as to its cultural meaning is to be found in a throwaway reference to 'the author of Rouge et Noir' in her letter to Rosina. Letitia was alluding to a book published in 1821 by William Read, a fellow *Gazette* contributor (not to be confused with Stendhal's later masterpiece *Le rouge et le noir*). It was an adroit *Don Juan*–style verse satire, with prose interludes, on gambling. The title alluded to the card game *rouge et noir*.

Throughout her career, Letitia gambled on her reputation. She manipulated her culture's clichés of emotional femininity with the insouciance of a high-stakes poker player. As she wrote in 1833, in a private letter to a worldly man of letters, Crofton Croker: 'when in doubt, lead trump—so I have taken refuge in sentiment, the court card of the poet's hand.' Had she allowed herself to feel for real, she would have fallen off her tightrope.

With the *Sunday Times,* Fred's birth, and *The Wasp,* the stakes had grown higher, the danger greater. In allowing nothing to ruffle her outer composure, she was like Read's gambler who hazards his whole fortune 'with that *au fait* air which one assumes in doing something which might be thought uncommon quite as a matter of course; although a summersault from the *Pont Neuf,* or a black bench at the *Morgue,* would perhaps have been the consequence of an unfavourable turn in the instance of a single card.' In the honour cult of the *rouge et noir* player, suicide was the inevitable result of ruin. According to Thomas De Quincey, the same went for the sexually shamed woman: 'there is no man, who in his heart would not reverence a woman that chose to die rather than to be dishonoured.'

Suicide had long been one of Letitia's favourite literary themes, but her pregnancy with Fred only made her more prolific as a writer. Using work as a distraction, she continued to pour out poetry 'by the pound'. By the end of 1826, she had finished a new collection, *The Golden Violet,* published at the start of 1827.

She strategically inscribed it to her Yorkshire uncle, insisting to anyone who might suspect otherwise that her recent absences from London had been due to respectable family visits to a country vicar, not to an untoward pregnancy:

To the Reverend James Landon,
Rector of Aberford and Amstery

My dear Uncle,

I inscribe to you this volume, the greater part of which was written under your affectionate roof, during the two pleasant

seasons I have passed with you. To have it deemed worthy of
your critical judgement, and your more partial approval, would
indeed be the pride and pleasure of

Your gratefully attached,
L.E.L.
December 1826.

Like *The Troubadour*, the new book's long title poem eschewed the
first-person mode that had first established L.E.L. as a cult figure. Its
conceit was a medieval poetry festival. Minstrels, both male and female,
convene at the court of a Provençal princess to compete for the trophy of
a golden violet by performing their songs. The structure gave Letitia the
opportunity to show off her skill at versification in a series of contrasting
lyrics and ballads in which her signature themes of love and bloodshed
could be treated in a detached manner, without her inhabiting a particular protagonist.

The narrative ended on an uncertain note, without the trophy being
awarded. Readers were invited to decide for themselves which poem
deserved the prize. Like the gambler in *Rouge et Noir*, Letitia was symbolically giving up her destiny to fate.

In a final envoi, she again stepped out of the narrative to speak in her
'own' first-person voice, adopting a faux-naïf style in a bid for sympathy,
this time alluding to the travails of her own career:

> *what art thou, fame?*
> *A various and a doubtful claim*
> *One grants and one denies; what none*
> *Can wholly quite agree upon.*
> *A dubious and uncertain path*
> *At least the modern minstrel hath.*

The very badness of the lines is shifty. What none could 'wholly quite
agree upon' was of course the truth of the allegations against her sexual virtue. The creaking versification only comes to life if one imagines Letitia speaking the words with coquettishly simulated wide-eyed
innocence.

By now, Letitia's high-wire act had become a compulsion. She continued to draw attention to her 'fall' and to invite confessional readings of her poetry, whose value, she asserted, was to be found in

Feelings whose truth is all their worth,
Thoughts which have had their pensive birth
When lilies hang their heads and die,
Eve's lesson of mortality.

The pure white lily hangs its head in shame at its own sexual corruption. L.E.L. knows, like Eve, that she is naked.

The poem in the collection of which she was most proud was 'Erinna', written at the end of October, just after *The Wasp*'s attack. Like *The Improvisatrice*, it had a first-person poetess heroine, this time an ancient Greek contemporary of Sappho. Letitia explained in a note that she was not attempting to reconstruct the historical Erinna but 'to draw the portrait and trace the changes of a highly poetical mind, too sensitive perhaps of the chill and bitterness belonging even to success'. In other words, the poem was designed to engage readers' pity for the assaults L.E.L. herself had endured in the wake of becoming a bestseller.

Unlike Letitia's usual heroines, Erinna has no lover. Her tragedy is played out not with a man but with the public. As an idealistic child, she believes that poetry will create an ideal bond between her and her readers. But she finds, on the contrary, that fame exposes her to 'mockery' and 'plague spot', bringing calumny on her head and causing her private agony, a clear allusion to Letitia's recent real experiences:

I have scorned myself
For that my cheek could burn, my pulses beat
At idle words.

Erinna confesses to have taken a 'deep and dangerous delight' in celebrity, but describes it as an addiction, 'the opiate of my heart'. She also represents it as a quasi-sexual violation: 'I do not hope a sunshine burst of fame, / My lyre asks but a wreath of fragile flowers.' To in-crowd readers looking for salacious hidden meanings, it must have seemed that Letitia was asking for the return of the virginity that she had traded with Jerdan for her career.

If 'Erinna' continued to offer fodder for gossip, so did Jerdan. On December 16, 1826, he gave *The Golden Violet* glowing prepublicity in the *Gazette*. His applause was indeed calculated to make Letitia's cheek crimson. 'When we . . . remember that this is the third work in the course of two years . . . by a young female, hardly of legal age to be considered more than a child,' he leered, 'we confess we are lost in amazement at what she has accomplished.' What, he continued, was the reason for her 'extraordinary popularity'? It was that her poetry was 'the bold adventure of a mere girl welling forth such strains (with all their imperfections) as the deepest natural feelings and the truest genius alone could inspire.' It was because, he wrote, 'She began to write so early in years, and having had so little intercourse with the world, that she wrote not only with freedom but without fear. The genuine sentiments of nature thus came to be expressed with a freshness, force and truth which, perhaps, her future works may want, but which were re-echoed by every heart where the best feelings were not obliterated.'

'Freedom,' 'genuine sentiments of nature', and 'truth' were treacherously suggestive signposts. The trainer was rewarding his songbird with punishment, humiliating her with praise. He probably hoped that salacious stories would actually boost the sales of the *Gazette,* while revealing him in the flattering role of a sexual conquistador.

In her everyday life, however, Letitia took practical steps to protect her reputation. When she finally returned to London from her hideout in Biggleswade at the end of 1826, she did not go back to her grandmother's apartment at 131 Sloane Street, where Jerdan was known to have been a regular visitor. Instead, she removed to lodgings above the girls' school at 22 Hans Place, where she herself had been a pupil a decade earlier. Now under the new management of two sisters called the Misses Lance, the school provided a potential refuge. Emma Roberts was already a lodger there. 'I look forward to the decided advantage of being under such a highly respectable roof as the Misses Lance,' Letitia told Miss Roberts from Biggleswade on December 19.

Letitia looked forward to the move as self-empowering: 'when I arrive at 22 . . . for the first time in my life [I] shall know what I am about.' The attic she moved into was later fictionalized by Elizabeth Barrett Browning in *Aurora Leigh* as a symbolic woman writer's 'room of one's own' *avant la lettre*. But it was a world away from the perfumed boudoir strewn with silks in which L.E.L.'s fans imagined her writing.

According to a contemporary visitor, it was a

> homely-looking, almost uncomfortable room, fronting the
> street, barely furnished with a simple white bed, at the foot of
> which was a small, old, oblong-shaped sort of dressing table,
> quite covered with a common, worn writing-desk heaped with
> papers, while some strewed the ground, the table being too small
> for aught besides the desk; a little high-backed cane chair which
> gave you any idea rather than that of comfort—a few books scat-
> tered about completed the author's paraphernalia.

Letitia's own feelings on arriving there are hinted at in a short story:

> I cannot describe to you how my heart sank within me when
> I first entered the gloomy attic, henceforth destined to be my
> home, my study, and where so much of my life was to pass. I gazed
> upon the low ceiling, which seemed to press the air down upon
> me; a slip of looking-glass, cracked and coarse-grained enough to
> make you discontented even with yourself, stuck in the plaster;
> the white-washed walls; the small stove, like that in the cabin of
> a ship; the wretched little wash-hand stand; the common check
> furniture of the bed; the parapet before the window—oh that
> parapet! . . . to the parapet my eye never became reconciled.

She would live and work in that room for a decade, while Jerdan carried
on carousing in his big house with his family and his wine cellar.

Hans Place was, conveniently, even nearer to Jerdan's home than
131 Sloane Street. After Letitia moved out, her complaisant grandmother
Mrs Bishop also relocated. By the time she made her will in 1829, she was
living a few steps from Hans Place at a new address in Queen Street (now
Hans Road), which may have provided a convenient love nest.

Despite the increased risk of scandal, the editor did nothing to protect his protégée, and she did equally little to protect herself. 'Mr Jerdan
is awful! Poor Miss Landon ought not to go home in a hackney coach
alone with him. The ill-natured who have read Miss Landon and *not seen*
Mr Jerdan will talk,' wrote Bulwer in the spring of 1827. The significance
of his comment comes into focus when one reads the courtesan Harriette
Wilson on the mores of Parisian society ladies at the same period:

As long as they will be hypocrites, in public, refusing, even, on a rainy night, to step into the carriage of the very man, whom they slyly slept with, the night before; and though these ladies are known for what they really are, they are, nevertheless, considered *femmes honnetes* until they no longer affect that virtue, which they, in reality, never possessed.

Egged on by Jerdan, the rebel in Letitia did not even bother to adhere to the outward rules. This was, Bulwer feared, to her own detriment. 'Miss Landon is amusing and would have passed anywhere for an extremely clever person, if she had never written a line; but she loses far more in interest than she gains in admiration. All women lose by wit if not very, very chaste and refined,' he wrote.

Letitia was indeed in danger of losing 'interest': social capital, the support of influential people. Her racy conversation was as risky as her sexually suggestive poems. Even without scandalmongering by the *Sunday Times,* the position of the literary lion was notoriously insecure. 'Let such a person's popularity only decline which is a very common case in the literary world and see how the aristocracy will treat him,' wrote James Grant in his early work of sociology *The Great Metropolis* (1836).

The very issue of the *Sunday Times* that contained the charwoman's revelations included a warning squib about the 'poet of fashion'. He begins by dining out in 'Park-lane' with dukes, dowagers and dandies, but soon finds his invitations sliding down the social scale, first to 'Sloane-street', then to Soho, and finally to 'Barge-yard', by which time the only admirers of his works are 'squab city misses' keen for him to inscribe their albums.

By now Letitia's equivocations were already wearing thin, but there was no one in literary London she did not attempt to cultivate. The sheer number of her contacts is dizzying. Anyone she met was a networking opportunity, and she was only too happy to offer Jerdan's services as a fixer. 'I think you might most advantageously communicate with Mr Jerdan, who I <u>know</u> is in the confidence of several of our leading statesmen,' she confided confidentially to one correspondent.

She continued to entertain, though her parties now took place in the Misses Lance's dingy downstairs parlour at 22 Hans Place. Fancy dress was sometimes required. On one occasion Letitia appeared as Perdita. Whether she was meant to be Shakespeare's innocent shepherdess, or the courtesan Mary Robinson who had made her name playing the role onstage, was left unsaid.

Letitia's visiting card survives, stuck into an album by a fan. The diminutive words 'Miss L. E. Landon' are dwarfed by the florid embossed border. The name is cheaply printed, not expensively engraved. It speaks of 'keeping up appearances'.

According to Katherine Thomson, Letitia's manic socializing left her with little time for intimacy: 'her usual regards never sank skin-deep into her heart. How could they? There were such large demands made upon her good-will; she had such dozens of very particular dear friends; such scores of admirers and worshippers.'

The true reason why she put so much effort into keeping so many contacts in play was precisely to avoid intimacy—and to control the spread of gossip. For the rest of her life, she had to contend with a constant drip-drip of low-level mockery in the press, and the possibility that a factual report as potentially damaging as that in the *Sunday Times* might again emerge.

After 1826, Letitia's position was in reality so compromised that she probably did not receive quite as many invitations as her memoirists later implied. When she *was* invited, she was sometimes snubbed. 'I avoided L.E.L., who looked the very personification of Brompton—pink satin dress and white satin shoes, red cheeks, snub nose, and hair à la Sappho,' Benjamin Disraeli recorded, having cut her at a party in 1832.

The table Letitia frequented most often was probably Jerdan's. Tom Moore sat next to her at a dinner party there in 1830. By way of making conversation, he averred to Miss Landon that no doubt she dined out all the time. Oh no, she replied. Most evenings she just wandered the local streets on her own, looking in the shop windows and watching the mail coach going by. Despite her bantering tone she was probably speaking something like the truth.

Moore summed up 'Miss L.E.L.' as 'girlish enough in manner (affectedly so indeed) but no girl at heart'. Like many of the male writers of the day, he regarded her as 'no exception to the bad opinion I entertain of such literary hermaphrodites—this sort of talent unsexes a woman.' By an unsexed woman he did not mean an unsexy woman, and certainly not a woman regarded as a male equal. He meant a woman who had forfeited her feminine claim on men's respect and chivalrous protection.

As the delicate balance of her reputation tipped inexorably from fame to shame, Letitia would find it increasingly hard to collect allies, especially among ladies. Mary Russell Mitford later took umbrage when she wrote to her as 'My dear Miss Mitford,' despite their both being former pupils of Miss Rowden. Although Miss Mitford admitted that she did not regard Letitia as a stranger, she took fright at the familiarity. Letitia was forced to apologize.

From 1826 on, Letitia was a constant butt of satire in the press. In this 1832 cartoon, *'Puff' and his Protegée*, Jerdan is shown smoking a cigar before a fireplace over which hangs a portrait of his 'Brompton Sappho' in a skimpy Grecian robe.

CHAPTER 7

Lyre Liar

'True' and 'false' are treacherous words in Letitia Landon's lexicon, miniature bombs that threaten to explode at any moment. She used them to play on ideas of veracity versus deceit, fidelity versus betrayal, the fallen versus the 'honest' woman. In her early lyric 'Truth', she even employed the title as a coy euphemism for sexual intercourse.

In the age of cant, the high-flown vocabulary of sensibility—truth and nature, soul and spirit—was reduced to a carnal code. Letitia would not have read the famous final lines of Keats's 'Ode on a Grecian Urn'—

Beauty is truth, truth beauty,—that is all
Ye know on earth, and all ye need to know

—as the gateway to some profound metaphysical mystery. She would have taken them as a teasingly empty tautology, gesturing towards an enigma that was in fact tragically banal: that in a fallen, materialist universe, art can aspire to nothing more elevated than the meaningless condition of sex.

From the start, L.E.L. deconstructed Romantic ideals, even as she constructed them. She embraced the fall into irony. 'O say not that truth does not dwell with the lyre / That the Minstrel will feign what he never has felt,' she wrote in 1822, employing for the first time the homonym on 'lyre' and 'liar' that became one of her idées fixes.

The lyre—from which 'lyric' poetry derives—was the ultimate Romantic symbol of unforced expressivity, adopted by Shelley and carved in stone on Keats's grave. As Sappho's iconic attribute, it was,

Keats's grave, with lyre, in the English cemetery at Rome

however, particularly associated with female genius. Madame de Staël, for example, was portrayed holding one in her 1809 portrait by the artist Elisabeth Vigée-Lebrun.

As conduits of creativity, women were supposed to be as natural and unselfconscious and passive as an Aeolian lyre or wind harp. However, the lyre was also a prop in the feminine masquerade. Chic Regency ladies, from actresses to aristocrats to Madame de Staël, were portrayed strumming on newfangled drawing-room variants, such as the harp-lute and lyre-guitar, exquisite examples of which survive, manufactured by Edward Light of London. As a fashion statement, the lyre straddled the symbolic fault line between authenticity and artifice, a tension brilliantly

The Marchioness of Santa Cruz by Goya, 1805

deployed by Goya in his portrait of the Marchioness of Santa Cruz holding a lyre-guitar (1805). The reclining sitter's awkward posture belies her
attempt to present herself au naturel. She has wild foliage in her hair, but
her feet stick out uncomfortably in pointy satin slippers from beneath
her faux-Grecian gown.

No poet was more alert to the contradictions of the lyre than Letitia.
But if she was an Aeolian lyre herself, what she channelled was not the
natural inspiration of Shelley's 'wild West Wind' but the 'spirit of the
age', to use a phrase coined in her lifetime. She knew her genius was not
transcendent but a product of the society in which she lived, which saw
the image of the lyre become a mass-produced design cliché, stamped on
innumerable book spines and incorporated into sofa tables, chairs and
wrought-iron railings.

Letitia's next collection, *The Venetian Bracelet,* published in 1829,
included a poem titled 'A History of the Lyre'. It features a poetess-
heroine whose imagination is compared to a stream whose 'wave' is 'lost
in artificial waterfalls' or 'coop'd up' to make the 'useless fountain of a
palace hall'. The new collection exposes how trapped as an artist Letitia

Madame de Staël with lyre by Elisabeth Vigée-Lebrun, 1809

had become in the work of spinning her 'public character', as she trod an increasingly tortured line between artifice and authenticity, disguise and self-exposure.

It opened with a prose preface in which, for the first time, Letitia Landon stepped outside her poetry to address her readers in what purported to be her own real voice. Blanking out L.E.L.'s erotic history, she offered a seemingly heartfelt apologia for her 'choice of love' as her 'source of song'. Seizing the moral high ground, she borrowed the poetess credo of her more respectable rival Mrs Hemans, who championed feminine sentimentalism as a bulwark against the selfish individualism of modern society. Letitia could thus reconfigure the titillating masochistic theatrics of her earlier work as altruism: she modestly asserted that her only purpose in engaging readers' feelings with stories of unhappy love was to help them become more ethical and empathetic.

That was, however, a politic act of gamesmanship conceived in response to the gossip about her private life. She went on to declare with wide-eyed innocence that if readers concluded from her verses that she 'must have an unhappy passion' of her own, she was wholly unconscious of the fact. Presenting herself as passive and unknowing as an Aeolian lyre, she even claimed to have no more access to her own authorial intention than any reader. The 'variety of opinions offered' on her poetry, she wrote, 'have left me somewhat in the situation of the prince in the fairy tale, who, when in the vicinity of the magic fountain, found himself so distracted by the multitude of voices that directed his way, as to be quite incapable of deciding which was the right path.' L.E.L. was reduced to a textual crux or rhetorical aporia. Letitia herself slipped silently away, leaving a disconcerting void.

Critics at the time were profoundly unsettled by the extreme moral and philosophical relativism they found in *The Venetian Bracelet*. It disturbed them far more than L.E.L.'s earlier innuendos had done. 'In reading many of her poems,' went one review, 'we caught ourselves saying instinctively, "There is falsehood here." But on a second perusal, in a different state of mind, we are sure that we might have said, "There is truth here." Is truth variable then? Is there no external standard to distinguish it from its contrary?'

The most striking piece in the volume was the deceptively simple 'Lines of Life', arguably Letitia's signature poem. The title was taken from Shakespeare's bitter and enigmatic Sonnet XVI, which casts doubt on the truth of art, and on the ability of 'barren rhyme' and 'painted counterfeit' to transcend time or even communicate.

'Lines of Life' reads like a perverse parody of an evangelical hymn, and draws us into such a vortex of multiple ironies that it becomes almost an antipoem. L.E.L. twines us, and is herself twined, in the classic philosopher's 'liar's paradox'. Is she, the poem asks, a truth-telling liar or a lying truth-teller? Either way, the reader is placed in an impossible position. So is the poet, who can only be true to herself by being false to herself, since personal honesty is an act of self-betrayal.

She begins with an aggressive refusal to reveal her inner self, which turns, paradoxically, into a confession of her complicity in the culture of lies:

Well, read my cheek, and watch my eye,—
Too strictly school'd are they,
One secret of my soul to show,
One hidden thought betray.

I never knew the time my heart
Looked freely from my brow;
It once was check'd by timidness,
'Tis taught by caution now.

I live among the cold, the false,
And I must seem like them;
And such I am, for I am false
As those I would condemn.

I teach my mouth its sweetest smile,
My tongue its softest tone;
I borrow others' likeness, till
Almost I lose my own.

I pass through flattery's golden sieve
Whatever I would say;
In social life, all, like the blind,
Must learn to feel their way.

I check my thoughts like curbed steeds
That struggle with the rein;
I bid my feelings sleep, like wrecks
In the unfathom'd main.

I hear them speak of love, the deep,
The true, and mock the name;
Mock at all high and early truth,
And I too do the same.

I hear them tell some touching tale,
I swallow down the tear;
I hear them name some generous deed,
And I have learnt to sneer.

I hear the spiritual, the kind,
The pure, but named in mirth;
Till all of good, ay, even hope,
Seem exiled from our earth.

And one fear, withering ridicule,
Is all that I can dread;
A sword hung by a single hair
For ever o'er the head.

We bow to a most servile faith,
In a most servile fear;
While none among us dares to say
What none will choose to hear.

And if we dream of loftier thoughts,
In weakness they are gone;
And indolence and vanity
Rivet our fetters on.

These lines are indeed an authentic dispatch from the heart of the hypocrisy culture in which Letitia actually lived. The trouble is that as the poem changes gear halfway through, she gives such an over-the-top performance of self-abnegation that we begin to doubt her sincerity.

She puts on a recital of such shrinking modesty—complete with reference to the blushing cheek, an image she so often used erotically—that we begin to wonder whether this poem too is just another act:

Oh! not myself,—for what am I?
The worthless and the weak,
Whose every thought of self should raise
A blush to burn my cheek.

We doubt her, yet at the same time we believe her. Her show of exaggerated non-self really does expose the flip side of fame's bloated ego, the vanishingly low self-esteem that results from living 'only in others' breath'.

At its turning point, 'Lines of Life' attempts to claim for art the capacity to transcend debased individuality and indeed time itself, in answer to the doubts expressed in Shakespeare's sonnet. L.E.L. makes a half-hearted Shelleyan gesture toward identifying herself as the vessel through which the transcendent spirit-power of poetic genius has poured. However, she instantly subverts the ideal. She can still only seek validation from her audience, to whom she gives the power to determine whether or not her art is 'vain' (literally, from the Latin root, 'empty'):

> But song has touch'd my lips with fire,
> And made my heart a shrine;
> For what, although alloy'd, debased
> Is in itself divine.
>
> I am myself but a vile link
> In earth's dark weary chain;
> But I have spoken hallow'd words,
> Oh do not say in vain!

The final stanzas yearn toward the only immortality available in an atheist's universe: posthumous fame. L.E.L. romantically rests her hope in being understood 'long after life has fled' by lovelorn young maidens and pale youths with poetic souls. Will such readers of the future, she asks, keep her alive by choosing, 'from many an antique scroll besides', that which bears her name? Letitia Landon lived in an age of mass print, not parchment scrolls. Even as she sought the understanding of futurity, she undermined her own hopes as futile.

When Virginia Woolf read 'Lines of Life' a century on, she thought it the most risibly 'insipid' poem she had ever seen. Influenced by her friend Doris Enfield's biography, she believed L.E.L. to be a wishy-washy schoolgirl virgin. Yet the ever-sensitive Woolf must have realized subliminally that something much darker was going on beneath the surface. Mere insipidity cannot explain either her fascination or her extreme reaction.

In Woolf's novel *Orlando,* the time-travelling, gender-bending protagonist enters the nineteenth century in a woman's body, to find herself sitting at a desk, pen in hand. She is viscerally nauseated when stanzas from 'Lines of Life' spew incontinently forth on the page before her. Nothing, Woolf writes, could be more 'revolting'. Orlando is relieved when she knocks over the ink bottle, blotting out the lines, she hopes, for ever.

Woolf recoiled in such disgust because she intuitively sensed the poem's submerged emotional violence and acerbic passive aggression, which were secretly rooted in Letitia's personal situation. She was also involuntarily sucked into Letitia's strange circle of self-harm, acting out the fear of 'withering ridicule' depicted in the poem itself. Only now that we know the truth about Letitia's double life can we begin to understand her literary voice. Like Heinrich Heine, she was an exponent of the Romantic irony that is more wretched in its emptiness than the tragic sentiments it erects only to mock and deconstruct. Orlando need not have spilt the ink. Letitia had already erased herself.

'Lines of Life' is a cry of nihilistic rage and despair. It is also a twisted torch song to the hypocrisy culture on which Letitia depended for her social survival. In this, she was aided and abetted by her 'respectable' friends, including Dr and Mrs Anthony Todd Thomson and, especially, Mr and Mrs Samuel Carter Hall. They publicly invested in her seeming purity, and denounced the slanders against her in the memoirs they published after her death. In reality, they were deeply entangled in her private life, effective codependents in her toxic affair with Jerdan.

After Letitia died, S. C. Hall and his wife returned to her story again and again in print with an assiduousness bordering on the obsessional. They had routinely seen her, they said, at least once a week, sometimes every day, and were therefore in a position to know that the rumours about her were false. However, Hall also let slip a telling reference to a 'blight in her springtime' (her original seduction by Jerdan) and admitted that the ' "bright ornament" of Truth' was never hers, and that 'secretiveness' was her 'bane'. Only in the light of recent revelations is it clear how much the Halls' published memories, like Katherine Thomson's, insinuate between the lines.

Not for nothing was the editor and art critic Samuel Carter Hall (1800–1889) later immortalized by Dickens as the arch-hypocrite Pecksniff in *Martin Chuzzlewit* (1843). According to Nathaniel Hawthorne's son, Julian, who met him in the 1850s, his 'unctuous solemnity', 'simpering self-complacency', and 'oily and voluble sanctimoniousness' needed 'no modification to be fitted to appear before the footlights in satirical drama'. Like Letitia herself, Hall was a walking paradox: 'an ingenuous hypocrite, an artless humbug, a veracious liar'.

In all his published memories of Letitia, Hall never described when and how he first met her, probably with good reason. He did not want to be associated with her disreputable beginnings in Jerdan's libertine circle. During the 1820s he and his wife, Anna Maria, whom he married in 1824, transformed themselves from rackety Irish literary adventurers into evangelical propagandists. The subtitle of the publication Hall edited from 1828 says it all: *The Amulet: A Christian and Literary Remembrancer.*

This metamorphosis is visibly apparent in Anna Maria's extant portraits. In a drawing made by Daniel Maclise in the 1820s, she appears bold and sassy with unkempt hair. In a photograph taken in later life, she kneels at a prie-dieu in an attitude of exaggerated piety, her hair covered by a black lace shawl.

S. C. Hall must in fact have first encountered Letitia soon after he came over to London, from Cork, in 1822, whereupon he immediately wormed himself into Jerdan's circle. Hall may even have helped inspire *The Improvisatrice,* as he soon found employment as secretary to the émigré Italian man of letters Ugo Foscolo, a well-known libertine who was said to keep a harem of attractive young female servants at his Regent's Park retreat, Digamma Cottage. Hall later paid tribute to Anna Maria for supposedly saving him from Foscolo's pit of vice, although Foscolo himself claimed that they parted company after Hall embezzled funds.

Like her husband, Anna Maria also smudged over when she first encountered Letitia. She told Blanchard that she did not meet her until 1828. But she later published a vivid account of their supposed first meeting at Mrs Bishop's Sloane Street apartment, soon after the publication of *The Improvisatrice* in 1824, in which she portrayed Letitia skipping around in a gingham frock. Intriguingly, the *Oxford Dictionary of National Biography* records that Anna Maria (née Fielding) attended the 22 Hans Place school after coming over to London from Ireland with her mother at fifteen in 1815. If so, her acquaintance with Letitia might have gone back to the period before she met Jerdan, and she may already have been Letitia's confidante during the very period in which the latter began her career-enhancing affair with the editor.

In their published comments, both Halls did all they could to reduce to the minimum linking Letitia's name with Jerdan's. But they were so intimately involved in the ménage that S. C. Hall and William Jerdan were the only friends Letitia invited to her grandmother's funeral in 1832, the time of which was arranged to their convenience. Elsewhere, Hall wrote pregnantly, 'I would gladly say more than I have felt justified in saying of William Jerdan. No doubt he was of heedless habits; no doubt he cared little for the cost of self-gratification.'

As Irish émigrés with a perilous hold on their social status, the Halls were hyper-aware that their position in London depended on their perceived respectability. As James Grant attested in *The Great Metropolis,* the middle classes staked their identity on their visible support for sexual morality, unlike the more freewheeling upper and lower orders. Hall himself admitted that he and his wife were not of 'sufficient rank' for there to be any leeway in the matter. He had particular scruples about female morals. It was not, he thought, sufficient for a woman to be 'pure'. She must also *seem* pure so as not to encourage impurity in others.

In pursuit of this ideal, he had a genius for reinterpreting the evidence before his eyes. After Letitia's death, he printed a warmhearted anecdote about introducing her to the Scottish writer James Hogg, who, he recounted, was so charmed by her innocence and grace that his suspicions of the dubious 'L.E.L.' were instantly dispelled. As Hall recalled, Hogg 'looked earnestly down at her for perhaps half a minute, and then exclaimed in a rich, manly "Scottish" voice, "Eh, I didna think ye'd be sae bonnie! I've said many hard things aboot ye. I'll do sae nae more."' The letter Hogg wrote to his wife at the time reveals what he was actually looking down at: Letitia's cleavage. He conceded that 'Miss Landon is a pretty girl' but was 'sorry to see' that she was 'quite naked all above the apron string'.

Hall had a particular interest in art criticism and later founded an art magazine. He was probably the author of the disapproving critique of Pickersgill's portrait of Miss Landon in the rakish Spanish hat that appeared in *The European* in 1825. In 1830, he published an engraving of another Pickersgill fancy portrait of Letitia, that was much more to his taste, in his annual *The Amulet: The Minstrel of Chamouni.*

Exhibited at the Royal Academy in 1828, this new take on Letitia combined elements from the artist's *L'Improvisatrice* of 1823 and his 'Spanish hat' portrait of 1825 (see plates). The costume is remarkably similar, down to the crucifix necklace, to the former. But the tone is completely different, the setting a clean Alpine landscape, not sultry Mediterranean heat. Instead of a female Don Juan, this new image showed Letitia as Hall wanted her to be seen: in the guise of a pure and simple peasant girl, wearing an unimpeachably innocent straw hat and a demure apron.

This more hygienic minstrel has attached prim pink ribbons to her lute, which she delicately plucks with a plectrum, as if afraid of touching the strings directly. The pose is so similar to that of the Spanish hat portrait of 1825 that Pickersgill probably went back to the original drawings he had made for that and simply changed the costume, as with a paper doll. Whoever commissioned the portrait—almost certainly Jerdan—clearly never paid for it, as it remained in the artist's possession. It was subsequently inherited by Pickersgill's niece Emily Maria. Her granddaughter married into the Benthall family, as a result of which the painting is currently on display in their ancestral seat, Benthall Hall in Shropshire, now a National Trust property.

The Minstrel of Chamouni (see plates) represented a belated change in Letitia's image, an attempt to desexualize her while keeping her in the fancy-dress realm of romance. The fact that the identity of the sitter was only visible to the in-crowd points to the paradox of the new mass marketing: the democratization of culture placed the emphasis more and more on exclusivity as the marker of fashion. Despite Hall's belated championship, the press was not taken in by the modest demeanour of *The Minstrel of Chamouni* at its first exhibition in 1828. *The Gentleman's Magazine* punctured its pose of innocence as yet another masquerade, describing it somewhat insinuatingly as a 'pleasing portrait under the disguise of one of those interesting minstrels so intimately blended with every romantic feeling and ardent passion'. The *London Magazine* was more direct in its brief and scathing review: 'No. 147. *The Minstrel of Chamouni*. H.W. Pickersgill,—This minstrel is an imposter. Shut the door upon him.'

Since the 'Spanish hat', Letitia's visual image had in fact had a bumpy ride. In 1827, the *Gazette* had attacked a 'pseudo portrait' of her by Adam Buck that had appeared as the frontispiece to the second volume of Richard Ryan's *Poetry and Poets* in 1826. More pert than pretty, it showed her in contemporary dress with an impressive embonpoint, a distinctive chin, and the short curly hairstyle she had recently adopted. If the *Gazette* wanted to distance itself following the *Sunday Times* debacle, it may have been because the Buck image subliminally showed Letitia as a seller of sexual secrets, her coiffure and dress aping the style of the kiss-and-tell courtesan Harriette Wilson as the latter had been portrayed in an engraving of 1825.

If the Halls were desperate to maintain Letitia's reputation, it was because they cared so much about their own. They regarded female impurity as contagious, especially from woman to woman. After the scandalous Countess of Blessington established her London salon at Gore House in Kensington in 1829, Mr Hall attended her glittering parties along with all the male elite of the day. But as no respectable lady would be seen there, Anna Maria stayed at home.

Although Lady Blessington was the widow of a fabulously rich Irish earl, she was also a former kept woman, having run away from a marriage to a violent abuser, into which she had been sold by her father at fifteen. Her first protector—for whose friends she was said to have danced naked on a table—had reputedly gone on to sell her to her noble husband. Following their marriage, she became notorious for sharing him with his effeminate young favourite Comte d'Orsay in an unconventional ménage à trois. In widowhood, she remained inseparable from d'Orsay, who co-hosted her salons and was believed to be her lover, despite concurrent rumours that he was gay.

For these reasons, Anna Maria could not countenance openly socializing with the widowed Lady Blessington. However, she was happy to pursue a private friendship with the countess, visiting her solo during the day for a cup of tea and a chat. Whatever Mrs Hall knew about Letitia in private, it would not have been in her own interests to admit it.

Sometime around 1834, Rosina Bulwer told Anna Maria Hall, in an exaggerated display of shocked horror, that she had burst in unexpectedly at 22 Hans Place to find Letitia sitting on old Jerdan's knee with her arm around his neck. Anna Maria responded, 'Oh, I don't *chuse* to believe anything against Miss Landon—that is, it's like Lady Blessington—it don't suit me to do so.' Her comment was almost a quotation from 'Lines of Life': 'none among us dares to say / What none will choose to hear.'

A complex system of Chinese walls ruled the society depicted in 'Lines of Life'. Rosina's horror at such ocular proof is unlikely to have been aroused by moral disgust. She was far from unworldly. The riotous parties the Bulwers hosted in the early 1830s were attended by a rag-bag of undesirables, including the late Byron's half sister and former mistress

The kiss-and-tell courtesan Harriette Wilson, 1825. Letitia had
more in common with her than her respectable friends
would have admitted.

Augusta Leigh. Letitia and Jerdan would turn up together. Disraeli
pranced around in velvet trousers, seeking attention for himself, even
though he avoided talking to the contaminating L.E.L.

Bulwer had in fact already told Rosina that he had heard Jerdan
boasting in his cups about his sexual conquest of Letitia at a drunken
dinner, coupled with 'some disgusting toast'. As a result, Rosina had
warned Letitia to forbid Jerdan's visits. Rosina was outraged to find them
in a clinch because Letitia had not followed her advice. Moreover, she
may have been furious that her supposed friend—whose reputation she
had defended 'against all the world, and firmly at that time believing in
her innocence'—had not confided in her openly, face-to-face. She did
not consider that Letitia might have held back from full disclosure for
the more generous motive of avoiding explicitly compromising her. Intimacy was the first casualty of the hypocrisy culture.

Letitia aping Harriette Wilson's hairstyle in Adam
Buck's portrait, engraved for Richard Ryan's *Poetry and
Poets* in 1826. The *Gazette* later dismissed it as pseudo.

The Halls, however, must have been privately apprised of Letitia's
affair from an early stage. They were, by their own admission, her daily
intimates. They took her under their wing, offered her hospitality at their
nearby Brompton home, and, around 1831, even helped fix up a curacy
in Devon for her feckless brother, Whittington (probably with Jerdan's
complicity), in an attempt to sort him out. Jerdan summed up his long-
standing relationship with the couple in the jovial pun '(H)all's well.' It
was rather more complicated in reality.

Despite depending on them, Letitia could never quite trust the
Halls. She was always careful in her dealings with them to pass her words
'through flattery's gilded sieve'. Scurrilous articles could be shrugged off,
but there was always the possibility that she might be betrayed by members of her own inner circle.

The Halls were keen to save Letitia from her own recklessness, to
protect their own respectability by association. The trouble was that the
ever-rebellious poetess continued to betray herself in print, in what looks

more and more like a cry for help. According to S. C. Hall, she was 'slow to believe that . . . evil words could harm her. At first they seemed but to inspire her, with a dangerous confidence, and to increase a practice we always deplored of saying things for "effect."'

By 1829, Letitia's addiction to risking her reputation was like that of a gambler who thinks he has found a 'system' to cheat fate and, as he is losing, puts his faith in it yet more. Letitia's 'system' was verbal ambiguity and the confessional hint. But while manipulating the selective blindness of her readers, she also blinded herself.

In *The Venetian Bracelet* Letitia referenced her private situation in acts of compulsive fictional projection more egregious than anything she had done before. Nothing could more literally dramatize the horror of losing 'face' than her depiction of the corpse of a woman so shamed by her forbidden love affair that she has kept it secret unto death:

> *still her face was bow'd*
> *As with some shame that might not be avow'd;*
> *They raised the long hair which her face conceal'd*
> *And she is dead, her secret unreveal'd.*

The most disturbing poem in the volume was titled 'The Dying Child'. Letitia presented it as a public poem, inspired by a newspaper report on the sufferings of the poor. It is written in the voice of a pauper unmarried mother who rejects medicine for her feverish little daughter and instead wills her to die:

> *Her cheek is flush'd with fever red;*
> *Her little hand burns in my own;*
> *Alas! and does pain rack her sleep?*
> *Speak! for I cannot bear that moan.*

> *Yet sleep, I do not wish to look*
> *Again within those languid eyes;*
> *Sleep, though again the heavy lash*
> *May never from their beauty rise.*

. . .

I may have sinn'd, and punishment
For that most ignorant sin incur;
But be the curse upon my head,—
Oh, let it not descend to her!

. . .

Tears—tears—I shame that I should weep;
I thought my heart had nerved my eye;
I should be thankful, and I will,—
There, there, my child, lie down and die.

As ever, Letitia had her finger on the pulse of social and political change. Attitudes toward single mothers were hardening, subsequently encoded in the 'Bastardy Clause' of the 1834 Poor Law Amendment Act. Prior to that, the absent fathers of illegitimate children were financially responsible for their upkeep, and could be chased for funds if the mother sought parish relief. The Bastardy Clause made the mothers instead financially responsible. It was part of a campaign designed to lower the illegitimacy rate—and the burden on the public purse—by stigmatizing single mothers.

But if the mawkishness of Letitia's poem repulses, it is because, alongside its public message, it channels so much suppressed personal rage. On June 20, 1829, just three months before 'The Dying Child' was published, she had given birth to her third illegitimate baby, Laura.

Like those of Ella and Fred, the circumstances of Laura's birth are clouded. She was probably born in Tunbridge Wells, which Letitia is known to have visited in the summer of 1829: a conveniently anonymous spa town with a ready supply of trained nurses. Contemporary clues suggest that she was by now relying on the Halls, the Thomsons and their allies to get her discreetly through the ordeal.

From Tunbridge Wells, Letitia wrote to a Mrs Tayler, who turns out to have been the wife of the Reverend Charles B. Tayler, a social reformer and contributor to S. C. Hall's *The Amulet: A Christian and Literary Remembrancer*. He later went on, with his 1835 tract *Live and Let Live: or, the Manchester Weavers*, to influence Elizabeth Gaskell's famous factory novel *Mary Barton*. Letitia told Mrs Tayler that she would soon be going home to London, where, after a few days at Hans Place, she would be spending a week staying with Dr and Mrs Thomson at their house in Hinde Street, presumably to recuperate.

The situation is reminiscent of another of Elizabeth Gaskell's classic philanthropic Victorian novels: *Ruth* (1853). Its story concerns a well-meaning Christian minister and his sister who find themselves entangled in a mesh of lies and deceit when they take in a young unmarried mother and try to protect her by passing her off as a widow. The buried interconnections between L.E.L.'s post-Byronic world and that of the Victorians offer much food for thought. It is odd to think that Dr Thomson's first wife was Elizabeth Gaskell's aunt. Katherine, his second wife, had taught at the boarding school in Warwickshire to which the eleven-year-old Gaskell was sent after her mother died. After the adult Gaskell finished *Mary Barton,* her first novel, she sent the manuscript to Katherine for literary advice. The latter, who may have resented the competition, responded negatively. It may be no coincidence that Gaskell's final novel, *Wives and Daughters,* features a widowed doctor who marries a second wife who is caustically presented as worldly, pretentious and a bad influence.

In her letter to Mrs Tayler, Letitia thanked Mr Tayler for inspiring her with the idea for 'The Ancestress', written for inclusion in *The Venetian Bracelet.* Its theme was a daughter cursed by her mother's sin. Letitia appears to have been vicariously dramatizing her own victimhood as a fallen woman to arouse the sympathies of the do-gooders on whom she by now depended for practical help. Ever aware of the transactional nature of such relationships, she later repaid the favor by puffing Tayler's *Records of a Good Man's Life* in the *Gazette* as a 'work calculated to do much good'.

Letitia had to rely on others because Jerdan was much less supportive than he had been back in 1823, when he had personally conveyed her to Canterbury for Ella's birth. 'I am disappointed at not being in town before this; the week after next you will receive the rest of my M.S. I want you very much to see the lost Pleaide,' she told him, referring to the title of one of the poems, 'The Lost Pleaide,' in her forthcoming *The Venetian Bracelet.* 'I am sure you will see to making the best arrangements, but I am ashamed to return to Hans Place with any remains of an harassment.'

The unspecified 'harassment' sounds like childbirth and its physical aftermath. Letitia did not want to go home to Hans Place until she was fully fit. The 'arrangements' must have had to do with the care of the child. 'But I am tresspassing [*sic*] upon you so addio,' she concluded mournfully. By the end of the year she would be telling him that she was anxious to know what he was doing and missed 'so very much not being able to talk to you'.

Jerdan's eye was wandering again. At twenty-seven, Letitia was no longer by any stretch of the imagination an infant genius. His taste was for very young girls. In the 1850s, Julian Hawthorne was astounded by the inappropriate attentions the by then ageing editor paid to his infant sister, Rose. Having secured the squirming child on his knee, Jerdan 'coquetted at her' until in desperation she finally offered a faint propitiatory smile, 'upon which he threw up his hands, emitted a hoarse cackle of triumph, and exclaimed, 'There—there it is! I knew I'd get it; she loves me—she loves me!' '

By 1829, Jerdan had developed an interest in a new teenage poetic prodigy named Mary Ann Browne, whose work he had begun to showcase in the *Gazette*. In his autobiography, Jerdan claimed unconvincingly that she and Letitia were firm friends. However, a torn-up fragment of a letter from Letitia to Mary Ann Browne survives in which the former coldly turns down an invitation from the latter on the unlikely grounds that she is such a slow writer that she cannot afford to take the time off work for socializing. A letter from Browne to Jerdan querulously compares the number of column inches she and Miss Landon have been given. He clearly enjoyed playing the poetesses off one against the other.

In *The Venetian Bracelet*, Letitia addressed a double-edged tribute to her younger rival, flattering Browne with faint praise while at the same time deflating her aspirations. Only those who truly suffer can be real geniuses, says L.E.L. Mary Ann's doting family provide her with too cocooning an environment:

> *With thine 'own people' dost thou dwell*
> *And by thine own fire side;*
> *And kind eyes keep o'er thee a watch,*
> *Their darling and their pride.*
> *I cannot choose but envy thee;*
> *The very name of home to me*
> *Has been from youth denied.*

The quotation marks around 'own people' seem twee until one reads the words aloud in a tone of vicious sarcasm. Letitia was covertly warning

Browne—and her proud parents—against the blandishments of the puppeteer Jerdan, while sending her Svengali a message to keep his hands off
the new prodigy.

With *The Venetian Bracelet,* Letitia began to get under Jerdan's skin.
Despite his libertinism, he had a sentimental weakness for little babies,
demonstrated by his sorrow at the death of Georgiana, and by a strange
short story he wrote in the first person from the viewpoint of a newborn,
with whom he clearly identified (the baby's desires are focused solely
on breasts). Indeed, Jerdan so loved babies that during the course of his
long life he fathered no fewer than twenty-three acknowledged children,
including those by Letitia and by a later mistress as well as by his wife,
Frances.

'The Dying Child' was calculated to hit home. In contrast to
the puffery with which he had greeted her previous collections, Jerdan's review of *The Venetian Bracelet* in the *Gazette* accused L.E.L. of
'nourishing of sickly aspirations'. He attacked the 'sentiment of self-
condemnation running through this volume', wishing it was merely an
'imagining' and not an expression of the poet's 'apparent moods'. The
mood of the volume as a whole was indeed more twisted than that of
her previous works. Most of her heroines die of broken hearts. But the
heroine of the title poem turns homicidal, murdering her love rival with
poison concealed in the eponymous Venetian bracelet, and framing her
unfaithful lover for the crime.

If this was a dig at Jerdan, Letitia was also cranking up the sensation-
alism in response to the fact that her actual sales were falling as the taste
for pseudo-Byronic poetry declined. 'The Dying Child' suggests that she
was prepared to take more and more risks with poetic semi-self-exposure
as her stock fell.

The sadomasochistic dynamic that infused L.E.L.'s poetic portrayals of romantic love was by now being reenacted in Letitia's real-life
relationship with the press. In publishing 'The Dying Child' she offered
fresh fuel for satirists. In December 1831, an unsigned titbit appeared in
the unlikely forum of *The Royal Lady's Magazine,* a publication usually
concerned with fashions and floristry. On this occasion it thrust in the
knife: 'It is very strange (and we only mention it on that account), but
it *is* very strange (and therefore we cannot help mentioning it), that
L.E.L. and Mr Jerdan should be so fond of writing about scandal and
little children.'

In February 1832, the same magazine went on to advise 'the injudicious friends of Miss L.E.L. not to talk too much about their "innocent female"—"virtuous girl"—"ornament of her sex"—"praiseworthy lady", &tc.' It concluded with 'The Lament: A Poetical Dialogue between L.E.L. and W. Jerdan, in the Manner of Both', which portrayed 'L.E.L.' bewailing the fact that she has forsaken the children her 'Willy' has given her. His response was not designed to reassure:

> *Then grieve no more—for here I swear—*
> *(Nay, smile, my love, you must—)*
> *I'll give again whate'er I've given,*
> *As freely as at first.*

Given the culture of anonymous publication, we cannot know who wrote this, but nor could Letitia herself. According to *The Royal Lady's Magazine* the satirist was a woman who had known her 'from early life'. The hint was sadistically calculated to increase Letitia's paranoia. The likeliest candidate for the false friend is Rosina Bulwer, whose taste for writing comic epigrams is on record, and whose husband openly flirted with Letitia in her presence.

As with Ella and Fred, there is no evidence that Letitia had any further contact with her third child after her birth. Jerdan, however, was in touch with Laura when she was a young adult, describing her in a letter to Ella as a 'dear Creature'. She is the only one of the children whose birthdate is recorded on her baptismal certificate. However, she was not christened until she was nearly twenty-one. This suggests that she only discovered her true parentage, and the fact that she had not been baptized as a child, on approaching her majority.

The baptismal certificate shows an interesting correction in the box for 'father's occupation'. The words 'silk manufacturer' are crossed out and replaced with 'gentleman', the word Jerdan used to describe himself on Ella's baptismal record and in some censuses. Silk manufacturer was in fact the profession of Laura's foster father, a man named Theophilus Goodwin. In the 1851 census Laura is listed as living with him and his wife, Mary Anne, at Rose Cottage in Dalston. She is described as their 'niece', a common euphemism for illegitimate foster children.

The childless Goodwins, who adopted Laura, were clearly able to offer her a comfortable home, as the census states that Theophilus was

Laura Landon's baptismal certificate. She was not christened until she reached adulthood. Perhaps she had only just learned the truth about her parentage. The words 'silk manufacturer'—her foster father's profession—are crossed out and replaced with 'gentleman,' the word her birth father, Jerdan, used to describe himself in some of the censuses.

successful enough to employ over two hundred people in his silk-manufacturing business. Further censuses show that she continued to live with them until she finally made a late marriage in her forties after Mrs. Goodwin died. On being widowed, she took in lodgers. Her existence was more circumscribed than Ella's, but clearly not so desperate as Fred's.

It seems likely that, prior to living with Theophilus, Laura was brought up with her elder sister, Ella, in early childhood. A census return for 1841 lists an Ella Goodwin and a Laura Goodwin of 'independent means' living with an Anne Goodwin in Regent's Park, along with other young people, also of independent means, all surnamed Goodwin. Although the ages are wrong for Letitia's daughters, the confluence of the two unusual Christian names is striking. Laura, who would in fact have been eleven going on twelve on June 6, 1841, when the census was taken, is listed as being ten. Ella, who would in fact have been eighteen going on nineteen, is listed as being nine, possibly a clerical error for nineteen. The Anne Goodwin with whom they were living seems to have taken in multiple children and registered them under her own surname for the purposes of the census. She does not appear to be the same woman as Theophilus's wife, Mary Anne, as she was older, single, and, unlike Mrs. Goodwin, born in India. Perhaps she made her living by fostering and subsequently placed Laura with Theophilus, a relative.

After the publication of *The Venetian Bracelet* in 1829, Letitia's private life became an ever more open secret among the literati. Soon after Disraeli cut her at a party in 1832, he heard from his writer friend Julia

Pardoe 'that it is well known to everyone that L.E.L. has no less than three children by Jerdan'. Yet Letitia continued to laugh off the gossip.

She managed to find a new niche among a group of ladies on the loucher, lower fringes of high society, who revelled in her whiff of scandal. They included Lady Emmeline Wortley and the wealthy, wilfully vulgar Mrs Wyndham Lewis, whom Disraeli himself married after she was widowed. In addition, Letitia also secured the patronage of the scandalous Countess of Blessington, who developed an affection for her and regarded her as a kindred spirit. Although no eyewitness accounts survive, it is likely that the reckless Letitia was one of the few females who risked being seen at the countess's soirees.

All the while, Letitia's 'respectable' lady friends not only lied for her to others, but to her face. As Mrs Thomson admits:

Lady Blessington in the 1830s. Men crowded to her salons but respectable ladies kept away. The portrait in the background, by Thomas Lawrence, shows the countess in her alluring youth. She regarded the wayward Letitia as a kindred spirit.

Our gifted friend defied slander, and gaily referring to the hosts of well-bred and titled dames who visited and caressed her, asked 'If any one believed it?' Could any one have the heart to answer 'Yes?' And yet the rumour grew and spread, and spread and grew; it ran its course underground: people were mighty civil to her face; but they inflicted on her friends the torture of hearing certain questions in her absence. Who could tell her of it? Not I—I couldn't have vexed her for the world.

By lulling Letitia into a false sense of security, they unwittingly fed her paranoia. 'How can . . . I trust / When I have full internal consciousness they are deceiving me?' says the poetess-heroine in 'A History of the Lyre', referring to the entourage of deceitful flatterers surrounding her. Reading the seemingly straightforward but insinuating memoirs later written by Katherine Thomson and the Halls, it is hard, as Letitia's biographer, not to feel forced into a similarly paranoiac position.

CHAPTER 8

The Cash Nexus

Money haunts Letitia's story like that of no other poet. From the Landons' ancestral losses in the South Sea Bubble to her own father's ruin, the vagaries of the market loom large. Her career coincided with capitalism's most rapid, unregulated growth spurt, which affected the publishing industry as much as any other sector.

'L.E.L.' was not just an author but a brand, as Thomas Carlyle registered when he responded to the news of her death in 1839 with his melancholy reference to her 'pictures in the Print shops'. Later that year, in *Chartism,* he gave voice to the growing fear that 'cash payment' had become the 'sole nexus of man to man', eroding the emotional bonds that had once held society together.

No writer's work is more demonstrably reactive to market forces than L.E.L.'s. Her poetry appeared to offer buyers the emotional capital— love—that, according to Carlyle, 'cash will not pay'. But the love in her verse is forever unrequited, mimicking the cycle of dissatisfaction inscribed in the dynamic of consumerism itself.

Letitia's writings are remarkable for the profound but subtle way in which they expose and surreptitiously subvert the commercial conditions of their own production. Her work makes the invisible hand of the market visible. Nothing could better embody the so-called contradictions of capitalism than the mutually assured destruction encoded in her paradoxes. Like the slave in the glass, she mocked the system that created her.

It is no coincidence that the conceit behind *The Golden Violet* is a poetry contest. Letitia knew what the 'principle of individual competition,' in the phrase of early-nineteenth-century economists, meant for the 'modern minstrel'. 'Alienation' and 'false consciousness' were later codified into Marxist theories, but the ideas are already there as inchoate metaphors in poems such as 'Lines of Life'. When L.E.L. wrote of poetic genius that its victims were its votaries, she could have equally been addressing the market, a similarly abstract and arbitrary taskmaster.

Victorian moralists such as George Eliot later spurned L.E.L. for commercializing poetry. Yet how much money Letitia personally received from her work is uncertain. She was said by James Grant to have accrued both 'fame and profit' as a result of William Jerdan's support. Yet according to her memoirists, there was something mysterious, if not murky, about her finances, especially in the second half of her career.

'A record of L.E.L.'s personal expenses would have astonished many who were acquainted with the amount of the sums she earned,' wrote Emma Roberts. Katherine Thomson made the same point more insinuatingly:

> But in spite of great and constant success, she was always poor. I asked not why:—in my opinion 'tis a direct insult either to the dead or the living to dive into their money matters . . . or to meddle with their cash accounts. . . . So, dear L.E.L., I will not touch upon thy difficulties, in detail. I merely repeat, 'She was not rich.'

From the early 1830s, stories of Letitia's day-to-day struggles with poverty abound. She was placed in the humiliating position of having to accept gifts from the wealthy Mrs Wyndham Lewis, who gave her a black velvet dress, and also handed her a diamond ring, 'saying gently that she need not keep it, thus tactfully implying that . . . Miss Landon might sell it to raise money for herself.'

Yet in his autobiography, Jerdan estimated that Letitia made on average £250 a year from her books. That would have been almost enough to keep a whole family on the right side of respectability. According to James Grant in *The Great Metropolis*, 'the Middle Classes consist of those families whose annual expenditure exceeds 250*l*. or 300*l*. a year, and who have no accident of birth or station in society which would justify in us ranking them among the higher classes.' Some in middle-class professions earned far less. A clergyman, according to Grant, could be paid as little as £100 a year. Patrick Brontë's annual salary as perpetual curate of Haworth was £200. Although Letitia was well known to have supported her mother following John Landon's death in 1824, that alone cannot have eaten up all her earnings. Far from maintaining a full household, Catherine scraped by in down-at-heel rooms, living as the lodger of Thomas Carlyle's postman at one stage.

Rumours later circulated that Letitia was a victim of blackmail. Extortion was certainly common in the age of cant. Owing to a legal loophole, it was not at that time a criminal offence to demand payment for not publishing a story. Harriette Wilson, the courtesan, notoriously charged former clients to delete their names from her memoirs. The scandal sheet *The Age* was said to base its entire business model on the practice. In 1826, Letitia lied her way out of the *Sunday Times* crisis, but it was uncertain whether her luck would hold a second time.

The Age's editor, Charles Westmacott, is certainly on record as having waged a long-standing campaign of ridicule against Jerdan. As early as 1822, when he was editing the short-lived *Gazette of Fashion*, a direct competitor to the *Literary Gazette*, he published a squib on Jerdan's reputation for puffery and his in-hock relationship with Longman. *The Age* itself later jibed at 'Miss Landon in swansdown muff and tippet, acting The Improvisatrice, with a necklace of Jerdan mock brilliants; her appearance is more of the gazelle than the gazette, although much puffed by the latter, a man-milliner.' However, no evidence has so far emerged to suggest that *The Age* did more than mock her.

The rumours regarding Letitia's money problems are much more likely to have originated in the messy financial ties that yoked her to her Svengali. In Anna Maria Hall's 1850s novel *A Woman's Story*, L.E.L.'s fictional surrogate, the poetess 'H.L.', has to hand over her literary earnings to a mysterious older man who is threatening to expose her shameful secret, which, in the novel, is that she is illegitimate herself, rather than the mother of illegitimate offspring. In the 1860s, it was also alleged that some editor had 'made use of his influence in the literary world to obtain power over her for her personal seduction' and had gone on to extort Letitia's literary earnings under threat of exposure.

William Jerdan's incorrigible indiscretion, and his keenness to boast about his sexual conquest of Letitia, make him an unlikely blackmailer by any conventional definition of the term. Nevertheless, there is evidence to suggest that he exploited his songbird financially. Some more recent critics have attempted to portray L.E.L. as a self-empowered literary businesswoman. Sadly, that was not the case.

The surviving accounts for the *Literary Gazette*, now buried in the British Library, reveal a surprising absence. The names of regular contributors, such as the art critic and the medical columnist Dr Thomson, appear like clockwork, along with those of occasional writers such as 'Mrs [Mary] Shelley'. Jerdan's salary as editor (seven guineas a week) is also regularly logged, along with his profits as third shareholder.

But Miss Landon's name does not occur once, even though during the period covered by the extant records (January 1826 to December 1829), she contributed around fifty individual poems to the magazine, far fewer than in previous years but still a substantial quantity, plus an unknown number of unsigned reviews, in addition to providing other editorial support. Jerdan described Letitia in his autobiography as his effective coeditor. It appears he omitted to pay her a salary.

At the very start of her career, Letitia was effectively taken on as an unpaid apprentice or intern. It seems she continued to repay Jerdan for his tuition by filling his column inches gratis long after the initial training period. It is hard not to conclude that her sentimentalized portrayals of poetesses as exotic slave girls had as much of a tawdry real-life undertow as her depictions of overblown love agonies.

Although Mrs Landon hoped that her talented daughter would take on the role of family breadwinner, she had raised her to identify upward in the social scale. The young Letitia wanted to be like the moneyed Romantic rebel Lady Caroline Lamb, not like the middle-class professional writer Mary Russell Mitford.

At eighteen, she had never had to worry about money. Following the Landon bankruptcy, she went along with Catherine's plan to sue for Jerdan's patronage. But she resisted being turned into a cash cow. Implicitly pushed onto the casting couch by a mother in denial of the sexual quid pro quo, she rebelled by showing as little interest in financial reward as she had done as a child when she handed over her shillings to Whittington.

According to Shelley, 'poets' food' was only 'love and fame'; breadwinning played no part. He was able to bypass the literary cash nexus because he could raise funds on the prospect of his future inheritance. Byron refused payment for his poetry out of aristocratic disdain, at least in the earlier part of his career. Letitia had no such financial backup. Yet in her early poetry it is always marriage that is the grubby bargain, while transgressive affairs are represented as the existential ideal.

Jerdan, however, proved to be as interested in cash as Catherine. In fact, one of Letitia's early *Gazette* poems shows her chafing at his demands when he exploited her talent too blatantly for commercial ends. In 1823, he commissioned her to produce a series of poems promoting a set of wafers manufactured by Messrs. Thomson of Wellington Street: gummed paper stickers used on letters in the days before envelopes as a cheaper alternative to sealing wax. In a frank exercise in product placement, Jerdan's advertorial encouraged readers to purchase the wafers for use in 'lovers' correspondence'.

Letitia obliged by providing a series of copybook verses describing the lovers from classical mythology, such as Hercules and Iole, shown disporting themselves on the wafers. However, she ended the series with a first-person 'Conclusion' that is very different in tone from the third-person decorative fripperies that had gone before.

Addressed to an unnamed lover whose 'name is breathed on every song', this angry, paradox-infused lyric turns out to be one of her knottiest: a personal poem privately inscribed to Jerdan but slippery enough to remain generalized to a general audience. She will, she tells him, achieve artistic renown once her apprenticeship is over, though she predicts it will be compromised by her gender and her sexual fall:

> *I will be proud for you to hear*
> *Of glory brightening on my name;*
> *Oh vain, oh worse than vanity!*
> *Love, love is all a woman's fame.*

For now, however, she has decided to break her lute and retreat into 'silence'. It is as if Letitia is threatening to go on strike at the humiliation of being required by her patron-lover to write advertising copy to order.

This lyric defines itself through ambiguity; its verbal simplicity is a sliding surface that becomes a brainteaser if scratched. When 'reality' is an 'echo', actuality and illusion merge:

> *I did not dream, when I have loved*
> *To dwell on Sorrow's saddest tone,*
> *That its reality would soon*
> *Be but the echo of my own.*

But the most interesting buried 'echo' here is to be found in the last line: a seeming verbal allusion to an almost identical line at the end of a stanza in Shelley's 'The Mask of Anarchy' of 1819, his radical response to the Peterloo Massacre.

> *'What is Freedom?—Ye can tell*
> *That which slavery is, too well—*
> *For its very name has grown*
> *To an echo of your own.'*

Shelley's next stanza makes an explicit link between power relations and economic oppression:

> *''Tis to work, and have such pay*
> *As just keeps life from day to day*
> *In your limbs, as in a cell*
> *For the tyrants' use to dwell.'*

Although 'The Mask of Anarchy' was unpublished at the time Letitia was writing, it was known in London, having been sent by Shelley to Leigh Hunt in 1819, though the latter declined to print it in the *Examiner* because of the prevailing political climate. In fact, many of Shelley's antiestablishment political poems enjoyed a limited samizdat-style circulation in manuscript in the aftermath of his death, under the auspices of his widow, Mary, herself an occasional contributor to the *Literary Gazette* in the 1820s. Letitia may have come across 'The Mask of Anarchy'—spelled 'masque' in the version that was finally published in 1832—through her now buried connections in 'Cockney' literary circles.

It was only through the masquerade and subterfuge of buried allusion that Letitia could tangentially express her resistance to playing slave to Jerdan's sultan, although it is unlikely that the busy Tory editor would have picked up on her Shelleyan reference. Certainly, Letitia's situation meant that she was little able to detach herself from the economic and power nexus Jerdan represented. Despite her threat to withdraw both her love and her labour, two weeks later we find her publishing a new series of verses in the *Gazette,* promoting the pictures in a commercial gallery in Soho Square. It is unlikely that the gallery owner, Mr Cooke, recompensed her for the poetical publicity, any more than did the wafers' manufacturer, Jerdan himself, or the *Gazette*'s other shareholders, Long-man and Colburn, who were implicitly in on the deal.

In real life, Letitia was able to cocoon herself from economic reality and dismiss money matters with pseudo-aristocratic disdain as long as she was living rent-free with her grandmother, and before her estranged father's death made her responsible for her mother's upkeep. In 1824, she grandly rejected a fee from fellow *Gazette* contributor A. A. Watts for a contribution to his new annual *The Literary Souvenir:*

> As to pecuniary recompense, for poems given with so much pleasure, I cannot hear of it. I really did think you had been too much of a poet yourself to think of linking pounds, shillings and pence to my unfortunate stanzas. . . . Henceforth I put a bar on the subject.

Her de haut en bas manner would rile the ambitious but ultimately dis-appointed Watts, whose own attempt to set himself up as a 'Cockney' poet from lowly origins failed, where hers succeeded. She then added to his humiliation by boasting with studied unconcern that she had made over £900 from *The Improvisatrice* and *The Troubadour* combined. Her lack of diplomacy with Watts was a strategic error that later came back to haunt her.

As this last boast suggests, despite the fact that Letitia was not paid for her *Gazette* work, her books indeed commanded publishers' fees (with the exception of the first, *The Fate of Adelaide,* which was brought out at her grandmother's expense). Jerdan provided a list in his autobiography:

For the Improvisatrice [Hurst and Robinson, 1824] she received	£300
For the Troubadour [Hurst and Robinson, 1825]	600
For the Golden Violet [Longman, 1827]	200
For the Venetian Bracelet [Longman, 1829]	150
For the Easter Offering [Fisher, 1832]	30
For the Drawing-Room Scrap Book, per vol. [Fisher, 1831–38]	105
For Romance and Reality [Colburn and Bentley, 1831]	300
For Francesca Carrara [Bentley, 1834]	300
For Heath's Book of Beauty [1832]	300

And certainly from other Annuals, Magazines and
    Periodicals, not less in ten or twelve years than   200

In all   2,585

However, with Jerdan as her agent, it is uncertain how much Letitia personally saw of these earnings. Those who imagined that she was
his 'ward', when she made her salon debut in 1824, were not far wrong.
'L.E.L.' was effectively a family business in which Jerdan played the role
of patriarch and banker.

When, for instance, Jerdan negotiated Letitia's contract with Hurst
and Robinson for *The Improvisatrice* in late 1823, he so regarded 'L.E.L.'
as a joint project that he even had to remind himself that she should be
permitted to revise the text herself:

> [T]hough I will correct the press and do everything in my power
> for the work, I should wish every page to be revised by the sweet
> writer whose intelligence will probably be beneficially exercised
> on the printed copy.

'I have written to Miss L.,' Jerdan went on, 'to say I have concluded the
arrangement with your House, that I shall, as soon as is agreeable to
you, have the pleasure of enclosing her a draft of 30 guineas.' It does not
sound as though Letitia received the full £300.

In the wake of the *Sunday Times* exposé of 1826, Letitia dismissed
the rumours about her sexual intimacy with Jerdan by stating that 'circumstances' had made her 'very much indebted' to the 'gentleman' concerned, but only as her financial manager:

> I have not a friend in the world but himself to manage anything
> of business, whether literary or pecuniary. . . . Place yourself in
> my situation. Could you have hunted London for a publisher,
> endured all the hot and cold water thrown on your exertions;
> bargained for what sum they might be pleased to give; and, after
> all, canvassed, examined, nay quarrelled over accounts the most
> intricate in the world? And again, after success had procured
> money, what was I to do with it? Though ignorant of business,
> I must know I could not lock it up in a box. Then for literary

assistance, my proof sheets could not go through the press without revision. Who was to undertake this—I can only call it drudgery—but some one to whom my literary exertions could in return be as valuable as theirs to me?

If Letitia's writings were indeed as valuable to Jerdan as they were to her, he must have been taking a fifty per cent cut, which sounds rather steep.

Jerdan seems to have held the purse strings, giving Letitia handouts from her own earnings. In one surviving note, undated but probably from around 1824–25, she politely asks him for a banker's draft:

Dear Sir,

So many thanks—an order if procureable—would be gratefully received—sent here—

He was, however, a very poor choice of 'treasurer'.

Despite his genius for generating marketing ideas, Jerdan was no accountant. In his own estimate, his 'blunders in attempting numbers, reckonings or accounts have been so hideous, that a schoolboy of ten years old would have been whipt for making them'. This is borne out by the fact that, in adding up Letitia's book fees as listed in his autobiography, the total he comes to is out by £100. His fiscal irresponsibility and wild credit addiction were such that his autobiography reads unintentionally like a Victorian moral treatise on the evils of debt.

He is unlikely to have felt any compunction about 'borrowing' from Letitia's earnings. He did not even pay his tailor. The actor William Macready's diary is indicative: 'A note from Jerdan asking me to withhold the cheque for £70 upon the faith of which he had borrowed that sum of me. The fact cannot be disguised; he is a man who has no conscience obtaining the means of other men. The money is gone!'

Plotted as a graph, L.E.L.'s fees as listed by Jerdan show a sharp spike followed by a decline. The success of *The Improvisatrice* was such that he was able to secure double the fee, also from Hurst and Robinson, for Letitia's next work, *The Troubadour,* published in 1825. However, Hurst and Robinson then went bust.

Letitia's next book, *The Golden Violet* (1827), was published by Jerdan's *Gazette* partner Longman, but for the reduced fee of £200, on the basis of what turned out to be an accurate sales prediction. Two thousand copies were printed, but the publisher still had 640 in stock after the first six months, which did not sell out for ten years. The yet lower price of £150 paid for *The Venetian Bracelet*, also by Longman, reflected the fact that even fewer were printed, only 1,500. If 'L.E.L.' was a speculative venture, its value did not hold up.

Why Longman—who had refused *The Fate of Adelaide* in 1821—should have taken on L.E.L. at the moment her stock began to fall is intriguing. The answer is to be found in the fact that by 1827 Longman was not only William Jerdan's fellow *Gazette* shareholder but also his creditor. A surviving unpublished letter from Jerdan, in which he asks Bulwer to do him the favour of guaranteeing a new loan from a moneylender, reveals that a large tranche of the £4,000 debt he had taken on 'in purchasing and furnishing Grove House' was owed to Longman, to whom he still owed £1,000 in 1830. It is hard not to conclude that the Svengali was selling on Letitia's labour as collateral to service his own debts.

Jerdan prided himself on being L.E.L.'s puppeteer, but he himself was also the 'puppet' (as H. F. Chorley put it) of the *Gazette*'s co-owners, Longman and Colburn, whose publishing businesses depended on a steady stream of good reviews in the magazine. Jerdan's lack of editorial independence from them—and later from Colburn's partner Richard Bentley—was a constant topic of snide discussion in the press at the time. The role of these sinister éminences grises in Letitia's life and career is barely documented, although it must have been greater than recorded. Unlike the profligate peacock Jerdan, they were hard-nosed businessmen with no urge for self-publicity and did not leave posterity with colourful accounts of their careers. Colburn's long relationship with Jerdan was, however, testy, its tensions exacerbated by the fact that Colburn was also the proprietor of both the *Sunday Times* and *The Wasp*, which exposed and mocked Letitia's pregnancies. He was also involved in *The Athenaeum*, which was set up as a rival to the *Gazette* in 1828. Jerdan's full interrelations with Colburn and Longman remain shadowy, but the key fact is that he borrowed money from both. They had more leverage over him as his creditors than as his colleague.

Longman gave up on publishing Letitia after *The Venetian Bracelet* in 1829 because L.E.L. was no longer commercially viable in her original form, and her poetry had ceased to be so valuable as collateral. By the end of the 1820s, the demand for the 'poet of fashion', and for pseudo-Byronic poetry collections, was indeed diminishing. The appetite for the strutting poetic ego was replaced in popularity by the so-called silver fork novel, prose fictions that provided peep-show glimpses of modern-day high life. The newcomer Benjamin Disraeli had made a splash with *Vivian Grey* in 1826, which Bulwer had equalled if not trumped with *Pelham* in 1828. Neither author was in reality quite so aristocratic as the milieu they described, but appetiteful provincial readers who longed for access to the exclusive in-crowd—such as the young Brontës in Yorkshire—were not to know that.

Commercial motives alone can explain why Letitia herself now turned to prose, publishing her own first novel, *Romance and Reality*, in 1831. No longer able to call on Longman, Jerdan turned to Colburn and his new partner Bentley to publish it, despite the fact that Colburn had recently set up *The Athenaeum* as an explicit competitor to the *Gazette*. By owning two competing magazines, Colburn figured he could generate controversy and boost the sales of both. Jerdan was no match for his Machiavellian business strategy.

In February 1830, Jerdan wrote to Colburn's new partner Bentley to clinch the contract for *Romance and Reality*, enclosing a document signed by Letitia in which she formally appointed him her 'Treasurer and Agent'. However, Jerdan's negotiating position was weak. 'I am afraid it is out of order, but if you cd make the date of the bill three months it would facilitate what I am asked to do,' he begged Bentley, desperate to see the money as soon as possible.

The fee Jerdan secured was £300, twice as much as for *The Venetian Bracelet*, but only the same sum as Letitia had started out with for *The Improvisatrice*. Compared to the £1,500 Bulwer got for *Devereux* at about the same time, it was pathetic. Bulwer himself lamented that Jerdan had sold Letitia's talents short. But Jerdan was by that time already touching Bentley for petty loans of £50 or £100, complaining to him about Longman's demands. He was in no position to ask for more.

Letitia did not personally benefit from the deal. In 1832, Anna Maria bumped into her outside Youngman's shop in Sloane Street. Letitia had just been in to buy a pair of gloves. She told her it was 'the only money I spent on myself out of the £300 I received for *Romance and Reality*'. In resting her hopes on Jerdan she had made as much of an error as her forlorn heroines, who yearn for lovers who can never fulfil their needs.

As a novel, *Romance and Reality* is a failure. Although Letitia's short stories are masterful, long-form fiction was not her forte. The plot—if it has one—is derisory: an engagement that never happens, leading to the heroine dying of a broken heart. More a series of picaresque sketches than a sustained narrative, the book only comes to life in its fly-on-the-wall scenes of social satire. They cynically depict a world ruled by the cash nexus.

'Now society is a market place,' the author tells us. Nature, once worshipped by the Romantics, now exists just to provide the raw materials for consumerism: the glistening shells of beetles are transformed into jewelry to be hawked in the high-end shops of Burlington Arcade. Sheet music for a new tune is marketed as danced by a duke. An aristocratic lady sells tickets for a private concert in her own home. Everyone is in the business of image-making. 'A part is to be played in company. . . . The natural face may be a thousand times more attractive, still a mask must be worn.'

The world of samizdat Romanticism, with its secret allusions to Keats or Shelley, had been transformed into the coded culture of the silver-fork roman à clef. The new genre was defined by its hidden references to real-life high-society figures, many of whom were by now penning their own post-Byronic novels, including Lord Normanby, whose *Yes and No* receives a glowing puff in *Romance and Reality* as an 'especial favourite'. The world of the Regency 'Exclusives'—those able to get into the exclusive Almack's Club in St James's—was being mass-marketed.

Letitia bucked the trend by attempting to make literary rather than aristocratic society the *coterie du jour*. She invited readers to test their inside knowledge by identifying the originals to her cameo characters, including flattering fictional versions of writer allies such as Mrs. Hall and the Bulwers. Belatedly trying to move her own image away from its hypersexualized origins, she also teasingly portrayed herself as 'Miss Amesbury', the celebrated author of '*The History of a Modern Corinne*'. The character, a great beauty with a brow fit for Madame de Staël, is said to make the error of creating poetess heroines tortured by love, when everyone knows that female writers have to work so hard that they have no time for romantic relationships.

Letitia was still playing a game of liar lyre. When the subject of truth comes up during a salon scene, she offers a proto-Wildean quip on the importance of being earnest:

'Mr Lillian,' observed Mr Morland, 'is one of the most brilliant supporters of paradox I ever met. His conversation only requires to be a little more in earnest to be perfectly delightful . . . we like and require truth—always supposing and allowing that the said truth interferes neither with our interests nor our inclinations.'

Yet Letitia's underlying cynicism was by now perilously close to the surface. Not just equivocation but self-deconstruction had become a habit. She self-sabotaged even in her preface, by making it insultingly clear to readers that she had only switched from poetry to prose to please the market: she informed them archly that 'the novel is now . . . the popular vehicle for thought, feeling, and observation, the one used by our first-rate writers.'

Her attitude was not lost on the *Westminster Review*. It opined that 'the fair accountant' must have been 'under the necessity of forcing herself to business', but eventually 'the book was full, the balance struck and the publisher arrived at his first stage of satisfaction'. Its critic cast an unrelenting eye on the L.E.L. brand and at the hollow commercial narcissism of celebrity culture:

The title page should simply contain the three magical letters which she has immortalized, opposite to which we would have engraven the portrait of a smart girl whose picture was hung up in the Exhibition a few years ago, and next by way of vignette in the title there should be a little piece not larger than a medal: in the distance on a throne should be sitting with brows encircled with laurel a Sappho or a Corinne surrounded by as many heads of kneeling adulators as Martin [John Martin, painter of sensational panoramas] could crowd into an inch square.

The sheer quantity of words produced by L.E.L. had once been viewed as a sign that she was a natural genius from whom poetry flowed as from a songbird. Now her prolific output was reconfigured as industrial production, 'L.E.L. at her spinning jenny.' The critic pointed out that Letitia's very preface mocked the idea of authorial integrity, by exposing the production-line nature of modern literary genius. When she thanked the compositor for correcting her errors, the 'division of labour' was 'carried even into authorship'.

No writer was in fact more consciously alert than Letitia to the idea that poets were not Shelleyan nightingales singing alone in the forest, but constructions dependent on a nexus of economic interrelations. Authorial identity was a function not of the author alone, but of publishers, critics, typesetters, booksellers, and especially of the readers whose consumer choices could determine whether a writer's voice lived or died. It is perhaps no accident that L.E.L.'s work features so many dead poets: in her awareness of the impact of commercial mass culture on literature, she anticipated the postmodern notion of 'the death of the author'.

Privately, Letitia was under increasing pressure, with her brand value in decline and her sexual hold over Jerdan decreasing. In early 1831, she also became the subject of a petty attempt at extortion, when a former maid, Sarah Clarke, who had left her service five years previously, turned up at Hans Place demanding money in a 'most insolent manner'. Clarke must have left Letitia's service around the time she left off living with her grandmother in 1826, pregnant with Fred and on the run from the *Sunday Times*. Servants, like the Jerdans' charwoman, had access to their employers' daily lives and often little to command their loyalty save the cash nexus.

Not daring to say what none would choose to hear, the maid exploited the insinuating power of the unsaid: she 'alleged no grounds for the demand only that she should swear a debt against me and led me to suppose it was for a large sum. . . . I particularly recollect one expression "five pounds Miss won't pay me nor five to the back of that."' However, Letitia stood her ground and refused to pay.

The maid retreated. Having scaled down her demands, she later tried to bring a case against Letitia in the small claims court for £1 11s for outstanding wages and purchases she had supposedly made on Letitia's behalf, but her case was scuppered by Jerdan, who pulled strings with the magistrate, Thomas Hill, a bibliophile and literary hanger-on. Writing to Hill, enclosing Letitia's formal written statement of the case, Jerdan expressed the hope that the maid's 'sheer imposition' would not prosper. Instead of offering a vulgar pecuniary backhander, he rewarded Hill in the coinage of L.E.L.'s fame and Letitia's privacy, ending his letter with a postscript: 'If you are an autograph collector, the enclosure will reward you.'

Jerdan enclosed Letitia's scrawled covering note to himself, forwarding it without her knowledge:

My dear Sir,

I herewith send my statement and the summons. Is there nothing I can do for you in the <u>live way</u> [?] I am still quite lame.

Your most obliged,
L. E. Landon

It is hardly a love letter, but the phrase 'Is there nothing I can do for you in the <u>live way</u>' could easily have been interpreted salaciously, given the prevailing culture of coded sexual language. Hill was known among contemporaries as a man addicted to 'defamatory gossip' and 'all the petty details'. He was 'supposed to know, everything about everybody, and was asked to dine everywhere in order that he might tell it. Scandal was, of course, the great staple of his conversation.' Letitia might simply have been referring to the fact that a foot injury would prevent her from attending court, but her interrogative word order, the personal 'for you,' and the underlined 'live way' comment could have been taken as suggestive. Whatever she actually intended, Hill could have crudely surmised that she was offering Jerdan sex in exchange for sorting out her court case.

Meanwhile, Letitia's attempt to recast herself as a novelist with *Romance and Reality* was not wholly satisfying to either her readers or herself. She always found verse easier to write than prose, and she remained desperate to find a new outlet for it once the appetite for traditional poetry collections had dried up.

After around 1830, the only commercially viable format for verse was to be found in a new publishing phenomenon: the 'annual' or 'gift book'. Letitia jumped on the bandwagon. Most of her prolific post-1830 poetic output is to be found in the annuals, large-format compilations of poetry, pictures and occasionally prose: the coffee table books of the day. Designed to be given as presents, they typically came out in the run-up to Christmas, and were invariably found, as Thackeray disdainfully put it in 1840, 'upon the round, rosewood, brass-inlaid drawing-room table of the middle-classes'. Their cozy titles, such as *Friendship's Offering*, appeared to bypass the cash nexus. But Charles Heath, who founded the most prestigious, *The Keepsake,* in 1827, made no bones about his 'motive': 'to get the *Profit* of my own Labour and Talent'.

Nothing better exemplifies the concept of the 'commodification of culture' than the annuals. Previously, individuals had had to copy out chosen extracts into their private albums or commonplace books. Now they could get a literary compilation ready-made.

The first English annual, *The Forget-Me-Not,* was initiated in 1822 by Rudolph Ackermann of *Ackermann's Repository,* the Regency fashion and interior design bible. Indeed, the annuals were furnishing items in themselves. They came ready-bound in spectacular jewel-coloured silks, at a time when most books were sold in plain paper covers, requiring the purchasers to go to the bother of taking them to the binders' themselves. Ackermann had been inspired by German models, including the almanac *Urania,* in which Franz Schubert first encountered the *Winterreise* poems that inspired his masterpiece. The line between high and commercial art was flexible in the 1820s. Letitia took advantage of that ambiguity.

Letitia contributed occasionally to the annuals from their inception, including Ackermann's *Forget-Me-Not.* But in 1831, she was hired by the publisher Robert Fisher to provide the entire content for his annual *Fisher's Drawing Room Scrap Book.* Its very title sums up the genre, with its deceptive message of informal domesticity, as if its readers had curated the contents themselves in the privacy of their own living rooms. She continued to write for Fisher's scrapbook year after year until her death, contributing all the texts, effectively a new poetry collection annually. But her brand value had by then diminished so far that the title page subordinated her name to that of the publisher, relegating her to the role of putative 'editor': *Fisher's Drawing Room Scrap Book, edited by L.E.L.*

L.E.L. was well placed to become the voice of the annuals, as their target audience was primarily female. Although the nameless melodist's early admirers had been young men without neck-cloths, her fan base became increasingly feminized, as is demonstrated by surviving ladies' albums of the period, in which forgotten fans—with names such as Mary Groom, Elizabeth Duncan and Mary Ann Payne, among others— copied out her poetry in their best handwriting. Although Letitia's annuals poetry was later disparaged by the Victorians, it struck a chord with women readers because it reflected their sense of thwarted agency in an era that saw the public discourse of feminism, once spearheaded by Mary Wollstonecraft, contract to the point of nullity.

Outsider readers, such as the adolescent Brontë sisters in Yorkshire, were entranced by the annuals because they seemed to give free rein to their imaginative yearning for wider horizons. In late 1830, fifteen-year-old Charlotte and thirteen-year-old Emily both made painstaking copies of the illustration to a poem by L.E.L., 'The Disconsolate One,' from the new *Forget-Me-Not* for 1831, which had been given to them as a present by their aunt. The picture showed a young woman leaning her head on her arm in an attitude of despair, a letter dropping from her other hand. Letitia's accompanying text has a diluted, pattern-book feel, compared to her early Satanic effusions. Yet its themes of forbidden love and jealousy would later reecho in the Brontës' published works.

George Eliot, on the other hand, denounced the annuals. Her novel

Pencil copy made by Emily Brontë at thirteen of the illustration to L.E.L.'s poem 'The Disconsolate One' in *The Forget-Me-Not*

Middlemarch—set in the late 1820s and early 1830s, though written between 1869 and 1871—includes a scene in which the naïve provincial youth Ned Plymdale attempts to impress Rosamond Vincy with the latest *Keepsake*. Rosamond is only too eager to see it, though she carefully curbs her enthusiasm as soon as the sophisticated Dr Lydgate dismisses it as trash. She is in fact a secret fervent admirer of L.E.L.

In making the monstrously shallow and narcissistic Rosamond a fan, Eliot delivered the ultimate insult to Letitia Landon. The Victorians in general looked askance at their immediate predecessors of the 1820s and 1830s, a period they regarded as a bankrupt age devoted to Mammon and lacking in moral vision. As an accomplished amateur singer who 'only wanted to know what her audience liked', Rosamond embodies the performative notion of femininity that had been L.E.L.'s undoing.

Had Eliot given any attention to the 1829 *Keepsake* (probably the one Ned shows to Rosamond), she would however have found that L.E.L.'s contribution, 'The Altered River', offered a thoughtfully ironic take on the annuals' consumerist aesthetic. The poem follows the course of a river through the countryside, then into a dismal, smoke-filled industrial landscape. It ends with a poet leaning over the water, a modern Narcissus poised to drown himself. In doing so, it secretly exposes the self-defeating, circular dynamic driving the industrialized literary economy. L.E.L. was only too aware that the job of cultural producers was to reflect consumers' sentimental tastes back at them, ultimately to be displayed on the drawing-room table as commodified symbols of status and emotional refinement.

Although Letitia continued to rely on Jerdan as agent for her book contracts, her correspondence shows her haggling with annuals' publishers on her own. By the 1830s, she had abandoned her pseudo-aristocratic unconcern with filthy lucre and was looking for a separate income stream independent of her Svengali. This placed her in a weak position, as women writers were rarely taken seriously as business negotiators. Jane Austen, for example, had had to rely on her banker brother Henry to broker her contracts.

In 1832, Fisher attempted to extend the seasonal market by commissioning Letitia to produce the entire poetic content for a new volume, *The Easter Gift: A Religious Offering*. Letitia agreed, keen to change her dubious image in the eyes of respectable bourgeois readers. But her lack of religious faith made her ill placed to recast herself as a Christian proselyte.

Clearly feeling unable to call on Jerdan, she wrote to another male literary crony, the antiquarian Crofton Croker, for advice. Her letter reveals how cynical she was in her desperation to please the publisher by reflecting readers' prejudices back at them: 'The Madonna puzzled me the most, I had in mind a vesper hymn, when I suddenly recollected that rosaries crucifixes etc were abominations in the sight of the good Protestants for whom the Easter offering is destined and so I have taken quite the opposite side.' The hymnlike verses in the collection jangle emptily. Only the poem on Mary Magdalene reads with anything like commitment.

By now Letitia was, according to Katherine Thomson, writing 'with the loathing of a slave' to fulfil publishers' deadlines. On one occasion she fell asleep late at night before completing a commission. She was only woken in the morning when the boy arrived to collect her copy. In fifteen minutes, she hurriedly produced a polished verse.

The rise and fall of the annuals as a literary phenomenon echoes that of L.E.L. herself. When Charles Heath created the idea for *The Keepsake* in 1827 he intended it as a high-end product. The deluxe version, bound in tooled morocco, cost a whopping £2.12.6. He employed the latest steel-engraving technology to reproduce the illustrations at the highest possible quality. The originals were provided by Turner, no less.

Fat fees enabled Heath to attract top names. The 1829 *Keepsake* included new writing from Walter Scott, Thomas Moore, Robert Southey, Samuel Taylor Coleridge, William Wordsworth and Felicia Hemans. Mary Shelley provided a previously unpublished text by her dead husband, in an effort to rehabilitate his reputation. Letitia and Jerdan also had their fingers in the pie, contributing a poem apiece.

In their heyday, the annuals were the most lucrative format in publishing. General sales of annuals generated £90,000 in 1828 alone, according to S. C. Hall, who cashed in on the craze with his own *The Amulet: A Christian and Literary Remembrancer*. However, publishers soon became hard-pressed to find new ways to differentiate their products and resorted to gimmicks. *Schloss's Bijou Almanac,* for which Letitia provided the entire poetic content in 1834 and 1835, was a miniature three-quarters of an inch long and half an inch wide. Although it was a triumph of Lilliputian book production, the text was unreadable by the naked eye. Letitia had sought to exploit her readers' selective blindness. Now they could not even read her without a magnifying glass.

Schloss's Bijou Almanac: a triumph of Lilliputian book production, but the text was unreadable by the naked eye.

Eventually the annuals spawned so many downmarket imitators that they lost their status as exclusive markers of taste and fashion. By about 1850 they had almost petered out. Like Narcissus, or L.E.L. herself, they ended up destroyed by their own success.

Letitia's need to diversify into the annuals was created by Jerdan's weak grip on money matters. He had as little capacity for relating pecuniary paper promises to actual circumstances as he had in connecting L.E.L.'s stylized poetic cries of erotic rage and despair with their everyday relationship. In 1834 his inability to compute reality resulted in a financial crisis that impacted on them both.

According to the vague and convoluted account he gave in his autobiography, Jerdan had got to know two brothers, sons of an apparently wealthy man who had just returned from India. He began negotiations with one of the young men to make him a partner in the *Literary Gazette,* which he unconvincingly claimed to have been prepared to do out of the kindness of his heart. The other brother wanted to 'enter into a co-partnery with one of a reputedly very rich Jewish family in the city' and apparently persuaded Jerdan 'in an evil hour' to put his name as security against certain bills 'to enable him to show something against the Leviathan fortune in the administration of which he was about to participate as a broker'. Jerdan signed a document guaranteeing the young man's stake in the brokerage business. The upshot was that Jerdan was sued for between three and four thousand pounds when the young man fled to the Continent. In a replay of John Landon's crisis a decade before, he faced bankruptcy.

Although Jerdan does not name the family with whom he was dealing, they must have been the Twinings, whom he named as his main creditors in an unpublished letter to Bulwer of December 1830. The Twiningses' long-standing tea concern was intimately connected with India, although they also diversified into banking in 1825. To this day, Twinings Tea still has a shop on the Strand near to the former premises of the *Literary Gazette*.

Back in 1825, it was the Twinings who had persuaded Jerdan to take the lease on Grove House, having briefly considered taking it themselves. They offered him an instant loan, telling him that it was essential to his professional status to be seen to live in a grand house, and that they hoped that he would promote their banking services among his numerous acquaintances. However, the loan mounted as Jerdan fitted out his impressive new residence.

By the end of 1830, Jerdan was asking Bulwer to underwrite a new loan he wanted to take out with a professional moneylender. 'I suppose troubling a friend on one's private affairs is something like the confession of a lady's love—after the first blush is over there is no stint,' he wrote, in an apparent allusion to L.E.L.'s endless love poetry. He complained that his prospects were not solidly vested in real estate but in 'copyrights', which adds to the impression that he was using L.E.L. as collateral. By the time of the Twiningses' final demand in 1834, Jerdan was in no position to pay.

All accounts of the extreme money troubles Letitia faced in her latter years coincide chronologically with Jerdan's bankruptcy. After Colburn published her next novel, *Francesca Carrara,* in 1834, she complained that she 'lost the whole of the proceeds . . . at one swoop', because of 'the debts to which it had been appropriated'. It is hard not to conclude that her debts were joined at the hip with Jerdan's. She had not done enough to separate her finances from his.

CHAPTER 9

French Connections

Jerdan's financial embarrassments took some time to result in a fait accompli. But they were common gossip by April 23, 1834, when he attended a supper party at the Garrick Club in honour of Shakespeare's birthday. 'I thought (not, I hope, uncharitably) that it would have been more graceful to have absented himself from a festive meeting under his peculiar circumstances, which he evidently cannot feel very strongly,' commented the actor William Macready in his diary.

In June, Letitia jumped at an impromptu invitation from a Hans Place neighbour, Miss Turing, to accompany her on a visit to Paris. As she put it in a note to Jerdan, 'it would be something to be out of the perpetual worry here [money short]' (the words in brackets were supplied by Jerdan in his autobiography in the 1850s). Miss Turing (a forebear of the computer genius Alan Turing) was the spinster daughter of a Scottish banker, some years older than Letitia. Like many respectable ladies, she was prepared to overlook any hints of the untoward as regarded Miss Landon's reputation.

The 1830s saw what Thackeray called an 'invasion of France' by English tourists. Visitors flocked to Paris for its buzzing nightlife and for its shopping, made all the more attractive by a favourable exchange rate. Miss Turing was particularly keen to visit the fashionable boutiques, but Letitia had literary reasons for wanting to go.

She had a half-formulated idea of writing a novel about the French Revolution and was keen to visit the scene. The projected tale, which was never written, was to feature an Icarus heroine: Charlotte Corday, the Girondin sympathizer who was guillotined after murdering Marat in his bath in 1793 in a desperate attempt to stem the tide of Jacobin extremism.

Letitia was still as interested in the corruption of political ideals as she had been when her first published poem, 'Rome', appeared in 1820.

Letitia and Miss Turing took the steamer to Boulogne. It picked up passengers on the Thames in the heart of the City, near London Bridge, as described in Thackeray's *Paris Sketch Book,* written in the late 1830s. Thackeray vividly depicted the social potpourri on deck in which distinctions of class and respectability were thrown into carnivalesque confusion. In Thackeray's account, English gentility is represented by a mother corralling her children, a couple of trainee governesses and a clergyman, who rub shoulders with a racy *danseuse* from the Paris opera and a pair of dubiously overdressed French milliners returning from a sales trip to London. Two young Englishmen, desperately growing their moustaches to emulate the French dandies, ogle the *danseuse* in anticipation.

Many tourists were attracted by the perceived hedonism of Parisian society compared to relatively straitlaced England. The onboard lunch, according to Thackeray, was, however, unappetizingly English for those looking forward to champagne and ices at the Café de Paris and Tortoni's: boiled beef, pickles, a 'great, red raw Cheshire cheese', and 'little dumpy bottles of stout'. Only about a dozen passengers choose to partake, he tells us. The rest are feeling queasy.

Letitia was prostrated with seasickness when she arrived at Boulogne on June 22. She and Miss Turing travelled from there to Paris by coach. The start of the journey was 'delightful', the road a long avenue through the countryside, roses landing in the carriage flung by urchins asking for *sous.* After Abbeville, however, Letitia was paralysed by fatigue. On arriving in Paris, she had to be lifted out of the *diligence* to be conveyed into the 'pleasant apartments, looking on the Boulevards' they had booked in the rue Louis le Grand.

The street view seemed 'gay' at first. Letitia expressed surprise that the people looked so clean and neat, a nod to Paris's reputation as a moral swamp. But the lodgings proved far noisier than anything in London, with a print works above, a carpenter opposite, and clattering carriages on the cobbles below. She and Miss Turing then moved, more satisfactorily, to 30 rue Taitbout, where they had delightful bedrooms, a little antechamber, and the prettiest saloon looking out on a charming garden. Those of the houses in the *rue* that still survive today as they were in the 1830s have courtyarded spaces behind large street-side double gates.

Rue Taitbout, photographed in the 1850s. Letitia stayed here in 1834 at number 30. Only a few of the houses in the street today retain their original appearance, the street doors opening onto inner courtyards.

Rue Taitbout was located in the heart of Parisian haut bohemia, near the theatres, the Café de Paris and Tortoni's. The Rothschilds' glittering mansion was nearby. A few years later, Balzac installed his fictional high-class courtesans in glamorous apartments in the rue Taitbout, while Chopin set up residence there in real life with George Sand. In G. W. N. Reynolds's Dickens spin-off *Pickwick Abroad; or, The Tour in France* (1837–38), rue Taitbout is where a dubious English hostess, implicitly on the run from British society, hosts her rackety salon.

The series of long letters Letitia wrote to Jerdan from Paris in 1834 are the only writings of hers that give anything like a sustained impression of the daily texture of their relationship. Not until over a decade into their affair do we get such intimate access. The originals have, typically, disappeared, but the texts were printed by Jerdan in his autobiography.

Their tone suggests an easy, quotidian familiarity, although they always begin formally 'Dear Sir'. Unlike L.E.L.'s poetry, they contain no high-flown passion, but they testify to Letitia's emotional dependence on Jerdan. At the start of their relationship, she had used all the wiles at her disposal to seduce him into publishing her. Three children later, their relationship had become an attachment as non-negotiable in her eyes as a family bond.

She wrote to him as soon as she reached Boulogne: 'We parted on Thursday, though not at all too soon, much as I regretted it. You cannot think how I missed you. . . . However, I have taken two things for granted, first that you would expect my first letter, and also that you would be glad to hear how I was.' As soon as she reached Paris on June 26, she wrote again, and then again the next day. 'Pray write to me,' she begged, longing to hear from him.

Yet when she finally received Jerdan's tardy response the following day, she violently upbraided him for having enclosed the *Gazette,* rather than sending it separately as printed matter, because she had had to pay extra postage costs as a result. Her bickering tone offers more proof of intimacy than any of L.E.L.'s extravagant declarations. This is the only occasion, outside her poetry, on which she used the word 'love' in relation to her feelings for Jerdan:

Love and fear are the greatest principles of human existence. If you owed my letter of yesterday to the first of these, you owe that of today to the last. What, in the name of all that is dreadful in the way of postage, could induce you to put the 'Gazette' in your letter? Welcome as it was, it has cost me dear, nearly six shillings. I was so glad to see your handwriting that the shock was nearly lost in pleasure; but truly, when I come to reflect and put it down in my pocket-book, I am 'in a state'. The Gazette alone would have cost twopence, and the letter *deux* francs; but altogether it is ruinous. Please when you next write let it be on the thinnest paper, and put a wafer. Still I was delighted to hear from you, and a most amusing letter it was. The Gazette is a real treat. It is such an excellent one as to make me quite jealous.

She ended with heartfelt postscript: 'I was so glad of your letter.'

Jerdan was not so assiduous a correspondent as she wanted him to be. His replies are not extant, but from Letitia's letters it appears that they were derisory. 'I hope you will not think that I intend writing you to death,' she wrote on June 30, well aware that she was sending him more letters than she received. The unfulfilled yearning of her childhood had repatterned itself.

She niggled and nagged. 'I write on purpose to scold you,' she wrote to Jerdan a few days later in peremptory tones. 'Why have you not sent me the "Gazette"; it would have been such a treat,' she complained. He was probably still smarting from her previous reaction. 'Also, you have not (like everybody else) written to me,' she carped. This was the everyday banality behind the woman wailing for her demon lover.

Letitia's visit to Paris is significant in terms of literary history because it highlights the French connections in her career and her international reputation in her lifetime. If her brand value as 'L.E.L.' was declining in England by 1834, her cult status was still in the ascendant in Paris, where her work had recently been showcased in a long article in the prestigious *Revue des deux mondes*. Posterity later consigned L.E.L. to a feminine ghetto unconnected with wider cultural currents. But her voice was in reality both more embedded in Romanticism and less Anglocentric than has previously been supposed.

The international fallout from Byronism meant that Anglomania was raging in Europe, where English writing was so admired that the greatest composers of the day looked to it for inspiration, often creating works that outlived their sources in popularity. Scott's *Lady of the Lake* inspired Rossini's *La donna del lago*. Byron's *Childe Harold* was reworked by Berlioz in *Harold en Italie*. Schumann's *Paradise and the Peri* was a musical interpretation of Moore's *Lalla Rookh*. Even Bulwer's now unread 1836 novel *Rienzi* inspired Wagner's first opera, of the same name.

Letitia's contacts with the European literary world went back a long way. At the time she began to publish her verses in the *Gazette,* its Paris correspondent was Stendhal, although he transferred his allegiance to the *New Monthly Magazine* (also owned by Colburn) in 1822 because Jerdan cut his copy when it became too overtly political. However, it may have been through Stendhal that Jerdan secured a glowing front-page review of *The Improvisatrice* in *Le Globe* in 1824.

In many ways, Letitia's real-life career seems as much a parable of 'ambitious mania' as Stendhal's 1830 novel *Le rouge et le noir*. Its parvenu antihero Julien Sorel fuels his social rise from obscure origins on a combination of talent, hard work, risk-taking, deception and sexual seduction. He ultimately overreaches himself and ends up on the guillotine.

Another French author who fascinated Letitia was her contemporary Balzac, although she was already an established writer when he began to publish. Her short story 'The Talisman' (1833) was inspired by a review of his early work *La peau de chagrin* that she read in *Le Globe*. Her enormous productivity and ironic references to the mechanics of the literary marketplace match those of Balzac himself. Both writers were fascinated by the theme of corrupted literary aspiration.

In verse, Letitia rendered the price of fame as stylized tragedy, but in prose she was more of a realist. Her late novel *Ethel Churchill*, published in 1837, features an impoverished, idealistic young poet, Walter Maynard, who is ultimately destroyed by the cash nexus. It has something in common with Balzac's *Illusions perdues*, which appeared in serial form between 1837 and 1843. The efforts of Balzac's poet-protagonist Lucien Chardon to promote himself on the literary and social stage lead him to debt, crime and a suicide attempt. As a historical figure, Letitia is not Shelleyan nor Dickensian, but more like a power player out of a Balzac novel, one of his writers or one of his courtesans.

Letitia's French sensibility almost certainly had family roots, given that her mother stated in the 1851 census that she was born in France. Catherine may even have been educated there, possibly alongside Mrs Siddons's daughters, Maria and Sally, her contemporaries, who were sent to boarding school in France to get them out of the way while their mother pursued her acting career. Sally was clearly close enough to Catherine to embroider a baby cap for Letitia, although she died the year after she was born.

Letitia spoke French well. She was complimented on her accent while in Paris and had no trouble understanding people. Indeed, she was confident enough in the language to suggest to Jerdan that she should put together an 'annual, consisting entirely of French translations', which she could get ready 'in about a month', although the idea never reached fruition.

In one of her Paris letters Letitia makes a curious throwaway reference to 'an old friend and relative' whom she had been seeing there, a Colonel Fagan. This, it turns out, was Christopher Sullivan Fagan, later a general, whose wife, Marie, was the addressee of Letitia's last letter from Cape Coast Castle. All researches into a possible family connection between the Irish Fagans and the Herefordshire Landons draw a blank. He must have been related to Letitia on her mysterious maternal side.

Colonel Fagan, who was involved in the East India Company, was the nephew of the Irish cavalry officer Christopher Alexander Fagan (1733–1816). Known as the 'Chevalier Fagan', the latter served in the Irish Brigade of the pre-revolutionary French army, and went by the title *comte*. Letitia's mother, Catherine, was said by Jerdan to be descended illegitimately from a nobleman. The Chevalier himself may have been Catherine's father, although his brother Andrew, who was also involved with the French army before transferring his allegiance to the East India Company, is another possible candidate. Given the fact that Letitia found so many Irish-born allies—from the Halls to Lady Blessington—it would make sense if she had an Irish family connection. The Chevalier Fagan was a close family friend and mentor of the Irish radical leader Daniel O'Connell. In October 1797, a few months after Catherine and John Landon married and settled at 25 Hans Place, Daniel O'Connell is on record as living at 12 Hans Place, from where he addressed a letter to his brother Maurice.

The Fagans were also connected to the theatrical demimonde, which looms so large in Letitia's story. The Chevalier's most significant love affair was with the French courtesan-actress Hyancinthe Varis, which produced an illegitimate daughter, Hyacinthe-Gabrielle Roland, who also appeared on the stage, before becoming the mistress of the Duke of Wellington's brother, the Earl of Mornington.

The image of L.E.L. Letitia initially created had much in common with the French culture of the *'femme libre'*, epitomized by actresses such as the two Hyacinthes. Her early work shows an uncanny similarity to the poetry of Marceline Desbordes-Valmore (1786–1859), whose *Elégies et romances* (1819) and *Elégies et poésies nouvelles* (1825) feature flowers, songbirds, secrets and lyres. Desbordes-Valmore's youth was also defined by her father's bankruptcy, but by the time she published her first book, she had been on the stage and to Guadaloupe and back. She drew a calculated veil over her early life, but was an adept manipulator of her own enigma. Her work addresses a mystery lover, 'Olivier', but her real secret was, in the view of a recent critic, 'her ability to play the secret for all it was worth'. Like L.E.L., she transformed herself into a 'poem authored by pain', a 'chronically wounded enigma of second hand literary production'.

Balzac, who knew Desbordes-Valmore in later life, made her the model for the chillingly cynical middle-aged protagonist of *Cousin Bette* (1846). Nadar made a startling deathbed photograph of her bony corpse in 1859. Her poetry was worshipped by Baudelaire, and she became the only woman allowed by Verlaine into his pantheon of *poètes maudits*, or accursed poets. Twentieth-century critics later despised the poetess tradition as vapid, but its sadomasochistic, self-deconstructing theatrics fed surreptitiously into modernism via Verlaine and Rimbaud.

The influence of Desbordes-Valmore on L.E.L. can only be hypothesized on stylistic grounds. However, Letitia was demonstrably *au fait* with the work of another French poetess, Amable Tastu (1798–1885): she

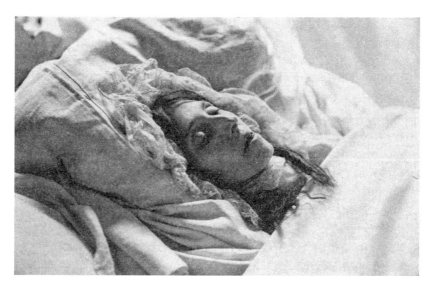

The poetess Marceline Desbordes-Valmore (1786–1859) on her deathbed, photographed by Nadar. Although a generation older than Letitia, she lived on into the age of photography.

Sabine 'Amable' Tastu, Letitia's most assiduous
companion in Paris

published a verse translation of Tastu's poem 'Les Feuilles de Saule' ('Willow Leaves') in the *Gazette* in 1827. Amable Tastu was married to the editor Joseph Tastu, who promoted her career, just as Jerdan promoted Letitia's. Her choice of the masculine first name 'Amable' as a nom de plume presaged Amantine-Lucile-Aurore Dupin's later adoption of her more famous masculine pen name, George Sand.

Madame Tastu was the anonymous author of the admiring piece on L.E.L. in the *Revue des deux mondes* of 1834. Arguing art for art's sake, it demanded in typically French fashion that a poet's private life should be kept off-limits to criticism. Talent, wrote Tastu, did not imply personal virtue any more than it excluded it. Poets should not need a certificate of good conduct. It was only of importance to Miss Landon's family, and irrelevant to her art, whether she was a woman of honour or not.

It was a statement of support in the face of the personal gossip that had by now become an integral aspect of Letitia's public image in England, initially at her own provocation but increasingly to her detriment. In France, on the contrary, 'gallantry' was so institutionalized as 'to create no remark', according to Thackeray in his Parisian sketches. He contrasted the English need for 'the decency of secrecy' with French sexual attitudes.

In Paris, Madame Tastu became Letitia's most assiduous companion. L.E.L.'s prestige abroad was such that she was able to attract the cream of literary society in France—at least those who were in town. It was a disappointment to her that Parisian party season was over, curtailing her networking opportunities. 'The soirées are where I should have met all the French *littérateurs,* but none are being given just now,' she complained to Jerdan on June 30. However, Madame Tastu took her to a friend's country retreat where one gentleman, in an act of surreal whimsy, 'was seized with such a fit of poetry that he wrote some verses in my honour, with a pea-pod on a cabbage leaf'.

Despite being in Paris in the dead season, Letitia was charmed by the attentions paid to her by Prosper Merimée and Odilon Barrot, received a flattering call from the über-critic Sainte-Beuve, and met Chateaubriand at Madame Recamier's. The latter was still very beautiful, with exquisite manners, according to Letitia. But the man who impressed her as 'the wittiest and most original person' she encountered in Paris was the German poet Heinrich Heine, then a political exile. Having heard she was in town, he wrote to her and then paid her the compliment of a call on June 29.

In a letter to Jerdan, Letitia rendered her encounter with Heine as a comic vignette. She depicted herself as responding in tongue-tied monosyllables to the German poet's attempts at small talk:

He said, 'Mademoiselle donc a beaucoup couru les boutiques?' 'Mais non.' 'A-t-elle été au Jardin des Plantes?' 'Mais non.' 'Avez-vous été a l'opéra, aux théatres?' 'Mais non.' 'Peut-etre Mademoiselle aime la promenade?' 'Mais non.' 'A-t-elle donc apporté beaucoup de livres, ou peut-etre elle écrit?' 'Mais non.' At last, in seeming despair, he exclaimed, 'Mais Mademoiselle, qu'est que ce donc, qu'elle a fait? 'Mais—mais—j'ai regardé par la fenetre.' Was there ever anything *si bête*?

Heinrich Heine, the 'wittiest and most original person' Letitia encountered in Paris in 1834. Portrait by Moritz Daniel Oppenheim, 1831.

Things clearly warmed up enough for Heine to show Letitia his wit and originality. Perhaps his sense of irony was tickled by the parodic aspect of their opening dialogue, its dance of dead-end commonplaces. Both poets' work reveals their awareness of the tragic absurdity of the social mask.

In humorously depicting her supposed social ineptitude with Heine, Letitia told Jerdan, 'you know it takes a long time with me to get over the shame of speaking to a stranger by way of conversation.' Despite her reputation as a society wit, she remained underneath as insecure as the tongue-tied little girl in 'The History of a Child'. 'I have seen a good many strangers, and it would take a quire of paper to detail all the little agonies I have suffered from them, all the little 'states' that I have been in,' she told an unnamed 'intimate and valued friend' in another letter from Paris, quoted in Blanchard's biography.

'Though all my life I have lived in society, and had to make my own way, I never got accustomed to doing it,' she went on. 'I am unconquerably irresolute and shy. The utmost I can do, and that by force of long habit, is to conceal my embarrassment, and to feel it, for that very concealment, all the more.' With Heine, she transformed her very shyness into a mannered performance, neutralizing her anxiety by projecting it into play-acting. She could only express her vulnerabilities by transforming them into masquerade.

Letitia told Heine that she had not yet been to the theatre, but that state of affairs was soon remedied when the solicitous editor of the *Revue des deux mondes* got her a box to see the risqué opera-ballet *The Temptation of St Anthony* ('which said temptation is the being made love to by a very beautiful woman, created by his Satanic majesty for that very purpose'). At the theatre she was introduced to a handsome young poet, Antoine Fontaney. She told her unnamed correspondent that he answered very well to her beau idéal of the French genius: 'pale, dark, sombre, and with a sort of enthusiasm of which we have no idea in England. . . . His conversation is very intellectual, and very spirited—or let me use the French word, *"spirituel."'*

Although still yoked familially to Jerdan, Letitia was eager to flirt with younger men. She was getting her own back for Louisa Costello, Mary Ann Browne, and whatever casual sexual couplings Jerdan pursued. Fontaney, however, was not interested. He was in fact smitten with an adolescent girl half Letitia's age, Gabrielle, the daughter of the famous French actress Marie Dorval. They went on to elope to London, to the distress of Madame Dorval, who would have preferred her daughter to have made a more advantageous match. The couple both ended up dying of consumption in a garret in true *La Bohème* style.

Despite her interest in the handsome Fontaney, Letitia's comments on French poetry matched the hypocrisy of English society. 'As far as I can judge,' she wrote, 'it is full of novelty, vivid conceptions, and I must say, genius, but what we should call blasphemous and indelicate to the last degree.' Though in reality a fallen woman, she cleaved to English social norms, even when they restricted her freedom. She complained that 'of course it is impossible for me to go out by myself, or accept the attendance of a gentleman alone, so that I am surrounded with all sorts of little difficulties and embarrassments.'

By 1834, Letitia's contemporary George Sand (born 1804) had left her husband and embarked on her famous period of Romantic rebellion in

Paris, where she threw off the shackles of marriage to become a writer, commit adultery, and tramp the streets alone in men's clothes. Her first foray into fiction was cowritten with her first lover, Jules Sandeau, just as Letitia created L.E.L. in partnership with Jerdan. However, she soon left him for a string of other sexual partners of both sexes, including Chopin and Marie Dorval.

Both Sand and L.E.L. based their literary voices on their treatment of thwarted female passion, 'love dashing her head blindly against all the obstacles of civilisation', as Sand put it in the 1832 preface to her novel *Indiana*. They had much in common: sexual transgression; a 'fatal facility' for producing page after page; a public personality cult to manage; a lack of faith in the feminist political project. However, Sand pursued her career with a ruthless independence Letitia lacked. By the time she died, of old age in 1876, she was a national treasure.

Sand's aristocratic background, and the fact that she had been married before she rebelled sexually, bolstered her sense of entitle-

'George Sand' at ease in her role as a betrousered, smoking rebel in the 1840s

ment. She was a twenty-six-year-old escapee wife by the time her first work was published jointly with Sandeau, whom she soon jettisoned once his usefulness had been exhausted. In contrast, Letitia, who began writing for the *Gazette* as a teenager, remained tied to Jerdan, who had taken her virginity, long after he ceased to be valuable as a springboard.

French mores were also more accommodating to the *'femme libre'* than was English society. They continued to be so long into the nineteenth century. Colette (born 1873) began her literary career in a situation not dissimilar to that of the young Letitia. When her family was in reduced circumstances, she was married off at twenty to the rakish publisher and writer Willy. He flagrantly exploited her talents, reputedly locking her in a room to make her write her *Claudine* books, which he initially published under his own name. The novels' combination of naiveté and sexual sophistication titillated the public in much the same way as L.E.L.'s early poetry.

Like Sand, Colette ultimately felt powerful enough to assert her autonomy and split from her Svengali. Having left Willy, she went scan-

A young Colette with Willy, c. 1890s. Unlike Letitia, she first married her Svengali and then left him to pursue her career solo.

dalously on the stage, and pursued a string of other lovers, while tirelessly promoting her own career. When Colette died in 1954, she was given a state funeral. Had Letitia been French, she might have ended up in the literary canon, accepted as a female bohemian like Marceline Desbordes-Valmore, George Sand and Colette.

On the evidence of her letters to Jerdan, Letitia's French trip was not altogether happy. She frequently complained to him of languor and fatigue, and, on one occasion, of being so unsteady on her feet that she kept falling over on the slippery parquet, hurting her arm. Meals were ordered in from the nearby Café de Paris. Letitia enthusiastically told Mrs Hall that she was 'making an experimental voyage through the carte', having a different dish every day. But she admitted to Jerdan that she had no appetite: 'I am obliged to force a little down: ice is the only thing I enjoy.'

Letitia's letter to Jerdan of June 30 offered a litany of complaints, numbered from one to six: too many Parisians were out of town; the lack of a gentleman chaperone restricted her movements; her planned stay was too short to make proper acquaintances; her companion Miss Turing knew nothing of French customs and was only interested in seeing 'the dresses, shops etc.' 'Fifthly,' she went on, 'one ought to be married; and sixthly I wish myself at home again.' The penultimate grumble, slipped in surreptitiously, leaps out.

The codes that governed the sexual behaviour of women were nuanced, but the status of the unmarried mistress was the most perilous. A woman who lost her virginity out of wedlock could wipe out the stigma by marrying her deflowerer, as does Jane Austen's Lydia Bennett. In Letitia's own circle, sex before marriage was not unknown. Rosina Wheeler slept with Edward Bulwer before their wedding, perhaps to inveigle him into marrying her (she later accused him of having pressured her into anal sex, an activity 'which women cannot tell even to their lawyers').

Even a mistress from the demimonde could aim at social acceptability by marrying her lover, although it was often a vain hope. Hyacinthe Roland eventually married the Earl of Mornington at St George's Hanover Square in 1794, but she was miserable in London because no one would visit her. Lady Caroline Lamb was particularly warned by her mother against acknowledging Hyacinthe in society.

Marceline Desbordes-Valmore, George Sand and Colette had a double advantage. Not only were they French, but all three had been married before embarking on their adventurous literary and sexual careers. Letitia, in contrast, was English and had become a mistress without ever having been a wife and with little hope of ever marrying her lover.

Could Letitia's relationship with Jerdan have worked out differently? At a time when divorce in England required an act of Parliament, and was restricted to a tiny minority of the very rich and well connected, far more unmarried couples from lesser backgrounds cohabited informally than one might assume. The life of the Victorian 'sensation' novelist Mary Elizabeth Braddon (1835–1915) offers an intriguing counterfactual parallel to Letitia's story.

A generation younger than L.E.L., Braddon went through a similar family crisis in her teens when her solicitor father suffered financial ruin and her parents' marriage broke up. She briefly went on the provincial stage under a pseudonym and found the protection of an older man, before embarking on a career-enhancing relationship with the publisher John Maxwell, who encouraged her literary talents and became her lover.

Like Jerdan, he was older and married. However, his wife was safely out of the way in a mental institution in Ireland. Braddon quietly moved in with him, gave birth to six children, and succeeded in passing as his wife in society, while simultaneously achieving wild commercial literary success as 'Miss Braddon'. They finally married in 1874, after the first Mrs Maxwell's death, by which time Mary Elizabeth Braddon had become both rich and respected as a result of her literary endeavours. In her later years, she was even presented to Queen Victoria.

In contrast to Miss Braddon, whose works were written in the third person and who kept herself out of the public eye, Letitia's literary celebrity had been tied to her confessional voice and Byronic aura of personal scandal from early on. By the time she had been hyped as the 'English improvisatrice' and paraded in salons by Jerdan as his 'ward', the couple could not have quietly settled down in a discreet ménage, fudging over the fact that he was already married. More important, there is no sign that he ever wanted to leave his wife, Frances, during the 1820s. She clearly performed adequately to his needs as the mother of his legitimate children and as the chatelaine of Grove House.

Yet although Letitia did not have the respectability of marriage, or a husband to squire her about Paris, she still felt she could count on the security of Jerdan's protection. He might not have written as often as she would have liked. But for her return journey from France, in the last week of July, he offered to meet her at Boulogne to provide her with the gentlemanly escort she complained she had not had throughout her stay.

We cannot know whether he went through with the offer, but we do know that a mishap occurred on the journey home. In Paris, Letitia had bought Jerdan an expensive fancy waistcoat. In order to avoid paying duty on it, she put it on under her clothes. However, the offending item was revealed when she was strip-searched by a suspicious female customs officer at Dover. The urge to symbolize their illicit relationship had become part of the fabric of her everyday life. The couple collude to cheat the system, but it is she who is ultimately exposed, blamed and humiliated.

Perhaps the gift was a means of ingratiating herself with Jerdan to secure his wavering commitment. As the 'L.E.L.' brand declined, so did his interest. Letitia had to nag him from Paris to look over the manuscript of her novel in progress, *Francesca Carrara*. When it was published in November 1834, the three magical letters had so lost value that they did not even appear on the title page. It was marketed as 'by the author of *Romance and Reality, The Venetian Bracelet* etc.'

Letitia had made her name as a poet with stylized portrayals of emotionally starved and voracious women. In real life, Jerdan increasingly regarded her as cumbersomely needy and fragile. When he quoted her Paris letters in his autobiography, years later, he made a point of commenting on her 'excess of feminine timidity' and 'long[ing] for protection'. Clearly, that protection was beyond what he was prepared to give.

One problem was that Letitia came with Whittington attached. We cannot trace their sibling dependency as adults in any detail, as little relevant correspondence remains extant. However, a surviving letter from Whittington to Jerdan, written on July 14, 1834, when Letitia was still in France, reveals that he continued to regard his sister's protector as his meal ticket, despite being shunted off to a Devon curacy in 1831. Whittington announces that it is of 'vital consequence' that Jerdan clear a £15 debt of his at Drummond's bank, promising that this shall be the last time he duns him for money, and insisting unconvincingly, in the voice of a prodigal son, that he has 'done all I could for the last three years to recover former errors and faults'.

Jerdan later described Whittington as a clever young man, who could have done as much as his sister in literature, but instead reserved his talents for penning comic epigrams designed to persuade his host to bring out another bottle. Mrs Bray, the wife of the Devon vicar to whom Whittington was curate, thought him 'a character of no ordinary cast', whose 'superior talents' had been 'cultivated . . . by the opportunity of mingling much in the literary circles of London'. She was herself an aspirant writer who, like so many others, valued Jerdan's patronage.

By Christmas 1834, Letitia was feeling neglected by Jerdan, even though she was still producing copy for his *Gazette*. In December, while staying at Aberford with her uncle James, she sent him some German poetry translations for the magazine. But she complained crossly that he had failed to give sufficient review space to a new volume of sermons just published by her brother. Letitia particularly singled out for approval Whittington's sermon against 'drunkenness'.

'I cannot get over my disappointment about Whittington's book,' she complained. 'You should have made one or quotations. . . . Can you not say omitted last week by mistake? and give a column or so— I almost despair of hearing from you—I have now been away all but three weeks—except two days—and I have only had a very brief hurried note.' She was clearly counting the days.

'Well good bye or I lose the post,' she concluded. 'I have lost the post . . . no letter today again,' she added underneath. Letitia's fictional heroines writhed with unrequited love. This was the commonplace of being ignored.

By the end of 1834, Jerdan was bankrupt. He had lost his Brompton mansion and seen its contents auctioned, replaying the Landons' fate of nearly fifteen years before. In a further uncanny repetition, his ruin precipitated the breakdown of his marriage, although his autobiography is characteristically silent on that point. Following the loss of the family home, he moved into bachelor lodgings in Parliament Street close to the *Gazette*'s offices.

By the time of the 1851 census, Frances was living alone with one of her daughters in a modest labourer's cottage in her ancestral Hampshire, near the village of Elstead, where she had been christened in 1781. She pointedly described herself as both 'married' and 'head' of the household. In contrast to her neighbours, all agricultural workers, she described herself as a 'gentlewoman'.

Jerdan was already experiencing Letitia's emotional demands as a problem, but the collapse of his marriage dislodged the geometry of what had been for around twelve years a secure triangle. Although his autobiography waxes lyrical on the early phase of his infatuation with his songbird, he remains silent on the long, slow process of its disintegration, as he sought—unsuccessfully—to extract himself.

The most significant clue as to the crisis in their relationship lies in a baptismal record for a baby named 'Marion Jerdan Stuart', who was christened on February 24, 1836, at St Peter's church, Walworth, in the London borough of Southwark. The baby's birthdate is given as January 17, 1836. Her father is recorded as 'William Stuart', a 'gentleman'. Her mother's name is given as Mary Ann.

Jerdan's new woman was not the poetess Mary Ann Browne (who had perhaps listened to L.E.L.'s veiled warnings), but another Mary Ann. This new character is a young woman of obscure origins whose surname was Maxwell. Given that her baby must have been conceived in the spring of 1835, Jerdan was probably already seeing her by the time Letitia wrote to him on December 23, 1834, complaining of his neglect.

Very little can be established about Mary Ann Maxwell. Her baptismal record has not turned up, not has any marriage certificate for her parents, which suggests that she was illegitimate. We can tell from the 1841 census, however, that she was born circa 1817 in Bath, which was a mecca for members of the Regency entertainment industry at that time. It is possible that she and her mother were in some way connected to the lower echelons of the stage. Willing women who did not demand marriage could easily be found there, as Dickens later discovered when he established his ménage with the young actress Ellen Ternan, with the approval of her mother. The *Gazette*'s theatre reviews in 1834 express boundless admiration for the physiques of the young dancers at the Strand Theatre.

Public records show that after losing Grove House and retreating to bachelor rooms near his office, Jerdan also set up another discreet establishment just across the river in Lambeth, near the church in which Marion Jerdan Stuart was christened. It is there, in Hercules Buildings, that we find him in the 1841 census as 'William Stewart', domiciled with his supposed wife, 'Mary Ann Stewart', their four children under five, and Mary Ann's mother.

In contrast to Brompton, Lambeth was insalubrious, a place where the struggle to keep up appearances was often put under insupportable strain. In the late 1830s, Stendhal and a friend went back there for sex with a pair of amateur prostitutes. The men were taken aback by the shabby-genteel aspect of the girls' tiny house, their pathetic gratitude at being given a bottle of champagne, and also by their self-consciousness and residual shame. Stendhal's girl had a lovely figure, but in bed she insisted on blowing out the candle as she was too embarrassed for him to see her naked.

Although Jerdan no longer had an impressive residence, he now had two women on site to look after him: a young sexual partner in Mary Ann and a housekeeper in her mother. The contrasting roles taken by Letitia and Frances could be performed under one roof. Mary Ann would remain Jerdan's partner for the rest of her life, though they never married. After bearing him thirteen children, she eventually died in a lunatic asylum in Maidstone, aged forty-five.

Letitia had long specialized in stylized representations of abandoned heroines, including a 'maniac', but Jerdan had been faithful to her in his fashion for over a decade. Mary Ann Maxwell was eighteen or nineteen when her first child was conceived, around the same age that Letitia had been when her affair with Jerdan began. Now he gave Mary Ann the family life whose loss Letitia had bewailed in the voice of 'Eulalia', the poetess-heroine of her 'History of the Lyre' who laments that she has given up the prospect of a happy home life for the sake of her genius. (In another mood, Letitia was, however, relieved not to have to look after her offspring. *Romance and Reality* includes a comic vignette of a married authoress desperately trying to carve out writing time while her feral children run wild and her husband retreats behind the newspaper.)

The irony is that by this stage in her career, the alter ego 'L.E.L.' no longer provided Letitia with an outlet for expressing the misery of erotic abandonment. The poetry she was commissioned to write for *Fisher's Drawing Room Scrap Book* that year included verse descriptions of engravings that offered little scope for self-projection: a view of Beverley Minster; a portrait of the governor of Greenwich Hospital.

Yet buried in the final volume of her 1834 novel *Francesca Carrara* is the following appeal, composed at a time when her primary reader, Jerdan, was losing interest. She constructs a bond of imagined intimacy with her anonymous audience, while confessing that she is unable to confide in her everyday companions:

I have often been told that my writings are too melancholy. How can that be a reproach if they are true? . . . Good Heaven! Even to myself how strange appears the faculty, or rather the passion, of composition! how the inmost soul developes [*sic*] its inmost nature on the written page! I, who lack sufficient confidence in my most intimate friends to lay bare even an ordinary emotion— who never dream of speaking of what occupies the larger portion of my time even to my most familiar companions—yet rely on the sympathy of the stranger, the comprehension of those to whom I am utterly unknown. But I neither ordered my own mind, nor made my own fate.

It was a mannered performance, compared to her letters to Jerdan, but it was also a cri de coeur. In Letitia's story, theatrics and authenticity are never mutually exclusive.

However, unlike her heroines, Letitia did not instantly die of a broken heart. Having griped to Jerdan that 'one ought to be married,' she took a surprising new course of action. She became engaged to another man. This promised to give her the chance to become 'respectable' and to distance herself from her old identity. However, the engagement was not to last. Its dissolution would plunge her into further crisis.

Blanchard treats this episode in prose so contorted by embarrassment that it is hard to get his drift. He states that in 1835 Letitia's friends heard rumours 'that "L.E.L." would soon cease to be the designation of the favourite of the public,' that is, that she was going to change her name by getting married. Left anonymous in Blanchard's account, Letitia's fiancé was in fact John Forster, later known to posterity as Charles Dickens's intimate friend and biographer. He was a decade Letitia's junior.

The age gap was not so unlikely as it might appear. Toyboys were de rigueur among the women writers of the era. George Sand, the German poetess Annette von Droste-Hülshoff, and the American feminist writer Margaret Fuller all took younger lovers. Even the sainted Felicia Hemans may have been less pure than she pretended, owing to her discreet but 'tender' friendship with a younger man, Robert Perceval Graves, alluded to by his descendant Robert Graves in his memoir *Goodbye to All That*. (Letitia and Hemans were far from being sisterly sentimentalists, as was until recently assumed. L.E.L. slyly exposed Hemans's less than perfect marriage, while a lyric by Hemans, probably addressed to Mary Ann

Browne, urges a young poetess to avoid being 'like that lost lyre' or 'that lost flower', an underground reference to the less than virginal L.E.L.)

Letitia's engagement to a younger man was not, however, driven by passion. In her correspondence with world-weary male insiders, she made her cynicism only too apparent. 'When I have the good luck or ill luck (I rather lean to the latter opinion) to be married, I shall insist on the wedding excursion not extending much beyond Hyde Park Corner,' she wrote unsentimentally to the Irish writer Francis Mahoney at the end of 1834. 'As for falling in love, it seems to me quite out of place except in a book,' she told the publisher George Huntley Gordon on February 20, 1835.

No gentleman who knew about Letitia's past would have regarded her as marriage material. John Forster was convenient because he was such a new entrant into the literary world that he was not party to her open secret, which was by now such old news among the in-crowd that it barely passed as gossip and was therefore not a matter of constant comment.

Forster had been a twelve-year-old schoolboy in Newcastle when the *Sunday Times* exposé appeared in 1826. As Letitia herself later put it, the 'cruel slander was old,' had been 'forgotten by most—and scorned by all'. If Forster read any of the intervening satires, he must have convinced himself they were unfounded. He was transfixed by Letitia's fame and by the entrée she appeared to offer into the heart of literary London.

S. C. Hall later stated that Letitia first encountered John Forster at his house. It is only too possible that the Halls had a hand in the enterprise. It would have been in the interests of their own, as well as their wayward friend's respectability, to see her safely married.

The first recorded on-the-spot sighting of Letitia and Forster together occurs on August 18, 1834, not long after her return from Paris. It is to be found in the diary of the actor William Macready, who had taken the young theatre critic under his wing, a friendship that benefited both professionally. Macready and Forster joined Letitia in a box at the opera to see the diva Giulia Grisi in Rossini's *Anna Bolena,* along with 'two other nice girls', sisters called Nanon and Ellen Williams, who were Letitia's fellow lodgers at Hans Place.

The actor William Macready: a model of Victorian
respectability in a rackety profession

That Macready described Letitia and her companions as 'nice girls'
suggests that her sexual reputation was still intact in his eyes. Keen to
keep on the right side of the *Literary Gazette,* whose theatre reviews were
influential, he had no desire to register her fallen state. 'Jerdan was in the
box,' the actor added as an afterthought, clearly unwilling to draw any
conclusion from the coincidence even in his private journal.

Macready's diaries attest to his near-paranoiac desire to construct a
bubble of respectability around himself. As a family man in a rackety profession, he erected a bourgeois cordon sanitaire around his life. Personally,

he was so afraid of untoward gossip that on one occasion he refused to walk a young actress home after a show when her chaperone failed to turn up, regarding her safety in the dark London streets as less important than his own moral reputation. Whatever he suspected in private, Macready was committed to keeping up appearances. He was also painfully aware of the need to keep the press, including Jerdan, on his side.

When news of Letitia's sexual history finally began to reach John Forster, he was humiliated to discover that he had been duped into proposing to a woman who was regarded among the cognoscenti as damaged goods. We do not know exactly when in 1835 the couple became engaged. But we do know that by November 20 their relationship was over.

The evidence comes, again, from Macready's diary entry of that date:

> Called on Forster, and stayed some time listening to a tale of wretched abandonment to passion which surprised and depressed me. He told me that he had been on the point of marriage with Miss L——, but that rumours and stories pressed in such number and frightful quality upon him that he was forced to demand explanation from one of the reported narrators or circulators Mr A. A. Watts—that his denial was positive and circumstantial, but that it was arranged between themselves and their mutual friends that the marriage should be broken off. A short time after, Forster discovered that Miss L—— made an abrupt and passionate declaration of love to Maclise, and on a subsequent occasion repeated it! It has lately come to light that she has been carrying on an intrigue with Dr Maginn, a person whom I never saw but whom all accounts unite in describing as a beastly biped; he is married and has four children. Two letters of hers and one of his were found by Mrs Maginn in his portrait [pocket?], filled with the most puerile and nauseating terms of endearment and declarations of attachment! I felt quite concerned that a woman of such splendid genius and such agreeable manners should be so depraved in taste and so lost to a sense of what was due to her high reputation. She is fallen!

Maclise? Maginn? Where is Jerdan? What are these two other men doing in Letitia's story?

CHAPTER 10

Vile Links

Letitia's afterlife has been so contaminated by the smoke and mirrors of her self-creation as L.E.L., and by the censorship of her memoirists, that it is full of blind alleys and confusing evidence. This is nowhere more evident than in the case of these fresh allegations about her love life.

On the basis of Macready's diary entry, twentieth-century literary sleuths focused almost all their attention on Maginn, and to a lesser extent Maclise, in their attempts to get to the bottom of the 'slanders' against L.E.L. Emerging from the morass of contemporary hearsay with nothing definite, they concluded that *all* the rumours of sexual misconduct against her were probably false. Ironically, they took less seriously the slanders about Jerdan, who is in fact the only man we now know for certain slept with her.

The discovery that Letitia was no virgin makes the possibility that she was sexually involved with more than one partner worth entertaining; but no hard proof, such as that embodied by Ella, Fred, and Laura, has come to light to prove it. What is certain is that these fresh allegations take us deep into the incestuous, factional milieu in which she was by now up to her neck. It is appropriate that one of her first meetings with her fiancé John Forster took place at a performance of *Anna Bolena*. Literary London in the 1830s could be almost as risky as the court of Henry VIII for a public woman whose professional currency was flirtation.

Letitia had long been playing a double game. While cozying up to the Halls, who invested in her public purity, she had also been cultivating a male clique who, in contrast, took delight in her reputation for sexual availability. This 'set of coarse men' was centred on *Fraser's Magazine for Town and Country*, to give it its full name: a rambunctious

Giulia Grisi as Anna Bolena in the production
attended by Letitia and John Forster in 1834.

London-based Tory monthly, founded in 1830 as an offshoot of the Edinburgh *Blackwood's*—the most self-consciously sophisticated and provocative publication of the day.

The two men with whom Letitia was now accused of having had
improper relations were closely associated with *Fraser's*. William Maginn
was its de facto editor, contributing much of the copy under a variety of
aliases, including 'Oliver Yorke'. The artist Daniel Maclise provided the
illustrations under his Frenchified pseudonym 'Alfred Croquis'.

Like S. C. Hall, who knew them both, Maginn and Maclise came
originally from Cork in Ireland. Both worked their way into Jerdan's
circle—and thus into Letitia's orbit—soon after arriving on the mainland: Maginn in 1822, Maclise (who was younger) in around 1828. Like
L.E.L. herself, they were defining cultural figures of the 'strange pause'
between the Romantics and Victorians. Like hers, their work was too

embedded in the ambiguities of its own time to lend itself to posthumous recognition commensurate with their raw talents.

After its initiation in 1830, *Fraser's* soon established itself as a prominent and commercially successful periodical. Bulwer complained that its stock-in-trade was 'the personal scurrility—the coarse slander—the artful misrepresentation—the audacious lie'. He was a frequent object of its jibes, having aligned himself with the radical tendency and taken on the editorship of the rival *New Monthly Magazine*. But even Bulwer admitted that to 'take these from periodical composition, would be to take the seasoning from the sausage'.

Fraser's in-jokes were often so obscure as to be 'hardly intelligible (not at all so except to persons of the craft)' according to Carlyle, making it peculiarly tricky for modern historians to interpret. Even in its own time, outsider fans, such as the young Brontës, could not get all its

The teenage Brontë sisters, painted by their brother Branwell, c. 1834. As outsider readers, they admired both L.E.L. and *Fraser's Magazine,* but could not get all its gossipy references.

A 'set of coarse men': the Fraserians by Maclise (undated). Maginn (centre) stands over a clutch of bottles, while Jerdan clinks his glass in the foreground with the diminutive Irish antiquary Thomas Crofton Croker.

gossipy references. However, their sense of exclusion only enhanced their desire to enter its charmed circle, adding to its circulation.

No periodical did more than *Fraser's* to promote an image of the London literati as a raffishly glamorous in-crowd. The Fraserians, as the contributors and their allies called themselves, were a macho lot. In a sketch by Maclise they are portrayed sitting around a table piled with bottles. Jerdan himself is in the foreground, holding up a glass.

The true hold the Fraserians had over Letitia almost certainly was the fact that they had inside information on her sexual history. In throwing in her lot with them, Letitia was making yet another Faustian pact.

Although no letters or diaries exist to document Maclise's or Maginn's private relations with Letitia, their public portrayals of her and Jerdan speak volumes if read in context. The most popular series run by *Fraser's* was its 'Gallery of Illustrious Literary Characters,' a sequence of profiles with texts mainly by Maginn and portraits by Maclise. Jerdan's vanity must have been tickled by the fact that he made the number 1 slot, ahead of Walter Scott (number 7), Wordsworth (29), Coleridge (37), and Letitia herself (41). The naïve young Brontës, who longed to join the pageant of literary stars, took the series straight, as have many subsequent modern critics. But like L.E.L.'s own poetry, it was more underhand than it appeared.

Placing Jerdan in pole position was an in-joke. The text snidely insinuated he was a has-been by claiming he was born in 1730, which would have made him a hundred years old, while also accusing him of being in hock to Colburn and Longman. Praise for his 'just indignation against the vices of society' was a sarcasm, pointed up by Maclise in his accompanying portrait. It showed the 'satyr-Cannibal Literary Gazetteer' (to use Carlyle's phrase) reading a manuscript by the light of an oversized phallic candle that throws a sinister shadow on the wall. His hand is clenched in a fist at his crotch (see plates).

In her *Fraser's* profile, Letitia was lavished with unctuous praise for writing on the 'feminine' theme of love. At the same time, it implied not only that that the Fraserians considered the pen a male tool, but also that they were metaphorically ejaculating over her:

LETITIA ELIZABETH LANDON! Burke said, that ten thousand swords ought to have leaped out of their scabbards at the mention of the name of Marie Antoinette; and in like manner we maintain, that ten thousand pens should leap out of their inkbottles to pay homage to L.E.L. In Burke's time, Jacobinism had banished chivalry—at least, out of France—and the swords remained unbared for the queen; we shall prove, that our pens shall be uninked for the poetess.

The piece went on to claim disingenuously that *Fraser's* had no right to ask whether L.E.L.'s love poems were based on personal experience, inviting readers to suppose the opposite. She had little choice but to simper in response, despite the fact that she was trying change her once erotic image.

Letitia's complicity in the misogyny of the dominant culture inspired distaste even in her own day. In 1827, the *Westminster Review* attacked her poetry for its 'pernicious' practical effects on 'the happiness of women,' opining that she 'takes every opportunity of preaching up this perfect subordination, and of bestowing admiration on the qualities which fit women for being useful and agreeable slaves'. Her works, it argued, were only good for 'the vanity of men', while her stylized medieval fantasies of 'knights' and their pursuit of bloodshed revealed an unspoken gender politics of sadomasochism.

The anonymous critic was probably John Stuart Mill, Letitia's contemporary and fellow child prodigy. He later published *The Subjection of Women,* inspired by the woman he loved, Harriet Taylor, who was married to someone else at the time. Despite the fact that they later married after her husband died, Taylor's influence on Mill's work remained hidden during their lifetimes for fear of scandal. Long into the nineteenth century, the convolutions of the hypocrisy society continued to entwine even rationalist moralists in its net.

The Tory Fraserians had atavistic notions of medieval chivalry and regarded themselves as Romantic renegades. But they were essentially amoral contrarians with an instinct for media manipulation. Maginn even inspired possibly the earliest use of 'spin' in the political sense in a doggerel epitaph by Lockhart:

> *And, whoever was out, and whoever was in,*
> *For your Tories his fine Irish brains he would spin.*

More interested in power play than in ideology, he took his definition of 'Tory' from its original meaning; it was coined in the seventeenth century from the Irish word for 'outlaw'.

Letitia was, in contrast, a radical manqué, who had lost her faith by the time she was twenty. In 1834, she looked back nostalgically to the utopianism of her youth while admitting that she had gone over to the other side for expediency's sake. 'I am refreshing my Tory principles and beginning to doubt whether republics, equality, and our old favourites, are not very visionary, and somewhat reprehensible,' she wrote to Mrs. Hall. She added significantly, 'you know my mirror like propensities.'

It was her uncanny ability to reflect back whatever her interlocutor wanted to hear that made Letitia a spy in more than one camp. She conducted simultaneous alliances with the prudish, supposedly progressive Halls, with the Tory Fraserians, and with their enemy Bulwer, who had been elected to Parliament on a Whig Radical ticket in 1831.

In the days of William Godwin and Mary Wollstonecraft, sexual liberation had been connected with proto-socialist ideals of truth and liberty. By the 1830s, Tory libertarians offered perhaps the only available space—albeit a mocking one—for the fallen woman. What we might now call the 'Left'—abolitionists, pressure groups promoting the rights of the poor—had aligned itself with a religious tendency whose attitude towards sex was moralistic.

Was a *femme libre* liberated in the revolutionary Wollstonecraft mould, as Letitia may have wanted to believe at nineteen? Or was she a woman with whom men made free?

By the 1830s, Letitia's sexual reputation had become the arena in which men played out their political rivalries. While the Tory Fraserians claimed her as a sexualized trophy, their political enemy Bulwer fictionalized her as the embodiment of unsullied purity in his 1834 novel *The Last Days of Pompeii*. Ostensibly set in ancient Roman times, but actually a commentary on the decadent society of contemporary London, it transformed Letitia into 'Ione', a Greek poetess who holds literary salons, expresses Wollstonecraftian ideals, and regards herself as a reincarnation of 'Erinna' (a clear reference to L.E.L.'s poem of the same name).

Unlike Letitia, Ione escapes intact from the rapacious clutches of her guardian: the Egyptian high priest Arbaces. He is painted as a pantomime villain version of Jerdan, a sensualist with a taste for young flesh, whose favourite dish is nightingales' tongues.

'It has ever been my maxim to attach myself to the young,' says this evil genius. 'From their flexible and unformed minds I can carve out my fittest tools. I weave—I warp—I mould them to my will,' he leers. His project is to 'form the genius and enlighten the intellect of Ione,' but he also plans to groom her for sex, declaring that 'woman is the great appetite of my soul':

> I love to rear the votaries of my pleasure. I love to train, to ripen their minds—to unfold the sweet blossoms of their hidden passions, in order to prepare the fruit to my tastes. I loathe your ready-made and ripened courtesans; it is in the soft and unconscious progress of innocence to desire that I find the true charm of love.

Arbaces simultaneously attempts to corrupt Ione's naïve young brother by offering to induct him into the metaphysical mysteries of Egyptian religion. The supposedly transcendental rites, perhaps a metaphor for Shelleyan

Romanticism, turn out to be no more than a drunken orgy. The brother too escapes and converts to Christianity, a buried allusion to the fact that Whittington had in reality been sent off from London to be a country curate.

In contrast to Bulwer's loyal attempt to idealize Letitia, by 1834 most men in literary London were openly laughing at her. When she appeared at the theatre in a hair accessory topped with a black feather, Comte d'Orsay quipped to his companion that L.E.L. was wearing her inkwell on her head and had not even forgotten her quill pen. He was so pleased with his own witticism that he went on to repeat it to Letitia's face. She laughed 'like a hyena' at her own humiliation.

Letitia had to smile at the Fraserians' jokes and flatter their mascu-line vanity if she was to have any chance at all of controlling their anar-chic pens. This, then, is the context in which the allegations about her supposed sexual relationships with Daniel Maclise and William Maginn should be viewed.

In the case of the artist Maclise, the only primary evidence of his feel-ings is to be found in his portraits of her. Taking on the role of her por-traitist from Pickersgill after 1830, he made at least eight. The first, now lost, was an oil exhibited at the Royal Academy in 1830. Like those by Pickersgill, it must have been commissioned by Jerdan, as Maclise wrote to him asking for his permission to exhibit it. The editor also puffed it in the *Gazette* and went on to commission another portrait of Letitia from Maclise, which was subsequently engraved in 1835.

Jerdan's involvement in at least two of Maclise's portraits of Leti-tia indicate that her relations with the artist were conducted against the background of her established partnership with her Svengali. Taken together, Maclise's images of L.E.L. suggest that he took a detached but not unsympathetic attitude toward the feminine masquerade she was required by her situation to perform. As such, they do little to support the idea that they were involved in a romantic affair.

A highly finished sketch, now in the National Portrait Gallery collec-tion, may be a study for the lost 1830 oil. It portrays a somewhat blousy and fleshy Letitia staring out provocatively, hand on hip, dressed to the nines in the high fashion and extreme coiffure of the time. However, a much more candid, quick-fire pen-and-ink drawing—apparently made at the same sitting, given the similarity of costume and coiffure, and now in the Harry Ransom collection—exposes Letitia shorn of her

Letitia as fashionable and flirtatiously forward, in a highly finished sketch by Maclise

masquerade. She appears in profile as the little woman whom Bulwer described in 1826 as being 'short and ill-made'. It is not how a man in love, or even in lust, would have presented the object of his devotions.

Maclise's caricature of L.E.L., made for the *Fraser's* Gallery in 1833, offers an oblique commentary on her reputation, contrasting ironically with the accompanying text's aggressively masculine imagery. It shows her

Letitia shorn of her masquerade: an uncharacteristically candid
undated sketch by Maclise

as the incarnation of ladylike fragility, with huge doelike eyes, a minute
wasp waist, and tiny hands and feet. As Maclise's pre-Raphaelite admirer
Dante Gabriel Rossetti later put it, 'the kitten-like *mignonnerie* required
is attained by an amusing excess of daintiness in the proportions.'

As such it promulgated an image of unfeasible girlishness, given that
Letitia was by then in her thirties, had toughed it out on Grub Street
for over a decade, and had given birth to three children. The face is so
expressionless as to support the famous eighteenth-century satirist Alexander Pope's contention, in his *Epistle to a Lady*, that 'most women have
no Characters at all.' Letitia indeed had no 'character', in the sense that
her reputation was besmirched. The overblown rose in the vase beside
her was the only hint that she was not in her first flush. The irony, which

'Kitten-like *mignonnerie*': Maclise's portrait
of Letitia for the *Fraser's* Gallery, 1833. The
accompanying text was ribald and mocking.

Maclise perceived, was that Letitia knowingly manipulated her hyper-
feminine image, but was in reality vulnerable.

In other moods, Maclise portrayed Letitia as overtly sexually available. In one unpublished sketch, probably a discarded study for a public
image, she appears as a flirty equestrienne, whip in hand (see plates).
Her liveried groom, in a cockaded hat, stands in for all men. He ogles

her from behind, while the mare's long eyelashes mimic the rider's. The animal's huge peachy buttocks are presented to the viewer in such a way as to suggest that they are standing in for hers. It could be a picture of a high-class courtesan in the Bois de Boulogne. Maclise must have given the sketch to Letitia's fiancé John Forster, as it is held today in the Victoria and Albert Museum archive as part of the Forster bequest.

In fact, Macready's diary entry does not allege that Letitia slept with Maclise, just that she made a pass at him on two occasions. That seems quite possible. Given her documented interest in the French poet Antoine Fontaney, she was attracted to younger men with the sort of pale, saturnine good looks she had given to Lorenzo in *The Improvisatrice*. A stupendous watercolour self-portrait Maclise made around this time shows him dark and handsome, as he gazes out at the viewer with a mix of

Letitia's face is as blank as a fashion plate in
this 1835 portrait by Maclise.

dandy arrogance and cautious self-containment, a ruby glistening on his finger, his waistcoat casually unbuttoned (see plates). Compared to the jejune John Forster, Maclise would have been a catch. He was good-looking, coming up in the world, widely regarded as brilliant, and only four years Letitia's junior.

The year 1835 saw Maclise working on his magnum opus to date: a massive medievalist canvas portraying *The Chivalric Vow of the Ladies of the Peacock,* which secured his election to the Royal Academy later that year. Letitia expressed her interest by composing a companion volume, *The Vow of the Peacock,* in homage. Conceived as a lengthy poetical illustration of Maclise's painting, it turned out to be her last independent poetry collection. Published by Saunders and Otley, as Longman had by then given up on her, it did not sell well, even though Jerdan tried to obtrude a review copy on *Blackwood's* and commissioned a portrait from Maclise for the frontispiece. A clear attempt to present her as demure, the image shows Letitia standing in a garden in a bonnet, her figure enveloped by her ballooning walking dress, her face as blank as a fashion plate. Jerdan failed to pay the ten guineas Maclise charged him for the picture, so the artist took it back. Letitia said that she supposed Mr. Maclise could keep it.

Letitia summed up the subject of *The Vow of the Peacock* as 'a lady in distress applying to some renowned knight for assistance'. If she indeed indicated to Maclise her need for assistance, he is unlikely to have responded positively. As fellow strivers in the creative professions, she and Maclise were peers. But Letitia was a Grub Street hack who had slept her way to fame. In medieval courtly love the lady was supposed to be unattainable.

Gossip about Letitia's relationship with Maclise certainly set the spiders of society spinning. In March 1837, the *Rural Repository* of Hudson, New York, reported, tardily and inaccurately, that the 'spirituelle' L.E.L. and 'the celebrated Croquis of *Frazer's* [*sic*] *Magazine*' had just got engaged, though it admitted, 'We give it as London gossip which as the papers say yet wants confirmation.'

But by then Maclise had in fact shown where his true romantic tastes lay, having embarked on an affair with an unattainable upper-class married woman, Lady Henrietta Sykes, Disraeli's former mistress. As the son of a Cork shoemaker living on his wits, he was probably initially drawn to Henrietta as much by her status as by her other attractions. But the affair ultimately ended in disaster when Henrietta's husband discovered them in bed and avenged himself by publishing 'an extraordinary advertisement' in the public prints, informing the world of his wife's adultery with the painter.

Following his calamitous affair with Lady Henrietta, Maclise never married. Taking refuge in work, he went on to establish himself as the artistic face of Victorian triumphalism, with his murals of Wellington and Nelson in the Houses of Parliament designed to boost national pride. In this he was helped by his fellow Corkonian S. C. Hall, who promoted him in print. The opposing factions surrounding Letitia in the 1830s were in fact incestuously close.

Maclise's earlier paintings from the 1830s, often based on literary, historical, or mythological subjects, are much more discomfiting. While his intimate pencil or watercolour portraits get to the heart of their subjects with extraordinary subtlety, his public oils thrust their Technicolor kitsch at the viewer with a covert aggression which, like L.E.L.'s poetry, seems as much designed to repulse as to enthrall. As with her poetic medievalism, Maclise's paintings suggest a covert acknowledgment that the taste for historical fantasy had something rotten at its heart.

His Shakespeare-inspired *Disenchantment of Bottom* of 1832 assaults the viewer with its mesmeric ugliness (see plates). It exposes not just the private madness of sexual obsession, but, more subtly, the public culture of delusory perception in the age of cant. In his autobiography, Jerdan blithely went on to portray himself as Bottom to Letitia's Titania. Unlike Bottom, Letitia always knew that she was dreaming when she used her literary skills to transmogrify Jerdan into the object of her readers' dreams.

Letitia's relations with William Maginn are far harder to unravel than her non-affair with Daniel Maclise. According to Macready's diary, they had an actual 'intrigue', and Mrs Maginn found love letters to prove it. No corroborating evidence has come to light to support that allegation, but Letitia certainly had a long-standing and twisted connection with the editor of *Fraser's*, who also moonlighted for the blackmailing scandal sheet *The Age*.

William Maginn is one of the strangest characters thrown up by the periodical culture of the 1820s and 1830s. Like Letitia, he embraced masquerade as the condition of the times. If every hack wanted a cult of personality just like Byron, Maginn deconstructed the idea from the inside with his multiple fictional identities.

The son of a Cork schoolmaster, he was a preternaturally precocious linguist, who gained his doctorate from Trinity College Dublin before he was twenty-one. He and Letitia had in common their extraordinary facility with words. Both treated literary composition as a conjuring trick. She could turn out a poem to order in double-quick time. He was said to be able to converse intently on one subject while simultaneously writing an article on another.

Maginn first made his mark in *Blackwood's* in 1819 through the unlikely medium of an anonymous metrical Latin translation of the medieval folk ballad 'Chevy Chase', which included a footnote accusing Professor Leslie of Edinburgh University of a lack of proficiency in Hebrew. Leslie sued and received a farthing in damages. Maginn got attention. When he finally appeared in person at the *Blackwood's* Edinburgh offices in 1821, he adopted a pantomime Irish brogue and pretended to be the victim of libel by the magazine. His chutzpah and thespian talents endeared him to the editor. He went on to develop the ribald *Noctes Ambrosianae* column in *Blackwood's,* cast in the form of a tavern dialogue in which the contributors discoursed rumbustiously from behind pseudonymous masks on topics such as pugilism and Byron's sex life.

Although Maginn made himself a central figure in the British periodical culture of the day, the slippery voices he created indicate a liminal outsider. No one doubted his brilliance. But, addicted to personal invective and increasingly hampered by a drinking problem, he never completed a major work.

William Maginn first met Letitia Landon in London in 1822 when she was still the nameless melodist and he was suing for Jerdan's patronage at the *Literary Gazette*. According to his contemporary biographer Shelton Mackenzie, he was so smitten by her that he proposed, only to be turned down. Given the content of the poetry Letitia was publishing at the time, it is much more likely that Maginn made a ham-fisted sexual overture and withdrew when he realized she was already Jerdan's property. He returned briefly to Ireland, where he picked up a conventional domestic wife, before returning with her to the mainland to pursue his career, first at *Blackwood's* and then at *Fraser's*.

Unlike Jerdan, Maginn had no reputation for priapism. Wine rather than women was his weakness. The one recorded instance of his sexual appetite is of a halfhearted visit to a low-rent brothel with Thackeray. However, he retained a psychological obsession with Letitia. When he was dying of consumption in 1842, he imagined he had a visitation from her ghost.

Fraser's offers no evidence that Maginn was Letitia's lover but ample proof that he used his inside knowledge of her sexual history to subject her to salacious bullying. In 1833, when she was trying to shake off the scandal of L.E.L. and reinvent herself as the respectable voice of the annuals, he mocked her in the attempt by publishing an obscene squib. It suggested that she was smuggling unmentionable sexual secrets into middle-class homes by stealth, and in doing so surreptitiously undermining the morals of the nice girls for whom genteel parents bought *The Keepsake*. It is intriguing to think that the young Charlotte Brontë read both the annuals and the following:

Papa and ma delighted that I'm getting on so well,
Were good enough to send me for a year to L.E.L.;
Where, a 'Keepsake' being bought me,
All the new effects were taught me,
Besides some useful secrets, which I promised not to tell.

One only that I feel myself at liberty to name,
Was 'always make the leading words of every verse the same';
I got so good at this,
That I wrote a little piece
Of four and twenty stanzas, and they each began 'She came!'

In this conjugating *style I also proved a great adept,*
The next piece published was 'She's gone!' *soon after which,*
   'He wept!'
Till each number, tense, and person
I'd a separate piece of verse on.
'She sighed!' *produced* 'We laughed!'—'He wrote' *was followed by*
   'They slept!'

Yet although Maginn subjected Letitia to lubricious ridicule, in other moods he addressed her tenderly as his Shakespearean 'dark ladye'.

Letitia, for her part, exploited Maginn's obsession, getting him to help her with her incessant annuals' workload. He was widely alleged to have written some of the contributions for her.

The letters Mrs Maginn found—supposedly filled with 'nauseating terms of endearment' (according to the credent Macready) and addressed by Letitia to her 'dearest William' (according to the skeptical Shelton Mackenzie)—are unlikely to have been genuine billets doux. As Letitia's letters to her authenticated lover, William Jerdan, begin formally 'Dear Sir', it seems most unlikely that she would address another lover in such tones.

Given that Maginn was well known for his literary practical jokes and powers of ventriloquism, it is far more likely that the letters were yet another tease designed to make Letitia squirm, possibly intended for publication. The 'William' to whom they were addressed is more likely to have been William Jerdan than Willian Maginn.

Such jokes were apparently considered funny in those circles. A little later, Mr and Mrs Samuel Laman Blanchard, a devoted couple, became the objects of a similar cruel epistolary tease at the hands of none other than John Forster, who sent Anne Blanchard the following message: 'You must no longer call that little perfidious S.L.B. "Jack" or "Sam" or any other such familiar and loving name, for he is wholly unworthy of you. . . . I have just detected him in writing to a lady whom he terms "My dearest Eliza". I have done the duty of a friend—my heart bleeds for it.'

According to Shelton Mackenzie, Mrs Maginn put the offending letters in a blank envelope and sent them on to Letitia's fiancé. But she never seriously believed that her husband had been unfaithful with Letitia, and retracted her allegation as soon as she realized it had done real harm to the latter's marriage prospects.

Letitia's on-the-spot response, in a letter to Anna Maria Hall, is very different in tone from the considered self-defence she wrote to Katherine Thomson in 1826 in the wake of the *Sunday Times* exposé. It is more natural, more bitchy, and much less like a calculated attempt to hide the truth.

Letitia rebuts the idea of an 'attachment' with Maginn as too absurd even for denial, and lays cattily into Mrs Maginn, putting her actions down to 'sheer envy' and recounting with a toss of the head that she has since seen and cut her decidedly. As a downtrodden housewife, excluded from her husband's professional circle, Mrs Maginn may indeed have felt resentful of a woman such as Letitia who appeared to move freely among literary men, unencumbered by domesticity.

'The letters, however, I utterly deny,' Letitia went on. 'I have often written notes, as pretty and flattering as I could make them, to Dr Maginn, upon different literary matters, and one or two of business. But how any construction but their own could be put on them I do not understand. A note of mine that would pass for a love-letter must either have been strangely misrepresented, or most strangely altered. Dr Maginn and his wife have my full permission to publish every note I ever wrote—in *The Age* if they like.'

Letitia also admitted, however, how scared she was of Maginn's unpredictable pen. 'The fact was,' she confessed, 'I was far too much afraid of Dr Maginn not to conciliate him if possible; and if civility and flattery would have done it, I should have been glad to do so. As it has turned out, I have, I fear, only made myself a powerful enemy; for of course, on the first rumour that reached me, I felt it incumbent on me to forbid his visits, few and infrequent as they were.' It seems likely that Maginn was dangerous not because he was sleeping with Letitia, but because he knew her secret.

In fact, the 'rumours and stories'—which, according to Macready, 'pressed in such number and frightful quality' upon John Forster—must have come from more than one direction. Shelton Mackenzie says that Forster also received anonymous letters reviving the old Jerdan slanders, prior to his receiving Mrs Maginn's blank envelope containing the supposed love epistles. Macready's diary also refers to an unspecified 'tale of wretched abandonment to passion' that reached Forster *before* he was informed about the additional allegations concerning both Maclise and Maginn. That can only have been the old story about Jerdan, which was far more damaging since it had, as we now know, produced three actual children, all of whom were recognized by him as his.

In the honour culture of the day, the anonymous letter was the ultimate weapon. In 1837 the Russian poet Pushkin died in a duel after receiving anonymous letters accusing him of being a cuckold. The anonymous letters that reached John Forster were almost certainly written by the poet, journalist, and annuals' editor Alexander Alaric Watts, the man named in Macready's diary as the supposed source.

Letitia had known A. A. Watts since the early 1820s when each was contributing 'Cockney' poetry to the *Literary Gazette*. However, she had gone on to alienate him by boasting about how quickly she wrote and how much money she made, adding insult to injury by refusing to accept payment for her contribution to his annual *The Literary Souvenir*. We can now establish that Letitia was not in charge of her own earnings, which may have been largely pocketed by Jerdan. But Watts did not realize that her comments were bravado. He smarted at the thought of being outdone by a female contemporary, and his resentment rankled.

Watts was aspirational, sensitive about his status, and was well known for bearing grudges. Like many others at that time, he was a struggling striver in the literary trade, but he lacked Jerdan's easy manner or Maginn's talents. A surviving drawing by Maclise of Watts's wife, Priscilla, known as Zillah, shows her attired in the most expensive fashions, her clothes clearly regarded as a status symbol by the couple, though their son went on to marry the daughter of the Quaker Mary Howitt.

Thin skin and an inability to conceal his desperate literary ambition made Watts a magnetic target for Maginn, who had known him since 1823, and who went on to mock him constantly in print as 'the principal fribble among the namby-pambies of the annuals'. Watts might have fared better had he adopted a pose of Olympian detachment, but anger management was not his forte. In a memoir, his own son devoted a chapter to 'Temper' in which he said his father suffered from 'some obscure form of disease more or less akin to hysteria'.

Watts's enraged responses to mockery led to him being satirically rechristened Attila by Maginn ('pray, Alaric Attila, where do you find those fine names—your own and Zillah Madonna? I'm told you hope to supply posterity with sugar-plums, and that they'll say the sweet, sweet Watts was the very one worth all the rest'). He tried to fight back with his own insults, accusing Maginn of 'despicable treachery', but they never seemed to hit the mark. Instead, he became irately litigious. In one of the cases he pursued, he sought legal damages against the printer and publisher of *Fraser's*. When his annual *The Literary Souvenir* was parodied in its pages in November 1834, Watts claimed that it had led to loss of circulation and earnings on his count, but at the close of the trial, in December 1835, the jury dismissed his case.

Fraser's remained conspicuously unrattled throughout. In the run-up to the trial, it showcased Watts in its Gallery in June 1835. Maclise's

A. A. Watts, scurrilously caricatured in
Fraser's as an art thief, 1835. He may have
been responsible for alerting John Forster to
Letitia's sexual history.

caricature portrayed him as an art thief, sneaking out of a grand house with
pictures under both arms, an allusion to the fact he was having to supple-
ment his literary earnings by dealing in pictures. Watts, who was privately living on a financial knife edge, wanted recognition as a serious
player in literature and in society. The caricature was so much the last
straw for him that even its republication fifty years later caused 'conniptions' in his son.

On November 20, 1835, when Macready recorded that John Forster
turned up to tell him that his engagement was off due to his discovery
of Letitia's sexual secrets, Watts's legal case against *Fraser's* was gearing up

More worldly than godly: Letitia's paternal uncle Whittington Landon, dean of Exeter and provost of Worcester College, Oxford.

The great actress Sarah Siddons, shown here reading in a grotto, was an old friend of Letitia's grandmother. L.E.L. was raised to see poetry as a performative art.

A Regency girls' school, such as the one at 22 Hans Place that Letitia attended from 1807, satirized by Edward Francis Burney (1805). Note the embryonic tragedienne to the right, the lascivious dancing master, the pupil eloping in the background, and the mechanical devices for improving posture.

William Jerdan by Daniel Maclise, 1830. The 'satyr-cannibal Literary Gazetteer' is portrayed reading by the light of a huge candle, which casts a sinister shadow on the wall; his right hand is clenched in a fist at his crotch.

Fashion plate from
Ackermann's Repository,
1819.

L'Improvisatrice by H. W. Pickersgill,
1823, possibly an early 'fancy portrait'
of Letitia dressed as a Neapolitan
poet-performer. It recalls the well-
known portrait of Byron in Albanian
dress (below) and also reflects
contemporary fashion trends.

Byron in Albanian dress by
Thomas Phillips, 1813.

Portrait of Letitia by H. W. Pickersgill, 1825. The original oil was first exhibited at the Royal Academy at the height of her fame. This engraving was commissioned for Jerdan's autobiography in the 1850s.

Letitia's 'Spanish hat' suggested she was a female Don Juan, referencing the headgear worn by the racy actress Madame Vestris in the contemporary vaudeville hit *Giovanni in London.*

MADAME VESTRIS as DON GIOVANNI.

London. Published by G. Hodgson.

Letitia appeared again in masquerade costume in Pickersgill's *The Minstrel of Chamouni,* first exhibited at the Royal Academy in 1829 and then engraved for S. C. Hall's annual *The Amulet* in 1830. The artist reprised elements from both *L'Improvisatrice* and the 'Spanish hat' portrait, but made her look much more demure. 'This minstrel is an imposter,' opined the *London Magazine.*

Bulwer's wife, Rosina, by A. E. Chalon. Letitia flattered her as a supposed best friend, but they later fell out.

The novelist and future politician Edward Bulwer Lytton by Pickersgill, c. 1831. As a Cambridge undergraduate, he was excited by L.E.L.'s poetry before he even met her. Although they flirted in public, there is no evidence to support the rumour they were lovers.

A young Anna Maria Hall looking bold and sassy with unkempt hair in an informal portrait by Maclise made in 1833.

Letitia's daughter Ella Stuart in later life. She grew up to defy the odds.

Smug marrieds: the 'Pecksniff' Halls invite their dear friends to their fiftieth wedding anniversary. Although they began as rackety literary adventurers, they transformed themselves into models of Victorian propriety.

A hyper-feminine Letitia, portrayed by Maclise in a watercolour study for *Fraser's Magazine*'s 'Gallery of Illustrious Literary Characters,' 1833. According to Dante Gabriel Rossetti, 'the kitten-like *mignonnerie* required is attained by an amusing excess of daintiness in the proportions.'

Portrait by Daniel Maclise of Letitia's jejune fiancé John Forster, early 1830s. Their ill-fated engagement broke up after he discovered her sexual history.

This unpublished and undated drawing by Maclise presents Letitia as a sexy equestrienne, crop in hand. The mare's long eyelashes mimic the rider's, while her groom observes her from behind.

Self-portrait by Daniel Maclise, made around the time he knew Letitia. She was rumoured to have made a pass at him, and may well have done so, if this likeness is anything to go by.

A 'rattling mad Irishman': William Maginn of *Fraser's Magazine,* by his fellow Corkonian Maclise, 1830. Although he was accused of seducing Letitia, wine rather than women was his weakness.

The Disenchantment of Bottom by Maclise, 1832. The mesmeric ugliness of this Shakespearean painting reveals the artist's insight into sexual illusion.

This picture by Maclise, 1837, portrays his married upper-class lover Lady Henrietta Sykes with her husband and children in medieval mode. He was more interested in impossible courtly love than in throwing in his lot with a female colleague such as Letitia.

Letitia's husband, George Maclean, governor of Cape Coast Castle, probably commissioned in London in 1836–38 by Matthew Forster, the businessman who introduced them.

A crushingly opulent gift: the grand silver centrepiece commissioned from Garrard's by the merchant committee for George Maclean in 1836.

View from Cape Coast Castle, October 10, 2017. 'I like the perpetual dash on the rocks—,' Letitia wrote in one of her letters home; 'one wave comes up after another, and is for ever dashed in pieces, like human hopes.'

Unfinished first sitting of Letitia made in 1838 by the great American portraitist Thomas Sully, shortly before her marriage.

Plaster medallion of Letitia by Henry Weekes, 1837. Her biographer Blanchard said it was a good likeness if only the shoulders had been a little higher.

for trial. His enmity with Maginn was long established. Getting at the *Fraser's* female mascot, L.E.L., who had already humiliated him, was a way for Watts to get at its editor.

However, given the widespread knowledge of Letitia's open secret, there must have been other informants too. In a desperate but far from fully candid letter she wrote to Bulwer in the midst of the crisis, Letitia referred to the 'gossiping of Mr Hall' as a supposed source, although she affected not to take it seriously. Hall had apparently pointed the finger at Watts when he himself was accused of spreading smut about her, but had gone on to 'eat' his 'words'.

Although 'Pecksniff' later boasted of having set up the match with John Forster in the first place, it is only too easy to imagine him switching sides as soon as hints of Letitia's past began to reach her fiancé. If he joined in the muckspreading, it was because he was fearful of being seen to have inveigled a callow young man into marrying a woman with an unsavory past.

Jerdan's presence in the theatre box at the first on-the-spot sighting of Letitia with Forster suggests that Hall may not have been the only backstage prime mover. By now, the bankrupt Jerdan was ensconced with Mary Ann Maxwell and finding Letitia a burden. He himself, despite their long-standing intimacy, may well have wanted to marry her off, perhaps convincing her to go along with the plan by promising that they would remain lovers.

Laman Blanchard descends into incoherence at this point in his 1841 biography. From the moment John Forster receives untoward information about Letitia, the narrative disintegrates. Blanchard states that a group of Letitia's allies sought to investigate the source of the slander in order to refute it. He then wordily announces that "the refutation which the evil report met, in the course of that investigation, was as effectual and complete as in the nature of such charges—charges so brought and circulated—it was possible to be.' He then goes on to claim, somewhat circularly, that the 'refutation consisted in the utter disbelief in the charge, and the honourable zeal to trace the source of the calumny, that were everywhere evinced.'

The 'sole object' of the friends' inquiry, Blanchard said, was 'to trace the false accuser, and to drag him forward.' However, they failed. That is unsurprising, given that the charges were actually true, and indeed an open secret among insiders. If the loose-tongued Jerdan himself was one of the gossips, it would have been impossible to finger him without calumniating Letitia.

That the crisis indeed led to frantic negotiations behind the scenes is evident from Macready's diary entry in which he says that it was agreed among the couple's friends that the engagement should be called off. It was Letitia, not Forster, who officially made the break. Although she was in no position to bring an action for breach of promise, an accepted proposal of marriage was a binding contract, unless the woman chose to withdraw. It was up to Letitia to do so.

Writing to Bulwer, Letitia dismissed the slanders but expressed a genuine desire to put 'all connection between myself and Mr Forster at an end' because of the aggressive way in which he had been questioning her over the 'shameful calumny'—and because she feared he had been questioning others, spreading the rumours further in the process.

Her letter offers an insight into the culture in which, as 'Lines of Life' puts it, 'none of us will choose to say / What none will choose to hear.' Forster had failed to stick to the rules. His worst crime, in Letitia's view, was to have made the unspoken spoken, by repeating to her face the rumours that *she* could not bear to hear: 'I cannot get over—the entire want of delicacy to me—which could repeat such a slander to myself. In no way has Mr Forster spared my feelings—The whole of his conduct to me personally has left behind almost dislike—certainly fear of his imperious and overbearing temper.'

Anthropologists define dirt as matter out of place. Sexual so-called secrets only became explosive if they were spread through the wrong channels to the wrong people in the wrong language. Letitia could laugh off ribald verses in the press, but she could not deal with direct interpersonal communication. She may have hoped for a no-questions-asked union of convenience with John Forster, imagining she could exchange her literary contacts and professional know-how for the title 'Mrs', just as her mother had traded her fortune for John Landon's name. However, once the allegations reached Forster, his male pride was stung.

Letitia's letter to him breaking off the engagement speaks the language of cheap melodrama, as if she is writing for the stage. She claimed she was retreating to save her fiancé, not herself: 'Why should you be exposed to the annoyance—the mortification of having the name of the woman you honour with your regard, coupled with insolent insinuation?'

She descended to near parody: 'The more I think, the more I feel I ought not—I cannot—allow you—to unite yourself with one accused of—I cannot write it. The mere suspicion is dreadful as death.'

Letitia was trying to control the situation through desperate casuistry. To Forster, she bemoaned what must privately have been a great relief: that the only evidence against her was hearsay. 'Were it stated as a fact, that might be disproved,' she wrote. 'I might say, look back on my life—ask every friend I have—but what answer can I give, or what security have I against the assertion of a man's vanity, or the slander of a vulgar woman's tongue?' We see her clinging to the fiction that she had no dubious past, notably alluding only to Maclise's supposed claim that she made a pass at him, and to Mrs Maginn's flimsy allegations. She makes no reference at all to the Jerdan rumours.

In his *Book of Memories,* S. C. Hall spilled much ink in sagely shaking his head over Letitia's supposed lack of decorum in her dealings with Maginn, whom, he opined, she had treated without the respect due to an older, married man. It is hard not to conclude that Hall gave space to the false allegation to distract attention from the truth. He took great care to excise the Jerdan allegations from his account.

When Laman Blanchard was researching his biography of Letitia, he interviewed Maginn at length. As private correspondence shows, they agreed that Maginn's name should not be mentioned at all in Blanchard's *Life.* In an odd turn of phrase, Maginn pronounced himself prepared to spare Letitia at his 'own cost'. This cryptic statement suggests that rather than have Blanchard explicitly clear him of seducing Letitia, Maginn opted to let the accusation against him remain abroad in the vague but swirling cloud of rumour. That would help to protect the dead L.E.L.'s reputation because the thicker the cloud, the less likely it would be to disperse, leaving the true facts about her affair with Jerdan visible. As his own deathbed hallucinations suggest, Maginn ultimately felt guilty about his treatment of Letitia. Having subjected her to the psychological torture of sexual mockery, while knowing full well about her struggling private situation as a mistress and single mother, he had every reason to feel guilty.

In the wake of the crisis, Letitia had a breakdown. Stress had been the motor of her life for years, but now she finally collapsed. By the time she wrote her letter formally breaking off the engagement, she was under the care of her regular doctor.

'I have suffered for the last three days a degree of torture that made Dr Thomson say, "you have an idea of what the wrack is now,"' she told John Forster. 'I look back on my whole life—I can find nothing to justify my being the object of such pain—but this is not what I meant to say,' she added pregnantly.

Her medical complaint, she explained, was 'inflammation of the liver'. The illness was considered at the time to be connected to the 'pains of thought'. In his *Elements of the Pathology of the Human Mind,* published in 1838, Thomas Mayo describes curing a case of 'melancholia'—in which the patient exhibits 'hysterical crying', 'shocking thoughts', and a suicide attempt—by treating the subject's 'torpor of the liver'.

Mrs Thomson later referred to Letitia's 'feverish illness; with no other source but a harassed and over-wrought mind, a wounded spirit that disdained, on that one point, sympathy, and shrunk, on that one point, from confidence'. Even to her doctor's wife, she could not bring herself to discuss her situation openly.

The John Forster debacle was calculated to render Letitia in reality the outcast woman she had so often ventriloquized through the mouthpiece of L.E.L. At the time of the *Sunday Times* crisis a decade earlier, she had had Jerdan as her partner in crime and could ride the storm on the back of his talent for effrontery. Now he was financially struggling and deep into his live-in relationship with Mary Ann Maxwell, who gave birth to their second child, Matilda, in 1837.

Jerdan was also poised to start dandling a new teenage poetic protégée before the world in the *Gazette:* Eliza Cook, the precocious self-taught daughter of a Southwark brassworker. He was evidently as keen to 'cultivate the divine organisation of her being' as he had once been to nurture Letitia's. The youthful Eliza told him excitedly, 'My "fastidious master" has a pupil, who deems herself honoured by the trouble he has bestowed on her, and begs to tell him his kind and just criticism is well appreciated; my muse is wild, and my judgement very immature and crazy.'

In the honour culture, men could fight duels, but suicide was the only way out for women. After so many poetic rehearsals, Letitia may well have considered it as a real life option at this juncture. After she was finally found dead in Africa, many thought it suspicious that the Colonial Office failed to investigate. A private memo shows why the colonial secretary, Lord Normanby—whose silver-fork novel Letitia had puffed in

Eliza Cook (1818–1889), Jerdan's
new poetic protégée, was sixteen
years Letitia's junior and a teenager
when he first took her up. Here she
is painted by William Etty in 1845.

Romance and Reality back in 1831—decided not to pursue the matter. The
reason was that his old friend Edward Bulwer had called to tell him that
he was bound to state that Letitia had once before attempted suicide
when in England.

Emma Roberts later told Mary Howitt's husband, William, about
the 'agonies of mind' her housemate L.E.L. had suffered at Hans Place
when 'calumny' was 'dealing freely' with her name:

> 'Have those horrible reports,' she eagerly inquired, 'got into the
> papers, Miss Roberts?' Miss Roberts assured her they had not.
> 'If they do,' she exclaimed, opening a drawer in the table, and
> taking out a vial of Prussic acid, 'I am resolved—here is my
> remedy!'

The date on the bottle found in Letitia's hand at her death was 1836. It
may have been the same one.

Letitia's mask was slipping. As Katherine Thomson recalled,

I found her, as I have said, variable in spirits, and so far uncertain in temper, that she would sometimes break forth in a bitter invective upon the hollowness of society—the worldliness of all mankind—'everybody was selfish and cold—there was no one to be trusted—no one to be believed.' But, the instant afterwards, her fine heart redeemed itself. She made exceptions to her censure, spoke warmly . . . upon the merits of some friend—and often, suddenly breaking off the middle of her harangue, would burst into a flood of tears—check them—walk about the room, and sit down again.

Letitia was by now desperately in need of allies as she sought to buttress her increasingly exposed position. She cultivated Lady Blessington, but it is uncertain how much social protection the notorious countess could provide. By the mid-1830s, Letitia was becoming persona non grata. 'The truth of Miss Landon's story and her situation had for some time oozed out; it was felt that her literary reputation had been exaggerated; that her social position was, so to say, not the pleasantest in the world,' H. F. Chorley, editor of the *Gazette*'s rival *The Athenaeum*, recalled guardedly in his 1873 memoirs.

Katherine Thomson later compared Letitia at this point in her life to the heroine 'in the exquisite novel of "Violet"'. This obscure allusion was to the anonymously published succès de scandale of 1836: *Violet; or the danseuse*. The heroine of the novel is a naïve young ballerina, brought up by doting but cash-strapped artistic parents, who put her on the stage in nothing but a flesh-coloured body stocking because they need the money. Violet falls desperately in love with an upper-class admirer and runs off to become his mistress. Her more worldly-wise friend meanwhile refuses to sleep with her admirer unless he marries her.

In one late scene, Violet goes to the theatre alone and sees her protector in a box. He is flirting with her former friend, now a high-society married lady, with whom he is on track to form a discreet adulterous dalliance. Realizing her own pariah status, Violet kills herself by taking an overdose of laudanum.

During the period of Letitia's incapacitating illness, however, *Fraser's* kept up its toxic banter. The issue for January 1836 contained a group portrait by Daniel Maclise of celebrated women writers. Although Letitia's swelling white bosom is clearly visible, she is portrayed turning away from the viewer, as if trying to hide her face in shame. Directly behind her is a black liveried servant, an avatar of the 'Negro' in her early squib. Maginn's accompanying doggerel slips in a sly joke about her relations with Maclise: 'isn't she painted *con amore?*'

In an article in the same issue on Greek pastoral poetry, Maginn (under the pseudonym Oliver Yorke) added an insinuating footnote to the phrase 'the virgin's melting kiss': 'Why does the pretty L.E.L. not take it for a motto? Would she like to learn Greek? Would she like OLI-VER for a tutor?' These sarcastic references make it highly unlikely that Maginn was actually Letitia's lover, but they show how insensitive he was at a time when he must have known that she was under extreme pressure. To the Fraserians, she was not a person but a persona.

Letitia's few published works of 1836 include her volume of short stories *Traits and Trials of Early Life*. Designed as a book of moral tales for young girls, it was a last-ditch attempt to move her public image away from its former eroticism. The book contained her melancholy autobiographical sketch 'The History of a Child', in which she tried to puzzle out the psychological causes of her fate.

John Forster, meanwhile, retreated into male bonding. His humiliation was turned into a rite of passage, proving his entrée into the 'freemasonery' of gentlemen. Inside knowledge of Letitia's dubious past was the glue that held male alliances together. At a Garrick Club dinner in June 1836, William Macready 'begged to propose a toast' to two 'earnest supporters of the cause of the drama'. They were John Forster and William Jerdan.

The incestuous carnival of pre-Victorian periodical culture was, however, about to implode. In the summer of 1836, Maginn's talent to annoy reached its apogee and its nemesis. Back in 1824, De Quincey had briefly considered challenging Maginn to a duel, after the latter cast aspersions in a review, accusing him of bedding his servant-maid and claiming (accurately as it happens) that Mrs De Quincey had given birth to their first child out of wedlock. However, he thought better of it.

Now Maginn succeeded in penning a book review that provoked a genuine challenge. This time the author in question was not an opium-eating hack but an upper-crust, moneyed Whig MP and sporting enthusiast, the Hon. Grantley Berkeley, who had leapt on the 'silver fork' bandwagon by publishing a novel, *Berkeley Castle*. His untalented foray into fiction represented everything the self-made Tory Maginn despised.

Instead of focusing on the novel's literary shortcomings, Maginn got personal. He hit Berkeley, a 'man of honour', in the most taboo region: that of illegitimacy. 'There could be,' Maginn wrote, 'no indelicacy in stating that Mr Grantley Berkeley's mother lived with Mr Grantley Berkeley's father as his mistress, and that she had at least one child before she could induce the old and very stupid lord to marry her.' That Berkeley's uncertain birth had already been proved by a legal case in the House of Lords mattered to him not a jot. He only cared that Maginn had printed it. The definition of 'slander' had less to do with the facts than with the act of publication.

Incensed at the slight, Grantley Berkeley and his brother Craven turned up at the offices of *Fraser's Magazine* on August 3, 1836, where

James Fraser, the managing editor of *Fraser's Magazine,* at his desk in an undated, unpublished drawing by Maclise, 1830s. In 1836, Grantley Berkeley surprised Mr Fraser in his office and assaulted him. Fraser later died as a result of his injuries.

they found the managing editor, James Fraser, at his desk. While the aptly named Craven kept watch, Grantley viciously assaulted James Fraser with a weighted whip, causing grievous bodily harm. Two days later, he and Maginn met in a field near the Edgware Road. Shots were exchanged, but neither party was hit.

Maginn was forced to publish a grudging apology, but his glory days were numbered. He left *Fraser's,* which had paid him well ('sixteen guineas per sheet' at the minimum, according to James Grant), and sank deeper and deeper into alcoholism and debt. James Fraser was eventually awarded (inadequate) damages by a court, but he never recovered from his injuries, dying in 1841. An impoverished Maginn followed him to the grave in 1842.

The incident demonstrates with crass literalism how close to the surface violence and cruelty were in the literary culture in which L.E.L. made her career. But it also bears more closely on her history, for when Grantley Berkeley came to publish his colourful *My Life and Recollections* in 1865–66, he claimed that he had fought the duel on her account.

Berkeley recalled how he had been introduced to Letitia after wangling an invitation to one of her literary salons at 22 Hans Place. The following day he called on her, whereupon, in his account, she burst into tears and, without naming names, told him that in her youth 'a certain person . . . had made use of his influence in the literary world to obtain power over her for her personal seduction'. This unnamed powerful magazine editor had demanded her acquiescence to his 'vile proposition' as the 'price of her public praise'. Now he was threatening to ruin her reputation if she did not hand over the 'greater portion of the proceeds of her pen' to pay his debts.

Taking the reprobate to be Maginn, an outraged Berkeley proposed himself as Letitia's defender. He believed that it was in revenge for his chivalrous intervention on her behalf that Maginn went on to write the offensive review of his novel that resulted in their duel.

Given her history, and the culture of the unspoken in which she operated, it is impossible to believe Letitia confided directly in Berkeley, who was no insider. However, his depiction of her suddenly dissolving into tears fits with other accounts of her unstable state of mind by 1836. In fact, his story is so clearly a garbled version of what we now know to have been Letitia's actual relationship with Jerdan that he must have confused the Irish editor of *Fraser's* with the Scottish editor of the *Gazette.* Berkeley may have hinted to Letitia what he had (mis)heard on the grapevine, and then took her humiliated, tearful response as confirmation.

After Berkeley published his account of his acquaintance with Letitia in the second volume of his memoirs, S. C. Hall leapt into print to dismiss him as a fantasist. In the ensuing debate, Berkeley pounced on Hall's unguarded reference to a 'blight' in Letitia's 'springtime,' asking, quite reasonably, 'what blight?' But he never realized that he had fingered the wrong editor in Maginn.

Nevertheless, Berkeley's claim that Letitia had invited his attentions—on the advice of her patroness Lady Blessington—may not have been wholly unfounded. His anecdotal memories of spending an evening with her and a female friend in the parlour at 22 Hans Place are convincingly circumstantial. On one occasion, he recalled, a small ornament fell down. When Letitia bent to retrieve it, the friend told her not to move as she was presenting such a beautiful tableau in the candlelight. This was probably Letitia's spinsterish fellow lodger Emma Roberts, who was, according to Crofton Croker, slavishly in love with her.

Letitia is certainly on record as flattering Grantley Berkeley. She wrote a gushing review of his awful novel in the *New Monthly Magazine,* telling him in a private letter, 'I could not praise a work as I have done yours unless I really admired it.' In this enterprise she was encouraged by Lady Blessington, who numbered Berkeley among the Whigs in her salon, and told him that Miss Landon 'should be proud of her bard'.

Since childhood, Letitia had had to defend her fragile identity by playing off different factions against one another. She had long since been trying to keep both the Whig Radical Bulwer and the Tory Fraserians on her side. If the Fraserians continued to mock her in print about her supposed love affairs, following her failed engagement to John Forster, it would not be surprising if Letitia had sought a new Whig ally in 1836.

In the event, the crisis of the duel put paid to Berkeley's chimerical protection. Yet in the wake of the debacle, Letitia continued to maintain her gambler's insouciance, pretending that nothing had happened, just as she had done after the *Sunday Times* exposé. Clinging to her increasingly threadbare position in society as a literary lion, she desperately accepted whatever invitations still came her way, while firing off studiously flippant correspondence. On November 1, 1836, she wrote to the Fraserian Crofton Croker, puffing herself desperately, boasting of the supposed sales for her latest volume for *Fisher's Drawing Room Scrap Book* and of her recent social conquests:

> I have been so gay lately—visiting at one place then at another. I have been staying at Sydenham with Lady Stepney—at Shirley Park with Mrs Skinner—at Harrow—at Dulwich—and at Ham[p]stead, wither, whither, there I have spelt it at last—I go again on Friday.

The hostesses to whom she referred were not in fact of the first rank, but she was keen to show that she was still in demand both as a guest and as a writer. Nor was her self-conscious spelling correction casual. Literary men had long since hated overtly intellectual women. Coleridge had once praised a female correspondent's poor spelling, explaining, 'The longer I live, the more I do loathe in stomach, and deprecate in Judgement, all, *all* Bluestockingism.' The faux-naïf style of L.E.L. had always been consciously fashioned. It was the price she had to pay to be accepted in the male-dominated world of literature.

However, Letitia now had a genuine cause for excitement. A possible escape route had emerged. At a dinner party in Hampstead, she had caught the eye of the man she would eventually marry: George Maclean, the governor of Cape Coast Castle in West Africa.

CHAPTER II

The Governor

George Maclean's entry into Letitia's narrative opens up a new seam of conflicting evidence and suspicious lacunae. The truth about her surprising marriage, which led her to Africa and ultimately to her death, sinks almost out of sight beneath the gabble of gossip, speculation and disinformation that subsequently flooded the public prints.

As with the mysteries surrounding her affair with Jerdan and her three children, those surrounding this last act of her drama often turn out to be the product of deliberate occlusion. Via Maclean, Letitia was about to be vicariously drawn into a new and separate web of lies and corruption far more significant in global terms than anything in literary London: the history of illegal involvement by British business in the slave trade following abolition. From this point on, her story is mired in overlapping conspiracies of silence, in which she herself forms the absent centre, as ambivalently abdicating of her own agency as she was as a teenager when her governess first thrust her in Jerdan's direction.

The contradictions begin with the retrospective testimonies of her 'friends' on the subject of her marriage. Her housemate Emma Roberts described the union as a love match that 'promised . . . lasting happiness.' Katherine Thomson attested that Maclean was the only man Letitia ever loved. But other contemporaries took a less sentimental view. According to S. C. Hall, Letitia's only motive was to 'change her name, and to remove from that society in which, just then, the old and infamous slander had been revived'.

For once, 'Pecksniff' was telling something like the truth. By now, Letitia was truly a woman on the edge: harassed by debt, her star status in decline, her social position in free fall, her allies melting away.

William Jerdan, for one, privately had no doubt as to why she married George Maclean. When he first received the news of her death in early 1839, he confessed to Lady Blessington, in an unpublished letter marked 'Private', that Letitia had only gone through with the marriage because she was 'annoyed and depressed by the inconveniences and humiliations of her own position'. He showed no sign of holding himself in any way responsible.

Katherine Thomson and Emma Roberts had good reason to bathe the marriage in a retrospective glow. Their eyewitness accounts of the courtship indicate how closely they were involved in what looks like a concerted effort on their part to find an honourable exit route for their beleaguered friend. Letitia had by now become an 'inconvenience' in herself, a social contaminant and an emotional drain. Faced with her increasingly chaotic mood swings, Miss Roberts and Mrs. Thomson reassured her to her face that no one believed the rumours. But they were also placed in the embarrassing position of having to answer ever more awkward questions about her in her absence.

The only way in which Letitia could realistically recoup her honour was through marriage. But any new potential husband would have to be an outsider, ignorant of the slanders: a man who could take her away. George Maclean must have seemed the perfect candidate when he turned up in London in the late summer of 1836. His arrival on August 31 was noted in the *Morning Advertiser* on September 5, along with the interesting fact that he had brought with him two young Ashanti 'princes' in the care of a tutor to be educated in Britain.

Maclean was just a year older than Letitia. Born in the Scottish Highlands in 1801, the son of a clergyman, he had joined the Royal African Corps in his early youth. As a result, he had spent all his adult life far away from the spiders of society: first at Sierra Leone, and since 1830 as governor of Cape Coast Castle, the most important British trading fort in West Africa.

The first meeting between the couple took place at a dinner party in Hampstead, once Keats's Cockney stamping ground but increasingly colonized by the new rich. The party was given by a wealthy merchant named Matthew Forster, no apparent relation to Letitia's former fiancé John Forster, though both came originally from the northeast of England where the surname is common. Matthew had a long association with George Maclean, as his firm, Forster and Smith, was the leading

British player in the West Africa trade at the time. One of the precursor companies of the modern Unilever, in the 1830s it had a fleet of at least fourteen—possibly as many as seventeen—ships. The commodities Forster and Smith imported from West Africa included gold, mahogany, coffee, peanuts, and, in particular, palm oil, used in the preparation of soap. Matthew and his brother William were sophisticated operators whose business combined commodity trading with complex finance and numerous other interests. Matthew was, for example, on the board of the Liverpool and London Insurance Co., the York and London Assurance Co., and the South Eastern Railway Co., while his bulging portfolio also included investments in Berwick Salmon Fisheries, South Hetton Colliery and Hartlepool Docks.

There is no sign that Letitia had ever met her wealthy host before she agreed to spend a few days at his house, Belsize (or Belle Size) Villa, later known as Belsize Court. Set in bucolic grounds, it has since been demolished but is revealed in a late Victorian photograph to have been a substantial mansion in the late Georgian neoclassical style. In Matthew's day, it boasted two gatehouses and, at the time of the 1851 census, eight live-in servants.

How anyone in Letitia's literary circle came to know Britain's premier palm oil importer is a conundrum, one of the many niggling mysteries in her story, but there is just a hint that the indefatigable fixer Jerdan may have played a role. Comically, given his grubby reputation, in 1834 he acquired a stake in the largest soap factory in London, Hawes Soap Works, the family firm of Benjamin Hawes, M.P., a man of wide cultural interests and acquaintance. Hawes's company is likely to have had dealings with Forster and Smith, as it supplied the soap trade with raw materials (though in 1835 Forster and Smith decided to go it alone by financing a new mill in London to extract oil from peanuts for making soap).

Perhaps Jerdan continued to proffer Letitia generally around as a celebrity guest, as he had done in the past, although without anticipating her marriage. In the wake of her shocking death, he assured Lady Blessington that he had so 'deprecated' her engagement to Maclean that he had tried to persuade her to break it off.

More likely, the connection may have come through a couple named Mr and Mrs John Liddiard, who are revealed in their daughter Maria's unpublished diaries to have already known Letitia well by 1831. The Liddiards' other friends included Emma Roberts, while Dr and Mrs Thomson are also on record as recurrent visitors to their home. John Liddiard (born c. 1779) is recorded in the 1851 census as a retired warehouseman, which meant a wholesale trader. Wealthy enough to have a substantial villa in leafy Streatham and a house in town in Hyde Park Gate, he may have had business connections with West Africa, and thus an entrée to Matthew Forster. The shadowy substratum of Letitia's nonfamous acquaintance is hard to penetrate, the interstices of her social web too often erased. The scattered and fragmented sources conjure only a faint sense of the anonymous lives of the era, lived in humdrum bourgeois respectability: the turning of a blind eye to Letitia's 'fallen state' and the quiet machinating to correct it by promoting her marriage.

Letitia's stock was falling fast in literary and high society, but in mercantile circles she retained a sprinkling of stardust, just as the 'poet of fashion' in the *Sunday Times* squib of 1826 finds a niche in the business community after losing cachet among upper-class patrons. Her value as a trophy guest might alone explain why Matthew Forster wanted the celebrated L.E.L. to grace his dinner party in honour of the governor of Cape Coast Castle's London visit. But it cannot explain why the merchant proved as eager as Emma Roberts and Katherine Thomson to matchmake Letitia with George Maclean. As we shall see, he had good reason to suppose that it might suit his business interests.

Matthew was so keen to make the match that on the morning of the dinner party he came up to Letitia as she was sitting in the library at Belsize Villa and thrust a sheaf of papers into her hand, telling her that they would form an introduction to the man she was about to meet. The texts contained Maclean's own account of an expedition he had led against a rebel tribe.

Letitia was being invited in advance to perceive the governor in a heroic light: to play the same role as her audience had once played in the idealized construction of L.E.L. 'If Miss Landon still retained her prejudice in favour of heroes, the perusal of Mr Maclean's dispatches was well calculated to awaken the first strong feeling,' Emma Roberts later put it.

Roberts herself was probably being naively romantic in helping to encourage the marriage. But there were other issues at stake behind the scenes. They can only be assessed by probing the backstory of Cape Coast Castle, George Maclean and Matthew Forster, even before we bring L.E.L. and her future husband together for the first time over Matthew's dining table, with its impressive array of fine silver.

Letitia's story was about to intersect with the history of British interests in West Africa during its most complex and ambiguous phase: the
transition period between the height of the British slave trade in the
eighteenth century and the establishment under the Victorians of direct
imperial rule. The port of Cape Coast had been an important trading
post for centuries and had become the hub of the British slave trade by
the 1700s. But the surrounding region did not formally become a British
colony, the Gold Coast, until the 1860s.

Prior to the Abolition Act of 1807, the castle's precincts had provided
a marketplace in which slave dealers did business above the heads of
the human cargoes held in its underground silos. The model was that
of a government-sponsored 'public-private partnership', as the historian
William St Clair puts it. Trade was conducted at the castle under the protection of British armed forces, under the aegis of the African Company
of Merchants, analogous to the East India Company.

After the Abolition Act of 1807, the castle and its satellite forts lost
their historical raison d'être, however. It became unclear as to what the
British should do with them or with the influence they had built up in
the surrounding region. The African Company of Merchants was dis-
solved in 1821 owing to its slaving associations. Yet the British government continued to underwrite the garrison at Cape Coast, perhaps more
out of inertia and uncertainty than as a result of any positive policy.

In the 1820s, it considered withdrawing entirely, but was unwill-
ingly drawn into a local war after the Ashanti, much of whose wealth
was bound up with the slave trade, attacked, probably in resentment
at the Abolition Act. Once hostilities calmed down, the British government again considered withdrawal but was pressured into continuing to
fund the garrison by two separate interest groups. Abolitionists wanted
a British military force in place to fight the slave trade, which continued to operate openly out of non-British ports in West Africa long into
the nineteenth century, as nations such as Portugal and Brazil had not
signed on to the ban: at Whydah, for example, in what is now Benin, the
notorious Portuguese-Brazilian slave trader Francisco de Sousa—subject
of Bruce Chatwin's classic book *The Viceroy of Ouidah*—held sway. On
the other hand, West Africa merchants such as Matthew Forster, who
were involved in growing what was then called 'legitimate trade'—that
is, in commodities rather than slaves—needed military support to keep

the trade routes into the West African interior open, as the region was plagued by tribal wars.

In response to such pressure, the British government agreed to keep funding the garrison, shortly before Maclean was appointed as governor of Cape Coast Castle in 1830. As such, he was expected to support official British policy by policing the slave trade; to stamp out the local custom, inimical to British values, of 'human sacrifice', the execution of prisoners as part of elite funeral rites; and to exercise soft power through supporting missionary work and education.

Yet despite the new abolitionist policy, the old public-private model, dating back to the days of the African Company of Merchants, continued. Central government outsourced Maclean's appointment to the new merchant committee, the 'Council of Merchants', that had been formed following the demise of the old company. Its chief spokesman was Matthew Forster, the man who introduced Maclean to his future wife.

Although he was in reality the merchants' placeman, Maclean interpreted his own role as political and judicial. Often acting on his own initiative, he succeeded in extending the sphere of British influence in West Africa. As a lawbroker, he settled local disputes and punished criminals in the courthouse at Cape Coast Castle. More widely, he nurtured a détente between the Fante and Ashanti so successfully that he is still remembered in Ghana today with admiration as a peace broker.

It was useful to the local nations to have a skilful independent mediator, but Maclean's role was informal, not underpinned by international law (which did not yet exist), nor even with any clarity by the British legal system of the day. One reason for his success in creating a Pax Britannica was that he embedded himself in the local culture, unlike later British colonial officials who barricaded themselves in their compounds and made 'going native' taboo.

Yet Maclean was not a colonial ruler in the Victorian imperial sense, with political powers direct from London. The West African region for which he was responsible did not yet have fixed borders or a clear system of law and governance, though it formed the original template for what later became the colonial Gold Coast and, after independence, modern Ghana. He was governor of the castle, the commanding officer in charge of its garrison, not governor of a country, his other official title being 'President of the Council of Merchants'. Indeed, his mercantile connections were almost certainly what recommended him to the job in the first place. His previous posting had been to Sierra Leone, where Matthew's brother William ran the local Forster and Smith operation. The very ship on which Maclean sailed for London for his rare home leave in 1836 suggests the closeness of his client relationship with the firm. Owned by Forster and Smith, she had been flatteringly christened the *Governor Maclean*.

Although the Colonial Office had rubber-stamped Maclean's appointment in 1830, its commitment to the region remained uncertain. Matthew Forster felt he had to keep pressuring the Colonial Office to support British business, afraid that the grant for the garrison might be withdrawn at any moment. In 1832, he pressed the point that only by supporting the 'legitimate' economy on the ground could Europe pay the 'heavy debt' it owed Africa 'for the crimes that have been committed under the slave trade'.

At the time he introduced George Maclean and Letitia Landon in 1836, Matthew was still a mere outsider lobbyist. Although his trading activities had made him rich, he was a gritty northern businessman with no entrée into London's political elite. The Whig cabinet of the time was dominated by aristocrats with liberal sympathies with whom he had no social connection and little in common. The only conceivable reason why Matthew should have been so keen to promote the governor's union with L.E.L. was because he surmised that she might provide useful contacts.

Despite her falling stock, Letitia still moved in circles close to the seat of power. Government ministers frequented the Whig salon of her patroness Lady Blessington. The countess had a particular fondness for the then colonial secretary, Lord Glenelg, in whose 'highly polished manners' she delighted. Matthew must have figured that an alliance between her protégée L.E.L. and his own George Maclean might just give him the political access he craved. Letitia's personal connections among the Whig elite clustered around Lady Blessington also included Lord Normanby, who went on to take over from Glenelg in February 1839. Had Letitia lived just three months longer, Matthew would thus have achieved not just an indirect connection but a direct personal channel to the colonial secretary via Letitia as governor's wife.

Back in the autumn of 1836, Matthew's need to cultivate the Colonial Office was particularly intense. In the summer of 1836, it had received untoward correspondence from someone at Cape Coast, alleging that the

British West Africa merchants were flouting the antislaving laws with the governor's collusion. In particular, the merchants were accused of contravening the 1824 Slave Trade Consolidation Act, which had been brought in to bolster the original 1807 legislation. Its purpose was to close a loophole by making it illegal not only for British subjects to trade directly in slaves, but also to do so indirectly: by trading with slave traders, whether by supplying them with goods, or doing business with them even in the most abstract of ways, such as by insuring their ships.

The Cape Coast correspondent alleged that the governor was helping British merchants to break the 1824 law by letting them use the storage facilities at the castle to hold goods destined for use in the slave trade. As he concluded, 'Thus is Cape Coast Castle, supported as it is by British funds, and bearing the flag of a country that has paid twenty millions of money for the abolition of slavery, made a warehouse for the supply to these dealers in human flesh and blood, of the very articles they require for the prosecution of their detestable traffic.'

The whistleblower was a man named John Burgoyne. His personal history does little to support his claim that he was acting idealistically on behalf of the oppressed African. However, it does offer some insight into the sort of person likely to seek refuge at Cape Coast Castle in the 1830s, providing a context for Letitia's subsequent decision to go there.

Burgoyne was an opium addict and bigamist, who had previously been court-martialled in Jamaica for striking a brother officer, before briefly managing to secure the post of captain of the guard at Cape Coast Castle. Having hoped to be promoted to governor himself, he channelled his resentment into a long-running smear campaign against Maclean, conducted both in private letters to the Colonial Office and pseudonymously in the press. He was a disaffected renegade, out of control and determined to stir up trouble. Maclean constantly had to defend himself against similar charges, mostly issuing from Burgoyne, right up until he was finally relieved of his post in 1844.

Not only was Maclean accused of turning a blind eye to business corruption, but he was also accused of ordering inhumane floggings. One named African prisoner, Kobina, a runaway slave, property of a merchant called Hansen, was given five hundred lashes in 1835, a punishment regarded as lethal in the British navy at the time. The miscreant, who had committed burglary after absconding, was found dead the next day in his cell. A 'somewhat perfunctory inquest' recorded that Kobina had died not of his injuries but because he had taken poison in prison 'in rage at his public humiliation'. Letitia's death a few years later would likewise generate controversy and conflicting accusations.

Although neither knew it at the time they met, then, the one thing Letitia and Maclean had in common was that they were both on the receiving end of 'slander'. Burgoyne's motives were no purer than those of the 'enemies' who sexually smeared Letitia. But recent research suggests that, like theirs, his allegations had some basis in reality.

The history of the slave trade and its aftermath is still in the process of being uncovered. Marika Sherwood's seminal 2007 study *After Abolition: Britain and the Slave Trade Since 1807* makes no reference to Letitia Landon and barely mentions George Maclean. But it includes Forster and Smith among its case studies of businesses that continued to make their wealth from the slave economy after it was made illegal. In particular, she exposes Matthew's firm as an egregious but secretive flouter of the 1824 Slave Trade Consolidation Act.

Indeed, it is hard to see how the company could have made such profits without doing business with the slave traders who continued play a powerful role in West African commerce after 1807. That Matthew was chairman of the London Committee of Portuguese Bondholders shows that he had close links with a slaving nation. The goods that Forster and Smith is on record as taking out to Africa to trade for palm oil and other commodities are identical to those fingered in contemporary abolitionist reports as destined for the slave trade: iron, guns and powder, 'machinery', and cotton piece goods. Guns and powder could have been used on slave raids or in slave ships. Iron and machinery could have been euphemisms for slave manacles and collars. The latter continued to be openly manufactured for export in Birmingham long after 1807, according to the *British and Foreign Anti-Slavery Reporter* in 1840. Cotton cloth was so popular in West Africa that there was an official exchange rate between it and the local slave price.

No historian of West African trade has so far been able to trace the origins of Forster and Smith—or indeed the identity of Smith. According to Martin Lynn, 'The origins of the Forster & Smith partnership are unclear and there is no evidence as to who the "Smith" was.' It is possible that the firm began life as a straight slaving operation and later covered its tracks. That Matthew's family had an estate in the West Indies adds to that impression.

In her memoir of Letitia, Emma Roberts portrayed Maclean as a human rights crusader. No one, she averred, could appreciate better than L.E.L. his 'chivalric energy' in suppressing the slave trade, his 'philanthropic and unceasing endeavours to improve the condition of the natives of Africa,' and his efforts 'to prevent the horrid waste of human life by the barbarian princes in his neighbourhood'—an allusion to the local practice of ritual executions. However, Roberts's remarks, designed to protect her own role in encouraging Letitia's marriage, were an intervention in a pre-existing propaganda war. The truth was somewhat more complex.

Caught between eighteenth-century laissez-faire and Victorian hegemony, Maclean is a liminal, transitional figure, just like Letitia herself. His story too is mired in slipperiness and spin. His voluminous dispatches to the Colonial Office, now in the National Archives, are often as hard to interpret as the ambiguous poetry of L.E.L., their relationship to the truth as contentious. He frequently resorts to legalese and hairsplitting. Like Letitia's, his survival depended on his capacity for equivocation.

Maclean proved himself a skilful tribal mediator in the Palaver Room at Cape Coast Castle, but he was much less confident in dealing with his remoter British masters. With them, he was placed in as impossible a position as Letitia was in her different world in London. She had to play the innocent in some circles and the sexualized woman in others. He had to keep both local tribal leaders and Forster and Smith happy, while convincing the Colonial Office of his commitment to abolition.

From his own perspective, Maclean's career was far from certain, even despite his local successes in promoting peace between the Fante and Ashanti. In his youth he had joined the army in the uncertain period after Waterloo, and had only been commissioned into the Royal African Corps, then regarded as the last resort of no-hopers, after a failed earlier career in two other regiments. London expected Maclean to police its antislavery laws, but its mandarins did little to make him feel appreciated. They constantly required him to defend himself against suspicion and paid him a pittance. In contrast, he was love-bombed by Matthew Forster and the merchant committee.

Maclean's relationship with Matthew offers curious parallels with that between Letitia and Jerdan. It was ambiguous as to who was the client and who was the patron. In both cases, the one who held the economic power made a great play of flattering the public figure on whom he depended. That Matthew Forster was two decades older than Maclean adds to the parallel.

Two surviving artifacts, now in a private collection, reveal the extent to which Matthew and his fellow merchants were determined to bludgeon Maclean into submission through flattery. The first is a portrait that must have been commissioned during Maclean's London sojourn in 1836–38. It shows the governor in his red army coat and grand gold epaulettes. In his hand is a scroll on which appears the elephant and castle crest of the African Company of Merchants, together with the date, 1751, at which that organization was incorporated. Given that the company was disbanded in 1821 because it was too identified with the by then outlawed slave trade, no symbol could indicate more forcefully that Maclean was being presented as in hock to the merchants, who continued to feel connected to their ancestral organization. The governor's oddly sensitive face contrasts with his uptight uniform. His chin is awkwardly off-centre in his collar.

The second artifact is yet more telling, an even clearer indication that Matthew Forster's efforts to cultivate the governor knew no bounds. A crushingly over-the-top gift, it is a silver table centrepiece of grandiose proportions, imposing and highly wrought. Over two feet high, and set on a mirrored ground designed to make it sparkle all the more, it consists of two tiered bowls, with elaborate foliate decoration, held up by undulating plant stems and negro putti. At the top is the elephant and castle crest of the African Company of Merchants, surrounded by flags bearing the names of the various British forts on the West African coast (see plates).

The inscription states that it was given to Maclean by the merchant committee with gratitude, although it gives no date. On examination, the hallmark reveals it was made by Garrard's in 1836, the year Maclean arrived in London and met Letitia. The extraordinary craftsmanship suggests that it was designed by the leading silver sculptor of the day, Edmund Cotterill, who worked for Robert Garrard at that time. In 1842–43, he was commissioned by Queen Victoria to make a centrepiece for Prince Albert, this time in silver gilt, at a fee of £1,200. This outsize bauble would have cost far more than Maclean's annual income.

The inscription pays testimony to Maclean's support of the merchants. It ends with a capitalized flourish stating that 'victims were sacrificed in sight of the Castle walls'—an allusion to the governor's attempts to discourage the practice of ritual killings, which he in fact managed with some diplomatic skill. Clearly Matthew was keen to promote Maclean as a force for moral regeneration and civilization. In reality, the West Africa merchant community took a much more relativistic line towards 'human sacrifice'. In his memoirs, the Forster and Smith agent Brodie Cruick-shank expressed acceptance of such 'time-honoured customs, however repulsive they might be to an European', pointing out that public executions still took place in England.

George Maclean's uncomfortable position, caught as he was between the merchants and central government, is amply demonstrated by his dispatches to the Colonial Office. He frequently plays semantics as he ducks and dives over the allegations that he was wilfully turning a blind eye to corruption. The 1824 legislation was so poorly drafted that it contained its own loophole. To be guilty of trading with slave traders, the defendant had to have 'prior knowledge' of the eventual use to which his goods or services were destined. That could easily be denied, and frequently was.

Maclean himself often resorted to using ignorance as a defence especially in response to reports that slave ships docked at Cape Coast to buy supplies en route to picking up cargoes of slaves farther down the coast. During one such later controversy over a Portuguese ship, the *Dos Amigos*, he even declared himself ignorant of what constituted equipment for slaving, as he had received no instructions from the Colonial Office in London on the matter. London should surely have been able to rely on him—the man on the spot—for such information.

Maclean was less slippery when it came to a further piece of British legislation that came in during his tenure: the Slavery Abolition Act of 1833. This law made not just slave trading but the institution of slavery itself unlawful in most areas of British control. Maclean made few bones about the impossibility of stamping it out. Indeed his incarceration and flogging of Kobina, Hansen's slave, in 1835 suggests that he regarded maintaining the property rights of local slave owners as crucial to asserting his authority on the ground.

Varying degrees of slavery—including debt bondage or indentured labour, which was known by the euphemism of 'pawnage'—were an age-old institution in West Africa, where there was little tradition of a wage economy. Domestic work was done by house slaves, although their situation as feudal family retainers was not dehumanized like that of plantation slaves in the Americas.

How could Maclean possibly make peace with the local people while at the same time setting himself against their traditions, which the Europeans who had settled in the area, such as Hansen (probably a Dane), had also adopted? It is hard not to suspect that Maclean's cordial relations with the Ashanti were partly derived from a policy of minimal interference in their slave-trading activities. A young British naval officer, sent to police the West African ocean for slave ships in the early 1840s, was shocked by Maclean's workaday attitude to slavery. He noted with amazement that the governor did not turn a hair when acting as executor for the will of a local merchant of British origin whose estate included substantial slaveholdings.

According to Maclean's 1962 biographer G. E. Metcalfe, Maclean was alleged to have held slaves himself. Indeed, it is hard to see how any domestic work could have been done at the castle without them, although the workers there were referred to as 'prisoners.' A proportion of those incarcerated in the former slave dungeons were there for debt. It would not be far-fetched to speculate that the cash-strapped governor had bought their labour on at a discount from a previous local cred-itor. In his memoirs, Brodie Cruickshank, the Forster and Smith agent who acted as Maclean's secretary in Letitia's time, frequently complained about the double standards that made what was acceptable back home indefensible in Africa. Imprisonment for debt, admittedly without hard labour, was still common in England.

One irony rarely mentioned at the time was that even so-called legit-imate commerce in West Africa could not have functioned without local slave labour to work the palm plantations, and to transport commodi-ties, which could only be done by bearers through the roadless bush. In 1849, Cruickshank openly proposed that it was necessary 'to legalise the Slave Trade to a certain extent' because commodities could not, in his view, be 'profitably produced . . . without slave labour being sanctioned'.

Maclean, then, was caught up in the slavery controversy throughout the period of his relations with Letitia and beyond. Initially, the Colo-nial Office grudgingly accepted his assurances that the merchants were not contravening the law under his watch. The in-house government lawyer at the time was Virginia Woolf's grandfather Sir James Stephen. It took years for this upright intellectual with abolitionist sympathies to acknowledge that the wily merchants were actively lying when they reassured him that their aims were pure. Stephen was as bemused as his famous granddaughter when it came to the dark heart of pre-Victorian corruption. Not until 1840 did he finally conclude, 'There can be no doubt that the merchants at Cape Coast, including among them the members of the Council, have been systematically engaged in violating, to a large extent, the Slave Trade Abolition Act.' As a result, the Colonial Office finally decided to send out a government inspector, Richard Madden, to Cape Coast to investigate the allegations.

Back in 1836, we return to Letitia as she is preparing for the dinner party at which she will meet her future husband. Far from inspiring hero worship, Maclean's dour dispatches about his expedition against the rebel tribe initially left Letitia cold. She later admitted to Brodie Cruickshank that she was relieved to find Maclean younger and more fashionable-looking than his serviceable prose had suggested. Indeed, Maclean's careful, legalistic communiqués to the Colonial Office bear out Bulwer's impression of him as a 'dry, reserved, hard-headed Scotchman, of indefatigable activity—not of much perceptible talent'. Maclean lacked the very quality that Letitia had in abundance: charisma.

Nevertheless, Letitia set about hooking the governor from the start, wound up by her friends like the clockwork doll in Hoffmann's tale. According to Katherine Thomson, she dressed carefully for the dinner party, accessorizing her gown to flatter the Scotsman she was about to meet. 'In her enthusiasm she wore a Scotch Tartan scarf over her shoulders. She had a ribbon in her hair, and a sash also of the Maclean Tartan; and she set out for the soiree in great spirits, resolved on thus complimenting the hero.' She had clearly scoured the haberdashery shops well in advance with Mrs Thomson at her elbow.

Maclean is universally remembered as socially ill at ease in London. Mrs Thomson recalled that 'his dark-gray eyes were seldom raised to meet that of another.' But Letitia, who had made flirtation her life's work, did all she could to draw him out.

Over dinner she made him the centre of attention. She asked him about 'African habits, African horrors, and African wonders—the sea, the coast, the desert, the climate, and the people.' Perhaps Kobina's story featured in his answers. One can imagine her looking winningly at Maclean, then casting a semisatirical eye over her own Scottish getup as if to say, We both know this is absurd but I am doing it for *you*.

Katherine Thomson later described Letitia's manipulative charm. Her technique was to gush so exorbitantly that she created a secret bond of humour with the person she was flattering.

The governor could hold his own in dealing with seasoned Ashanti warlords, but he was, by his own admission, 'unaccustomed . . . to ladies'. Englishwomen of Letitia's conversational élan were outside his experience. Moreover, he was not immune to the cult of literary fame. Letitia later discovered that 'portraits of distinguished authors' were hung on the walls of Cape Coast Castle.

Maclean was also, as Katherine Thomson coyly recalled, 'much struck by her appearance'. By 1836, whatever personal attractions Letitia had ever possessed were in reality fading fast. The publisher Henry Vize-telly found her 'most unattractive . . . a pale-faced, plain-looking little woman, with lustreless eyes, and somewhat dowdily dressed, whom no amount of enthusiasm could have idealized into a sentimental poetess.' Another witness, who also met her around this time, remarked on her

Tired and drawn: Letitia in 1837 by John
William Wright

'plainness of looks and diminutiveness of form'. She looks tired and drawn in a portrait made in 1837, her hair slicked down under a band.

Yet Letitia knew that beauty was in the eye of the beholder. She had spent a lifetime perfecting her talents for audience manipulation. Maclean was smitten. Further meetings followed at the Hampstead mansion under Matthew's watchful eye. The Liddiards invited Letitia and Maclean to go to *Hamlet* with them on January 13, a bad performance by an American actor, apparently, but a 'pleasant evening' nonetheless. By now, Maclean was getting friendly with Whittington too, who joined his sister and the governor for a walk in Hyde Park with the Liddiards on February 14. Maclean then left to pay an extended visit to his relatives in Scotland, but a provisional understanding between the couple had apparently been reached.

Now that her marriage and departure were on the horizon, Letitia's first thought was for Whittington, to whom she had been bonded since childhood. She was concerned as to how her brother, who had lost his curacy, would cope without her. When the secretaryship of the Literary Fund, a writers' charity, fell vacant, she focused her energies on getting it for him.

Election to the post required the support of as many high-status signatories as could be levied. With the help of her patroness Lady Blessington, Letitia succeeded in signing up a host of grand names, including that of the former prime minister Sir Robert Peel. The list of powerful, titled men Letitia secured confirms that Matthew Forster would not have been wrong to think she had useful contacts. Her biographer Blanchard later pointed to the willingness of elite men to offer their support as proof of her unblemished position in society. It was nothing of the sort. Rather, it was a throwback to the courtesan's traditional informal access to male power.

The ever-present Jerdan had long since been involved with the Literary Fund and was on the committee. He also added his name to Whittington's slate and mustered his contacts. He must have been as keen as Letitia was to settle her penniless brother.

'You are canvassing for us do let me work for you—send me any books,' Letitia told Jerdan on March 8, 1837, offering her services in lieu as an unpaid reviewer for the *Gazette*. Her faith in Jerdan's influence, however, proved as misplaced as ever. The following month, the Literary

Fund instituted an inquiry into his suspected misappropriation of funds destined for the charity.

During this period, Letitia was less and less able to keep her social mask in place. Henry Chorley, of the *Gazette*'s rival *The Athenaeum*, witnessed its slippage when he called on her to offer his support for Whittington's candidacy. 'It was, for both of us, an awkward visit,' he recalled:

> She received me with an air of astonishment and bravado, talking with a rapid and unrefined frivolity, the tone and taste of which were most distasteful, and the flow difficult to interrupt. When, at last, I was allowed to explain my errand, the change was instant and painful. She burst into a flood of hysterical tears.

Letitia had previously published anonymous barbs against Chorley. She burst into tears because the sympathy of an erstwhile enemy made it humiliatingly clear that she was no longer considered a player but an object of pity. By 1837, male litterateurs had belatedly discovered a new vein of patronizing compassion for the woman they had previously regarded as unsexed. As Leigh Hunt put it, 'I believe she is very timid at least, & lives in perpetual fear of what the world will say of her. Besides, she has suffered, & is, I understand, very generous to her relations; and for these reasons, I think you will appreciate, that the good ought to comfort & praise her as much as they can.'

To Letitia's relief, Whittington was eventually elected to the secretaryship. She was so wound up that when the news came through she collapsed. 'I never shall forget waiting on Wednesday—I never suffered so much in my life—when I heard of our success the blood rushed from my nose and mouth in torrents,' she told Crofton Croker on April 14. Maria and Anne Liddiard had spent the day with her so that she should have some support at the moment of the announcement.

In his bitter first-person lyric of the 1820s, 'Warte, warte, wilder Schiffman', Heinrich Heine used the image of blood streaming from the eyes and body as a self-consciously over-the-top metaphor to describe the combined trauma of a lost love and exile over the seas from Europe: the exact fate that Letitia was now facing. Heine's poem was part ironic, part felt. Letitia—who had so enjoyed Heine's company in Paris, and published several poems based on German originals—may have known it. But there was neither irony nor romance in her real-life nosebleed.

CHAPTER 12

Engagement

Cape Coast represented escape, but to what? Letitia had long since played with ideas of the exotic. As a child, she had thrilled to her father's traveller's tales and had even fantasized about making her own voyage to Africa. But Cape Coast was in reality far from an ideal destination. The region's health risks were notorious, while the castle itself was associated in the public mind with the horrors of the slave trade. Unlike India, where Emma Roberts had spent some years, West Africa had no mixed-sex European society. Yet Letitia had no option but to clutch at it as her last chance.

Until her engagement was a fait accompli, she could not relax. The trouble was that Maclean began to get cold feet during his long absence in Scotland. As Katherine Thomson recalled,

> Mr Maclean had sought her hand in marriage; it was promised: and then, after a temporary separation, after a kind farewell, after several letters, written in the approved style of persons so situated in respect to each other, behold! the correspondence on the gentleman's part suddenly ceased. No explanation—no regrets followed.

According to Mrs Thomson (writing, of course, pseudonymously), Letitia made 'one false step' during the courtship. In nineteenth-century parlance, that meant only one thing: that she had slept with Maclean in the hope of entrapping him into matrimony. It was a high-risk strategy. The man's sense of duty might kick in, but he could equally reject the woman as a whore.

The breach-of-promise law was designed to prevent lusty men from reneging on vaguely pledged engagements after the event. In Dickens's *The Pickwick Papers,* published in 1836, the year Letitia met Maclean, an absurd breach-of-promise action is brought against Pickwick by his landlady, after a misunderstanding lands them in the same bed and leads her to believe that they are engaged. But Letitia was in no position to sue.

Two letters Maclean wrote to Matthew Forster in May and June 1837 expose his dithering and ambivalence, as well as his anxiety not to displease his patron. He may have been too embarrassed to send them, as they exist only in draft. '[E]very body makes a fool of himself once in his life, and I candidly admit that I have done so to perfection,' he confessed. '*A priori* I should have said that there does not exist a man in the world less likely to "fall in love" (as it is called) than myself. Nothing could be more "out of the way," I am free to acknowledge, and nothing could be more foolish. . . . [L]ooking at the matter as I now do . . . I am only surprised at my own folly in ever having dreamed such a plan.

'Nevertheless, it is equally true,' he went on, 'that both verbally and in writing, I am pledged to the lady; that is, I left her with the understanding that I was to marry her on my return to London, unless my love be cooled by the cold winds of the north. I must confess also, that I would have married her when in London—at least I think I would—and I must do the lady justice to say that she refused to allow me to enter into any engagement until I should have an opportunity of knowing my own mind.'

His reference to the 'cold winds of the north' must be a quotation from Letitia, as Maclean was not a man of metaphors. She had clearly subjected him to the strategies of paradox and equivocation she had perfected in her poetry, making it appear that she was giving him the right to retract, while at the same time making him feel contractually bound.

Maclean was cornered. 'What the devil I am *now* to do is another matter. I suppose, as you say, that I must pay the penalty of my own folly and precipitation, and marry the girl,' he concluded limply. 'I cannot, I suspect, recede honourably, & cannot go forward with safety.—However, I must make up my mind in some way or another,' he wrote.

'She possesses wit, talents, and powers of literary composition in no ordinary degree—but you have no conception of the violence of her temperament when excited,' he went on. Though a self-confessed 'ignoramus' as regards womankind, he wondered whether Miss Landon had 'a bee in her bonnet'. Was she mentally unstable?

When he happened to mention to her that a lady he had seen in Edinburgh had 'won' his 'heart' with her exquisite singing, Letitia had exploded with jealousy, as if she could not tell the difference between a throwaway remark and a serious expression of attachment. After manipulating so many romantic clichés in her poetry, perhaps she really could not. However, her insecurity was real. For fifteen years she had 'sung passionate songs of beating hearts' to a receptive public. Now she felt threatened by the drawing-room singing of an amateur.

Even the stability of Letitia's familiar long-term residence at 22 Hans Place had by now evaporated. Early in 1837, her landlady, Mrs Sheldon, who had taken over from the Misses Lance when they retired, moved out. Letitia had had to expend endless energy on winning the suspicious Mrs Sheldon over. She went with her to her new address in Upper Berkeley Street. Nevertheless, the change had been a blow.

When Maclean tried to cool things off, he received a note from Mrs Sheldon 'telling me that if I do not write Miss Landon will kill herself'. He did not take it seriously (perhaps he should have done so). But he found himself emotionally blackmailed into making fresh declarations of love at the very moment when he wanted to disentangle himself. 'What on earth' could he do under such circumstances, but 'say something very soothing and tender'?

Letitia's swinging moods were not, however, Maclean's only reason for wanting to withdraw. He had become 'acquainted with various matters which have somewhat altered my opinion of Miss Landon'. News of her dubious sexual reputation had finally reached him, whether through anonymous letters or oral gossip.

The prospect of a second broken engagement was terrifying for Letitia. 'Never shall I forget the anguish of my poor friend,' recalled Katherine Thomson. Letitia, desperate, told Maclean to apply to her respectable acquaintances for evidence of her virtuous character.

Proof that she did so rests in a long set-piece letter she wrote to Mrs Thomson in June 1837, defending herself against the 'invidious remarks of which I was made the object'. No doubt intended to reach the eyes of Maclean himself, it reads like a reprise of her 1826 apologia, though composed with less rhetorical bravura.

Letitia was brazenly deceitful in rebutting the 'slanders'—and pathetically honest in describing the pain they caused her:

To those who [to] indulge in a small envy, or a miserable love of gossip, talk away my life and happiness, I only say, if you think my conduct worth attacking, it is also worth examining. Such examination would be my best defence. From my friends I ask brief and indignant denial, based only on their conviction of falsehood. As regards myself, I have no answer beyond contemptuous silence, an appeal to all who know my past life, and a very bitter sense of innocence and injustice.

To Maclean's discomfort, Letitia also got Matthew Forster to plead her cause: 'her applying to *you* has . . . surprised and disappointed me exceedingly,' he complained. 'It shows a want of delicacy which I could not have conceived possible.' He was mortified by having to question not just Letitia's honour but, by implication, that of the rich and powerful man who had introduced them.

But as Maclean wavered, Letitia grasped the upper hand. After responding soothingly to her suicide threat, he was astonished to receive a cold reply, upbraiding him at his 'impudence in having written to her so kindly'. Letitia intimated *her* intention of closing the correspondence, alluding to 'various reports' about *him* that had reached her. This was an act of desperate gamesmanship.

Letitia had heard, probably from Matthew Forster, that Maclean was already involved with a local woman at Cape Coast. That was indeed the case. Such 'country marriages', as they were called, were the norm among European men in West Africa, who were often stationed there for years at a stretch. It was understood that the partnership was not for life. If the man went back to Europe, he was free to marry there, in line with the local practice of polygamy. But they were not casual relationships.

Although not married under British law, the women involved were regarded as wives, not mistresses, and as such had acknowledged rights. Their marriage contracts had typically been brokered by their families in financial detail. Many were of mixed race, the product of previous unions between European traders and local women. They typically lived family lives with their partners and any children they had together. The men were expected to compensate the women if they left the country and ended the relationship. 'Country wives' had a greater claim on their men than Letitia had on Jerdan as his mistress.

Little is known about Maclean's African partner, with whom he is said to have had an unspecified number of children. However, her name, 'Ellen Maclean', occurs in an 1837 list of Cape Coast female traders. This suggests she was not an exotic concubine with hot veins, but an entrepreneurial businesswoman.

One unintended consequence of the Abolition Act in West Africa was to increase the number of women involved in commerce. Reduction in slave exports created a glut in the local market and a consequent lowering of prices, widening the number of entrants into business able to afford slave bearers to transport goods. Ellen herself was probably one of them. Maclean may also have transferred to her the legal ownership of his own slaves, following the 1833 Slavery Abolition Act, in line with the typical behaviour of male British nationals with local 'country wives'.

According to Richard Madden, Maclean's country wife was the half sister of a Mr Bannerman, a man 'of colour, of respectability, living in Accra'. This was James Bannerman (1790–1858), a leading local merchant, himself the son of a Scottish father and a Fante mother. He married an Ashanti princess, Yaa Hom, and named his daughter 'Elen,' presumably after his half sister. The family remains to this day significant in Ghana. When I visited the country in 2017, the candidate on election posters in the impoverished Jamestown district of Accra was a Bannerman.

Maclean's 'country marriage' reveals the extent to which he had 'gone native'. It was not something he would have wanted to advertise in London. Such cross-cultural relationships became less and less acceptable in England as proto-Victorian notions of race replaced the laissez-faire attitudes of the eighteenth century. Ironically, as antislavery became the majority view, the horror of miscegenation increased.

In this respect, Letitia's own poetry acts as a mirror of the times. In the 1820s she romanticized a love affair between a white Crusader and a Moorish princess. But by 1832 we find her crystallizing the new attitudes in her mawkish poem 'The African', designed for her bourgeois annuals' audience. In it, an African prince is wrested from his homeland and sold into slavery. But he finds a new and better 'home' in his conversion to Christianity by a sexless, blue-eyed female child, a prototype of Little Eva in *Uncle Tom's Cabin*.

The African, from *Fisher's Drawing Room Scrap Book.*
Letitia's accompanying poem sentimentalized slavery
for her annuals' audience.

The poem shows L.E.L. cannily playing to both sides in the slavery
debate. She attempts to put across an abolitionist message, while carefully
avoiding alienating the large constituency of ordinary Britons who invested
at a remove in slaves. The year after she wrote it, many such small investors
would be claiming government compensation for the loss of their property
following the Slavery Abolition Act of 1833. L.E.L. did not want to rub her
readers' noses in the brutality of plantation life. In an act of breathtaking
denial, she described the Caribbean island, where her African prince is
exiled, as a tropical paradise hung with flowers. His sorrows are divorced
from material reality. They are only those of a sensitive soul.

Letitia was not in reality put off by the discovery that Maclean had
a country wife. She had spent her entire adult life as the 'other woman'.
Both in her poetry and in her daily experience, the love triangle was
her relationship norm. 'I can scarcely make even you understand how
perfectly ludicrous the idea of jealousy of a native woman really is. Sentiment, affection, are never thought of—it is a temporary bargain—I must
add that it seems to me quite monstrous,' she later told her brother. Yet

what had her affair with Jerdan been if not a 'temporary bargain'? There is no reason to suppose that Maclean's relationship with the mother of his children precluded affection any more than did Letitia's transactional relationship with Jerdan.

The information about Maclean's country wife came at an opportune moment for Letitia, when she most needed to distract his attention from the 'invidious remarks' he had heard concerning her. His squirming gave her further opportunity to hold him to the engagement. It was also to her advantage that his departure for West Africa was postponed for month upon month by official Colonial Office business. He was needed to lead a delegation to The Hague to discuss the Dutch settlements in West Africa.

The anxieties created by her on-off engagement made Letitia ill throughout 1837, reliant on Dr Thomson's care. That year she is repeatedly reported as 'ill' in Maria Liddiard's diary. She was without a fixed abode by now, having parted company with her landlady, and instead relying on the hospitality of the Thomsons and the Liddiards. The two families were clearly at one in their attempts to offer Letitia a refuge. In one of her anonymously published memoirs, Mrs Thomson pointedly praises Mrs Liddiard's respectability and Christian virtues, as well as her 'large fortune' and luxurious house.

Yet still Letitia's fatal facility continued unabated. At the end of 1837 she published her novel *Ethel Churchill*. Ostensibly set in the eighteenth century, it offered a chilling portrayal of the literary marketplace of the 1830s, with its tragic tale of the idealistic poet Walter Maynard destroyed by the literary cash nexus.

For the cynical publisher Curl, life is 'only a long sum', 'sentiment' and 'personality' are mere 'marketable commodities', the writer's only duty is 'to write what will sell,' and the publishers' advance is a form of debt bondage. Letitia took the name from Edmund Curll, the unscrupulous bookseller satirized by Alexander Pope. But she probably based him on Henry Colburn, who had been in the background throughout her career. If Letitia hoped to puncture him it was in vain. All Colburn cared about was the bottom line.

One reviewer of *Ethel Churchill* detected signs that L.E.L. was becoming 'a sort of Radical' because the novel exposed the sufferings of the poor. But the novel has no Victorian philanthropic optimism and decidedly no political idealism. Its view of life is materialistic, deterministic and pessimistic.

The verse epigraphs Letitia wrote as chapter headings—which survive in manscript in the Liddiard archive—would have been bypassed by the casual reader. But they offer a unique insight into her state of mind. Compared to the calculated equivocations of the early L.E.L., they are remarkable for their lack of ambiguity, suggesting she had finally lost faith in her own system of equivocation.

Taken out of context, they seem much more naked than any of her previous poems. She was no longer using the mask of L.E.L., either as a way of teasing readers or as a psychological distancing device. There are no playful double entendres, nor does she put her words into the mouth of a romanticized double. Her mask had become transparent.

In 'Gifts Misused', she looked back in bleak despair at her own career and the 'idol' she herself had created in 'L.E.L.':

> Oh, what a waste of feeling and of thought
> Have been the imprints on my roll of life!
> What worthless hours! . . .
> My power of song, unto how base a use
> Has it been put! With its pure ore
> I made an idol, living only on the breath
> Of idol worshippers.

In 'Life's Mask' she openly stated her cynic's creed of fatalism:

> Which was the true philosopher?—the sage
> Who to the sorrows and the crimes of life
> Gave tears—or he who laughed at all he saw?
> Such mockery is bitter, and yet just:
> And heaven well knows the cause there is to weep.
> Methinks that life is what the actor is—
> Outside there is he quaint and jibing mask;
> Beneath the pale and careworn countenance.

In another, yet more striking fragment, she reduced language and human emotion to mere physiology. Offering an irredeemably materialist message, she wonders at the capacity of words to redden the physical cheek and make the heart pulse, since they are nothing but a breath of air:

> *'Tis a strange mystery, the power of words!*
> *Life is in them, and death. A word can send*
> *The crimson colour hurrying to the cheek.*
> *Hurrying with many meanings; or can turn*
> *The current cold and deadly to the heart.*
> *Anger and fear are in them; grief and joy*
> *Are on their sound; yet slight, impalpable:—*
> *A word is but a breath of passing air.*

In 'Gossipping', she lashes out at the 'spiders of society' for spreading slander, while in 'Self-blindness' she admits that only self-deception can bring repose. In 'Life has dark secrets', personal secrets burrow into the heart, working to create incessant fear of future exposure. In 'The Marriage Vow', a wedding altar becomes a sacrificial slab. More sinisterly, 'Death in the flower' is addressed to the almond tree, in whose kernels are the raw ingredient for prussic acid.

Ethel Churchill in many ways anticipates the 'sensation' novels of Wilkie Collins and Mary Braddon, which were designed to titillate Victorian readers by shaking their comfortable assumptions. Unlike theirs, it does not seek its power directly from a mystery plot. Yet its moral ambiguities are equally destabilizing.

The one character in it who tries to resist determinism, by being 'mistress of my fate in this world', is the antiheroine Lady Marchmont. Equally enraged against her cold husband and her faithless lover, she plans to murder them both. In one phantasmagoric scene, worthy of Collins or Braddon, she is shown concocting prussic acid in a laboratory. Before simmering the crushed kernels of bitter almonds on the fire to create the poison, the villainess dons what Letitia was by now wearing: a 'glass mask'.

When Lady Marchmont's lover drinks the fatal cup of coffee that she has laced with the poison, Letitia spends several pages subjectively imagining what it must feel like to die of prussic acid, as the victim gasps for breath, feels his heart racing, experiences a fiery thirst, and staggers for support against a tree. After Letitia's own death by prussic acid, an

excited reader from Bedford wrote to *The Times,* pointing out the thrill-
ing coincidence.

The reviews of *Ethel Churchill* were generally good. Even *Fraser's,* perhaps realizing that it had gone too far in its mockery of L.E.L., admired
the novel's 'astonishing qualities', though it also complained of its insuf-
ficiently 'healthy' tone. The novel was also translated into German and
published in Leipzig. Letitia's low was replaced with a manic high once
her book was well received, although she was 'still on strict regimen, and
under Dr Thomson's care'. 'All the misery I have suffered during the last
few months is past like a dream,' she told Laman Blanchard, rhapsodi-
cally misquoting Coleridge's drug-induced poem 'Kubla Khan':

> *I on honey-dews have fed,*
> *And breathed the airs of Paradise.*

The 'opium of praise' had its effect.

Another reason for her better mood was that her engagement was
now decisively, and publicly, on. 'I saw L.E.L. today,' wrote Bulwer. 'She
avows her love to her betrothed frankly, and is going to Africa, where *he*
is governor of a fortress. Is that not grand? It is on the Gold Coast, and
his duty is to protect black people from being made slaves. The whole
thing is a romance for Lamartine. Half Paul and Virginia, half Inkle and
Yarico. Poor Miss Landon! I do like and shall miss her.'

Bulwer's comments were spiced with sarcasm. In *Paul and Virginia,*
Bernardin de St. Pierre's late-eighteenth-century best seller, the heroine
dies in a shipwreck en route from Mauritius. In the 1787 English comic
opera *Inkle and Yarico,* set in the Caribbean, an English trader's love affair
with a native woman turns sadistic when he plans to sell her into slavery.

Letitia and Whittington had by now been taken together under the
Liddiards' wing and were constantly at their house. Maclean was often
invited for dinner, or joined the group in outings to the theatre, according to Maria Liddiard's diary (one show they attended was *La Donna del
Lago,* based on Scott's *Lady of the Lake,* which Letitia had memorized in
childhood). Absorbed into the Liddiards' comfortable and respectable
family circle, Maclean did not spend much time alone with his fiancée.

Even Emma Roberts had begun to get cold feet. In a letter to the
Liddiards' daughter Maria, written on November 28, 1837, she expressed
her pleasure in the fact that Letitia's health seemed improved, but was

'unable to say' whether or not she desired 'the marriage to take place'. '[A]nxious as I am that she should have a protection, I do not like her going out to Africa,' she wrote. Her fear was that 'the climate and the dearth of books and other congenial entertainment may exercise an injurious effect upon her health and perhaps oblige her to return to England without him which would be a very disadvantageous circumstance'. Miss Roberts indicated in the most delicate fashion—calculated to go over the head of the innocent Maria, unless she was less innocent than her parents supposed—that she was afraid that Letitia would rebel against her exile and return to England as a renegade wife, yet more fallen than before.

In March, Matthew Forster gave a 'sumptuous' all-male dinner for Maclean and 'a select party of gentlemen connected with the African trade' at the Albion Tavern, Aldersgate Street, near the Forster and Smith offices in the City. Whittington attended. The highlight of the evening was the formal presentation to Maclean by Forster of the silver centrepiece, which according to the *London Evening Standard* was valued at 500 guineas. One of the guests was a leading Quaker abolitionist. He must have had as much of a talent for selective myopia as his fellow Quaker Bernard Barton, who had shut his eyes to L.E.L.'s sexual subtexts back in the early 1820s.

Blanchard attests that throughout the period of their acknowledged engagement, Maclean was Letitia's most loyal defender in the matter of her sexual reputation. Of course he was. Whatever he privately knew or suspected, he would not have wanted anyone to think he was marrying a dishonoured woman. As Bulwer's comments suggest, Letitia for her part trumpeted Maclean's antislavery credentials. Their very lack of intimacy enabled each to promote the other's reputation. However, all accounts suggest that Maclean continued to impress upon Letitia the discomforts and unsuitability for a lady of Cape Coast Castle.

From the viewpoint of some outsider observers, he was not an attentive fiancé. According to Lady Blessington, from 'the moment of his return from Scotland to that of their departure [for Cape Coast], he was moody, mysterious, and ill-humoured, continually sneering at literary ladies, speaking slightingly of her works, and, in short, showing every symptom of a desire to disgust her.' Yet Letitia was not to be disgusted; her 'pride shrank from again having it said that another marriage was broken off'. It was the lady's prerogative to withdraw from an engagement. Letitia refused to do so.

Pressed by further demands from a moneylender for a £75 debt of her brother's, Letitia applied to Richard Bentley on May 1, 1838, for an advance of £100. She had plans for another novel. However, her last major project apart from *Ethel Churchill* was a perversely doomed act of resistance to the cash nexus: an uncommissioned tragedy, *Castruccio Castracani*, about the toxic power of political factionalism.

Set in Renaissance Italy, inspired by Machiavelli's *Vita di Castruccio Castracani*, and based on Mary Shelley's 1823 novel *Valperga*, it was written in the manner of Shelley's own closet drama *Beatrice Cenci*. It was unperformable. Unrealistically hoping to get it put on, Letitia made vain efforts to get Bulwer to obtrude it on the notice of the actor-manager Macready, unaware that the latter had damned her in his diary as a 'fallen' woman.

During her last months in London, Letitia appears disconnected. Her mood seems labile, her sense of her own place in the world unstable. In wild optimism—and grandiose denial of her dubious social position—she addressed the opening poem of the latest *Fisher's Drawing Room Scrap Book* to the new queen, Victoria, going straight to the top, with Jerdan-like effrontery, in a quest for fresh patronage. According to Katherine Thomson, it was apparently suggested that Miss Landon herself should be presented at court. She was said to have declined the proposal because she was so modest she did not like to put herself forward. More likely, the palace felt that association with L.E.L. would be a public relations disaster.

The last poetry volume Letitia wrote, *Flowers of Loveliness,* was also inscribed to Victoria. Large-format, and illustrated with fine-quality, if disturbingly kitsch, engravings, it was published by Ackermann and featured a series of poems on different flowers and the female character types they supposedly represented. Despite the decorous dedication to the young virgin queen, the verse was decidedly more decadent than Letitia's standard annuals' offerings. She explained to her editor Robert Fisher at *Fisher's Drawing Room Scrap Book* that it could not possibly interfere with his comfortably bourgeois market as it was so 'utterly different'.

With its floral leitmotif, the volume was a throwback to Miss Rowden's botany treatise. The cloying sweetness of the engravings and the poetess's careful use of metaphor meant that innocent readers might still escape unscathed. Yet Letitia went riskily back to riffing on the dangerous themes with which she had originally created L.E.L.

In *Flowers of Loveliness,* Letitia portrayed a lovelorn woman as a
swooning opium addict.

The poem on the poppy, for example, featured a voluptuous woman
lying on a divan, under the gaze of a female friend, with her Turkish-style
bodice awry. The text explained, in politely poetical language, that the
heroine had become an opium addict as the result of a sexual trauma, her
life blighted by 'one huge serpent, and one only'. At this late stage in her
career, was Letitia returning to making anonymous digs at Jerdan as the
one lover who had defined and defiled her life?

Flowers of Loveliness is a work of cynical surface prettification. Like
the best kitsch, however, it is not blandly shallow but *deeply* shallow,
embracing shallowness as a form of covert rebellion. Its underlying per-
versity anticipates Baudelaire's similarly named 1857 shocker *Les fleurs du
mal,* which was itself influenced by the poetess tradition of Marceline
Desbordes-Valmore. The word 'loveliness' sounds twee to our ears, but in
1838 it was ambiguously on the cusp, not quite yet domesticated into the
wishy-washy semantics of today. 'Lovely' was the word used by Shelley

in *Adonais* to evoke Keats's rebellious sensualism back in 1821. *Flowers of Loveliness* was L.E.L.'s last stand.

Even at this late stage, Jerdan was still, in fact, involved behind the scenes in the business of creating L.E.L.'s image. Unable to let go of his songbird, he could not give up his Pygmalion habits. As late as 1838 he was puffing her latest *Fisher's Drawing Room Scrap Book* in the *Gazette* and was almost certainly involved in persuading the great American artist Thomas Sully (whose portrait of the seventh president, Andrew Jackson, still graces the $20 bill) to paint her.

Sully had come to London with his daughter Blanche in the hope of securing a sitting from the new queen. As he waited for a yes from the palace, picking up other commissions along the way, he joined the Garrick as a temporary member, which is where he probably first came across William Jerdan. Blanche Sully told her mother in a letter of January 1, 1838, that just as she and her father were leaving the house of the artist George Healy, who should walk in but 'a Mr Jordan [*sic*]—editor of some magazine here'. In March, Jerdan puffed Sully exorbitantly in the *Gazette* as an exceptionally talented American painter, proffering the insider knowledge that the new queen had sat for him the previous Thursday. The Marquess of Lansdowne, who knew Jerdan and had purchased *L'Improvisatrice* from H. W. Pickersgill in the 1820s, may also have been involved; Sully's diaries record how gratified he was to receive a dinner invitation from the marquess, as he wanted to get in with the nobility, so keen was he to paint the young queen.

Sully was eventually granted five sittings with Victoria at Buckingham Palace, resulting in his now iconic image of the young monarch in her coronation robes. The first sitting he made of Letitia—now in a private collection—was never finished. Like his English equivalent, Sir Thomas Lawrence, Sully was famous for his flattering portraits of female sitters. His take on Letitia is alluringly enigmatic. Her dark eyes are as expressionless as they are deep. The fact that Maclean did not leap at the chance to purchase a marriage portrait of his intended is further proof, if it were needed, that theirs was no standard love match.

According to Blanchard, another portrait was also commissioned during Letitia's last months in London in 1838: 'a medallion portrait, in plaster', by the sculptor Henry Weekes. The latter made his name later that year with a bust of Victoria, the first of her reign, but his image of Letitia was never, according to Blanchard, reproduced and marketed as planned, probably because no fee was forthcoming (a similar profile plaster medallion of Tennyson was made in the 1850s and sold as a souvenir to poetry lovers; in this, as ever, L.E.L. was before her time). Labelled 'Miss Landon', Weekes's plaster medallion shows Letitia wearing a flimsily girlish circle of flowers around her head, an ironic reminder of the wreath with which she had crowned Jerdan in the first flush of her fame.

This medallion appeared to have been lost until I found a reference to 'an early Victorian plaster cameo portrait of Miss Landon in an oval gilt matt and bird's-eye maple frame by Henry Weekes' in a sale catalogue for a small auction house in West London, where it went (as lot 507) for a pitiful £85 on March 30, 2010. Neither the auctioneers nor the buyer, whom I contacted, had ever heard of the poet Letitia Landon.

Blanchard regarded Weekes's effort, with reservations, as a good likeness. 'Although the profile was not the happiest view of her face, the likeness is sufficiently faithful to be very agreeable; and were the throat less long and the bust less broad and full, the resemblance would be perfect.' If Weekes lengthened Letitia's short neck, Sully must have stretched it to giraffe proportions. All her portraitists idealized her face, but in different ways, with the result that all her portraits look like different people. Her attractiveness was, as Anna Maria recalled, to be found in motion. The mobility of her face—an act of performance—was her emperor's new clothes.

Sightings of Letitia during her final few months in London are rare, but suggest she was less and less able to put up a social front outside the comfortable bubble of the Liddiards' home. In the run-up to her planned departure for Africa, Mrs Thomson took her to call on the writer Harriet Martineau, who had a cousin in Sierra Leone, to get advice about what to pack to take to West Africa.

Miss Martineau was dismayed by Letitia's detachment from practical realities and by her depressed and dissociated demeanour. 'I was at first agreeably surprised by Miss Landon's countenance, voice and manners,' she wrote, having clearly girded her loins to expect a brazen scarlet woman. Instead she was moved by the melancholy torpor of her guest:

[I]t was all so sad that my mother and I communicated to each other our sense of dismay, as soon as the ladies were gone. Miss Landon was listless, absent, melancholy to a striking degree. She found she was all wrong in the provision of clothes—was going to take out all muslins and no flannels, and divers pet presents which would go to ruin at once in the climate of Cape Coast. We promised to go to Dr Thomson's and hear the new play before she went; and I could not but observe the countenance of listless gloom with which she heard the arrangement made. Before the day of our visit came round it was discovered that she had been secretly married and I saw her no more.

As that last comment suggests, an atmosphere of furtiveness hung over the wedding, which finally took place at St Mary's, Bryanston Square, in Marylebone on June 7, 1838. Blanchard later painted a rosy picture of the bride at the altar surrounded by her friends, but it was a hole-in-the-corner affair. It took place by special licence, for which Maclean applied a week before the ceremony. That meant that the banns did not have to be read. Clearly, neither party wanted the wedding publicized in advance.

Letitia initially anticipated that the ceremony would not occur until just before they sailed for Africa, but Maclean later told his uncle it had supposedly been brought forward to accommodate the wishes of her 'two nearest relatives' who wanted it to take place, 'privately at least', before then. The Liddiard diaries, however, suggest that it was touch and go to the end. A wedding had been anticipated in April, but had come to nothing, leaving Miss Landon 'very strange and out of spirits' in May.

Whittington, as a clergyman, performed the ceremony. According to the marriage register, the other witness was 'Mary Elizabeth Landon'. The latter could have been Letitia's Yorkshire cousin but was probably the former governess, known as Elizabeth, who was living in London with Letitia's mother, Catherine, at the time of the 1841 census. She had been present, barely traceably but in the background, throughout Letitia's long career as Jerdan's mistress.

Bulwer gave the bride away. Maclean's brother was present but not his uncle, Sir John Maclean, the head of the family, who was not even informed until afterward. In an embarrassed letter to Sir John, Maclean later explained that he had not wanted to say anything as the marriage plans had been so on and off.

Letitia's signature on the marriage register leaps out. Her round, disconnected, childlike hand is shakier than normal. It contrasts vividly with the flowing, educated signatures of her husband, brother, and cousin.

Letitia's signature on her marriage register. Her round, childlike, shaky letters contrast with the educated signatures of her husband and brother.

After the service, according to Katherine Thomson, the couple spent the night at the Sackville Street Hotel, but then Letitia returned alone to the Liddiards' and continued to use her maiden name for at least a fortnight. Maclean later explained this away to his uncle by saying that they had not wanted the expense of setting up an establishment before leaving for Africa. 'In this way it was that Miss Landon *continued* Miss Landon *after* the marriage had actually taken place,' Maclean put it in some embarrassment. One wonders why she could not have stayed with him at his hotel, or he with her at the Liddiards', as her biographer Blanchard—erroneously, and in an effort to smooth away the irregularities of the situation—states he did.

The marriage was tardily announced in *The Times* on June 23. By then, the couple had gone out of town together, presumably to absent themselves at the moment of the announcement. The Liddiards, though they were providing Letitia with bed and board, do not appear to have been invited to the wedding itself.

Their daughter Maria, then in her early twenties and about to get engaged herself, was not even told it had taken place. Everyday life went on as usual on the surface in the Liddiard household. On June 10, three days after the marriage, Maria recorded in her diary that her father had taken her sister Louisa and L.E.L. to the zoo during the day, probably a welcome distraction for the latter. In the evening, however, 'Papa' had 'a long confab with Mr Maclean in his room—a crisis seems looming.' Whatever was said in Papa's room was not shared. Maria's diary is a testimony to how much was kept from her by her parents about Miss Landon's situation. Only on June 21, a fortnight after the wedding, was Maria finally informed: 'Miss Landon told me what surprised me greatly—her marriage!—I will make no comments. I said little talking by the conservatory.'

On June 23, after noting that the marriage announcement had been printed in the papers, Maria added that '2 strange notes came from Mr Maclean in the evening—not himself—what a wretched affair this is— she extremely angry.' Clearly it was no fairy-tale wedding.

The couple returned to London on June 27 for a small farewell party. The guests included the Earl of Munster—William IV's illegitimate son by the actress Dora Jordan—whom Jerdan had cultivated for two decades. The Thomsons could not come, but called at the Liddiards' in advance. The rest of the guest list recorded by Maria Liddiard includes the minor novelist Lady Stepney, whose books were claimed by Mary Russell Mitford to have been honed into publishing shape by Letitia. Otherwise, it comprises a select clutch of unknowns or hardly knowns, including the elderly novelist Miss Jane Porter (1776–1850), whose sister and fellow novelist Anna Maria Porter's romantic portrayal of goitered outcasts had long ago inspired Letitia, in a family joke, to compare the bankrupt Landons to the Cahets.

Bulwer and S. C. Hall both made speeches. The latter boasted of his affection, regard and respect for Letitia, 'which she could not have so long and continuously retained had they not been earned and merited'.

Maclean's response to such Pecksniffery was laconic: 'If Mrs McLean [sic] has as many friends as Mr Hall says she has, I only wonder that they allow her to leave them.' Even at their wedding party, Letitia's new husband could not disguise his conviction that he had been inveigled into taking away an inconvenient woman whose friends could not wait to get her out of the country. 'More disquietude about the party on Wednesday. What disagreeables this affair has involved,' noted Maria Liddiard in advance of the occasion.

The next day, June 28, was Queen Victoria's coronation. Letitia watched the procession from a balcony in St James's Street. It was her last public appearance in London and a symbolic moment for L.E.L. Despite her attempts to change her image, she remained mired in the rackety Regency, associated with the illegitimate Earl of Munster and not with the new queen, who would make such efforts to remould monarchy in the image of middle-class morality. Letitia, poised for exile, could not survive under the incoming regime.

Just before she was due to sail, Letitia wrote to Maclean's clergyman father. He had a volume of sermons just out—including one, ironically enough, on 'sincerity'—which he had arranged to have sent to her. 'I trust that Mr G. Maclean will at least not find his happiness diminished by being accompanied by one who has the sincerest affection and esteem for him,' she wrote. Sensibility, once a sign of Romantic rebellion, had become a sine qua non in respectable bourgeois marriage, but her double-negatived platitude was hardly a declaration of passion.

The newlyweds originally intended to board the *Governor Maclean* at London the day after the coronation. However, Letitia viewed the cabin and found it too basic. Nothing had been done to fit it out for female comfort. In the end, the couple boarded at Portsmouth a few days later, where Letitia found the cabin had been improved. Only at the 'eleventh hour' was a maid 'permitted' to join her on the voyage, she told Katherine Thomson. This was Emily Bailey, the wife of the ship's steward. She was destined to be the last person to see Letitia alive.

Whittington went with Letitia to Portsmouth. They missed the train, because she found it so hard to say goodbye to her London friends and kept putting off their departure. It was late in the evening when they reached Portsmouth, where they checked into a hotel.

In the morning, Whittington found his sister 'sitting on a hassock, on the floor, with the window-seat for a desk, busy writing a number of little farewell notes'. They discussed her plans for writing once in Africa. When asked, 'What will you do without friends to talk to?' she replied, 'I shall talk to them through my books.'

More farewell notes were written as they waited for the cutter that was to take them to where the *Governor Maclean* lay at anchor. Letitia gave a start when the guns fired a salute as Maclean himself stepped on board. But at the final farewell dinner on the ship Whittington remembered her as being in high spirits. Then her brother took his leave. As he sailed off in the cutter he watched her 'standing on the deck and looking towards us, as long as I could trace her figure against the sky'.

They set sail on July 2 or 3. Letitia had experienced seasickness crossing the English Channel in a steamer. The long voyage to Cape Coast was hellish. Not until after their brief stopover in Madeira—where Maclean but not Letitia briefly disembarked—did she feel able to write:

> Never is there one moment's quiet,—the deck is about a yard from your head, and it is never still; steps, falling of ropes, chains, and the rolling of parts of machinery, never stop: if you sleep you are waked with a start, your heart beating—by some sudden roll. . . . Till to-day I have attempted to do nothing, and even this scrawl is a labour of Hercules; the table rocks to which the sofa is tied, and the sofa rocks too.

The sofa was where she spent her days, retching, while Maclean busied himself with his scientific instruments, charting the ship's position. Her brief journal of the voyage—a mere handful of paragraphs—does not dwell on her new husband. He would be up at eight to 'take the sun'—to measure its altitude—before breakfasting with the captain. After that he 'generally comes for a moment to see how I am', which does not sound overly attentive.

But on deck there were moments of disorienting beauty:

> The sky is filled with stars, and there is a new moon—just Coleridge's description:—

> > 'The moon is going up the sky
> > With a single star beside.'

> All seem to be racing—I can use no other word—up and down the heaven, with the movement of the vessel. It is tremendous to look up, and see the height to which the sails ascend—so dark, so shadowy; while the ship seems such a little thing, you cannot understand how she is not lifted out of the water. The only light is that in the binnacle, where the compass is placed, by which the course is steered; it is such a speck of light for the safety of the whole to depend upon. The colour of the sea is lovely . . . we had a slight tornado last night, the lightning was splendid, the thunder appeared to me much louder than I ever heard; it was at night, and I was luckily on deck; it

was very striking—the sudden stir on the deck that had been so still—the men who start up, you cannot tell from whence, and the rapid furling of the sails!

The two poems Letitia wrote during the voyage were not designed to make her 'friends' in London feel easy. One was addressed to the Polar Star, which she watched sinking lower and lower in the horizon each night as they neared the equator, until at last it disappeared. It suggested that her own star was waning and prophesied a death:

> *But thou hast sunk beneath the wave,*
> *Thy radiant place unknown;*
> *I seem to stand beside a grave,*
> *And stand by it alone.*

The second, 'Night at Sea', dwelled in melancholy tones on her coming exile, each verse ending with the same two-line refrain:

> *'Tis Night, and overhead the sky is gleaming,*
> *Through the slight vapour trembles each dim star;*
> *I turn away—my heart is sadly dreaming*
> *Of scenes they do not light, of scenes afar.*
> > *My friends, my absent friends!*
> > *Do you think of me as I think of you?*

The open-endedness of the final question was a typical L.E.L. ambiguity. How *did* her absent friends think of her? Mrs Thomson, who had shepherded her to Harriet Martineau's to make sure she made the right preparations? Mr Hall, who had insinuated even in his farewell speech that her respectability was in doubt? Even the sympathetic Bulwer had given 'poor Miss Landon' away. And what of Jerdan? As H. F. Chorley later remarked, 'Those who had, in some measure, compromised her, were in no case to assist her; those who had stood aside, had become aware of the deep and real struggle and sorrow which had darkened her whole life, from its youth upwards, and the many, many pleas for forbearance implied on such knowledge.'

On Friday, August 10, they first sighted land. 'All I can say is, that

Cape Coast must be infinitely worse than my worst imaginings, if it does not seem paradise after this ship,' wrote Letitia. They reached the harbour on the night of the fifteenth.

Maclean went on ahead alone, in a small boat, at two o'clock in the morning. It was later surmised that he had gone to check that Ellen had left the premises, or to tell her to leave if she was still there.

He came back from his foray soaked to the skin and with bad news. The young man who had been acting as his secretary in his absence had died of fever and the castle was in confusion as a result. Letitia's first introduction to Cape Coast was thus an instant reminder of the 'white man's grave'.

But when, next day, she disembarked herself, she was relieved to have put an end to her sea sufferings. 'Cape Coast Castle! Thank goodness, I am on land again.' Two months to the day after they reached the harbour, Letitia herself was found dead.

CHAPTER 13

Heart of Darkness

Ellen had probably already left the castle with her children to join her family in Accra, alerted by letter in advance, as Thomas Hutchinson later reported (according to one of Letitia's own letters home from Cape Coast Castle, the locals were fond of receiving letters; if illiterate, they dictated replies). The sources offer no corroborative evidence to substantiate the rumours that she plotted to murder Letitia, possibly with Maclean's connivance.

Significantly, the government inspector Richard Madden found nothing to support the idea when he visited Cape Coast in 1841, despite his suspicious attitude towards Maclean. Although his official task was to investigate the allegations of illegal commerce, he had a sympathetic interest in finding out what he could about Letitia's fate, as he had met her in London through their mutual friend Lady Blessington. He was certainly no friend to Maclean or the merchants, against whom he eventually submitted a highly critical report. Nor was he immune from paranoia: while actually staying at the castle, he caught a fever and imagined in his delirium that the cook was trying to poison him and that Letitia's ghost was wafting through his bedroom. Yet even Madden dismissed the murder theory, having questioned the castle staff and interviewed Ellen in Accra.

Letitia's state of mind during the last eight weeks of her life is, however, crucial to understanding her death. One reason why the unsubstantiated murder theory was able to establish itself was that her letters home from Cape Coast Castle to friends such as Anna Maria Hall and Katherine Thomson, which were published in the newspapers in the aftermath of her death, offered no hint that she had been suicidal, or even ill.

Soon after her arrival, Letitia wrote to tell Mrs Hall that she had recovered from her seasickness and was now 'as well as possible'. Everything pleased her: the castle was a 'very noble building,' its rooms large and cool. The one in which she was writing, 'painted a deep blue, with some splendid engravings', would be 'pretty even in England'. This was probably the room—referred to by Brodie Cruickshank as her 'dressing-room'—in which she was later found dead.

Letitia was delighted with the castle's situation: 'On three sides the batteries are dashed against by the waves; on the fourth is a splendid land view.' The 'cocoa trees, with their long, fan-like leaves,' were 'very beautiful'. As for the 'natives', they looked 'very picturesque with their fine dark figures, with pieces of the country cloth flung round them.' They even had 'an excellent ear for music,' she enthused: 'the band plays all the old popular airs, which they have caught from some chance hearing.'

Letitia's only 'troubles,' she told Mrs Hall, were of the 'housekeeping' variety. At Hans Place she had been effectively infantilized. She had dined early with the schoolgirls and had never had to worry about how the meals appeared. Now she was expected to take charge of an unfamiliar domestic economy, where there was plenty of silver but nothing to clean it with, in which the mahogany furniture was expected to be constantly dusted, and where the diet consisted of unfamiliar foods such as yams and plantains. Although she does not mention it, her insecurity was compounded by the fact that the castle staff remained loyal to their previous, more competent chatelaine, Ellen. To add to her discomfort, other members of the Bannerman clan must have been frequently present in the castle, which, with its warehouses, remained the local centre for trade.

Yet Letitia told Mrs Thomson optimistically, 'I begin to see daylight. I have numbered and labelled my keys—their name is Legion—and every morning I take my way to the store, give out flour, sugar, butter, &c., and am learning to scold if I see any dust, or miss the customary polish on the tables.' She claimed to have taken in her stride the sight of half-naked black prisoners sluggishly scrubbing the floors overseen by a soldier with a bayonet, only complaining that they were less effective at the job than a single old woman in England.

She was even getting pastry-making lessons from Emily Bailey's husband, who had served as the ship's steward on the *Governor Maclean*. Both Baileys were happy to help as they waited for their passage home to England. 'I am very well and happy,' Letitia concluded, although she admitted that she missed her English friends.

In his 1841 *Life and Literary Remains of L.E.L.*, Laman Blanchard described Letitia's letters home as rehearsing 'without variation' and 'in the strongest terms' her 'favourable impressions of the country, her satisfaction with her new abode, her enjoyment of health, and her cheerful hopes and prospects'. The lack of variation is indeed remarkable.

Soon after arriving, she told Whittington, 'The castle is a fine building. . . . I am very well.' 'I am very well and happy. The Castle is a fine building,' she reiterated in a letter to Blanchard himself. 'The [room] in which I am writing would be pretty in England—it is of a pale blue—and hung with some beautiful prints,' she added, reprising her earlier comments to Mrs Hall. West Africa was 'like living in the Arabian nights'. 'I am most uninterestingly well and happy,' she informed Bulwer.

On October 10, five days before her death, she told Katherine Thomson, 'I cannot tell you how much better the place is than we supposed. . . . I must again repeat how infinitely better the place is than we thought.' Her use of the word 'we' reveals Mrs Thomson's complicity in the enterprise. On October 12, she told Robert Fisher, publisher of *Fisher's Drawing Room Scrap Book,* 'I never was in better health and like the place exceedingly. The Castle is a fine building.'

In her letter to Marie Fagan, found on her desk the day she died, she repeated herself yet again: 'The castle is a fine building. . . . I do not suffer from heat; insects there are few or none and I am in excellent health. . . . The land-view, with its cocoa and palm trees . . . is like a scene in the Arabian Nights.'

The key phrase in that final letter is 'insects there are few or none'. One of the few European women ever to have visited Cape Coast Castle previously—Sarah Bowditch, who spent time there in 1816 and 1817 with her husband—was a keen naturalist. She left a detailed record of the insect life at Cape Coast Castle: the poisonous centipedes she found in her bed; the scorpions that hid themselves among her books; the tarantulas; the cockroaches; the plagues of red and white ants that devoured everything, including clothes packed in chests, and the wooden chests themselves, which had to be placed on well-tarred legs set in water to discourage them. Then there were the mosquitoes.

Letitia's letters home were her last exercise in puffery, her final masquerade. In equating Cape Coast with the fantasy vistas of the 'Arabian

Nights', she was playing Scheherazade to the end. Letitia's poetry had transformed her commonplace affair with William Jerdan into a grand passion. Now she was 'working up' her descriptions of Cape Coast to please her audience, to save her own pride, and to protect her 'friends' from their own guilt at having encouraged her to go.

In some of her letters, however, her resolve to mask the 'covered mass of care' wavers. The sheer physical discomforts were more trying than she admitted to Mrs Hall. She confessed to Whittington that the after-effects of seasickness went on for some time, leaving her 'stone deaf' on one side. Although she told most of her correspondents that she did not suffer from the heat, in her one letter to her mother she admitted that 'the nights are so hot you can only bear the lightest sheet over you. As to the beds, the mattresses are so hard, they are like iron—the damp is very destructive—the dew is like rain, and there are no fireplaces; you would not believe it but a grate would be the first of luxuries. Keys, scissors, everything rusts.'

Sleep, it seems, was as rare a commodity at Cape Coast Castle as it had been on board ship. The castle band did not provide unmixed pleasure. Letitia's old arch humour resurfaced when she described the noise disturbance in a letter to Bulwer: 'At first I thought it rather hard that they should fire the gun at five o'clock every morning—neither did I see the necessity of the bugle again at six—moreover—the band seemed to play all day long—but now I hear none of them.'

She was still able to put on her witty society voice, regaling Bulwer with a mildly racy anecdote:

> The people appear very intelligent—fond of getting letters which they dictate—having a passion for a dictionary in which they look out words—I was a little alarmed the other day—when a note came whose writer said he had sent Mr Maclean a quantity of—'darlings—' I thought he might have spared his present—however it only turned out to be some honey—Most indefatigable research into the said dictionary—having discovered some connection between the words, honey sweet—darling.

But, she went on, she had seen nothing beyond the 'batteries' that bordered the castle precincts.

Letitia needed to block out the noise of the band to carry on writing; perhaps she also used writing to block out the noise. She could not stop. 'You may suppose what a resource writing is,' she told Blanchard, explaining that she had already completed a series of essays on the female characters in Walter Scott for Fisher, as well as the first volume of a new novel. She had since childhood been 'addicted,' as her mother told Jerdan when she was still an adolescent, to the escape offered by literary composition. Now she had to write, whether or not she wanted to: she was still in debt.

Fisher's Drawing Room Scrap Book represented her steadiest income stream. Ironically, she did not know that Robert Fisher was planning to sack her. On December 15, 1837 (after Letitia died but before the news reached England), he wrote to Thomas Moore asking him to take the *Scrap Book* over. 'I found,' Moore complained, 'that the payment to poor L.E.L. for *her* 60 pages of verse . . . amounted at first to only £100, though afterwards to £120 or 130. On hearing this I could not help telling him laughingly that even if I *could* have agreed to write for him it was plain he knew nothing of the *scale* by which my prices (however undeservedly) had hitherto been measured.' Letitia had been selling herself short.

The one friend in literary London whom she treated with anything like 'confidence' was Laman Blanchard, her future biographer. But when her one surviving letter to him reaches the topic of her financial embarrassments it suffers complete syntactical breakdown. As if afraid of spelling out the situation, she takes refuge in dashes, expecting him to fill in the gaps:

> If my literary success does but continue—in two or three years—I shall have an independance [*sic*] from embarrassment—it is long since I have known—It will enable me comfortably to provide for my mother—who I made a point of seeing before I left England—whatever of complaint I might have—though all I had done had been in vain—still I thought—leaving my country—I would only consider—what might best be done for the future—Mr Maclean—besides what he did in England—leaves my literary pursuits quite in my own hands—and this will enable me to do all for my family that I could wish—I treat you—you see with all my old confidence—I hope you will write to me.

Letitia put a positive spin on her financial independence within marriage, a rarity at the time, since a wife was not a separate legal person from her husband. In fact Maclean would have been responsible in law both for her earnings and for her debts. She clearly had not told him how much she owed her creditors, probably because her debts were so entwined with those of Jerdan. Even in the run-up to her marriage she had been anxiously sounding out Bulwer as a possible sponsor for her future publishing 'arrangements', desperate to make some money. By then she had ceased to rely at all on Jerdan's editorial input, and was hoping to use Whittington instead as a proofreader ('My brother who has lately acquired the habit will look over the proofs').

Even in otherwise cheerful-sounding letters from Cape Coast, Letitia's isolation shows through. Lone but tellingly repetitive sentences, devoid of emotional affect, recur again and again. To Anna Maria Hall: 'You cannot think the complete seclusion in which I live.' To Laman Blanchard: 'The solitude is absolute—I get up at seven o'Clock—till I see Mr Maclean at our seven o'Clock dinner—I rarely see a living creature—except the servants.' To Bulwer: 'My solitude is absolute—from seven—when I rise—till seven when Mr Maclean comes in to dinner from the court—I rarely see a creature.' To Catherine Landon: 'At seven Mr Maclean comes in from court—till then I never see a living creature but the servants.' To Marie Fagan on the morning of her death: 'The solitude, except an occasional dinner, is absolute; from seven in the morning till seven when we dine, I never see Mr Maclean, and rarely anyone else.'

Though Letitia depicts herself, with a nod to childhood fantasy, as a 'feminine Robinson Crusoe,' the castle complex was in fact teeming with people: prisoners, house slaves and other local staff, merchants' agents, soldiers, the cacophonous band, and the two English servants, Mr and Mrs Bailey. Her isolation was a state of mind.

The courtroom, where Maclean conducted his official business, is in fact only a couple of doors down, along an outside veranda, from the room that Letitia adopted as her boudoir. Another wife might have been comforted to think that her husband's place of work was so near at hand. Another husband might have joined her for his lunch break.

Since her arrival, Letitia had also been introduced to the British merchants and merchants' agents living in the nearby hills. Those with whom she dined included Brodie Cruickshank, who later recalled her sparkling conversation at table the night before her death, and his shock at seeing her dead body laid out on a bed the following morning. She had in addition presided over two formal dinners for visiting dignitaries, the governor of Guiana and the commander of the nearby Dutch fort. Such occasions, however, stretched her housekeeping skills to the limit. It was also awkward, she confessed to her friends in London, being the only lady at dinner.

On the morning the Dutch delegation was due to depart, Maclean was ill and refused to leave his bed. Letitia had to see them off alone. She felt very uncomfortable taking the salute on the parade ground. Some women might have thrilled at the prospect of taking on such a masculine role. But Letitia's defense had always been the feminine masquerade.

The only human warmth Letitia expresses in her letters home was for the Baileys, he a 'godsend,' she a 'most civil, obliging person,' without whom 'I know not what I should have done.' The couple was planning to board the *Governor Maclean* for their return passage to England on the day Letitia was found dead by Mrs Bailey in the blue room, with the bottle of prussic acid in her hand.

That Letitia died from a self-administered dose of prussic acid is one of the least uncertain aspects of her story. The label on the bottle found in her room was carefully transcribed at the inquest: 'Acid Hydrocianicum Delatum, Pharm. Lond. 1836, Medium Dose Five Minims, being about one-third the strength of that in former use, prepared by Scheele's proof.' If the castle surgeon chose not to perform an autopsy, it was because he had so little doubt as to the cause of death. How and why she was in possession of the bottle, and her intentions on taking the drug, are the questions that remain to be answered.

Prussic, or hydrocyanic, acid is a compound of hydrogen and cyanide diluted in liquid. Derived from bitter almond kernels, it was first developed during the eighteenth century by Carl Wilhelm Scheele, from whom the name 'Scheele's proof' derived. It was initially hailed as a wonder drug but very soon developed a controversial reputation. Owing to its extreme toxicity, except in the tiniest of doses, it soon become a suicide's cliché. In June 1822, Shelley asked Edward Trelawny to get him some because, although he had 'no intention of suicide at present', it would be 'a comfort to me to hold in my possession that golden key to the chamber of perpetual rest.' Dickens subsequently made comic capital out of prussic acid as the romantic self-slaughterer's drug of choice in *The Pickwick Papers*.

After Letitia died, her doctor, Anthony Todd Thomson, queried how she could possibly have had access to such a dangerous drug. His objection, however, makes little sense. Prior to the Pharmacy Act of 1868, prussic acid was freely available over the counter. The ease with which it could be obtained is indicated by a coroner's report that appeared in *The Times* on December 23, 1839, relating to the suicide by prussic acid and laudanum of a maidservant from Kentish Town, in the northern suburbs of London. The coroner questioned the pharmacist's judgement in having sold her the poison, but maintained that he could not be held responsible because the 'law was very defective on this point'.

It is, however, unlikely that Letitia had to obtain the drug herself from the chemist. Maclean testified at the inquest that he had seen her frequently resorting to the bottle to calm her 'spasms and hysterical affections'. When he tried to take it away from her in alarm on the voyage out, she had told him that it was necessary for her very life, and that it had 'been prescribed for her by her medical attendant in London (Dr Thomson)'.

After her death, Dr Thomson denied he had prescribed it for her and released to the press the pharmacist's inventory for the travelling medical chest he had ordered for her to take out to Africa in 1838. It did not contain prussic acid. However, that does not preclude the possibility that he had indeed prescribed it for her at some earlier point. The date on the bottle found in her hand was 1836. Given the tiny dosage—a single drop in a glass of water—a bottle would have lasted a long time.

Maclean's evidence that Dr Thomson indeed prescribed it is corroborated by overwhelming circumstantial clues. By the 1820s, most of the medical profession had lost faith in prussic acid's supposed curative properties. But Dr Thomson is on record as remaining a fervent champion of the drug well into the 1830s, despite the fact that it had by then come to be regarded with caution if not suspicion among doctors.

Thomson was a long-standing proponent of prussic acid. His enthusiastic experimental use of it on a consumptive teenage girl at a boarding school in Brompton's Cadogan Place was recorded in his friend Dr Augustus Bozzi Granville's *Historical and Practical Treatise on the internal use of the hydro-cyanic (Prussic) acid*, published in 1820. The girl had died, but only, Thomson maintained, because she had not been given the acid early enough.

For years afterward, Dr Thomson's own publications frequently recommend prussic acid for conditions ranging from pulmonary disease, dyspepsia and palpitations to fainting fits and depression of spirits. He even found it 'extremely useful as an external application' to treat acne. In the 1830 edition of his popular medical textbook *The London Dispensatory: A Practical Synopsis of Materia Medica, Pharmacy and Therapeutics,* he described it as 'a remedy of great efficacy' for 'spasmodic coughs', 'palpitations of the heart,' 'painful and difficult menstruation, floodings, haemoptysis, and nervous diseases'.

By 1838, the ambitious Thomson had sold his private practice in Sloane Street and been elevated to the first Professorship of Materia Medica at the newly formed London University (even though he himself had never completed his own medical studies as a student at Edinburgh). Throughout his tenure, he was dogged by snide remarks on his clinical competence. His peers regarded him as 'pompous in his phraseology, indistinct and doubtful as to diagnosis, prognosis, or treatment of the cases which were under his care'. The only reason why Thomson published the pharmacist's inventory after Letitia was found dead was to protect his professional reputation from the imputation that he had negligently caused the death of his celebrity patient by supplying her with a dangerous drug.

Why he prescribed it for her is another question. The list of diseases for which he recommended it is long. Yet the 'spasms' and 'hysterical affections' to which she was subject seem vague. At no point did Dr Thomson offer any account of an existing medical condition that might on its own have explained her death.

In fact, Letitia was using prussic acid because, 'if properly diluted and dispensed', it was, in the words of a modern historian of medicine, 'by far the most efficient alternative to narcotic opium'. According to Thomson himself, it 'certainly is a very powerful sedative; and may be employed in all cases in which sedatives and narcotics are indicated with decided advantage'. Letitia was an addict. The frequent opiate images in her work had as much of a squalid real-life undertow as her romanticized portrayals of forbidden love.

On January 22, 1839, soon after the news of her death hit London, an anonymous paragraph appeared in *The Times* under the headline

'L.E.L.,' describing her drug use. 'We all know, whatever anyone says,' confided the writer, 'that she was subject to the most violent spasms in the head and stomach, and that when on a visit four years since she used laudanum so very carelessly that Mrs —— told her she would certainly poison herself.' It was said that Letitia had gone on to try prussic acid on the advice of an acquaintance who claimed to have benefited from it himself.

The anonymous writer's purpose was to insist that Letitia's death had been accidental, not suicide. Emma Roberts—who later told William Howitt that Letitia had shown her a bottle of prussic acid at Hans Place—was probably responsible. Some of the phrasing echoes her 1839 memoir of Letitia almost word for word.

Letitia's drug dependency was in fact well known in literary London. According to Lady Blessington, she could not sleep without 'the aid of narcotics and that violent spasms and frequent attacks of the nerves left her seldom free from acute suffering'. After Letitia's death, it was common gossip at Cape Coast that she took prussic acid non-medicinally to 'stimulate her energies, a use probably unknown to Scheele'. For those so addicted to laudanum that it no longer worked for them, prussic acid was the next step.

Letitia's addiction cannot preclude the possibility of an undiagnosed underlying medical condition, but her 'spasms' could have been caused by the drug use alone. Withdrawal was not then well understood. Her unexplained blackouts and fainting fits, referred to by Roberts and by Madden, could have been the result of drug abuse too, analogous to the 'nodding' of the heroin addict.

Chemical addiction was widespread in the literary community. Many, such as Samuel Taylor Coleridge and Elizabeth Barrett Browning, became dependent on laudanum after initially using it for pain relief as it was the standard over-the-counter painkiller before the introduction of aspirin. However, it was also used to combat stress, especially by writers.

Harriet Martineau was told by a clergyman who 'knew the literary world of his time so thoroughly that there was probably no author of any mark then living in England with whom he was not more or less acquainted' that 'there was no author or authoress who was free from the habit of taking some pernicious stimulant. The amount of opium taken to relieve the wear and tear of authorship was, he said, greater than most people had any conception of, and *all* literary workers took something.'

Few writers of Letitia's generation had made themselves more vulnerable to the 'wear and tear of authorship' than she had. According to *The Times*'s anonymous correspondent, her drug use was already spiralling out of control by the beginning of 1835, even before the disaster of her broken engagement to John Forster. That might explain why she was so unsteady on her feet in Paris in 1834, constantly slipping over on the parquet, and why her appetite was so suppressed that ice cream was the only thing she could force down.

Letitia's drug use almost certainly began in the 1820s. Her early poems in the *Gazette* feature more drinking songs than opiate references. But by 1827, in the wake of the *Sunday Times* exposé, we find her using the vivid insomniac image of 'the opiate which may lull a while, / Then wake to double torture' in her dramatic monologue 'Love's Last Lesson.'

Although Letitia became dependent on narcotics to sleep, she may in fact have started as a recreational user. Though a sedative in larger doses, laudanum was a stimulant in smaller quantities. 'Many fashionable women attempt to light up their spirits previous to the reception of a party by a dose of Laudanum,' reported Dr Thomson in one of his popular medical texts, noting its popularity among English 'females' for 'exhilarating the spirits'. Letitia was painfully shy in childhood. Her social vivacity was probably chemically enhanced.

She is also likely to have used laudanum as a literary stimulant. Coleridge's 'Kubla Khan' was supposedly composed under its influence, as was Mary Robinson's gothic poem 'The Maniac'. Shelley and Byron dabbled in laudanum for non-medicinal purposes, as did Keats, who in his 'Ode to a Nightingale' compared the creative poet's dissociated state to that of a laudanum user who had 'emptied some dull opiate to the drains'. De Quincey's *Confessions of an English Opium-Eater* came out in book form in 1822, Letitia's most productive year as the *Gazette*'s 'nameless melodist'.

Opium dreams like that supposedly recorded in 'Kubla Khan' were atypical. According to De Quincey, hallucinations were rare. Letitia did not use drugs to raise visions, but her addiction offers an illuminating angle on the English *improvvisatrice*'s method of composition. Her drug use was comparable to that of jazz improvisers such as Miles Davis and Charlie Parker, who used heroin as a facilitator, to dampen performance anxiety and to block out distraction, as too much conscious cognition could impede the improvisatory flow. In her repetitive but varied use of the same themes and phrases, Letitia treated language in the same way that jazzmen later employed melodic building blocks.

The earliest oblique allusion to prussic acid in her oeuvre occurs in a lyric of 1825, addressed to 'The Almond Tree', whose kernels were used in its preparation: 'Fleeting and falling, / Where is the bloom / Of yon fair almond tree? / It is sunk to its tomb.' It was no doubt through Dr. Thomson that she first encountered it. On December 6, 1823, shortly before he initiated his regular medical column, the *Gazette* featured a reference to his friend Granville as the pioneer of prussic acid, just above a pre-puff for *The Improvisatrice*. The frontispiece of *The Improvisatrice*, published the following year, depicted a girl receiving strange roots from the hands

The Improvisatrice, frontispiece. A girl accepts from a wizened magician strange roots that turn out to be poison.

of an evil, wizened magician. She believes they are the raw ingredients for a love potion, but they turn out to be poison.

Letitia's long-standing drug addiction explains why by 1838 she needed prussic acid 'for her very life'. Whether she took her fatal overdose by accident or by design remains to be asked. As with her entire poetic oeuvre, an unresolved issue of intentionality hovers.

Mrs. Bailey told the inquest that on the evening before her death, Letitia had seemed 'affected' at the thought of her leaving her. She had 'had the spasms rather badly' and signaled her intention of taking some of 'the medicine in the bottle'. Without the Baileys, Letitia would have no allies in the castle.

Letitia could have chosen to sail home with the Baileys. Before she left England, Matthew Forster predicted that she would not be able to take the hardships of Cape Coast Castle and would be back by the next ship. But a few days before her death, on October 12, she wrote to him, in a tone of forced jollity, 'No my dear Mr Forster, you will not see me back by the Maclean, I never was in better health.' She had made the decision to stay.

It would have been humiliating for Letitia to return. Having been effectively cast out, she could not crawl back. All that would await her would be her 'one fear, withering ridicule': more gossip, more 'slanders', questions about why her marriage had failed. She no longer even had a home in London. Nor could she expect her old friends to welcome her with open arms, since they had propelled her into exile. She might also have simply recoiled from the prospect of reliving the physical horrors of the long voyage, the seasickness that had caused her such unbearable suffering.

On the night before she died, Letitia handed Mrs Bailey two letters to deliver in London. One was for Whittington, the other for an unnamed Mrs —— (probably Mrs Thomson or Mrs Liddiard). She also cut off a lock of her hair, which she handed to Mrs Bailey to give to her brother.

After the tragedy, Mrs Bailey passed the letters to Maclean, but they subsequently disappeared. They were later said to have been mere letters of introduction. It is hard to see how Mrs Bailey would have needed a letter of introduction to Whittington, as she must have met him at Portsmouth when he came to see Letitia off. Mrs Bailey kept the hair, rather than passing it immediately to the widower, as one might have expected. She finally gave it to Whittington in London over a year later when, having changed her plans for departure, she finally returned to London.

If Letitia's lost letters were indeed formal suicide notes, they would have contrasted startlingly with the upbeat tone of the letter to Mrs Fagan found on Letitia's portable writing desk. Up until she died, she continued to live in a world of split perspectives and alternative realities.

By now she was exhausted. Unbroken rest had been impossible on the passage out, even with narcotics. Sleep had been no easier at the castle, with its iron beds, its cacophonous band, and the constant noise of the Atlantic waves. In the fortnight before her death, the sleep deprivation had been even worse. For ten days, probably around the beginning of October, Maclean had been very ill. Letitia had had to sit up with him for 'four nights' running, only able to rest for the odd half hour on the floor beside the bed when he was 'still with opiates'.

By the morning of her death, however, he was on the mend. According to Maclean's testimony at the inquest, she brought him his arrowroot drink as usual at 6 a.m. but complained of weariness, which he attributed to her 'attendance upon himself while sick, and want of rest for three previous nights'. Despite her inability to sleep, she appeared to him to be 'in her usual spirits'. She then returned to bed for about an hour and a half before removing to her so-called dressing room, where she had her own cup of morning coffee.

Mrs Bailey soon looked in on her and found her 'well,' whereupon Letitia gave her a leaving present and then dismissed her, intimating that she would send for her later to help her dress. According to Brodie Cruickshank's later recollections, the maid then went to attend to some errands, including fetching some pomatum, used as hair oil or skin cream, from a store cupboard. When she returned to the dressing room around thirty minutes later, between eight and nine o'clock, she found Letitia's body blocking the door.

In her last moments Letitia was alone, without witnesses. She must have taken her final dose direct from the bottle, as it was found in her hand: not a drop in a glass of water, as was her usual habit according to Mrs Bailey. That suggests a firm intention to die, but perhaps she was simply trying to still worse symptoms than usual. The fact that Mrs Bailey would soon be coming back to help her dress suggests she half hoped to be stopped or revived. The maid thought Letitia's body was by the door because she had been trying to open it to summon aid.

If Letitia had indeed attempted suicide on a previous occasion in London, as Bulwer later told Lord Normanby, she may not quite have believed that she was going to succeed in a repeat performance. Or perhaps she changed her mind and panicked. It was a messy ending to a career built on poetic ambiguity.

Laman Blanchard devoted his 1841 *Life and Literary Remains of L.E.L.* to protecting Letitia's memory from the stain of suicide. But at the moment he first received the news of her death, he privately had no doubt that she had killed herself. On January 2, 1839, 'poor Blanchard' appeared in Macready's dressing room 'in dreadfully low spirits' to tell him that 'poor L.E.L., that gifted creature, perished by her own hand!'

Blanchard's anguish at the time is apparent from an unpublished letter he wrote to Lady Blessington on Friday, January 4, 1839, shortly after receiving the news. He confided his conviction that Letitia's true experiences at Cape Coast Castle had been very different from the positive spin she had put on them in her letters home:

Dear Lady Blessington,

She was indeed worthy of the praises and honour which your liberal feelings award her. But her fate is more pitiable and shocking than you even yet suppose. The depositions relating to her death [i.e., the inquest transcript] . . . tell us clearly how she died but they do not tell us why. The tale is one of wretchedness indeed—and perhaps may never be told. The letters to . . . friends are awfully contrasted with the story of her real feelings during her short sojourn in that living grave—the Castle.

Her whole life was one of sacrifice and sorrows—of calumnies on the part of others, and incautiousness on her own part. But its end was a concentration of suffering. What an effort must that last letter have cost her—that horrible resolution to be gay and happy in addressing Mrs Fagan—

while the one sole servant that reminded her of England was being sent away and the desolate scene was becoming yet more desolate. Who can wonder that her strong pride gave way, and the noble mind was on the instant overthrown by the recoil. Without seeing what she had previously written, the misery of the story cannot be imagined.

Little survives of 'what she had previously written,' but it includes a passage from an undated letter to Whittington that depicts Maclean as coldly refusing to let her have a room of her own, as she had had at Hans Place, and of treating her like a servant:

> There are eleven or twelve chambers here empty, I am told, yet Mr Maclean refuses to let me have one of them for my use nor will he permit me to enter the bed-room from the hour I leave it, seven in the morning, until he quits it at one in the afternoon. He expects me to cook, wash and iron, in short to do the work of a servant. I never see him till seven in the evening when he comes to dinner; and when that is over he plays the violin till ten o'clock when I go to bed. He says he will never cease correcting me till he has broken my spirit, and complains of my temper, which you know was never, even under heavy trials, bad.

Her allegation about not being allowed a room seems strange since she clearly had the use of the room in which she died. Perhaps she wanted a separate, more private space farther away from the governor's apartments. Perhaps she simply felt oppressed that she had no say in the choice.

Maclean was a man who wanted to feel in control. He was obsessed with scientific instruments and charting the position of the sun. 'That poor Sun, he never seems to get a moment's rest,' exclaimed Letitia during the voyage. But his sense of autonomy was under continual threat: from Matthew Forster and the merchant committee; in his subordinate relation to the British government, with its unrealizable diktats on slavery; and in his relationship with the slippery Letitia. His initial sexual infatuation with her had made him feel a fool, but he had been trapped into taking her away. No wonder if he became chilly and controlling on his own turf. As Letitia herself put it in a newly discovered letter to the

Liddiards' daughter Fanny, written from Cape Coast Castle, 'no wonder that a man whose whole life is past in the exercise of authority and who sees every hour the advantages arising from its exercise should be somewhat of a disciplinarian even in what with most men is a matter of sentiment and careless yielding. You would no longer wonder at the way of his marriage—"such is Jove's will and what he wills is fate." '

Yet Letitia, who was inured to being badly treated by men who professed to be her friends, kept up such a complaisant and accepting countenance that Maclean had no intimation of the impact of his coldness on her. In a household bustling with staff, she was personally in the habit of bringing him his morning arrowroot. Her own breakfast coffee was brought by a young black boy.

On the day of her death, Brodie Cruickshank recalled Maclean's state of total shock and disbelief, sitting staring into space over her dead body. Back in 1837, Maclean had dismissed her threat to kill herself as no more than a 'bee in her bonnet'. Although he was alarmed to discover her taking prussic acid on the voyage out, he never anticipated he would end up with a suicide on his hands.

'I must have seen it, had she been so unhappy. She could not, would not, have so concealed it,' he wrote to Whittington after her death, unaware that she had long since regarded concealment as her survival

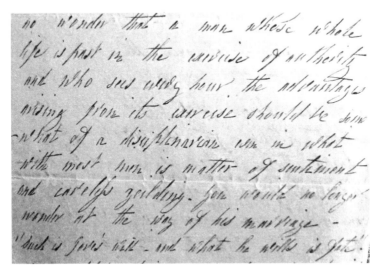

Letitia describes Maclean as a 'disciplinarian' in this manuscript letter to
Fanny Liddiard from Cape Coast Castle.

route. He recalled Letitia's very words to him during his illness, at a moment when he feared he might die. 'And do you really think that I could survive you? Never believe it or take any thought about my fate, for I am sure I should not live a day after you,' she had told him, in the stilted clichés of romantic melodrama.

Life for Letitia had long been a two-faced masquerade. She complained to her brother about Maclean's coldness. But to her husband's face, she continued to keep up a front, as she brought him his arrowroot, charmed his guests, and tended him when ill. 'And yet this is she who *had* written but a few days before, that her existence was insupportable on account of my "cruelty and indifference"!' Maclean wrote to Whittington in incomprehension, apparently quoting from another lost letter. He was unable to process the disjunction. Cut off from intimate knowledge of her previous fifteen years' experience, he had never been able to read Letitia. She showed him only the face she thought he wanted to see.

Their relationship had always been a muddle. Both parties were in denial about the transactional substratum, and the fact that neither was quite a free agent.

At the inquest, Maclean testified, somewhat otiosely, that an unkind word had never passed between him and his wife. However, hearsay evidence suggests that a cause of matrimonial tension might in fact have arisen shortly before her death. In the 1920s, Sir William Brandford Griffith (1858–1939), a former chief justice of the Gold Coast, recalled what his father had told him relating to the death of L.E.L. In 1886, Griffith senior, who was governor of the Gold Coast in the 1880s, heard the following story from a mixed-race Cape Coaster: Edmund Bannerman, the son of Ellen Maclean's half brother James, who said he had been told it by a relative who was actually in the castle on the day Letitia died. That a Bannerman was present reinforces the testimony of Richard Madden, who depicted Letitia as isolated at the castle amid a community loyal to Ellen, who, as we have seen, was a Bannerman herself.

Edmund related the following story. One day, the post arrived during dinner. After Letitia retired, Maclean opened a letter addressed to her that she had overlooked. Its contents convinced him that she had a child by another man. He showed her the letter and accused her, soon after which she poisoned herself.

It is hard to see how such gossip could have come from a published source. The scandal sheets of the 1820s and early 1830s, with their insinuating references to Letitia's 'baby', were not circulated at Cape Coast, and had gone the way of ephemera by the 1880s, when this story was told. Yet knowledge of Letitia's secret past was clearly current in the area for decades after her death. In his *Wanderings in West Africa* (1863), the explorer Richard Burton declared:

> The true history of Mrs Maclean's death is known to many, but who, in writing the life of 'L.E.L.,' would dare tell it? Owning that *de mortuis nil nisi verum* should be our motto, how would it be possible to publish facts while actors in the tragedy are still on the stage of life. And after their death it will be forgotten.

By 'actors in the tragedy' Burton could not have meant George Maclean, who had died in 1847. Those still alive in 1863, whose privacy Burton felt honour-bound as a 'gentleman' to protect, can only have been Letitia's illegitimate children. Her status as a fallen woman made men who knew about it feel bound to protect her privacy.

Brodie Cruickshank recalled that Mrs Maclean had been as charming as ever at dinner on the night before her death. Perhaps the incriminating letter was opened after he left. A ship from England had recently docked, bearing mail.

The possibility that Letitia's true past was revealed to Maclean via a letter from London is supported by Blanchard's gnomic comment in his *Life and Literary Remains* that her enemies pursued her even to Africa, and also by an unpublished letter from Bulwer in response to a lost letter from him. 'I conclude from your letter that her persecutors were not contented with exile, and that their malice found her in Africa,' Bulwer told Blanchard on January 6, 1839. 'I should like much to hear more of this mournful event. Can you dine with me on Tuesday, six o'clock? Let me know.' As *we* cannot know what was divulged over dinner, the identity of the so-called persecutors remains unknown. Some unnamed creditor may have threatened to expose Letitia to her husband if she did not pay up. However, the person most likely to have contacted her about her children is their father, Jerdan.

Exposure to Maclean would have left Letitia undefended, without a mask. An honour suicide would have been the logical consequence of such a loss of face, echoing that of the humiliated slave Kobina. In the European context, Balzac explained the psychology of suicide in his novel *Lost Illusions:*

> Suicide results from a feeling which if you like we will call self-esteem . . . the day when a man despises himself, the day when he sees that others despise him, the moment when the realities of life are at variance with his hopes, he kills himself and thus pays homage to society, refusing to stand before it stripped of his virtues and his splendour.

However, given her previous form, Letitia would have lied, lied, and lied again to her husband in the face of any incriminating letter, assuring him it was all 'slander'. Her ambiguous end had none of the glory of the Roman falling on his sword. She could have chosen to reenact the dramatic death of Sappho by throwing herself from the castle battlements into the ocean in an unequivocal grand gesture. But there was no poetry in the befuddled circumstances of her final overdose.

Balzac's analysis of suicide divides it into three types: 'firstly the kind which is no more than the last bout of a longstanding sickness and surely belongs to the domain of pathology; secondly suicide born of despair; thirdly suicide which is reasoned out.' Whatever factors prompted Letitia to put the bottle to her lips in the moment, her self-induced death resists a final, single definition, just like her poetry. It may have been one of those cases in which, as Balzac puts it, 'the three causes come together,' but without the two lost letters we cannot be sure how premeditated it was.

In addicts, the line between active suicide and suicidally reckless drug use is notoriously hard to define. Even now, coroners' verdicts often err on the side of accident to spare the feelings of survivors. The merchant jury at Letitia's inquest was composed of men who were Maclean's close daily associates. No doubt they wanted to spare his feelings by recording a verdict of accidental death. But they were also keen to deflect negative publicity. A celebrity suicide scandal had the potential to shine an unwelcome spotlight on their 'dark nook of colonial dependency'.

CHAPTER 14

Cover-up

The fact that Cape Coast was weeks away by ship from England meant that Letitia's death was already old news by the time it was announced in London. Distance added to the sense of public uncertainty since there was no easy way of getting or checking information. Yet the atmosphere of mystery, subsequently handed down to posterity, arose because so many of those connected with her had something to cover up that they feared her death might expose. The result was a confusing web of concealment, consisting of separate, differently motivated strands.

After the burial, Maclean departed for Accra in the dark, presumably to seek solace with Ellen. Two days later, he wrote a letter to his uncle in Scotland, telling him that 'a great blow has fallen on me so dreadful and so utterly unexpected, that it has almost broken my heart. My dearest wife is no more!—I cannot tell you the particulars, I am so ill, and ill at ease.'

Maclean was indeed shocked that Letitia had taken her life. But his uneasiness was not simply the grief of a stunned widower. He instantly realized that news of her death might fuel other, unconnected suspicions surrounding his role at Cape Coast. Even before writing to his uncle, he took time out to pen a letter to an anti-slavery campaigner, Thomas Fowell Buxton, for inclusion in the latter's forthcoming treatise *The Africa Slave Trade and Its Remedy*. Written on October 16, the very day after Letitia's death, it shows Maclean conspicuously trying to tie his colours to the anti-slavery mast, but dolefully questioning that it would ever be possible to suppress the trade:

> My neighbour (as I may call him) De Sousa at Whydah, still carries on an extensive Slave Trade; judging by the great numbers of

vessels consigned to him, he must ship a vast number of slaves annually. He declares, and with truth, that all the slave treaties signed during the last 25 years have never caused him to export one slave fewer than he would have done otherwise.

A further signatory to Buxton's book, which was published by John Murray in 1840, was W. Forster: Matthew's brother William, who was in charge of the Forster and Smith enterprise in Sierra Leone and Gambia and clearly felt no compunction at all over his hypocrisy.

Maclean would not have been wrong to suppose that the news of Letitia's death might exacerbate pre-existing suspicions surrounding his governorship. However, neither he nor the merchants anticipated that it would spark the unsubstantiated allegations of murder that were soon doing the rounds in London. They came from a surprising source, unconnected with the slavery controversy: Letitia's brother Whittington. In January, he wrote to the Colonial Office to lodge, in the words of an official's memo, a 'complaint in which he charged a former mistress of Mr Maclean with the murder of that gentleman's wife, not obscurely intimating that Mr Maclean had some participation in the act'.

The newly installed colonial secretary, Lord Normanby, failed to reply. He did not believe a murder investigation was necessary because he had been confidentially informed by Bulwer that Letitia had previously attempted suicide in London. If he did not answer Whittington's letter—which he even managed to lose after taking it home for discretion's sake—it was because he was too embarrassed to spell out to the bereaved curate what the latter did not want to hear: that his sister had killed herself. Suicide was still illegal and regarded as a sin in the eyes of the church.

Whittington was indeed resistant to accepting that the sister on whom he had been emotionally dependent since childhood had chosen to abandon not just life but him. 'My darling Whittington . . . I feel selfish in leaving you,' she had written to him from Cape Coast Castle, subordinating her own needs to his almost to the last. He was traumatized by her demise. Any death other than suicide would have been preferable from his viewpoint.

Ellen's existence had clearly made Whittington uncomfortable from the start, since Letitia had to explain to him that country marriages were, as she put it, a 'temporary bargain'. Why he made the leap to murder becomes apparent when one reads his two follow-up letters to the Colonial Office, which, unlike the first, survive in the archives. They reveal that he was not acting alone, but in concert with Dr Thomson.

Desperate to absolve himself of the charge of having prescribed Letitia with prussic acid, Dr Thomson was at the weak-willed Whittington's shoulder, encouraging him in his lurid suspicions. According to a surviving letter from Whittington to the Colonial Office, it was the doctor's 'medical comment' that convinced him to request an inquiry. Dr Thomson was, he said, 'most anxious' to go in person with him to the Colonial Office to make a deposition on oath, presumably to the effect that he had not supplied the prussic acid, leaving the way clear for a homicide allegation (the offer was not taken up).

The doctor was desperate to lay the blame on anything—and anyone—other than prussic acid. Ellen was a useful scapegoat. He gambled on the probability that even if inquiries were initiated, which would take months if not years at such a distance, his word as an English gentleman would carry more weight than that of any 'native woman'.

When Maclean belatedly got to hear of the murder allegations, he told his uncle that he had little to fear on that score, but that he was astonished that Whittington 'of all men' had propagated them. The unpublished Liddiard diaries attest to the frequent contact between Maclean and Whittington in the long run-up to Letitia's marriage. Unaware of Dr Thomson's input, Maclean simply could not understand how his brother-in-law could have conceived the idea.

Within a year of Letitia's death, Whittington himself had abandoned all notions of a homicide inquiry, which he had not in any case pursued with much determination. Grudgingly accepting Maclean's assurances, he skidded over the fact that he had originally accused his brother-in-law of being an accessory to murder, and made out instead that the investigation he had initially sought was into her alleged suicide. As he put it in a mealy-mouthed, syntactically slippery letter to Blanchard, 'I do not hesitate to say that George Maclean's narrative is marked by the desire, and goes to remove any impression of suicide from my sister's memory, and is just so far acceptable as it is calculated to attain the end which alone I had at heart in soliciting investigation by Government.'

The murder rumours soon began to lose traction, though they remained abroad. It can be no coincidence that the person who tried hardest to keep them alive in the coming years was Dr Thomson's wife,

Katherine. In her 1860 book *The Queens of Society*, which she published under a pseudonym that disguised her personal interest, she vigorously reiterated that there was no prussic acid in the medical chest and went further than her husband had done back in 1839 by explicitly extrapolating from that fact that Letitia's London doctor could never, ever, at any stage have prescribed it for her. She shifted the focus onto the cup of breakfast coffee, which had been brought to Letitia by a 'little native boy' on the morning she died, asserting that it must have been poisoned with some mystery agent on Ellen's orders. More than twenty years on, Katherine still felt the need to finger the first Mrs Maclean to cover up her husband's medical incompetence.

The murder allegations were able to continue rumbling because Letitia's death had been purposefully wrapped in a veil of obscurity from the start. The inquest jury's efforts to cover up an apparent suicide had unintentionally opened the door to more lurid suspicions. In the immediate aftermath, the merchant community at Cape Coast also took steps to prevent the spread of gossip to London about Maclean's cold treatment of his wife, which might damage his personal reputation and rebound on them.

The English servants, Mr and Mrs Bailey, who had been so sympathetic to Letitia, had been about to sail home on the day she died. Instead, they were given an offer they could not refuse to remain at Cape Coast for another full year. Mr Bailey was found employment as an overseer, presumably on a palm plantation. It was not a job for which his previous experience as a ship's steward—which required the skills of a butler—had prepared him. In an attempt to deflect suspicion, the Baileys' initial change of plan was later put down to no more than the fact that they had had an argument with the captain of the ship that was to take them home; even if so, they need not have waited a whole year for another passage. Forster and Smith alone had at least fourteen vessels plying the seas between England and West Africa.

After her return to London over a year later, however, Mrs Bailey began to talk, putting it abroad that Maclean had mistreated his wife. According to Brodie Cruickshank, who described her as a 'malignant woman', she was the main source responsible for the 'calumnies which were circulated of [Letitia Landon's] self-destruction'.

Forster and Smith did all it could to silence and discredit her.

In December 1840, an unusual story appeared in *The Times* among the police reports. A Mrs Moroner, living in the Mile End Road, had been robbed of various household articles by a servant, hardly newsworthy in itself. However, during the course of the ensuing case, the victim's daughter-in-law asked the magistrate's advice on another, unrelated matter. This was Emily Bailey, who was staying with her mother-in-law because her husband had gone off to sea again on another job.

Mrs Bailey told the magistrate that she had been intimidated by some 'gentlemen', who had on repeated occasions come to their house. Refusing to give their names, they had demanded that she hand over any documents relating to Letitia Landon: notes she had taken on the voyage out, and at Cape Coast, and even letters she had written to her husband after he was again at sea. The men's conduct was 'offensive' and 'not at all becoming gentlemen', although 'they came in their carriage'. They made verbal threats; they were 'abusive' and 'annoying'. Although they represented themselves as 'mercantile travellers', they had the appearance of 'persons of distinction'.

A few days later another item appeared in *The Times:* a letter to the editor dated from the offices of Forster and Smith, signed 'W. Forster.' Matthew's brother William announced himself as 'the only friend of Mr Maclean at the moment in town', and claimed he had investigated Mrs. Bailey's allegations of intimidation with 'the care required by the woman's position and past conduct'. Having forced Mrs. Bailey to go to a police station, William Forster had leaned on the officers to make her sign the following statement:

> I hereby declare, that the statement which I made to Mr Norton [the magistrate], at the Lambeth-street Police-court, on Thursday last, to the effect that I have been visited by different persons, some of them apparently of distinction, coming in their carriages, and requiring me to give up documents which I alleged to have in my possession, in reference to the death of the late Mrs Maclean, is entirely unfounded; and that I am possessed of no such documents or papers of importance. . . . I very sincerely regret having been led by the public excitement on this subject to invent these stories. It is true that I embarked with Mrs Maclean as her personal servant at Portsmouth and attended her

in that capacity up to the time of her death at Cape Coast Castle, but I hereby solemnly declare that I never saw or heard of anything to justify the calumnies which have been circulated against her husband on the subject of her death. I neither saw nor heard of any ill-treatment, nor do I believe Mr Maclean capable of any of those things which I have heard laid to his charge by public rumour.

'It is singular,' continued William Forster in *The Times*, 'that the first of the calumnious fables founded on the death of Mrs Maclean . . . should have been terminated in so speedy and complete an exposure of the author.' Singular indeed. 'I am sorry to add,' he concluded,

> that I have reason to believe that the extraordinary fabrications of Mrs Bailey are not the last links in the chain of falsehood by which it has been sought to enthral the character of my friend [Maclean], for the sake of pandering to the public appetite for scandal. But his absence from this country, added to the indefinite nature of the charges against him, have hitherto afforded impunity to his libellers, which it may not be safe for themselves to rely upon.

That last clause sounds like a threat.

By the time this appeared in *The Times*, the merchants had reason to feel particularly vulnerable. No doubt galvanized by the high-profile coverage surrounding Letitia's death, the Colonial Office had finally decided to get to the bottom of the allegations of illegal trading by appointing Richard Madden to conduct his inspection tour of West Africa. A fervent abolitionist, who had recently overseen the dismantling of slavery in the West Indies, he was not the man Matthew Forster would have chosen. That Madden was also a friend of the dead Letitia's patroness Lady Blessington only made matters worse.

Once he arrived at Cape Coast Castle in 1841, Madden investigated and dismissed the murder rumours, as we have seen. However, when it came to breaches of the slave trade laws, he was not reassured by what he found. While he was actually staying in the castle, one of Forster and Smith's ships, the *Robert Heddle*, commanded by a Captain Groves, anchored just beyond the harbour. She was fitted out with equipment for slaving and reported to have traded along the coast at Whydah with the notorious slave trader De Sousa.

Dr Madden thought this justified the ship being seized, but Maclean declined. 'All I was worth in the world would not pay the damages that must inevitably be given against me,' he told Madden, apparently afraid that the merchants would sue him. He would not change his mind when Madden told him that the British government would take the legal responsibility, and then even offered to do so himself.

Madden then sent for the ship's captain, who said that all he had done was to deliver goods for which he received cash. He expressed the view that De Sousa had been calumniated, as he had not personally seen him selling slaves while at Whydah. As with adultery in London, only ocular proof counted. The captain said he had been given permission by Maclean before taking the goods on to Whydah, although Maclean denied it. Madden believed that Maclean was reluctant to interfere because the vessel belonged to Forster and Smith.

When Matthew Forster discovered what had been going on, he became apoplectic, bombarding the Colonial Office with lengthy diatribes in which he insisted that the office itself would have to furnish him with information on which traders along the coast were slave traders. 'It was no part of Captain Groves' duty to sit in judgment on his customers,' he thundered. Matthew may have initially hoped that an alliance between Letitia and Maclean would help him cultivate the Colonial Office. Her unexpected death, followed by the Madden inspection, had rattled him.

On returning to England, Madden wrote his damning report, in which he repeatedly queried the business activities of Forster and Smith. However, by the time it was presented to Parliament, the government had changed. In the election of 1841, the Whigs lost and the Tories came in. One of the new MPs was Matthew Forster himself, who was elected on a free-trade Tory ticket for the constituency of Berwick in Northumberland, where he had family roots. Finally achieving the political heft he had long craved, he now found a more sympathetic colonial secretary in the new incumbent, Lord Stanley.

The Parliamentary Select Committee that was convened to consider the Madden report rejected most of its findings. It comes as no surprise to discover that the Select Committee's most assiduous member was Matthew Forster, MP. Richard Madden meanwhile was subjected to a campaign of press vilification, which included the charge that he had failed to complete his medical studies as a student (not something that had ever held Anthony Todd Thomson back) and thus had no right to call himself 'Dr'.[*]

Having seen off Madden, Matthew Forster became ever more hubristic. By 1843, he no longer felt the need to disguise his attitude to the slave trade laws, openly telling a House of Lords Select Committee that 'it was painful to hear the twaddle that is talked on the subject of the sale of goods to slave dealers on the coast of Africa. People forget that there is scarcely a British merchant of any eminence who is not proud and eager to deal as largely as possible with slave importers in Cuba and Brazil, and slave buyers and sellers in the United States.' The fallout from Letitia's death had made Forster and Smith nervous, but for now Matthew was riding high.

In contrast to its tangential effect on the world of international business, the tragedy hit at the heart of literary London. Not only was it a shocking personal bereavement for those who had been close to Letitia, but her fate had the potential to implicate the entire ecosystem that had colluded in the creation and destruction of L.E.L.

On Monday, February 4, just over four weeks after the story of Letitia's death broke, Charles Dickens attended an all-male dinner party at the home of the novelist William Harrison Ainsworth. He noted the guest list in his diary. It included Letitia's former lover William Jerdan, her former fiancé John Forster, and her friend and future biographer Samuel Laman Blanchard. The others present were the ageing Cockney Leigh Hunt, the cartoonist George Cruikshank, and the *Literary Gazette* contributor Richard Harris Barham.

The fact that there was no woman at Ainsworth's dinner table is an indication of how much literary networking had changed in the fifteen years since Letitia made her social debut in the bluestocking salons of Miss Spence and Miss Benger. By 1839, literary men were choosing to

---

[*] By coincidence, Madden studied medicine at St George's Hospital, and may have been there in 1822 when Letitia wrote her early poem on the subject.

meet in the new male-only clubs, such as the Garrick. In his recent hit, *The Pickwick Papers,* Dickens had ridiculed the very idea of the female salon. His fictional literary hostess, Mrs Leo Hunter, makes her name by publishing rickety sentimental poetry under the coy moniker of an 'L' followed by eight stars, and gives a fancy-dress breakfast at which she recites her effusive 'Ode to an expiring Frog'. One female guest plans to go as Apollo but is dissuaded by her embarrassed husband from appearing in a mini-tunic. She agrees to cover her legs in a long dress but worries that no one will know what character she is supposed to be. Don't worry, they'll see your lyre, he reassures her. Nothing could satirize Letitia's milieu more bitchily.

Dickens's brief diary entry does not record the conversation at Ainsworth's table. However, an absent woman, L.E.L., is likely to have been the main topic. Her death, reported only a month before, was still 'great talk' in London, to quote Carlyle's gossipy letter to his brother, written that very same day.

No one around the table had a more intimate interest in the subject than Jerdan. His immediate response to the tragic news can be gauged from the unpublished letter he wrote to Lady Blessington on January 5 in reply to a condolence note from her. It offers his most explicit admission of his affair with Letitia. But it is very different in tone from the agonized letter that Letitia's devastated friend Blanchard wrote to Lady Blessington at the same time.

Jerdan descanted in orotund phrases on the 'miserable calamity' that had 'closed the earthly career of our wonderfully gifted friend'. But he continued, Pygmalion-style, to deny Letitia's gifts by taking the credit for her work:

My poor, dear all but adored L.E.L.—the creature whose earliest and precocious aspirations it was mine to cherish and improve, whose mind unfolded its marvellous stores as drawn forth and encouraged by me—well did she sweetly paint it when she said

'We love the bird we taught to sing.'

He rose to a rhetorical pitch as he summed up her life, but showed no apparent awareness that he had contributed to her demise. It was a textbook example of the attitudes summed up in *Violet; or the danseuse,* in which gentlemen who ruined 'poor unfortunate women' did not feel morally to blame, but instead regarded themselves as the deserving beneficiaries of the natural female tendency to self-sacrifice:

A life of self-sacrifice from infancy to the grave—of sufferings vainly concealed under mocking brilliancy and assumed mirth—of a heart broken by mortifications, of spirits always forced, of the finest of human chords ever crushed and lacerated by the rudest handling, of sensitiveness subjected to perpetual injury—in features such as these are to be read the sad story of L.E.L. Men are exposed to unhappiness, but, alas what else is there for their beautiful and gentle companions?

Hard is *the fate of womankind;*

and the serpent who contends with the heel of the one, gnaws the hearts and drains the lifeblood of the other.

'Truly . . . did I love her for fifteen eventful years,' Jerdan confessed, his choice of adverb uncomfortably if unconsciously recalling L.E.L.'s poetic equivocations on the word 'truth'. He went on to explain to Lady Blessington that he had written 'Private' at the top of his letter because he had 'been led to unbosom myself to you in a manner that would not do for many in our bad world'. He reminded the countess that he could depend on her discretion because he knew that she too had things to hide, employing the coded language of sensibility in what almost sounds like a veiled threat: 'Yes, I do know how it is! It is because I am writing to one, every emotion in whose heart is attuned to the dearest and loveliest sympathies of our nature.

'Could her life be told, what a history would there be of Woman's fated wretchedness and of the woes which genius must endure,' Jerdan wrote theatrically, as if the mother of three of his children had been an abstraction not an individual. However, he raised a pertinent point. There was no way in which Letitia's true history could be told, not just for the sake of her memory but to preserve the reputation of the literary industry as a whole.

Authorship was at a crossroads. When Letitia started her career, the Byronic model of literary fame, based on illicit hints of sexual transgression, was dominant. But by 1839, Dickens was on his way to creating a new image for the celebrity writer, defined in terms of 'Victorian' family values. His bestseller *Oliver Twist*, published in instalments between 1837 and 1839, literally marginalized the 'fallen woman', once L.E.L.'s poetic stock-in-trade, by killing off the hero's unmarried mother in the first chapter. In the early days of her affair with Jerdan, Letitia associated her own bohemian antics with upward mobility and the aristocratic pecca-dilloes of Byron and Lady Caroline Lamb. As it turned out, her trajectory had been downward towards that of Violet the *danseuse*.

Around Ainsworth's table, the ageing Leigh Hunt represented the old guard, providing a backward-looking link to the sexually transgres-sive world of Shelley and Byron. But Dickens and John Forster were the coming men. With the new queen poised to import bourgeois morality into monarchy, the younger generation was determined to turn the rack-ety trade of letters into a respectable middle-class 'profession'.

By 1839, the Regency culture of so-called *demi-connaissance* was hardening into full-blown Victorian denial. In private life, a deeper level of secrecy had already begun to govern literary men's sex lives. In the 1820s, Jerdan had paraded Letitia as his trophy mistress, handing her into a carriage at the end of an evening in full view of party guests. But his new liaison with the invisible Mary Ann Maxwell was a sign of the times. Victorian men wanted silent women who could provide domestic retreats, not flamboyant lovers with careers of their own.

Following the breakup of his marriage, Bulwer too had a new mis-tress, whom he kept so discreetly that he referred to her by an alias in his will. Although she gave him several children, all his modern biog-rapher can discover about her is that her real name was Laura Deacon and that she worked for a while as a teacher in Brompton. A jealous and angry Rosina spittingly noted that Laura was friends with Letitia, which is confirmed by references to Miss Deacon in Maria Liddiard's diaries.

A similar secrecy later surrounded Charles Dickens's relationship with his much younger mistress, Ellen Ternan. Their affair was later stu-diously suppressed by John Forster when the latter came to write his clas-sic Victorian biography of the novelist in the 1870s. Forster was equally discreet about his own private life, leaving no published remarks at all about his embarrassing youthful engagement to Letitia. If Byron had fetishized the confessional hint, and L.E.L. had commodified it, the Victorians pulled a cordon sanitaire around the private life.

The men at Ainsworth's dinner were quite used to the idea of keeping each other's sexual secrets. According to Rosina 'that patent Humbug Mr. Charles Dickens' and his 'clique' were notorious for practising 'that freemasonry which exists among "gentlemen," that each gentleman's vices should be held sacred by any other gentleman, as there is no knowing when their own turn may come.' But in Letitia's case more was at stake than was usual. Her history was not just a potential embarrassment to Jerdan, who was in fact constitutionally unembarrassable, but to the industry as a whole.

The pressing question was how to manage the story as it spread through the public prints. As editor of the evening paper the *Courier,* Samuel Laman Blanchard had already been attempting to do that, though in a zigzag, stumbling fashion. His early reporting of Letitia's death hinted at his private conviction that she had been unhappy. But he had then been prevailed upon to call for a moratorium on all public commentary.

Soon afterward, Blanchard lost his job at the *Courier.* His literary confrères may have convinced themselves that they were doing him a favour by proposing him as Letitia's official biographer. With a wife and children to support, and no job, he needed the commission. It came from Henry Colburn, the shady éminence grise who had founded the *Literary Gazette* back in 1817, had played a long-term but mostly unrecorded role in L.E.L.'s literary career, and now had some stake keeping her sales posthumously afloat. However, the main reason why Blanchard was chosen had to do with his personality. In a world in which duels could be fought over book reviews, he was known for his soft, sweet, pliable nature. The biography would prove his poisoned chalice.

Laman Blanchard's story is as emblematic of the times as Letitia's own. Born in Lambeth in 1804, the son of an impoverished painter and glazier from a Jewish background, he began his career as an aspirant 'Cockney' poet. In his youth he dreamed of following Byron to Greece (which he did not do) and of going on the stage (which he did briefly, in Margate). After struggling as a clerk, he briefly secured a sinecure as secretary to the Zoological Society, which enabled him to publish his one and only poetry collection, *Lyric Offerings,* in 1828. It includes a sub-Shelleyan ode on liberty, and a clunky courtly lyric to an unnamed 'earthly beauty' who is probably L.E.L. since she is 'more Sappho than Eve' and inspires 'sweet sighs for the wrong'.

Letitia was taken with Blanchard from the moment they first met sometime in the mid- to late 1820s. She told Mrs Hall how good-looking he was. He was her type. His 'dark, handsome jewish features' were similar to those she gave Lorenzo in *The Improvisatrice* and appreciated in the French poet Fontenay.

Yet Blanchard was in fact uxorious. Having married his childhood sweetheart Ann at nineteen, he became a devoted father of three sons and a daughter: Sidney, Walter, Edmund and Lavinia (in one touching surviving letter, he expresses concern for one of his little boys, who had been injured by flying fragments of glass from a bursting soda water bottle). Instead of flirtation, a friendship sprung up between Letitia and Blanchard that was perhaps the most disinterested she ever experienced in the literary world. The way in which she writes to him, given her self-confessed 'mirroring tendencies', reveals much about his own kindness and good humour. One of her warmest and funniest letters was written to Blanchard from 22 Hans Place in 1837:

> Do you, my dear Mr. Blanchard, know of any person in want of a 'young woman, sober, honest, and good-tempered,' 'would not object to waiting on a single gentleman?' If you do, for mercy's sake, recommend me. For the last fortnight I have been qualifying for the situation. Everybody has been ill and in bed but myself; one servant gone home, the other turned out at a moment's notice for too great devotion to 'ardent spirits,' and we are left alone!—desolate as Babylon, or the ruins of Palmyra. I have run about with a saucepan of gruel in one hand, and a basin of broth in the other. I have not yet lost the keys, and have only broken one candlestick. I hope my patients are recovering, and then I shall leave the kitchen for the attic.

Blanchard's life was, however, a constant struggle. To keep his family afloat he turned from poetry to journalism. He was appointed to a number of short-lived editorships that were well paid, but he could not hold them down. As a writer he became known for his humorous columns on the so-called sunny side of life, but he was haunted by depression. As with the essayist Charles Lamb, who befriended him, his upbeat

whimsy disguised a troubled soul. In his youth he had experienced suicidal thoughts, threatening to throw himself off Westminster Bridge, and
writing a sonnet on Werther. In an unpublished letter of 1832, thanking
Bulwer for a belated review of *Lyric Offerings* in the *New Monthly Magazine*, he complains about the pressures of daily journalism. His letter is
dated from an asylum.

Blanchard was, in Bulwer's view, quite unfitted for the Darwinian
struggle of the literary marketplace. He did not have the mental tough-
ness required of the literary 'free lance', a metaphor whose martial-
mercenary implications were very much alive. Starstruck by 'noisier
aspirants of fame', he was renowned for 'monstering' Letitia with a blind
devotion that made more cynical contemporaries cringe.

No one was less likely to dig the dirt than Blanchard. Despite his
intimate, insider knowledge of her private life, his stated aim was to

Too sensitive for the Darwinian struggle of the literary
marketplace: Letitia's friend and biographer Samuel
Laman Blanchard, after Maclise, published 1846

'keep her memory as a pleasant odour in the world'. As his son-in-law Blanchard Jerrold later put it, the 'domestic fight this gallant little woman made alongside her literary battle was known to very few, if to any, save Laman Blanchard'. The cloying Dickensian image of the gallant little woman twisted the seedy L.E.L. into a virtuous Little Nell, convincing unsuspecting future commentators that her domestic fight involved no more than dutifully supporting her widowed mother.

In the course of his research, Blanchard interviewed everyone intimately connected with Letitia, but he omitted Maginn entirely and redacted John Forster's name from the book. References to Jerdan were kept to a minimum. When he was mentioned it was as a respectable family man and father figure.

As keen not to offend anyone as he was to protect Letitia's reputation as a virtuous woman, Blanchard was put under pressure from all sides. In deference to Dr Thomson, for example, he repeated the latter's assertion that there was no prussic acid in the medicine chest, although he could not quite bring himself to cast doubt on the presence of the bottle altogether, given the clear evidence of the inquest. In increasing desperation he flailed around for an explanation to avoid the conclusion she had knowingly dosed herself with prussic acid. Perhaps, he suggested unconvincingly, it was an old bottle, which had been recycled to contain a more innocuous drug? Perhaps Letitia did not know what 'hydrocyanic acid' meant? Perhaps she had merely applied some of the contents topically to her jaw and been overcome by the fumes?

Forster and Smith also exerted its will. A curious note appended on the back flyleaf of Blanchard's biography, clearly added just before it went to press, tells readers not to trust any testimony offered by Emily Bailey.

Letitia's official biography was the most high-profile project Blanchard ever undertook, but it was a critical failure when it was published in May 1841. 'We have rarely opened a more painful or unsatisfactory book than this,' opined *The Athenaeum,* censuring the biographer's reluctance to give 'a full and unanswerable statement in explanation' of the slanders against L.E.L. The sententious reviewer was probably H. F. Chorley, who had seen Letitia dissolve into tears when he condescended to offer her his support for Whittington's job application to the Literary Fund in 1837. In his memoirs, he later moralized over literary London's failure to support L.E.L. in her hour of need. Yet he failed to offer Blanchard forbearance for the impossible task he had undertaken.

Another disappointed reader was the housebound poet Elizabeth Barrett. She was dismayed not only by the gaps in Blanchard's biographical narrative, but also by his critical comments on Letitia's work. Blanchard bent over backward to deny that there was any connection between the tragic emotions in L.E.L.'s poetry and her own life experience. Barrett was disappointed to discover that the poetess she so admired had not written from the heart: that her 'passion' was 'pasteboard', that she was 'the actress and not Juliet'. And yet when she heard the 'Jerdan rumours', she hoped them 'into slander'. She wanted it both ways: for L.E.L.'s love agonies to be authentic, but for Letitia to remain unsullied. Both Barrett and Blanchard were caught in the trap that Letitia herself had set. She could not be read as both an honest poet and an honest woman.

Blanchard knew he had failed as a biographer because he had had to keep silent about the sexual relationship that had underpinned Letitia's poetic career from the start. 'If I have failed,' he told S. C. Hall gnomically, 'it is because there were difficulties in the way that I cannot explain; and if some of her enemies escape, it was because I was fearful of injuring her.' In the wake of the failure of *The Life and Literary Remains of L.E.L.*, Blanchard never got another salaried editorial post or another major book commission. His once idealistic, generous nature became increasingly bitter and cynical, according to his contemporary Peter George Patmore. Struggling to make an increasingly precarious freelance living, he used to walk the streets, desperate to come up with ideas for articles, troubled by constant anxiety attacks, which increased when his wife fell ill with a paralytic condition in 1844. When she finally died in 1845, Blanchard collapsed. He was seized by attacks of psychosomatic paralysis, 'sudden attacks of tears', night-after-night insomnia, and 'fits of hysteria' so extreme that it required 'several persons to hold him down'.

At 1 a.m. on February 15, 1845, Samuel Laman Blanchard slit his throat in the upstairs bedroom of his home in Union Place, Lambeth, just around the corner from Hercules Buildings where Jerdan was by then living with Mary Ann Maxwell and their growing family. He was forty years old. As he grabbed the cutthroat razor, he called out to the hired nurse, who was supposed to be minding him, that she had better not leave him as he felt a strong desire to throw himself out of the window. She ran downstairs to get his burly elder son to help restrain him. But it was too late. While she was still on the stairs, she heard a scream.

It came from his younger son, Edmund, aged thirteen, who had been asleep in the bedroom and had woken to witness his father's final act.

Although the immediate trigger for Blanchard's suicide was the death of his wife, Bulwer believed that it had longer-term origins in the 'sores and evils' of commercial literary culture 'where mind is regarded but as a common ware of merchandise'. In his memoir of Blanchard, he also pointed to the coincidence by which both Letitia and her biographer had killed themselves, the only acknowledgment in print by any of Letitia's circle of her suicide. It was a hint that her death and the stress of writing her biography for money to support his family had reawakened Blanchard's old suicidal tendencies. After becoming a father, he had told friends that he would never give in to the temptation of suicide for fear of the impact on his children. But suicide, as Dr Forbes Winslow argued in his 1840 *Anatomy of Suicide,* could be contagious.

Despite the appalling details, reactions to Blanchard's death were universally sympathetic. No attempt was made to hide the fact that he had killed himself 'during a moment of temporary insanity' when his mind was disturbed by grief. A pious Victorian monument was eventually erected in Norwood cemetery as a 'tasteful tribute to the genius and private worth of Laman Blanchard'.

Immediately after his death, literary colleagues rallied round to support his orphans. Bulwer, John Forster, and Harrison Ainsworth joined forces to get Blanchard's eldest child, Sidney, a job as secretary to Disraeli, although he then 'drifted away into London journalism'. The daughter, Lavinia, was found a place to study at the Royal Academy of Music and later married William Blanchard Jerrold, son of the journalist Douglas William Jerrold, Dickens's friend.

The death of a family man's beloved wife was an acceptable Victorian excuse for self-slaughter. Letitia's suicide in contrast was mired in a life shaming not just to herself but to all who had been complicit in it. By no stretch of the imagination could her motives be made to concord with the ideology of 'the angel in the house', even though she did not subject any of her children to a trauma comparable to that visited on Blanchard's youngest son, who saw him slit his throat.

In another, unrelated case, L.E.L.'s poetic idealizations of lovelorn female suicides, and the highly publicized reports of her death, may have prompted an act of copycat behaviour: that of the servant girl in Kentish Town who poisoned herself with a cocktail of prussic acid and laudanum in 1839, whose death was ruled by the coroner to be a clear-cut instance of self-destruction through love.

The victim, Elizabeth Abbott, was said by her employers to have been somewhat eccentric and 'fond of copying poetry'. What she read is not recorded, but it is highly likely that it included the work of L.E.L., the most popular female poet of the day, whose readership was by then slipping down the social classes as the annuals went mass-market, often through cheap pirated versions. Elizabeth Abbott's last note, found on the kitchen table, was a semiliterate verse epistle to the object of her unrequited passion, a James Roberts. It was a pathetic echo of the 'passionate songs of beating hearts' with which Letitia had made her name:

> It is not the blood of my body i do wish to wear
> But the heart of James Rogers i do wish to tear
> Hopeing he may never sleep or happy be
> Untill he comes & speaks his true sentiments to mee.

Letitia's death by prussic acid had been one of the major news stories of 1839. Was this the ultimate act of reader response?

Within the charmed circle of literary London, from which lower-class readers such as Elizabeth Abbott were excluded, the dead Letitia aroused guilt. A fund was set up to support her destitute mother, who rejected an offer of money from Maclean because she was afraid it would look as though she had been paid off. The subscribers included Letitia's onetime fiancé John Forster and his friend Charles Dickens. A leading role was played by Edward Bulwer, who told Blanchard shortly after Letitia's death, 'I have heard too much calumny to believe various stories, however plausible, relative to one whom calumny can torment no more; I never, indeed, would listen to them—true or false; . . . Even if partially true—what excuses! Friendless, alone, with that lively fancy; no mother, no guide, no protection. Who could be more exposed? Who should be more pitied?'

Lord Normanby also felt some duty to Letitia's memory. Her death had been one of the first problems he had had to deal with after taking over as colonial secretary in February 1839. Having been privately told by Bulwer that she had a history of attempting suicide, he had ignored

Whittington's letter and shrunk from making any public comment on the matter. He made amends by fixing up a governess job for Letitia's eldest daughter, Ella, with his family in Paris.

By the 1840s, census records show that Catherine Landon was living in poverty as the lodger of Thomas Carlyle's postman in Chelsea, together with Letitia's former governess Elizabeth Landon. Catherine wrote a series of pathetic letters to Bulwer dating into the 1850s, thanking him for his 'donations'. They open a window onto the humiliations of nineteenth-century charity, showing the onetime mistress of Trevor Park reduced to beggary, addressing her benefactor in mawkish tones of self-abnegation, larded with stilted religious clichés.

'Sweet indeed is the bread I partake of from your bounty,' she told Bulwer; 'how thankful I should be to hear you are well God bless Sir Edward, may the kindness you have shown to me and others be returned ten fold to yourself that my prayers are ever offered at the throne of mercy that God will give you comfort.' Her eagerly expressed concern for Bulwer's health makes it only too patent how afraid she was that he might die, leaving her without funds.

Catherine was by now in a genuinely destitute position, but her letters show her playing up to the role. Like the poetry of L.E.L., they are a performance. For street-corner *improvvisatori,* the line between busking and begging was thin. The only time when Catherine's voice relaxes at all is when Bulwer invites her to stay at his family seat, Knebworth, clearly a Potemkin offer as she was by then too old and infirm to travel. Suddenly, for a moment, the status-aware Mrs Landon experiences the illusion that she is being treated as an equal.

Despite his sister's efforts to procure it for him, Whittington resigned shortly after her death from the secretaryship of the Literary Fund, having been detected in petty embezzlement of around £10. It had turned out to be 'not worth having', an honorary post without a proper salary. However, he remained hopeful that he would find a more prestigious position.

A fortnight after he heard the news of Letitia's death, he began bombarding Lady Blessington with requests for patronage. His illustrious uncle, the provost of Worcester College, had died on December 29, 1838. Whittington imagined that with Lady Blessington's support, he would be a shoo-in as his successor. The failed curate was out of touch with reality. Lady Blessington wrote back that it was beyond her powers. But

Whittington continued to bother the countess with demands for the next couple of years.

Among Lady Blessington's papers, preserved today in the British Library, is a lock of L.E.L.'s hair. In an effort to cultivate her, Whittington must have handed over the last keepsake Letitia had entrusted to Mrs Bailey on the night before her death. A part of Letitia's physical body had become a currency of exchange, even though it did not in the end reap any career benefits for the brother who parted with it.

However, Whittington did succeed in marrying the Liddiards' daughter Anne, an outcome that would have pleased Letitia, who had always worried about his prospects. In 1840, Whittington began his married life in a fashionable villa in bohemian St John's Wood, presumably funded by his father-in-law. By the time of the 1851 census he had moved to Wales, as perpetual curate for the parish of Slebech, and was the father of three children. He appears to have remained dependent on his father-in-law, as he had once been dependent on Jerdan. Records show that in the 1850s 'John William Liddiard of Streatham' brought a suit in chancery against the lord of the manor of Slebech relating to the financing of the parish church and rectory.

Whittington named his eldest daughter Letitia. On his mother Catherine's death in 1856, he wrote to Bulwer, formally thanking him for supporting her, and apologizing for his own inability to do so. His tone was that of a pained but entitled gentleman.

Jerdan did not contribute to the fund set up to support Catherine Landon, although unpublished correspondence shows that Katherine Thomson wrote inviting him to do so. In her letter, Mrs Thomson explained that 'united contributions of several old friends of dear L.E.L.' made £85, but that her own contribution was not secure, as its value had declined from £30 to £15—which suggests that she herself was trying to extricate herself from the commitment. 'Any aid would therefore be acceptable,' she concluded.

Given Jerdan's own parlous financial situation by this point, he cannot have had much spare cash. The children he kept fathering by Mary Ann Maxwell were a drain on his resources. He did, however, succeed in making some small profit from the dead Letitia. On December 8, 1846, he received confirmation from Richard Bentley that the latter was willing to buy from him the copyrights of Letitia's novels *Romance and Reality*,

Francesca Carrara, and *Ethel Churchill* for a mere £25 apiece. Presumably the copyrights had reverted as the original editions had by then sold out, but there is no reason to suppose that Jerdan had the right to them. Legally they should have gone to her next of kin, but it may be that Jerdan had always been regarded informally if not formally as the copyright holder. The initial advances for her last novels had probably been earmarked from the start to pay off his debts to Colburn and to Bentley, their publishers, from whom Jerdan had separately borrowed.

In July 1862, the by then octogenarian Jerdan wrote to Bulwer, revealing how much the past was haunting him. L.E.L. and the world she represented had become ghostly memories:

> When the lamp is flickering out, there are shadowy intermittent periods during which the reflections of its early light and burning assume vivid hues from their nature imperceptible to the world. It is at such times that I am apt to recall the memory of friends who were near and dear to me—much in Communion—and of circumstances once so deeply interesting.

After his partner Mary Ann died in 1862, in the asylum at Maidstone, Jerdan lived on for another seven years, finally dying himself at the age of eighty-seven in 1869.

Mr and Mrs Hall, who had treated Letitia as their surrogate infant, remained childless. Throughout their long lives they continued to promote their own moral superiority and married bliss. In 1874 they sent out an invitation greeting their 'friends' on the occasion of their golden wedding. The card featured photographic portraits of themselves. Dr. and Mrs. Thomson also continued to keep up their place in society. Their grandson married Nancy Mitford.

After the collapse of their marriage, the Bulwers remained locked in a lifelong war of attrition. Rosina became ever more unstable, drinking all night, sleeping all day, and taking whatever opportunity she could to embarrass her estranged husband, who responded with equal vitriol. He tried to have her committed to a lunatic asylum. She wrote an autobiography called *A Blighted Life*. Having switched sides to the Tories, Bulwer succeeded in becoming a cabinet minister and continued to write novels. Neither he nor Rosina showed any interest in their two children.

Their daughter died young of tuberculosis in lodgings. However, their son managed to shake off his childhood and grew up to become viceroy of India.

John Forster never said anything in public about his embarrassing youthful engagement to L.E.L. He became Bulwer's factotum, supporting him in his battle against Rosina. In 1856, he married Eliza, the widow of the shadowy Henry Colburn, who had left an estate valued at around £35,000. Thereupon, he reputedly became 'an exacting husband, a despot in his own house'.

In 1840, two years after Letitia died, Lady Blessington expressed concern that no monument had been erected to her. Writing to Richard Madden on the eve of his departure for his inspection tour of Cape Coast, she confessed that she 'entertained such a deep affection for her' that she was prepared to defray the expense herself for any such memorial.

When, shortly after arriving, Madden duly brought up the issue, Maclean told him that he had in fact already commissioned a handsome marble tablet from England, but had not yet got around to putting it up. It was an index of the widower's ambivalence to have ordered a memorial stone but kept it in storage. In February 1841, during Madden's visit, the plaque was finally set up on a wall near Letitia's grave on the parade ground of Cape Coast Castle. The inscription commissioned by Maclean was composed in formal Latin. It ended:

> *Quod spectas, viator, marmor,*
> *Vanum heu doloris monumentum*
> *Conjux moerens erexit.*

> *(What you see, traveller, is a marble,*
> *Vain, alas, a monument of pain,*
> *Erected by her doleful spouse.)*

Even on her gravestone, Letitia was defined by the eye of the beholder.

George Maclean remained governor of Cape Coast Castle until 1843. That year, in a typical official fudge, the British government simultaneously 'exonerated and demoted' him: he was absolved of corruption but relieved of his post. In an atmosphere of controversy, it was decided that the only course was to take the Cape Coast settlements under direct central government control. The British imperial project in West Africa thus began. Soon after the new governor, Henry Hill, took up his post in 1844, complaints were made that he had alienated the tribal chiefs and was at loggerheads with the merchants. He had perhaps underestimated the political challenge of the post. Maclean stayed on in the region, but lived only another two years, dying at the age of forty-six in May 1847. He was buried beside Letitia on the parade ground.

Matthew Forster lived on until 1869. His subsequent career, during which he switched from the Tories to the new Liberal party, was not without incident. In 1857 he was deselected as MP for Berwick on being found 'guilty of bribery' after conspicuously offering sweeteners to voters in his constituency.

More embarrassing was a petty episode which reveals that he was just as capable as Jerdan of effrontery. Travelling to or from his office on the omnibus, he was caught fare-dodging between City Road and Broad Street. As a result he was taken to court and forced to pay not just the fare, but three shillings costs and four shillings to the conductor for loss of time. As a man who at his death left £120,000 in his will, this escapade could hardly have been prompted by necessity. There is perhaps some poetic justice in the fact that in 1852 his butler at Belsize Villa was jailed for stealing silver worth between £200 and £300.

The two Ashanti princes, whom Maclean had brought to London in 1836, were shown 'the moral beauty of England' by their clergyman guide. After several years of being tutored, they finally returned to West Africa in 1841 with a pension of £100 apiece, on the understanding that they would promote British values. One of the men, Kwantabisa, was soon detected in adultery with a tribal chief's wife. As in England, the penalty was worse for the woman. Kwantabisa was spared, but the chief's wife was put to death.

CHAPTER 15

Hauntings

The Victorians wanted to forget L.E.L., and yet she haunted them. She was the scapegoat whom the literary profession had had to eject in order to recast itself in a more respectable mode. An entire culture had been complicit in her rise and fall.

After her death, her memory was hard to process, not simply because her true story could not openly be told, but because she herself had been so ambiguous, both as a poet and as a person. The friends who took on the management of her posthumous image were of course keen to suppress the scandal about her affair with Jerdan and her self-induced death—to protect their own reputations as much as hers. But they were also unable to let her go because she had been so slippery in life that they had never been able to grasp her fully. She remained unfinished business, her history open-ended. There could be no closure.

The least restrained of Letitia's many memoirists was William Jerdan himself. His brief memoir, written for the 1848 reissue of *Romance and Reality*, offered some new tidbits about Letitia's family and also some previously unpublished poetic fragments, dating from the very early days of L.E.L., written in the voice of a lovesick girl bewailing the fact that her 'ruin'd wall / Lies worn and rent.' The lines, in his view, were worthy to be placed by those of Eloise to Abelard. They had, he coyly revealed, been inspired by a real-life 'flirtation'. He went on to explain that the 'feelings conjured up in the composition, compared with those inspired by the occasion, were as death from spontaneous combustion, instead of a casual burn from a particle of hot sealing-wax'. Perhaps even the narcissistic Jerdan never believed that Letitia had fallen passionately in love with him when she first traded her body for career advancement.

Jerdan's autobiography, published in the 1850s, was yet more indiscreet, boasting of Letitia's Sapphic warmth, and claiming that he was the only begetter who had inspired all her delicious verses. When it came out, reviewers recoiled from directly engaging with the sections on L.E.L. They were clearly embarrassed by Jerdan's shamelessness, and wanted to draw a Victorian veil over the literary industry's sleazy past.

Yet the rumours continued to arouse fascination, especially among those at the fringes of British literary gossip, keen to enter its penetralium. When posted to Liverpool as American consul in the 1850s, Nathaniel Hawthorne was intrigued to meet Jerdan. The author of *The Scarlet Letter* was unable to 'see how such a man . . . attained a vogue in society, as he certainly did,' but he was fascinated by sexual secrets. Hawthorne salaciously cross-examined Jerdan's neighbour, Francis Bennoch, as to whether there was 'any truth in the scandalous rumours in reference to Jerdan and L.E.L'. Bennoch replied that he thought there had been 'great looseness of behaviour,' but that it had 'fallen short of the one ultimate result', saying that he had been assured by Jerdan 'on his honour' that 'L.E.L. had never yielded her virtue to him'. However, it is also on record that Bennoch knew about Fred Stuart, Jerdan's son by Letitia, and probably about the other children too. Bennoch was teasing Hawthorne, just as L.E.L. had once teased her readers.

It was not only in nonfiction memoirs—including those by Blanchard, the Halls, Katherine Thomson, Grantley Berkeley, and A. F. Chorley—that Letitia lived on. Her self-fictionalizing tendencies proved contagious. In 1857, Anna Maria Hall's novel *A Woman's Story* transformed L.E.L. into the mysterious poet H.L., filling the tale with personal details about Letitia's family background, but making the heroine sexually pure, targeted by a blackmailer over her own illegitimacy, not over having illegitimate children.

Anna Maria's fictional take was personally motivated, but L.E.L. had so long existed 'in others' breath' that her image continued to replicate at the hands of writers who had had little or no contact with her. In 1847, for example, George Eliot's future lover G. H. Lewes created an unsympathetic portrait of a poetess with distinct echoes of L.E.L. in his novel *Rose, Blanche and Violet* (the title was taken from George Sand's *Rose et Blanche*). Lewes was probably too young to have met Letitia personally, since he was born in 1817, but their paths could conceivably have crossed before she left London in 1838, as he began his ascent of the literary greasy pole while still in his teens. However, he later became intimate with both Daniel Maclise and John Forster, who would have been able to tell him much about her in private. As Isaiah Berlin once reputedly remarked, a 'secret' is something you tell to one person at a time.

Lewes's early novels embrace the theme of the writer's career in the uncertain world of the literary marketplace, following in the footsteps of L.E.L.'s *Ethel Churchill* and Balzac's *Lost Illusions*. He was so fascinated by Letitia as an emblem of the literary trade that in his first novel, *Ranthorpe* (1847), he made the hero, an aspirant poet, live in lodgings in Hans Place. *Rose, Blanche and Violet*, his next novel, was published in 1848. However, its action begins in 1835. It was an attempt by the young Lewes to show his in-crowd credentials by revealing his cognizance of the seamy side of 1830s literary London.

Like Letitia's, the career of Lewes's fictional poetess Hester Mason is kick-started when she becomes the mistress of an older married man. She 'falls with her eyes open'. Like Letitia, she writes with a 'fatal facility', and her poetry is 'daring and extravagant'. 'Doesn't it strike you as wery stwange,' says a character with a Dickensian speech impediment, 'that a young woman should wite in such twemendous misery? Nothing but seductions, delusions, bwroken hearts, pwoswrated spirits, agonies of wemorse, tewible pwedictions, wetched weveries, and all that sort of thing!'

Hester announces herself as a disciple of Wollstonecraftian free love, as, frustrated by her ageing protector, she attempts to engage the sympathies of a young male writer. She flips open her negligee to reveal her magnificent bust, but he makes his excuses and leaves. Her work does not sell as well as she hopes. She is plagued by the difficulty of finding ladies willing to attend her London salons. She ends up a streetwalker on Piccadilly Circus, a crude metaphor by Lewes for the prostitution of talent.

When G. H. Lewes met Charlotte Brontë in London in 1850 at a lunch given by the publisher George Smith, he enraged her by intimating that they had something in common, as they had both written so-called naughty books. His was *Rose, Blanche and Violet;* hers was *Jane Eyre*. Given that Lewes's novel contained a portrait of an ambitious woman writer who comes to London from the provinces only to become a prostitute, it is hardly surprising that the nervous, though best-selling, Yorkshirewoman was displeased.

Charlotte had read *Rose, Blanche and Violet* not long after it came out. She had been particularly struck by the character of Hester. 'He gives no charming picture of London Literary Society, and especially the female part of it,' she wrote to William Smith Williams, her publisher's assistant, who supplied her with a steady stream of the latest books. When Williams hinted that Hester's tawdry story was based on a real-life model, Charlotte told him, 'I never for a moment doubted the whole dreary picture was from the life.' It is hard to tell whether or not she explicitly connected Hester Mason's story with that of L.E.L., the poetess whose work had inspired her in her youth, and about whom *Fraser's* had made so many ribald remarks. But reading Lewes's novel certainly increased her awareness of the opprobrium attached to women who wrote about passion in a confessional female voice, as she herself had done in *Jane Eyre,* which she had published under the pseudonym Currer Bell because she believed that critics were prejudiced against women writers.

Despite being a runaway success, *Jane Eyre* was a controversial book in its day. The male nom de plume fooled no one, because of the intensity of its first-person female voice. Its tortured romantic plot and, especially, the abrasive passion of the heroine led to it being attacked by critics as unfeminine, coarse and immoral.

When Charlotte finally made her identity known and visited London as an acknowledged author, she found herself constantly at the mercy of male mockery, and not just that of Lewes. The Fraserian Thackeray thrust a phallic cigar in her face and asked her insinuatingly whether she knew its significance. He treated the Yorkshire parson's daughter to the sort of banter that had not long before been L.E.L.'s daily diet. An embarrassed Charlotte put up the shutters.

London critics did not, as was once assumed, turn on *Jane Eyre* because it was unheard-of for a woman to write about love in the first person, but rather because it was an only too well-trodden path that had ultimately led Letitia Landon to Cape Coast. They read the original title *Jane Eyre: An Autobiography* (the subtitle was chosen not by Charlotte but by her publisher) as a calculated 'puff mysterious', assimilating it into the scandalous tradition of publicity-hungry semi-confession that L.E.L. had embodied. In fact, Charlotte and her sisters adopted pseudonyms because they sincerely wanted to walk invisible, as Charlotte put it. However, as provincials they were out of touch with metropolitan literary culture and did not fully appreciate how discredited the discourse of female Byronism had become in London by the late 1840s.

Jane Eyre, first published in 1847, bears the imprint of L.E.L. in its first-person confessional voice, in its gothic extremes, in its love triangle plot, and in its emphasis on sadomasochistic romantic passion. What it does not share is L.E.L.'s fatalistic pessimism, mannered narcissism, and self-irony. In contrast, it is about as authentic as literature ever gets. As such, it resists as much as it draws on the model offered by L.E.L. Jane refuses to become Rochester's mistress and consistently stands up for herself. She becomes a character with an inner life and moral integrity, qualities alien to L.E.L.'s play of masquerade.

Charlotte Brontë's use of the confessional first person, and her choice of love as her prime subject, did not endear her to her fellow women writers, who were striving to detach themselves from the image of female genius promulgated by L.E.L. The hyperrational Harriet Martineau—who had been portrayed by *Fraser's* as a witch, and who had gone on to express concern over Letitia's depressed demeanour shortly before the latter left for Cape Coast—wrote Charlotte a stiff letter after she published her searingly confessional novel *Villette* in 1853. Although Martineau did not know the details, the novel was indeed based on Charlotte's real-life unrequited passion for her mentor Constantin Heger, who had taught her in Brussels in the early 1840s. Martineau objected to its focus on frustrated female desire, and feared that Brontë was not only exposing herself but giving women writers per se a bad name.

Amazingly, the scandals surrounding L.E.L. were sufficiently suppressed outside the in-crowd that she remained an aspirational figure for young women writers into the 1840s. In 1847, the same year as *Jane Eyre* appeared, L.E.L. was frequently name-checked in admiring tones by a naïve first-time novelist, Rose Ellen Hendricks, in *The Young Authoress*. Hendricks's unsophisticated and deservedly forgotten novel projects a starry-eyed vision. It promotes the unrealistic notion that literary fame will set a woman on the path to true love and eventually reward her with a perfect marriage.

Charlotte Brontë was both more talented and more conflicted than Rose Hendricks. The daughter of an Irish Tory, she had been schooled in her youth by *Blackwood's* and *Fraser's,* imbibing their misogyny from an early age, yet wanting to assert herself in writing like the female authors of the annuals. At twenty, Brontë wrote to the poet laureate Robert Southey, confessing her desire to be 'for ever known' as a poetess. Southey acknowledged her talent, but counselled her against putting too much value on 'celebrity' in a letter that has often been read over-reductively as an act of simple male sabotage. As his comments on Lucretia Davidson show, Southey was genuinely concerned about the way in which the dominant culture schooled ambitious girl writers into a desperate need for external approval that could eat away at their self-esteem. In the long run, Southey's warnings enabled Charlotte to make art out of her conflicted position as a female outsider.

However, the first-person voice she created in *Jane Eyre* and *Villette* did not become the norm among Victorian women writers. It was too dangerous. Katherine Thomson's stepniece Elizabeth Gaskell, who published under her respectable married title 'Mrs Gaskell', eschewed it in her philanthropic, social conscience, third-person fiction. Mary Anne Evans, a.k.a. George Eliot, also adopted a third-person aesthetic. As she was privately living in sin with G. H. Lewes by the time she began publishing fiction, she could only assert her moral authority by publishing her novels under a male pseudonym. Her masterpiece *The Mill on the Floss,* based on her childhood memories, suggests that she would have been an astonishing first-person confessional writer. But she knew that a third-person perspective was essential if she was to achieve her goal of being accepted alongside men as a serious author. Following the scandalous death of L.E.L., the female 'I' became unpalatable.

By making L.E.L. the loathsome Rosamond Vincy's favourite writer, Eliot detached herself from the literary culture in which she herself had in fact first made her way. Her early career as Marian Evans was not in reality that dissimilar to that of Letitia Landon. Indeed, she narrowly avoided a similar fate when she came to London from the provinces in 1850, long before she began to publish as 'George Eliot'.

On arriving in the metropolis, she ensconced herself in the household of the publisher John Chapman, located in the Strand, not far from the offices of the *Literary Gazette*. A Jerdan-like figure, he already had both a wife and a mistress on site. Nevertheless, he went on to seduce the young Marian, to the annoyance of both the other women in his life, a fact that only surfaced after Chapman's private diaries turned up in a bookstall in the twentieth century.

Luckily for Marian, she did not become pregnant. Chapman moreover did not think her pretty enough for it to be worth his while to continue pursuing her, given the reaction of his wife and mistress, who joined forces to eject the newcomer. But Chapman was so convinced of

George Eliot, aged thirty-nine in 1858.
As a young woman in her twenties
she had been in the thrall of the
editor John Chapman, a Jerdan-like
figure. She went on to express her
disapproval of L.E.L. in *Middlemarch*
(1871–72).

Marian's intellectual value that he persuaded her to come back to act as de facto editor of the *Westminster Review*, which he had recently acquired. She agreed to do so, gratis. Like L.E.L., she began her career as the unpaid intern of a libertine editor who was her inferior in talent.

In G. H. Lewes, Marian subsequently found a male muse who was prepared to subordinate himself to her career, although they could not marry, as he and his wife were not able to divorce under the restrictive laws of the time, since he was held to have condoned his wife's adultery with Leigh Hunt's son. Sexual bohemianism continued in literary London into the Victorian age but under discreeter rules. Unlike Letitia, George Eliot kept herself offstage and under wraps.

Nevertheless, female poets continued to regard L.E.L. as a necessary touchstone into the Victorian age. Elizabeth Barrett (later Browning), the one scion of the 'poetess' tradition who remains a famous name today, acknowledged L.E.L.'s influence. Although she was only four years younger than Letitia, her talent was comparatively slow-burning; she only came to public prominence in her thirties with the publication of her *Poems* in 1844. Yet she had followed L.E.L.'s work since the

1820s. Stuck in her invalid's retreat in Wimpole Street, she seized on whatever gossip came her way via visitors such as Mary Russell Mitford and L.E.L.'s onetime enemy H. F. Chorley.

Distressed by the news of Letitia's death, Miss Barrett instantly wrote a tribute, 'L.E.L.'s Last Question', which Chorley published in *The Athenaeum*. Inspired by the latter's shipboard poem, with its equivocal refrain to her absent 'friends' ('do you think of me as I think of you?'), it portrayed L.E.L. as an incarnation of loneliness despite her fame, a woman for whom sympathy came too late, whose poetic obsession with 'love' was a cruel irony, and whose 'inward oracle' should have been God:

> *Hers was the hand that played for many a year*
> *Love's silver phrase for England,—smooth and well!*
> *Would God, her heart's more inward oracle*
> *In that lone moment, might confirm her dear!*
> *For when her questioned friends in agony*
> *Made passionate response,—'We think of thee'—*
> *Her place was in the dust, too deep to hear.*

'I fancy it would have worked out better—had it been worked out—with the right moral & intellectual influences in application,' wrote Elizabeth Barrett in the wake of L.E.L.'s death. Barrett acknowledged her '*raw* bare powers', but she failed to register the extent to which L.E.L. was a knowing chronicler of her own complicity.

L.E.L. later became the inspiration behind Barrett's verse novel *Aurora Leigh,* published in 1857, 'an autobiography of a poetess—(not me)'. Like L.E.L.'s Improvisatrice, her heroine Aurora is from Florence, although of English parentage and living in the present day. Filled with idealistic literary ambition and a spirit of independence, she rejects an offer of marriage from her rich cousin Romney and instead goes to London to live alone and make her living by her pen. There she occupies an attic like Letitia's at Hans Place, and finds a commercial readership for her romantic verses. Yet she becomes hollowed out by the demands of the marketplace, as she turns out poem after poem to feed the superficial demands of publishers.

Romney meanwhile becomes a fervent evangelical, devoting himself to Bible study and social work. He rescues a working-class prostitute, Marian Erle, whom he plans to marry in an act of Christian charity. In

Aurora and Marian, Barrett splits off the two sides of Letitia into separate characters: the professional authoress and the sexually exploited woman. In the end, Marian selflessly sets Romney free from their engagement so that he can marry Aurora. On marriage, the latter stops writing to please the market, and instead devotes herself to becoming a 'true' poet whose work will explore serious matters of spirituality. She thus becomes a real Victorian and redeems the figure of the poetess from the sleazy past of L.E.L.

The irony is that the only way Barrett can make that happen is by removing Aurora's need to make a living. Romney's wealth enables her to sidestep the cash nexus in her quest to write meaningful poetry. In this, she presages the view of Virginia Woolf, who asserted that a woman must have not just a room of her own, but money of her own, in order to write fiction.

Another poetess, Emily Brontë, who was sixteen years Letitia's junior, cut herself idealistically off from the world. Never making a penny from her writing in her lifetime, she lived as a recluse in Haworth, supported by her family, only venturing out when forced. She summed up her attitude in her now famous poem 'The Old Stoic', first published in 1846:

> *Riches I hold in light esteem*
> *And Love I laugh to scorn*
> *And lust of Fame was but a dream*
> *That vanished in the morn—*
>
> *And if I pray, the only prayer*
> *That moves my lips for me*
> *Is—'Leave the heart that now I bear*
> *And give me liberty.'*

Riches, Love, and Fame—money, sex, and celebrity—had been the leitmotifs of Letitia Landon's career. The reclusive Emily, in contrast, only agreed to publication, under a pseudonym and at her family's own expense, after days of pressure from her more ambitious sister Charlotte.

L.E.L. continued to haunt the imaginations of women writers into the 1860s, even though by then the plates for *The Improvisatrice* had been melted down. Christina Rossetti—whose father, Gabriele, gave popular lectures on Italian literary culture in London the 1820s, and whose artist

Christina Rossetti, drawn by her brother
Dante Gabriel Rossetti in 1866. In her
poem on L.E.L., she imagined her as an
outcast.

brother Dante Gabriel later praised Maclise's hyperfeminized portrait of
L.E.L.—imagined Letitia as an outcast, 'whose heart was breaking for a
little love'. Rossetti's poem 'L.E.L.' is an act of religious wish fulfilment.
Letitia had been a Shelleyan atheist in her youth, but Christina Rossetti
imagines her finding peace and trust in Christian faith and with God.
The full implications only come to the surface in context. Christina, who
worked in a refuge home for former prostitutes, is imaging Landon as a
fallen woman:

> *Yet saith a saint: 'Take patience for thy scythe';*
> *Yet saith an angel: 'Wait, for thou shalt prove*
> *Time best is last, true life is born of death.*
> *O thou, heart-broken for a little love!*
> *Then love shall fill thy girth,*
> *And love makes fat thy dearth,*
> *When new spring builds new heaven and clean new earth.'*

Soon after writing 'L.E.L.,' Christina Rossetti composed her more famous poem 'Goblin Market,' whose sexualized imagery of flowers, fruits, and their juices were surely employed with less blind unconsciousness than some modern critics have assumed. They harked back to the young L.E.L.'s use of Della Cruscan erotic symbolism. However, Rossetti redeployed the technique in the service of a moral fable exposing the dangers of narcissism and self-indulgence.

In contrast, among male writers, L.E.L.'s Della Cruscan influence worked its way through early Tennyson to the more deviant Swinburne, who in his private life sought sexual excitement through pain. Obsessed with flogging, he constructed a sensual poetic universe in which sound trumped sense, and sadomasochism was represented via floral imagery, the 'raptures and roses of vice', as he put it in his hymn to Dolores, the lady of pain. An echo of 'Letitia Landon' might just be detectable in the title of his posthumously published pornographic novel *Lesbia Brandon,* although the heroine's interests are more Sapphic in the modern sense.

In the later nineteenth century, L.E.L.'s post–Della Cruscan sensibility most notably survived in the writings of underground gay poets, who used her buzzword 'shame' as a code word for the 'love that dare not speak its name' and were equally addicted to floral euphemisms, although they tended to prefer the symbolism of hyacinths and narcissi to that of rosebuds and lilies. Their shadowy position in society was similar to Letitia's as a semi-acknowledged fallen woman. Her subversive performativity, which exposed sexual identity as built on artifice, became grist to their mill.

Oscar Wilde's quip that sentimentality was the bank holiday of cynicism could have been designed to describe Letitia's mind-set. It sums up her double-faced persona as much as it reflects the two sides of Wilde, seen in the contrast between the glittering wit of his plays and the mawkish emotionalism of his fairy tales, such as 'The Nightingale and the Rose', in which the songbird self-impales on a thorn. When he organized a posse of camp young men to turn up to one of his premieres sporting mysterious green carnations in their buttonholes in 1892, he was playing the same game that Letitia had played over half a century before when she crowned Jerdan at a party with a floral wreath. Wilde's act of puffery increased the ambiguous aura of scandal around his name, inspiring a semisatirical novel, *The Green Carnation,* published by Robert Hitchens in 1894, the year before Wilde's trial.

L.E.L.'s rise and fall prefigures that of Wilde. Both walked a dangerous line between fame and shame, monetizing their literary notoriety to support their downwardly mobile families, while pursuing renegade private lives. As an Irish cultural adventurer making his name on the mainland, Wilde was a descendant of Thomas Moore, William Maginn, Lady Blessington, Daniel Maclise, Samuel Carter Hall, Anna Maria Hall and Rosina Bulwer. Even the Brontës fit the mould as their father was a displaced Irish Protestant. Letitia's identification with so many Irish émigrés—and her probable Irish heritage via the Fagans—points to her own marginal position in society.

During the second half of the nineteenth century, selections from L.E.L.'s less daring later poetry continued to be reissued sporadically. As cultural memories of her scandalous personal reputation receded, helped by the biographical cover-up, her sentimentalism was increasingly taken at face value. It is ironic that Bloomsbury regarded L.E.L. as an insipid virgin, since the real Letitia Landon lived in a literary subculture that was, at least in its sexual habits, quite as 'modern'. What Landon and her fellow literary hustlers of the 1820s lacked was the sense of entitlement and financial security enjoyed by Virginia Woolf and her circle in the 1920s, who could flout the establishment because they belonged to it.

Bloomsbury's modernist urge to blow apart bourgeois values was a reaction against Victorian complacency. But the Victorian values they perceived as so stultifying had themselves been a reaction against the fragmentation and free-for-all of the pre-Victorian decades. Those who promoted the new moralistic ideology, including Charles Dickens, had often experienced the insecurity of the previous era at first hand.

The Victorians not only idealized the family but created a professional caste as a bulwark against the Darwinian free-for-all. The sea green incorruptibility of Virginia Woolf's grandfather Sir James Stephen, the Colonial Office lawyer in the 1830s, became the standard in the new civil service bureaucracy, designed to combat the culture of 'interest'. His literary son, Leslie Stephen, helped transform the world of publishing into a new establishment when he initiated the *Dictionary of National Biography* in 1882, designed to reflect British cultural confidence in the era of empire.

As general editor, Leslie Stephen presided over the entry on Letitia Elizabeth Landon. It obscurely referred to a 'cruel scandal . . . destitute . . . of the least foundation', without ever detailing its content, while dismissing her work entirely, concluding that 'as a poetess . . . she had too little culture . . . to produce anything of great value.' The sole interest of her career was situated in its snuffing out, but its circumstances remained shrouded: 'No circumstance respecting L.E.L. has occasioned so much discussion as her sudden and mysterious death.'

Letitia's memoirists did a good job. By the twentieth century, her sexual history had completely slipped from sight. The problem was that any understanding of her literary sophistication went with it. In her entrapped, silenced, yet paradoxically public space, she had in fact developed an uncanny voice in which to chronicle and expose the post-truth culture of her day. She defined the contours of her age, yet had no faith that her work would outlive her. Despite its fantasy vistas of medieval minstrels and ancient Greek poetesses, her art was so embedded in its time that it embodied modernity in Baudelaire's sense of 'the transitory, the fleeting, the contingent'.

Vestiges of L.E.L.'s type—women on the edge, who accept their fate but attempt to cheat it—continued to echo at a remove through fiction during the Victorian age, at a time when Letitia's own voice was increasingly silenced. In narratives where issues of illegitimacy, class and gender were at stake, the theatre proved a staying metaphor for the masquerade of social identity. Shorn of the certainties of her respectable upbringing, the pointedly named Magdalen in Wilkie Collins's *No Name* (1862) takes to the stage in her quest to reestablish her birthright. The eponymous heroine of Thomas Hardy's *The Hand of Ethelberta* (1876), who has to conceal her lower-class family connections, performs in public as a poet and storyteller, an English *improvvisatrice* in the L.E.L. mould.

Down on her luck on the Suffolk coast, and afraid that her machinations have come to naught, Collins's Magdalen contemplates suicide. Gazing through the window out to sea, a bottle of laudanum in her hand, she tells herself that she will only drain the contents—and die—if a certain number of ships pass before her eyes in a specified space of time. Collins explicitly depicts Magdalen as a fatalist, no believer in Christian providence, a character whose intense drive coexists with a gambler's worldview that abdicates free will to chance. Luckily for Magdalen, the right number of ships pass by and she ultimately prospers, as does Hardy's Ethelberta. Both fictional women successfully manipulate every situation to their advantage. It's tempting to imagine Letitia playing a similar game of Russian roulette with the prussic acid bottle, looking out to sea at Cape Coast Castle. Just before she left England, she discussed her belief in fatalism with the Liddiards. But by the end of her life she was on a losing streak.

At every stage, she was a casualty not just of her personal circumstances but of her historical moment. The dying of Romanticism, the political repression of the post-Waterloo era, market forces, a press licensed to bully, the rise of moral hypocrisy, the coming of Victorian values, and the corrupt world of the illegal slave trade were as implicated in her tragedy as her father's bankruptcy, Jerdan's predation, and her dodgy doctor. It is as well to remember that Magdalen in Wilkie Collins's *No Name* is a figment of the male imagination, allowed to be alluringly gutsy and triumphant because she exists only in a book. In real life, Collins chose two poor, semi-literate women to be his concurrent mistresses, keeping them in such secrecy that their voices are completely lost to history.

In contrast, Letitia was a public figure with a voice, though that voice was compromised by her situation. She responded to her own embattled position, in a society in which the truth could not be told, by dissociating. Her larger-than-life tragic heroines were surrogates to shield her from the pain of 'feelings (if I have any)', as was her persona as a society wit. With her interior life under constant siege from external pressures, she used her brilliant mind to develop ambiguity and masquerade as a literary means of rattling her cage bars and obliquely offering a devastating commentary on her own situation and society. She became the most acute witness to the 'strange pause' of the 1820s and 1830s that we have. In the classical myth, Philomel became a bird whose song was fated to be forever misunderstood. Only now can Letitia Landon's voice be truly heard.

On October 10, 2017, I visited Cape Coast Castle. Letitia died on October 15, 1838, so it was the same time of year. On the day she died, storm clouds hovered, bursting into a downpour during her burial. The day I visit is, in contrast, sunny and clear, very hot. Uninterrupted blue sky merges with the calm ocean. The castle, its white walls coated in plaster and paint, indeed appears a 'fine building'. Only when the guide takes us into the slave dungeons below ground level is its traumatic history made visible.

In none of her letters home does Letitia mention the dungeons or the castle's history as a slave fort. The perpetual swoosh of the ocean waves—

pleasant enough for the hour or two I spend there, but inescapable—seems to echo the constant low-level interference of the suppressed. Letitia lived her entire adult life with the stress of the unspoken: 'none among us dares to say / What none will choose to hear.'

The room in which Letitia died is now an office, divided by a panel. Two men are looking at spreadsheets while an electric fan whirs. One green shutter is closed. Through the window you can see the edge of the castle batteries, bristling with cannon, and above them nothing but ocean and sky.

Acknowledgements

Before I got sucked in, I initially chose to work on Letitia Landon because I thought she might be relatively quick to dispatch, being a 'minor' subject. Making sense of her life and work turned out to be much harder than I anticipated. The fact that her first biographer slit his throat in 1845 was hardly a consoling thought during the nine years I spent entangled, on and off, in the project.

Although I often felt alone in L.E.L.'s hall of mirrors, I was, however, lucky enough to be able to draw on the materials collected by other researchers, especially F. J. Sypher, who has shown such dogged commitment to L.E.L. studies over many years. William Jerdan's biographer Susan Matoff was delightfully supportive when I met her just as I was finishing this book, and her research has proved invaluable.

Cynthia Lawford deserves recognition for publishing the first discovery relating to Letitia's children in the *London Review of Books*. However, the truth about L.E.L.'s hidden life would never have come to light were it not for Michael Gorman's interest in his own family's history; thank you to him for his spirited telephone conversations and email correspondence, and for allowing me to reproduce the photograph of Ella.

David and Tina Burgess offered me kindness and hospitality in Cornwall, where they let me see Maria Liddiard's diary, along with other unpublished materials connected with L.E.L. Veronica Maclean also provided warm hospitality at her home in Scotland.

Frances Wilson generously encouraged me at a very early stage, while Adam Gopnik, Simone Ling and John Barnard were amazingly kind to give up their time to read and comment on embryonic drafts or sections, as did William St Clair. Later on, Philippa Brewster's close reading of the manuscript was invaluable.

I am hugely grateful to Hermione Lee, who invited me to speak on L.E.L. at Wolfson College, Oxford, home of the Oxford Centre for Life-Writing. As a visiting scholar there, I enjoyed many fruitful discussions with fellow biographers. In Oxford, Helen Barr, Alan Rusbridger, and Lindsay Mackie also offered me succour at Lady Margaret Hall, at a time when (to my chagrin and embarrassment) I was not in the best shape to make the most of it.

Private conversations with many others—including Lyndall Gordon, Germaine Greer, Fiona MacCarthy and Claire Tomalin—had more of an effect on my ability to keep going than they probably realize. Thank you also to the Brontë Society, which invited me to give its annual lecture in 2014, and was gracious enough to put up with me talking about L.E.L. instead; to Diane Long Hoeveler and Deborah Denenholz Morse, who let me digress on L.E.L. in the Blackwell *Companion to the Brontës;* to Tamsin Shaw for generously inviting me to talk about my work in progress at NYU; to Gregory Dart, who allowed me to try out some of my ideas (equally digressive) at the 2015 Hazlitt conference at University College London; and to Caroline Pegum for inviting me to speak on L.E.L.'s visual image at the 2017 Understanding British Portraits conference at the National Portrait Gallery.

Jonathan Bate and Paula Byrne were welcoming at Worcester College, Oxford, where Letitia Landon's uncle was his predecessor as provost. John Styles and Marika Sherwood shared their erudition. For invaluable conversations, connections, and permissions relating to Letitia's portraits, I am indebted to Juliet Carey, David Ekserdjian, David Bindman, Tim and Jonathan Benthall, Ned Campbell, David Moore-Gwyn of Sotheby's and Anthony Greenwood. The skill and professionalism of picture editor Cecilia Mackay were invaluable.

The staff of the British Library, British Museum Print Room, London Library, Bodleian Library, New York Public Library, Hertfordshire Archives, Witt Library at the Courtauld Institute of Art, Heinz Archive at the National Portrait Gallery, and Harry Ransom Center at the University of Texas at Austin were unfailingly helpful. In Ghana, Mirwen Safi, who took me to Cape Coast Castle and showed me Accra, was the best of guides. Especial thanks to him, and to Alberto for his eloquence. Also to Anthony Appiah and to Isobel Appiah-Endresen for putting me in touch with them.

I suffer from the opposite of L.E.L.'s fatal facility. It's a very long time since I published a book, but I don't think I would have found a voice for this one without Lisa Allardice, who was a wonderfully enabling editor when I was writing profiles and literary commentary pieces for the *Guardian,* what now seems an age ago.

Those who selflessly endured listening to my endless, Ancient Mariner–style monologues on L.E.L. include both family and friends. Thank you to Lisa Miller, Charles Miller and Caroline McGinn, Mark Bostridge, Alexander Miller, the late Hugo Herbert-Jones, Kate and Benji Meuli, and Veronica Henty (with her book group); and also to Richard Sennett, John Mullan and Harriet Stewart, Natasha Lehrer, Sarah Christie-Brown, Emily Campbell, Lucy Morgan, Matt and Martha Hancock, Gus Gazzard and Tamara Oppenheimer, Jane Darcy, and Christopher Gayford. Working with Natasha Walter and the community at Women for Refugee Women kept me sane, with an especial mention for Monica Aidoo.

I owe a large debt of thanks to my publishers, Dan Franklin at Jonathan Cape and Victoria Wilson at Knopf, who kept faith with me for years, and to my agent Georgina Capel, who continued to believe in me long after I had ceased to do so. Thanks also to Marc Jaffee and Ryan Ouimet, and to Roland Ottewell.

My immediate family has been tolerant beyond the call of duty during my many mental absences due to L.E.L. I cannot thank my husband, Ian, or our beloved children, Oliver and Ottilie, enough.

Notes

ABBREVIATIONS

AWJ *The Autobiography of William Jerdan.* 4 vols. London: Arthur
　　Virtue and Co., 1852–53.

BL　British Library

CO　Colonial Office

DNB *Dictionary of National Biography*

Letters *Letters by Letitia Elizabeth Landon.* Ed. F. J. Sypher. Ann Arbor,
　　MI: Scholars Facsimiles and Reprints, 2001.

LG *The Literary Gazette*

LLR Samuel Laman Blanchard. *The Life and Literary Remains of L.E.L.*
　　2 vols. London: Henry Colburn, 1841.

NPG　National Portrait Gallery

PLG *Poems from the Literary Gazette by Letitia Elizabeth Landon.* Ed.
　　F. J. Sypher. Ann Arbor, MI: Scholars Facsimiles and Reprints,
　　2001.

TNA　The National Archives

I have used first editions of L.E.L.'s works.

PREFACE

xii 'did in truth resemble': S[arah] S[heppard], *Characteristics of the Genius
　　and Writings of L.E.L.,* p. 160.

xii 'female Byron': Rowton, *The Female Poets of Great Britain,* p. 425.

xii 'Sappho of a polished age': J. A. Heraud, quoted in Madden, *The Literary
　　Life and Correspondence of the Countess of Blessington,* vol. 2, p. 268.

xii 'Landon, or L.E.L.': Montgomery, *The Age Reviewed,* p. 147.

PROLOGUE

4 She later testified: *LLR*, vol. 1, p. 212.
4 'crushed': Cruickshank, *Eighteen Years on the Gold Coast*, vol. 1, p. 224.
4 The workmen finished the job by torchlight: Ibid., vol. 1, p. 229.
4 a discreet death notice: *The Times*, January 1, 1839, p. 8.

CHAPTER I   THE TANGLED WEB

6 'legendary figure': McGann and Reiss, *Letitia Elizabeth Landon*, p. 11.
6 'so identified with the literature of the day': S[arah] S[heppard], *Characteristics of the Genius and Writings of L.E.L.*, p. 10.
6 '*raw* bare powers': *Letters of Elizabeth Barrett Browning to Mary Russell Mitford*, vol. 2, p. 88.
6 'genius' . . . 'almost unnecessary to speak': Poe, 'Review of New Books.'
6 Goethe's family: In 1827, Goethe's daughter-in-law received Landon's book *The Troubadour* as a present from her mother, inscribed 'Ottilie von Goethe. Geschenk der Mutter.' Sypher, *A Biography*, p. 70.
6 Heinrich Heine: Heine called on Letitia Landon when she was staying in Paris in 1834. For Landon's account of the meeting, see *Letters*, pp. 107–8. See also Mende, *Heinrich Heine*, p. 116.
6 *Revue des deux mondes*: 'Une jeune poète anglaise,' vol. 6 (May 15, 1832): 404–18.
6 'strange pause': Young, *Victorian England*, p. 12.
6 'an embarrassment to the historian of English literature': Nemoianu, *The Taming of Romanticism*, p. 41.
6 'indeterminate borderland': Salmon, *The Formation of the Victorian Literary Profession*, p. 8.
7 'I have sung passionate songs': L.E.L. *The Venetian Bracelet*, p. 107.
7 'the fallen leaf': Ibid., p. v.
7 'No female poet before L.E.L.': Greer, *Slip-Shod Sibyls*, p. 275.
8 'not occasioned by any sickness': Quoted in *The Times*, January 3, 1839, p. 3.
8 'poor lady': *The Times*, January 10, 1839, p. 6.
9 'I must say': *LLR*, vol. 1, pp. 213–14. The text of this letter was appended to the inquest transcript.
9 first floated the possibility: *Morning Post*, January 3, 1839, unpaginated.
9 'remotest and darkest nooks': *Weekly True Sun*, January 20, 1839, unpaginated. This article was widely reprinted, for example in the *Southern Reporter and Cork Commercial Courier* on January 29.

9   'strange and dismal place' . . . 'fatal spot': *Mirror of Literature, Amusement and Instruction*, no. 933, January 26, 1839, front page.

9   'All manner of outrageous reports': Cruickshank, *Eighteen Years on the Gold Coast*, vol. 1, p. 230.

10   Such were the suspicions . . . the relevant documents had been lost: Whittington Landon's first letter to the colonial secretary was indeed lost, but much of the correspondence in fact survives in the National Archives, CO 267/157.

11   'What newspapers do you see?': Thomas Carlyle to John A. Carlyle, February 4, 1839, *Carlyle Letters Online*.

11   'I lived / Only in others' breath': 'Erinna,' *The Golden Violet*, p. 257.

11   'These are the spiders of society': *LLR*, vol. 2, p. 276.

12   'We have been a long time without letters': Eden, *Up the Country*, p. 302.

12   'elucidat[e] all that was mysterious in her fate': *LLR*, vol. 1, p. vi.

12   'After fully examining the evidence': Poe, 'Review of New Books.'

12   'There is a mystery somewhere': *Letters of Elizabeth Barrett Browning to Mary Russell Mitford*, vol. 1, p. 252.

12   In 1858, the printing plates: St Clair, *The Reading Nation*, p. 615.

12   'Do you know the story of L.E.L.?': Virginia Woolf to Lytton Strachey, September 3, 1927, *Letters of Virginia Woolf*, vol. 3, p. 418.

13   'sexually ignorant': Enfield, *L.E.L.: A Mystery of the Thirties*, p. 111.

13   In the 1940s, one critic: McGann and Reiss, *Letitia Elizabeth Landon*, p. 16.

13   Stokes-Adams syndrome: Watt, *Poisoned Lives*, pp. 129, 198–99, 224.

13   'virgin': Mellor, *Romanticism and Gender*, p. 120.

13   'knew only that she had never yielded' . . . 'fantasies': Greer, *Slip-Shod Sibyls*, p. 263.

13   'slander more utterly groundless': S. C. Hall, *A Book of Memories*, p. 264.

13   Gorman's claim was confirmed: Lawford, 'Diary.'

13   family correspondence: See Matoff, *Conflicted Life*.

14   'morbid symptoms': Gramsci, *Selections from the Prison Notebooks*, p. 276.

CHAPTER 2   THE THREE MAGICAL LETTERS

15   'We were young and at college': Bulwer, 'Romance and Reality,' p. 546.

16   'I know not who, or what thou art' . . . 'a lady yet in her teens': *LG*, no. 264, February 9, 1822, p. 89.

16   'We soon learned it was a female': Bulwer, 'Romance and Reality,' p. 547.

16   'stamp of originality': *LLR*, vol. 1, p. 40.

17   'In all the work of L.E.L.': Enfield, *L.E.L.: A Mystery of the Thirties*, p. 67.

17   'moon of our darkness': *Poetical Works of Thomas Lovell Beddoes*, p. xvii.

17 'all is vanity': S[arah] S[heppard], *Characteristics of the Genius and Writings of L.E.L.*, p. 165.

17 'no one sees things exactly as they are' L.E.L., *Romance and Reality*, vol. 1, p. 202.

18 'All things are symbols': *LLR*, vol. 2, p. 275.

18 'metromania': 'Of all the manias of this mad age, the most incurable, as well as the most common, seems to be no other than the Metromanie.' *Blackwood's Edinburgh Magazine*, vol. 3 (August 1818), p. 519.

18 Gowland's Lotion: *Ackerman's Repository*, November 1809, sourced from www.pemberley.com.

18 The success of Scott and Byron: On Scott's and Byron's new poetic methods, see Elfenbein, *Byron and the Victorians*, pp. 13–46.

18 the many fan letters he received from women: Corin Throsby, 'Byron, Commonplacing and Early Fan Culture,' in *Romanticism and Celebrity Culture, 1750–1850*, ed. Tom Mole (Cambridge, UK: Cambridge University Press, 2012).

19 Shelley had succeeded in shocking: On Godwin's relationship with Shelley, see St Clair, *The Godwins and the Shelleys*, also Sampson, *In Search of Mary Shelley*.

19 'paradise of exiles': Shelley quoted in Stabler, *The Artistry of Exile*, p. 15.

19 'the Godwinian colony': *Blackwood's Edinburgh Magazine*, vol. 10 (December 1821), p. 696.

20 'I had such projects for the Don': *Byron's Letters and Journals*, vol. 6, p. 232.

20 'men of diseased hearts': Southey, *A Vision of Judgement*, preface, pp. xix–xxi.

20 'Satanic mania': Bulwer, *Pelham*, preface, p. ix.

21 'sorrow, indignation and loathing': *LG*, no. 226, May 19, 1821, pp. 305–8.

21 'lay before our readers': Ibid.

23 'foolish young man': *LG*, no. 254, December 1, 1821, p. 772.

23 'daystar was even in dawning o'ercast': *PLG*, p. 14.

23 'bright star': *PLG*, p. 19.

24 'Sweet Poesy!': *PLG*, p. 23.

24 'cameleon [*sic*] poet': John Keats to Richard Woodhouse, October 27, 1818, *Letters of John Keats*, p. 157.

24 'Six Songs': *PLG*, pp. 9–14.

24 'I shall not shrink': *PLG*, p. 10.

24 'Oh! come to my slumber': *PLG*, p. 11.

25 'unfit for ladies': Rollins, *The Keats Circle*, vol. 1, p. 91.

25 'leafy couch' . . . 'bulbul': *PLG*, pp. 12–13.

25 'my heart sickens': *Collected Letters of Samuel Taylor Coleridge*, vol. 2, p. 905.

25 'foolish and profligate': *Blackwood's*, vol. 10 (December 1821), p. 696.

25 'I thought thus of the flowers, the moon': *PLG*, p. 13.

25 'He must be rich whom I could love': *PLG*, p. 13.

26 'combination of willed *naïveté*': Kramer, 'The Schubert Lied,' p. 218.

27 'die virgins': Greer, *Slip-Shod Sibyls*, p. 263.

27 'sweet ruin': *PLG*, p. 39.

27 'She leant upon her harp': *PLG*, p. 32.

28 'bold lover' . . . 'goal': Keats, *Complete Poems*, p. 345.

28 'Truly it has been thine': *PLG*, p. 493.

28 'Long may the sorrows of thy song': *LG*, no. 317, February 15, 1823, p. 107.

28 'sober Quaker': *Mary Howitt: An Autobiography*, p. 188.

28 'religion's cause': *LG*, no. 233, July 7, 1821, p. 428.

28 'obscenity': Quoted in Kelly, *Ireland's Minstrel*, pp. 65–66.

29 '[T]he wonderful precocity of her intellect': Roberts, *A Memoir*, p. 11.

29 'There were two Portraits': *PLG*, p. 34.

29 dramatic monologue: See Baiesi, *Letitia Landon and Metrical Romance*.

30 'I must turn from this idol': *PLG*, p. 131.

30 'Extracts from my pocket book': *PLG*, pp. 191–95.

30 'Farewell, farewell! Then both are free': *PLG*, p. 160.

31 'The chain I gave': *Poetical Works of Lord Byron*, vol. 3, p. 49.

32 'half in love with easeful Death': Keats, *Complete Poems*, p. 347.

32 'Twine not those red roses for me': *PLG*, p. 158.

32 'A deep, a lone, a silent grave': *PLG*, p. 228.

32 'restless little girl, in a pink gingham frock': S. C. Hall, *A Book of Memories*, pp. 268ff.

33 'I was surprised, and somewhat scandalised': Devey, *Life of Rosina Lady Lytton*, p. 41.

34 'She is, I understand, rather short': *Mary Howitt: An Autobiography*, p. 188.

34 'On Receiving a Laurel Crown from Leigh Hunt' and 'To the Ladies Who Saw Me Crown'd': Keats, *Complete Poems*, pp. 97–98. See also Barnard, 'First Fruits or 'First Blights,' ' p. 90.

CHAPTER 3   KEEPING UP APPEARANCES

36 'spiritual welfare': *Western Times*, September 5, 1829, p. 4. My thanks to Peter Selley for this reference.

37 'Mr and Mrs Spangle Lacquer' . . . 'paying for it': Quoted in Hilton, *A Mad, Bad and Dangerous People*, p. 37.

38 'had been elevated by her marriage': Anna Maria Hall, *A Woman's Story*, vol. 1, p. 49.

38 'Oh, what am I, and what are they?': L.E.L., *The Golden Violet*, p. 7.

38 Her will: TNA, Prerogative Court of Canterbury and Related Probate Jurisdictions, Will Registers: Class: PROB 11; Piece: 1807.

39 'genteelly': *AWJ*, vol. 3, p. 180.

39 '£14,000, her horse and her groom': [Thomson], *The Queens of Society,* p. 162.

39 'late marriage of convenience': Anna Maria Hall, *A Woman's Story,* vol. 1, p. 49.

39 'a treaty in which every concession is duly weighed': L.E.L. to Rosina Wheeler, November 30, 1825, *Letters,* p. 21.

39 'sentimentally recal [*sic*] the glories of Bond-street': L.E.L. to Katherine Thomson, August 1826, *Letters,* p. 33.

39 'Grasmere Lake': *Fisher's Drawing Room Scrap Book* (London, 1834), pp. 45–47.

40 'like the heart of all the universe': Thomas Carlyle to Alexander Carlyle, December 14, 1824, *Carlyle Letters Online.*

40 'my country, city of the soul': *Letters,* p. 24. The allusion is to Byron's *Childe Harold's Pilgrimage,* Canto 4, lxxvii: 'Oh Rome! my country! city of the soul!'

40 'there never was an age or any country': Southey, *Letters from England,* vol. 3, p. 290.

40 A single 'Mrs Bishop' is recorded: Highfill, *A Biographical Dictionary of Actors,* vol. 2, p. 138. She was in Samuel Foote's summer company at the Haymarket Theatre on September 18, 1776, playing Mrs. Wisely in *The Miser,* and appeared at the same theater in the out-of-season performances of 1778.

41 'would give all the reputation I have gained': Planché, *Recollections and Reflections,* vol. 1, p. 103.

41 'Love, love is all a woman's fame': *PLG,* p. 125.

42 'magnificent rocking-horse': *LLR,* vol. 1, p. 8.

42 'Mrs Siddons and the French fashions': Anna Maria Hall, *A Woman's Story,* vol. 1, p. 111.

42 'to sit at the open parlour-window': S. C. Hall, *A Book of Memories,* p. 274, note.

43 'fancy farm': Jerdan, 1848 memoir, p. ix.

43 'display' her reward: *LLR,* vol. 1, p. 7.

43 included the aristocratic future Lady Caroline Lamb: Douglass, *Lady Caroline Lamb,* p. 22.

44 Frances Arabella Rowden: *DNB.*

45 Fanny Kemble: David, *Fanny Kemble,* p. 26.

45 'amorous and botanical': *Athenaeum,* no. 216, January 7, 1832, p. 6.

45   immediately identified as St. Quentin: Mary Russell Mitford to her father, February 7, 1809, L'Estrange, *The Life of Mary Russell Mitford*, vol. 1, p. 63.

45   'grosser' . . . 'If the introduction of the passion of Love': Rowden, *The Pleasures of Friendship*, p. viii.

46   '[W]e do not agree with her in thinking': *Monthly Review*, April 1812, p. 434.

46   her little brother sitting astride the rocking horse: *LLR*, vol. 1, p. 8.

46   'robe of grace': *LLR*, vol. 1, p. 7.

46   'How little could Lady Caroline have imagined': [Thomson], *The Queens of Society*, p. 165.

46   Arabella Stuart: Page, *A History of the County of Hertford*, vol. 2, pp. 337–42, sourced from *British History Online*.

47   'toy' farm: Jerdan, 1848 memoir.

47   Flixton Hall: Suckling, *The History and Antiquities of the County of Suffolk*, vol. 1, p. 189.

47   'Who is not alarmed': Thompson, *An Inquiry*, p. xvii.

47   'respectability has various meanings': Wakefield, *Popular Politics*, p. 26.

47   envy-inducing book: *Views of the Seats of Noblemen and Gentlemen in England, Wales, Scotland and Ireland* (London, 1821). Flixton, the seat of Alexander Adair, Esquire, appears in vol. 4 as no. 20.

47   Adair's engraved portrait: Drawn by H. Edridge and engraved by H. Meyer, c. 1810, https://www.grosvenorprints.com/.

48   an income in 1800 alone: Jackson, 'British Incomes Circa 1800,' p. 257.

48   'Eton or Westminster': L.E.L., *Ethel Churchill*, vol. 3, p. 33.

48   'large, old, and, somewhat dilapidated place': L.E.L., 'The History of a Child,' *Traits and Trials*, p. 295.

48   'as phantasies do to facts': *LLR*, vol. 1, p. 22.

48   privately told another friend: L.E.L. to S. C. Hall, mid-1837, *Letters*, p. 167.

48   'original melancholy': *LLR*, vol. 1, p. 22.

49   push sweets under the door: *LLR*, vol. 1, p. 12.

49   'measuring stick': *LLR*, vol. 1, p. 10.

49   'lie awake half the night': *Letters*, p. 167.

49   'pothooks': *LLR*, vol. 1, p. 12.

50   'dear little fingers': *LLR*, vol. 1, p. 16.

50   'fine ladies' who 'were going to the devil': Austen, *Mansfield Park*, p. 409.

50   warm nature: [Thomson], *The Queens of Society*, p. 167.

51   'The Boudoir': *The Keepsake*, 1831, pp. 209–21.

51   'contributions to various periodicals': *Letters*, p. 168.

52   *'public character'*: *LLR*, vol. 1, p. 15.

52   'just to outshine': Anna Maria Hall, *A Woman's Story*, vol. 1, pp. 49, 131.

53 'Talk of education!': L.E.L., *Romance and Reality*, vol. 1, pp. 96–97.
53 Lucretia Davidson: Low, *The Literary Protégées of the Lake Poets*, pp. 19–20.
53 Elizabeth Smith: *LLR*, vol. 1, p. 28.
53 discarded mistress: L.E.L., *Romance and Reality*, vol. 1, pp. 118ff.
53 'stocks and dumbbells' and 'backboards and collars': L.E.L. to Rosina Wheeler, November 30, 1821, *Letters*, p. 21.
54 'certainly not beautiful': *LLR*, vol. 1, p. 290.
54 eyewitness anatomization of her looks: *LLR*, vol. 1, pp. 292–93.
55 'It was strange to watch': *LLR*, vol. 1, p. 292.
55 In a poem published in 1826: *LG*, no. 512, November 11, 1826, p. 705.
55 abused by his nurse: MacCarthy, *Byron: Life and Legend*, pp. 22–23.
55 'me, and only me': L.E.L., *Traits and Trials*, p. 287.
55 'tiresome' child: Ibid., p. 291.
56 'childhood . . . images forth our after life': Ibid., p. 312.
56 'It has always been my most earnest wish': L.E.L. to Elizabeth Landon, late 1820, *Letters*, p. 6.
56 forbade her charge to read novels: *LLR*, vol. 1, p. 10.
56 the books she enjoyed: L.E.L., *Romance and Reality*, vol. 1, p. 192.
56 'surrender of virtue': More, *Moral Sketches*, pp. 244–45.
56 'Happily for her': [Thomson], *The Queens of Society*, p. 188.
57 Harriet Beecher Stowe: See Caroline Franklin, *The Female Romantics* (London and New York: Routledge, 2012).
57 Charlotte Brontë later read: *Letters of Charlotte Brontë*, vol. 1, p. 129.
57 odd juxtapositions that appeared: L.E.L. to Bernard Barton, ?August 1824, *Letters*, p. 15.
57 '[r]emarkably neat and retired VILLA': Sypher, *The View from Rose Cottage in 1818*, p. 7.
57 'calisthenic exercises': L.E.L., *Romance and Reality*, vol. 1, pp. 96–97.
58 read as she ran: *AWJ*, vol. 3, p. 174.
58 Rose Cottage: Sypher, *The View from Rose Cottage in 1818*.
58 her 'plump' body: *AWJ*, vol. 3, p. 174.
58 'exuberance of form': Jerdan, 1848 memoir, p. x.
59 'delicate looking females driven from their home': Blessington, *The Magic Lantern*, p. 4.
59 'embarrassed state of my father's circumstances': *Letters*, p. 167.
60 'Miss Landon, though not having the pleasure': *Letters*, p. 3.

CHAPTER 4   THE SONGBIRD AND THE TRAINER

61 ignored by literary history until recently: Matoff, *Conflicted Life*, offers a wealth of documentation.

61 'satyr-cannibal Literary Gazetteer': Thomas Carlyle to John A. Carlyle, November 27, 1835, *Carlyle Letters Online*.

61 'drunken and rowdyish' . . . 'seduced innumerable women': Hawthorne, *English Notebooks*, pp. 282–83.

61 'liked and regarded without respecting': S. C. Hall, *A Book of Memories*, p. 285.

61 'It would be difficult now to comprehend': Ibid.

61 'pampered and petted': *AWJ*, vol. 1, pp. 21, 38.

62 In his teens he made his way to London: *AWJ*, vol. 1, pp. 41ff.

62 'indomitable effrontery': Julian Hawthorne, *Hawthorne and His Circle*, p. 143.

62 'no artifice by which notoriety can be obtained': Cited in *Wellesley Index to Victorian Periodicals*, vol. 3, p. 162.

62 'puppet of certain booksellers': *Personal Reminiscences by Chorley, Planché and Young*, p. 8.

63 'A friend of mine in whose literary fame': St Clair, *The Reading Nation*, p. 574.

64 'sallow clerks': Bulwer, *Pelham: or the Adventures of a Gentleman*, preface (to the 1835 edition, reprinted in the 1842 edition), p. ix.

64 'even our footmen compose tragedies': *Blackwood's Edinburgh Magazine*, vol. 3 (August 1818), p. 519.

64 'betaken themselves to literature': Bodleian Library, MSS. Eng. lett., d. 113–14, vol. 2, p. 342.

64 'addicted': *AWJ*, vol. 3, p. 175.

64 played with his own children: L.E.L. to S. C. Hall, mid-1837, *Letters*, p. 167.

64 'Oh! how thou art changed': *PLG*, p. 1.

65 epitaph on Letitia's great-grandfather's grave: *LLR*, vol. 1, p. 2.

65 Catherine was said to have loved: Anna Maria Hall, *A Woman's Story*, vol. 1, p. 10.

65 had been painted by George Stubbs: Royal Collection.

65 Hazlitt had a statuette of Napoleon: Cook, *Hazlitt in Love*, p. 85.

65 Keats had a Napoleon snuffbox: Roe, *John Keats*, p. 181.

66 'Should the favour Mrs Landon requests be admissible': Bodleian, MSS. Eng. lett., d. 113–14.

67 'West Indian dandy': *PLG*, p. 2.

68 'into endurance, and even love of slavery': Godwin, *Memoirs of the Author of A Vindication of the Rights of Woman*, p. 79.

68 'I do not dwell': *PLG*, p. 349.

68 'careless of the passion . . . in the bud': *PLG*, p. 3.

68 'I wished to pourtray': *Letters*, p. 6.

68 'I am too well aware of my many defects': *Letters*, p. 4.

69   'belov'd Inspirer of thy youthful minstrel's dream': L.E.L., *The Fate of Adelaide*, p. 7.

69   'bards of Greece' . . . 'not quite unworthy thee': Ibid., p. 35.

69   'Need I say how anxious she is': *Letters*, p. 5.

69   'troublesome' . . . 'no resolution to go on': *Letters*, p. 5.

69   'How happy I am!': *Letters*, p. 8.

69   a long-lost branch: Sypher, *A Biography*, p. 16.

69   a fabled race: Featured passim in Anna Maria Porter's novel *The Knight of St John* (1817), where they are described as heroic outcasts suffering from some vague congenital disorder; also as subject of a correspondence in *The Gentleman's Magazine* (September 1819, p. 225, and October 1819, p. 326). Letitia's reference to 'the frightful goitres' etc., *Romance and Reality*, vol. 2, p. 123.

70   'From day to day and hour to hour': *AWJ*, vol. 3, p. 169.

71   ' 'Twas my first': [Thomson], 'Memorials,' p. 183.

71   comic poem: *LLR*, p. 146.

72A   'mystery of L.E.L.' . . . 'devoted attachment': *AWJ*, vol. 3, p. 170.

72B   'Youth's deep and passionate idolatry': *PLG*, p. 33.

72B   'passions' mere 'pasteboard': *Letters of Elizabeth Barrett Browning to Mary Russell Mitford*, vol. 1, p. 252. See also Knowles, *Sensibility and Female Poetic Tradition*, p. 134.

72B   'to impress on the reader's mind': *LLR*, vol. 1, p. 38.

72C   'emotional honesty': Lawford, 'Thou Shalt Bid Thy Fair Hands Rove.'

72C   'Poetry always carries me out': *Letters*, p. 168.

72C   'the whole frame trembles': L.E.L., *Ethel Churchill*, vol. 3, p. 196.

72D   'We love the bird': William Jerdan to Lady Blessington, January 5, 1839, BL Add. 43688F, ff 64–65.

72D   'a nightingale, who sits in darkness': Shelley, *Selected Poems and Prose*, p. 657.

72E   'And you took my young heart': *PLG*, pp. 313–14.

72   'Dinner passed, and within an hour': Jerdan, 1848 memoir, p. xi.

72   'mawkishness': Keats, preface to *Endymion* (1818).

73   'Am Teetisch': Heine, *Werke*, vol. 1, p. 84.

73   'St George's Hospital': *PLG*, pp. 38–40.

73   Whittington went up to Oxford: He matriculated on March 8, 1823 (*Alumni Oxoniensis*, 1715–1886, vol. 3). Letitia's poem 'I must turn from this idol' was published on March 22. *PLG*, p. 131.

74   'Cockney' culture: See Dart, *Metropolitan Art and Literature, 1810–1840: Cockney Adventures*.

74   'rationalised or reformé': L.E.L. to Mr. Richards, May 15, 1822, *Letters*, p. 10.

74   Isabella Jones: Roe, *John Keats*, p. 109.

75 male keepers of the flame: Barnard, 'First Fruits or 'First Blights.' '

75 'I have an utter aversion to Bluestockings': Hazlitt, 'Of Great and Little Things' (1821), *Complete Works*, vol. 8, p. 236.

75 'kneel down in the front of the box': Roberts, *A Memoir*, p. 19.

75 'finest natural organ': L.E.L., *Romance and Reality*, vol. 1, p. 61.

75 Sicilian fairy . . . 'Venus of South America': Matoff, *Conflicted Life*, p. 148.

76 Sarah Baartman: Hall, *Macaulay and Son*, pp. 66–67.

76 Elizabeth Barrett complained: *Letters of Elizabeth Barrett Browning to Mary Russell Mitford*, vol. 1, p. 252.

76 'runs over the grass' . . . 'the death cup': L.E.L., *The Zenana*, ed. Emma Roberts, pp. 48–50.

77 left him her gold watch: *AWJ*, vol. 3, p. 185.

77 Her estate went to Letitia: TNA, Prerogative Court of Canterbury and Related Probate Jurisdictions, Will Registers: Class: PROB 11; Piece: 1807.

77 We know from the baptismal record: London Metropolitan Archives, Church of England Parish Registers, 1754–1906, ref. no. 87/js/006.

77 no record of exactly when Ella was born: Matoff, *Conflicted Life*, pp. 604, 640.

77 'clouded births are seldom correctly dated': Anna Maria Hall, *A Woman's Story*, vol. 1, p. 138.

77 'Canterbury of all places': *The Sunday Times*, March 5, 1826, third page (unpaginated).

78 'For the first two or three months': *Letters*, p. 11.

78 who died of consumption, aged fourteen: Parish Records of St. George Hanover Square, September 15, 1825, London Metropolitan Archives, ref. no. DL/T/089/020.

78 'few things are to my taste more tiresome': *Letters*, p. 13.

78 'Do you recall one autumn night': *PLG*, p. 259.

79 the unusual seal she used: L.E.L. to Bernard Barton, September 1823, *Letters*, pp. 11–13, note.

79 'child / Of sorrow and of shame': *PLG*, p. 142.

79 'a year' before she saw the proof sheets: 'I never saw the MS till in proof-sheets a year afterwards, and I made no additions only verbal alterations,' Letitia told A. A. Watts in 1824. *Letters*, p. 18.

80 Pickersgill portrait of Letitia: *LLR*, p. 290.

80 *Ackermann's Repository:* March 1, 1819, vol. 7, no. 39, plate between pp. 180 and 181.

80 instantly sold in exhibition: Graves, *The Royal Academy of Arts*, vol. 6, p. 142.

81 'less than five weeks': *Letters*, p. 18.

82 'M.E.' and 'L.E.L.' rubbed shoulders: *LG*, October 4, 1823, p. 635.

82 earned her living as a governess: Matoff records (p. 447) that Ella worked as a governess in Lord Normanby's family in the 1840s.

82 'prosperous and happy journey' . . . 'never be welcomed back': Matoff, *Conflicted Life*, p. 447.

CHAPTER 5   FAME

85 'Dutch improvisator': *LG*, no. 321, March 15, 1823, p. 169.

85 'court poet, show-woman, adventuress': Findlen, *Italy's Eighteenth Century*, p. 122.

86 'a sort of mental masturbation': *Byron's Letters and Journals*, vol. 7, p. 225.

86 'My hand kept wandering on my lute': L.E.L., *The Improvisatrice*, pp. 31–32.

87 'peculiarities of my own individual character': Anon., *Andrew of Padua*, p. 68.

87 'Softly, softly': Ibid., p. 186.

87 'blood was on her small snow feet': L.E.L., *The Improvisatrice*, p. 66.

88 'rubbishy sentimentality': Adam Roberts, in Wu, *A Companion to Romanticism*, p. 29.

89 Thomas Lovell Beddoes: Berns, *The Ashgate Research Companion to Thomas Lovell Beddoes*.

89 'As far as our poetical taste and critical judgment': *LG*, no. 389, July 3, 1824, pp. 417–20.

89 'extraordinary poetic talents': *Ackermann's Repository*, 3rd series, vol. 4, August 1, 1824, p. 122.

89 'young Lady just out of her teens' . . . 'vivid imagination': *Gentleman's Magazine*, vol. 94, July 1824, p. 61.

89 'There is . . . scarcely an image which is not connected': *New Monthly Magazine*, vol. 12, no. 44, August 1, 1824, p. 365.

89 in the Parisian *Globe*: 'The Improvisatrice,' *Le Globe*, September 15, 1824, p. 4. A further article, 'L'Improvisatrice de Mlle. Letitia Landon,' appeared in *Le Globe* the following year (August 9, 1825, p. 737).

89 also published in America: By Monroe and Francis of Boston in 1825.

90 The so-called review: *Blackwood's Edinburgh Magazine*, August 1824, pp. 189–93.

90 'in those days of leo-hunting': [Thomson], *The Queens of Society*, p. 171.

90 'litr'y abilities': Devey, *Life of Rosina Lady Lytton*, p. 44.

91 'rank' and 'opulence': *Letters*, p. 28.

92 'the instant L.E.L. was known': [Thomson], *The Queens of Society*, p. 173.

92 'Witty and conversant as she was': William Howitt, *Homes and Haunts*, vol. 2, p. 438.

92 'stroke of electricity': Anna Maria Hall, *A Woman's Story*, vol. 2, p. 38.

92 'the society of her own sex': [Thomson], *The Queens of Society*, p. 174.

92 'who had such a plethora of character and respectability': Devey, *Life of Rosina Lady Lytton*, pp. 42–43.

93 'drest upon an idea': [Thomson], 'Memorials,' p. 88.

93 'air of merry scorn' . . . 'sleeve': Howitt, *Homes and Haunts*, vol. 2, p. 154.

93 'short sleeve made very full': *Ackermann's Repository*, March 1824, p. 184.

94 a surviving lock of her dark hair: BL Add. MS, 43688; hair originally contained in folded paper (folio 69a) with note, in Lady Blessington's hand, reading 'The Hair of poor dear L.E.L.'

94 'by a crop curled in the neck *à l'enfant*': L.E.L., *Romance and Reality* (one-vol. 1848 edition), p. 274.

94 'martyrdom of curls': *Letters*, p. 42.

95 'Marry ma charmante rose': L.E.L. to Rosina Wheeler, November 30, 1825, *Letters*, p. 21.

95 Caroline Lamb's toy boy: Mitchell, *Bulwer Lytton*, pp. 13–14.

95 'only eighteen' . . . 'a Dean's daughter': Quoted in Sypher, *A Biography*, p. 10.

95 'cast-off' mistress: Mitchell, *Bulwer Lytton*, p. 51.

95 sodomy with Disraeli: Ibid., p. 62.

95 'Mr Jerdan says': Devey, *Life of Rosina Lady Lytton*, p. 142.

95 'witnessing the usual flirtation': Quoted in Matoff, *Conflicted Life*, p. 255.

96 a fellow guest noted with distaste: Sadleir, *Bulwer and His Wife: A Panorama*, pp. 149, 422–23.

96 'I have been quite a round of dinner parties': *Letters*, p. 21.

96 'Nothing could be more lively': [Thomson], *The Queens of Society*, p. 174.

96 'quadrille' party: *Letters*, p. 18.

97 'made a modest and retiring young lady': Quoted in Whitley, *Art of England*, p. 89.

97 Madame Vestris: Mandel, *The Theatre of Don Juan*, p. 399.

98 'When she was in the first flush of her fame': Anna Maria Hall, 'The Portraits of L.E.L.,' p. 3.

98 'Scarce possible it seem'd to be': L.E.L. *The Troubadour*, p. 246.

98 'My page is wet with bitter tears': Ibid., p. 252.

99 'surveillance': Ibid., title page.

99 'endowed by nature with talents so far above': Jerdan's expansive review is spread across three consecutive issues of the *Literary Gazette*: no. 443, July 16, 1825, pp. 449–50; no. 444, pp. 469–70; no. 445, pp. 484–85.

99 Elsewhere, *The Troubadour* was well reviewed: Sypher, *A Biography*, pp. 60–70.

99 'sickly thoughts clothed in glittering language': *Westminster Review*, April 1825, pp. 537–39.

100 drawing room: Croker, *A Walk from London to Fulham*, p. 47.

100 'ostensible wealth' . . . kitchen cooker: *AWJ*, vol. 4, p. 38.

100 'his house was ever open': Lord Lennox, *Celebrities I Have Known*, vol. 2, p. 35.

100 running a wheelbarrow: Scott, *The Poetical Works of L.E.L.*, Introduction.

100 £4,000 debt: Letter from William Jerdan to Edward Bulwer, December 23, 1830, Hertford Record Office, D/EK C/ 11/ 23.

101 'We are happy to be enabled to state': *The Sunday Times*, March 5, 1826, third page (unpaginated).

101 '*The Literary Jordan*': BL, General Reference Collection 1865.c.3 (166).

102 'so positive': *Letters*, p. 211.

102 'What malignity begins': *LLR*, vol. 1, p. 52.

102 'Unfortunately, the very unguardedness of her innocence': Ibid.

102 'And I,—I felt immortal': L.E.L., *The Golden Violet* (1827), p. 245.

CHAPTER 6   SHAME

103 'a reluctance which will at least ensure brevity': *LLR*, vol. 1, p. 57.

103 'A well-known English Sappho': *The Sunday Times*, March 5, 1826 (unpaginated).

105 '*hushed up*': Austen, *Mansfield Park*, p. 409.

105 a letter to her friend Mrs. Thomson: *LLR*, vol. 1 pp. 53–56.

107 'girlish days': *LLR*, vol. 1, p. 53.

107 'constant medical friend and advisor': S. C. Hall, *A Book of Memories*, p. 266.

107 In 1810 he delivered the future novelist Elizabeth Gaskell: *DNB* entry on Elizabeth Cleghorn Gaskell.

107 compared the personal physician to a confessor priest: L.E.L., *Ethel Churchill*, vol. 3, p. 200.

108 'Already I see you a regular lioness': *Letters*, p. 25.

108 glowing review of Mrs. Thomson's book: *LG*, no. 485, May 6, 1826, pp. 273–75.

108 *On Hypocrisy*: *LG*, no. 517, December 16, 1826, p. 793.

108 'No one knows but myself': *LLR*, vol. 1, p. 53.

109 'acquired so perceptible a degree of *embonpoint*': 'Quacks of the Day: William Jerdan,' *The Wasp*, no. 2, October 7, 1826, p. 22.

109 'L.E.L. (alias Letitia Languish)': *The Wasp*, no. 3, October 14, 1826, p. 36.

109 'I had intended, my dear Mrs Thomson': *Letters*, p. 29.

109 'Mr Ashwell': *Letters*, p. 37.

110 a boarding school in Uxbridge: It was located at Belle House, had thirty-seven pupils, all boys, and was maintained by a schoolmaster named Joseph Ibert. TNA, 1841 Census, Uxbridge District, Piece: 655; Book: 10; Folio: 51: page: 11.

110 In his autobiography: *AWJ*, vol. 1, p. 22.

110 Jerdan 'exported' him to the West Indies . . . 'going on prosperously in Trinidad': Family correspondence quoted in Matoff, *Conflicted Life*, pp. 488–89.

111 William and Frances's youngest daughter: Georgiana's death notice: *Morning Post*, April 20, 1826.

111 George Hogarth wrote to Jerdan: Matoff, *Conflicted Life*, p. 219.

111 'ingenious allegory': Jerdan, 'The Sleepless Woman,' *The Club-Book*, vol. 2, p. 54.

112 'Leaves grow green to fall': *PLG*, p. 352.

112 'When we can find nothing better to entertain readers with': *LG*, December 30, 1827, p. 828.

112 dismissed lawyers as pests: *LG*, December 30, 1827, pp. 817–18.

113 'the slightest idea of my original sin': *Letters*, p. 30.

113 'We have past divers rural days': *Letters*, p. 32.

113 'A heavy misfortune befell me': *Letters*, p. 34.

114 'utter cold worldliness': *Letters*, p. 31.

114 'feelings (if I have any)': *Letters*, p. 30.

114 'Why should I shed a single tear': *PLG*, p. 349.

114 'if such a novelty as a lover': *Letters*, p. 36.

114 'the author of Rouge et Noir': *Letters*, p. 32.

115 'when in doubt, lead trump': *Letters*, p. 96.

115 'with that *au fait* air': Read, *Rouge et Noir*, p. 8.

115 'there is no man': *De Quincey's Works*, p. 261.

115 'by the pound': *Letters*, p. 33.

116 'what art thou, fame?': L.E.L., *The Golden Violet*, p. 236.

117 'Feelings whose truth is all their worth': Ibid., p. 239.

117 'to draw the portrait and trace the changes': Ibid., p. 242.

117 'I have scorned myself': Ibid., p. 260.

117 'deep and dangerous delight': Ibid., p. 258.

117 'the opiate of my heart' . . . 'I do not hope a sunshine burst of fame': Ibid., p. 259.

118 'When we . . . remember that this is the third work in the course of two years': *LG*, no. 517, December 16, 1826, pp. 785–87.

118 'I look forward to the decided advantage': *Letters*, p. 37.

118 'when I arrive at 22': *Letters*, p. 37.

119 'homely-looking': *LLR*, vol. 1, p. 79.

119 'I cannot describe to you how my heart sank': *Tales and Sketches by Letitia Elizabeth Landon*, p. 77.

119 her will: TNA, Prerogative Court of Canterbury and Related Probate Jurisdictions: Will Registers; Class: PROB 11; Piece: 1807.

119 'Mr Jerdan is awful!': Devey, *Letters of the Late Edward Bulmer*, p. 196.

120 'As long as they will be hypocrites': Quoted in Peakman, *Lascivious Bodies*, p. 94.

120 'Miss Landon is amusing': Devey, *Letters of the Late Edward Bulmer*, p. 195.

120 'Let such a person's popularity only decline': Grant, *The Great Metropolis*, p. 256.

120 'poet of fashion': *The Sunday Times*, March 5, 1826.

120 'I think you might most advantageously communicate': *Letters*, p. 220.

120 Letitita appeared as Perdita: Roberts, *A Memoir*, p. 25.

121 Letitia's visiting card survives: William St Clair collection.

121 'her usual regards never sank skin-deep': [Thomson], 'Memorials,' p. 182.

121 'I avoided L.E.L.': Disraeli, *Letters*, vol. 1, p. 247.

121 Tom Moore sat next to her: *Journal of Thomas Moore*, vol. 3, p. 1305.

122 Mary Russell Mitford later took umbrage: *Letters of Elizabeth Barrett Browning to Mary Russell Mitford*, vol. 1, p. 253, note 9.

CHAPTER 7   LYRE LIAR

123 'Beauty is truth': Keats, *Complete Poems*, p. 346.

123 'O say not that truth does not dwell': 'The Poet,' *PLG*, p. 31.

125 'A History of the Lyre': L.E.L., *The Venetian Bracelet*, p. 95.

127 'have left me somewhat in the situation of the prince in the fairy tale': Ibid., Preface, p. vi.

127 'In reading many of her poems': *The Athenaeum*, no. 105, October 28, 1829, pp. 669–70, and no. 106, November 4, 1829, pp. 688–90.

127 'Lines of Life': L.E.L., *The Venetian Bracelet*, pp. 265–74.

131 She is viscerally nauseated: Woolf, *Orlando*, pp. 167–68.

131 'blight in her springtime': S. C. Hall, 'Memories of Authors of the Age,' p. 89.

131 ''bright ornament' of Truth' . . . 'secretiveness' . . . 'bane': S. C. Hall, *A Book of Memories*, pp. 263–64.

132 'unctuous solemnity': Julian Hawthorne, *Hawthorne and His Circle*, ch. 11.

132 he soon found employment: Vincent, *Ugo Foscolo*, ch. 10.

133 her grandmother's funeral: S. C. Hall, *A Book of Memories*, p. 270.

133 'I would gladly say more': Ibid., p. 285.

133 'sufficient rank' . . . 'pure': Sadleir, *Blessington-d'Orsay*, p. 200.

133 'looked earnestly down at her': S. C. Hall, *A Book of Memories*, p. 275.

133 'Miss Landon is a pretty girl': *Collected Letters of James Hogg,* vol. 3, p. 27.

133 *The Minstrel of Chamouni:* Graves, *The Royal Academy of Arts,* vol. 6, p. 145; the painting was no. 147 in the 1828 Royal Academy exhibition.

134 on display in their ancestral seat: The picture is currently miscataloged as a portrait of the artist's daughter Emily Maria (1837–1924). See www.british portraits.org.uk/events/annual-seminar-2017/ for a podcast of my presentation on Pickersgill's images of Letitia Landon at the Understanding British Portraits Annual Seminar of 2017 at the National Portrait Gallery: *The protean poetess: portraiture, masquerade, and celebrity in the post-Byronic era.*

134 'pleasing portrait under the disguise': *Gentleman's Magazine,* vol. 143, June 1828, p. 539.

134 'This minstrel is an imposter': *London Magazine,* 1828, 'Notes on Art,' p. 383.

134 'pseudo portrait': *LG,* March 31, 1827.

135 'Oh, I don't *chuse* to believe anything against Miss Landon': *Unpublished Letters of Lady Bulwer Lytton,* p. 129.

135 The riotous parties the Bulwers hosted: *Journal of Thomas Moore,* vol. 4 (1831–35), p. 1463.

136 Jerdan boasting in his cups about his sexual conquest: *Unpublished Letters of Lady Bulwer Lytton,* p. 128.

136 'against all the world': Ibid., p. 127.

137 helped fix up a curacy: *Autobiography of Anna Eliza Bray* (London: Chapman and Hall, 1884), pp. 235–36.

137 Jerdan's complicity: The vicar's wife, Anna Eliza Bray, records in her autobiography that Jerdan had given her first book, a travelogue, a warm review in the *Gazette* in 1820, which she put down to his good-natured desire to 'cheer and encourage a writer of the weaker sex' (p. 157). They remained in touch into the 1830s, as is shown by a surviving letter from Mrs. Bray to Jerdan, Bodleian, MSS. Eng. lett., d. 113–14.

137 '(H)all's well': *AWJ,* vol. 4, p. 327.

138 'slow to believe that . . . evil words could harm her': S. C. Hall, *A Book of Memories,* p. 264.

138 'still her face was bow'd': L.E.L., *The Venetian Bracelet,* p. 208.

138 'The Dying Child': Ibid., p. 247.

139 Letitia wrote to a Mrs. Tayler: *Letters,* p. 51.

139 contributor to S. C. Hall's *The Amulet:* Charles B. Tayler, 'Soldier's Wives,' *The Amulet* (1833), pp. 191–204. Other contributors to the same volume include Mary Howitt, Laman Blanchard, and L.E.L. herself.

139 to influence Elizabeth Gaskell's famous factory novel: Rudolph Beck, 'The Writing on the Cartridge: A Note on Elizabeth Gaskell's *Mary Barton* and Charles B. Tayler,' *Notes and Queries* 45, no. 2 (June 1998): 216–17.

140 Dr. Thomson's first wife was Elizabeth Gaskell's aunt: Uglow, *Elizabeth Gaskell*, pp. 21–22, 34–35, 182.

140 'work calculated to do much good': Puff quoted in an advertisement at the back of Thomas Taylor, *The Life of William Cowper* (London: Smith, Elder, 1833).

140 'I am disappointed at not being in town before this': *Letters*, p. 48. Letitia has not dated her letter. 'June 1828' has been added in pencil by another hand, but the reference to 'The Lost Pleiade' makes it far more likely to have been 1829, since Letitia rarely wrote so long in advance of publication, and that poem was published in *The Venetian Bracelet* in November 1829.

141 missed 'so very much not being able to talk to you': *AWJ*, vol. 4, p. 404. As in this case, Jerdan often reproduces letters out of context, and without commentary, leaving their actual import unspoken.

141 'coquetted at her': Julian Hawthorne, *Hawthorne and His Circle*, p. 142.

141 a torn-up fragment: L.E.L. to Mary Anne Browne, *Letters*, p. 201.

141 A letter from Browne to Jerdan: *AWJ*, vol. 4, p. 314.

141 'With thine 'own people' dost thou dwell': 'Stanzas to the author of 'Mont Blanc,' 'Ada,' etc.,' *The Venetian Bracelet*, pp. 287–94.

142 a strange short story: Reprinted in *AWJ*, vol. 4, appendix, pp. 411–20.

142 'nourishing of sickly aspirations': *LG*, no. 663, October 3, 1829, pp. 641–43; no. 664, October 10, 1829, pp. 660–61.

143 *The Royal Lady's Magazine*: Cited in Mason, *Literary Advertising and the Shaping of British Romanticism*, p. 111.

143 'dear Creature': Matoff, *Conflicted Life*, p. 533.

143 her baptismal certificate: London Metropolitan Archives, St Michael Queenhithe, Register of Baptisms, P69/MIC6/A/01/Ms 9150, Item 1.

144 the census was taken: Class: HO107; Piece: 680; Book: 4; Civil Parish: St Marylebone; County: Middlesex; Enumeration District: 4; Folio: 7; Page: 6; Line: 1; GSU roll: 438796.

145 'that it is well known to everyone': Disraeli, *Letters*, vol. 1, p. 408n.

146 'Our gifted friend defied slander': [Thomson], 'Memorials,' p. 182.

CHAPTER 8   THE CASH NEXUS

147 'cash payment': *Works of Thomas Carlyle*, vol. 4, p. 164.

147 'cash will not pay': Ibid.

148 'fame and profit': Grant, *The Great Metropolis*, p. 341.

148 'A record of L.E.L.'s personal expenses': Roberts, *A Memoir*, p. 16.

148 'But in spite of great and constant success': [Thomson], 'Memorials,' p. 186.

148 'saying gently that she need not keep it': Quoted in Sypher, *A Biography*, p. 337.

148 'the Middle Classes consist of those families': Grant, *The Great Metropolis*, p. 274.

148 Patrick Brontë's annual salary: *The Letters of the Reverend Patrick Brontë*, p. 46.

149 lodger of Thomas Carlyle's postman: Jane Welsh Carlyle to John A. Carlyle, November 15, 1851, *Carlyle Letters Online*.

149 squib on Jerdan's reputation for puffery: Matoff, *Conflicted Life*, p. 123.

149 'Miss Landon in swansdown muff': *The Age*, December 16, 1827.

149 'made use of his influence in the literary world': Berkeley, *My Life and Recollections*, vol. 2, pp. 47–48.

150 The surviving accounts: BL, Bentley Papers, Add. 44, Vol. CXV, ff. 314.

150 'poets' food': From 'An Exhortation,' in *The Poetical Works of P. B. Shelley* (London: C. Daly, 1839), p. 502.

151 'lovers' correspondence': *PLG*, p. 103.

151 'Conclusion': *PLG*, pp. 124–25.

152 ' 'What is Freedom?—Ye can tell' ': Shelley, *Selected Poems and Prose*, p. 362.

152 many of Shelley's antiestablishment political poems: Reiman and O'Neil, *Percy Bysshe Shelley*, vol. 8, p. 71.

152 promoting the pictures in a commercial gallery: *Poetical Catalogue of Pictures [to be continued occasionally.] Vandyke consulting his mistress in a Picture in Cooke's Exhibition. PLG*, pp. 125ff. See also note p. 503. W. B. Cooke (1778–1855), a publisher of engravings, had his place of business in Soho Square.

153 'As to pecuniary recompense': *Letters*, p. 26.

153 she had made over £900: *Letters*, p. 27.

153 Jerdan provided a list: *AWJ*, vol. 3, p. 185.

154 '[T]hough I will correct the press': MS in the University of Edinburgh quoted in Matoff, *Conflicted Life*, p. 145.

154 'I have not a friend in the world but himself': *Letters*, p. 28.

155 'an order if procureable': *Letters*, p. 211.

155 'blunders in attempting numbers': *AWJ*, vol. 4, p. 229.

155 'A note from Jerdan asking me to withhold the cheque': *Diaries of William Charles Macready*, vol. 1, pp. 482–83.

155 *The Golden Violet:* Matoff, *Conflicted Life*, p. 192.

156 *The Venetian Bracelet:* Ibid., p. 216.

156 'in purchasing and furnishing Grove House': William Jerdan to Edward Bulwer, December 23, [1830], marked 'Private,' Hertfordshire Archives D/EK C/11/23.

156 'puppet': *Personal Reminiscences by Chorley, Planché and Young*, p. 8.

157 'I am afraid it is out of order': Jerdan to Richard Bentley, February 1830, Harry Ransom Research Center, University of Texas at Austin.

157 'the only money I spent on myself': S. C. Hall, *A Book of Memories*, p. 274.

158 'Now society is a market place': *Romance and Reality*, vol. 1, p. 156.

158 An aristocratic lady sells tickets: *Romance and Reality*, vol. 1, p. 63.

158 'A part is to be played in company': Ibid., vol. 1, p. 157.

158 *Yes and No:* Ibid., vol. 1, p. 279.

158 'Miss Amesbury': Ibid., vol. 1, pp. 142–43.

159 ' 'Mr Lillian,' observed Mr Morland': Ibid., vol. 1, p. 283.

159 'the novel is now . . . the popular vehicle': Ibid., vol. 1, p. 198.

159 'the fair accountant': *Westminster Review*, vol. 16, January 1832, pp. 204–17.

160 Letitia's formal written statement: BL, Original Letters to Thomas Hill, Add. 20081, fol. 262–64.

161 'defamatory gossip': *Personal Reminiscences by Chorley, Planché and Young*, p. 89.

161 'upon the round, rosewood, brass-inlaid drawing-room table': Saintsbury, *Paris Sketch Book*, p. 170.

161 'to get the *Profit* of my own Labour and Talent': Heath, *The Heath Family Engravers*, vol. 2, p. 24.

162 Nothing better exemplifies: On the phenomenon of the annual, see Harris, *Forget Me Not*.

162 surviving ladies' albums of the period: William St Clair collection.

163 In late 1830: Alexander and Sellars, *The Art of the Brontës*, p. 15.

164 Ned Plymdale attempts to impress Rosamond Vincy: Eliot, *Middlemarch*, pp. 302–4.

164 'only wanted to know what her audience liked': Ibid., p. 190.

165 'The Madonna puzzled me the most': *Letters*, p. 73.

165 'with the loathing of a slave': [Thomson], 'Memorials,' p. 88.

166 Jerdan had got to know two brothers: *AWJ*, vol. 4, p. 358.

167 They offered him an instant loan: Matoff, *Conflicted Life*, p. 161.

167 'I suppose troubling a friend': Jerdan to Bulwer, December 25 [1830], Hertfordshire Archives and Local Studies, DE/K/C11/23.

168 'lost the whole of the proceeds': L.E.L. to Bulwer, Hertfordshire Archives and Local Studies, DE/K/C1/96.

CHAPTER 9   FRENCH CONNECTIONS

169 'I thought (not, I hope, uncharitably)': *Diaries of William Charles Macready*, vol. 1, p. 124.

169 In June, Letitia jumped: [Thomson], 'Memorials,' p. 183.

169 'it would be something to be out of the perpetual worry': *Letters*,

p. 101.

170 The onboard lunch: Thackeray, *Paris Sketch Book*, p. 3.

170 'delightful': *Letters*, p. 103.

170 'pleasant apartments, looking on the Boulevards': *Letters*, p. 104.

172 'We parted on Thursday': *Letters*, p. 102.

172 'Pray write to me': *Letters*, p. 105.

172 'Love and fear are the greatest principles of human existence': *Letters*, p. 105.

173 'I was so glad of your letter': *Letters*, p. 107.

173 'I hope you will not think that I intend writing you to death': *Letters*, p. 107.

173 'I write on purpose to scold you': *Letters*, p. 109.

174 'The Talisman': *Tales and Sketches*, pp. 61–90.

174 'annual, consisting entirely of French translations': *Letters*, p. 113.

175 'an old friend and relative': *Letters*, p. 118.

175 Christopher Sullivan Fagan: Made a colonel in the Bengal army 1815, and a general in 1837. See *Alphabetical List of the Officers of the Bengal Army*, pp. 102–3.

175 In October 1797: Mrs. Morgan John Connell, *The Last Colonel of the Irish Brigade: Count O'Connell and Old Irish Life at Home and Abroad, 1745–1833* (London: Kegan Paul, 1892), vol. 2, p. 216.

175 Hyacinthe-Gabrielle Roland . . . the Earl of Mornington: Farmer, *A Regency Elopement*, pp. 169–71.

176 'her ability to play the secret for all it was worth': Jenson, *Trauma and Its Representations*, p. 121.

176 'a poem authored by pain': Ibid., p. 117.

176 'a chronically wounded enigma': Ibid., p. 119.

177 'Willow Leaves': *PLG*, p. 353.

177 admiring piece on L.E.L.: *Revue des deux mondes*, vol. 6, 1832, pp. 404–8.

178 'gallantry': Thackeray, *Paris Sketch Book*, p. 143.

178 'The soirées are where': *Letters*, p. 109.

178 Heinrich Heine: Mende, *Heinrich Heine*, p. 116.

178 'He said, 'Mademoiselle'': *Letters*, p. 108.

179 'you know it takes a long time': *Letters*, pp. 107–8.

180 'I am unconquerably irresolute': *Letters*, p. 115.

180 'pale, dark, sombre': *Letters*, p. 115.

180 They went on to elope: See Knapp, *Marie Dorval*.

180 'As far as I can judge': *Letters*, p. 110.

180 'of course it is impossible': *Letters*, p. 110.

181 'love dashing her head blindly': Quoted in Miller, *The Brontë Myth*, p. 13.

183 'making an experimental voyage through the carte': *Letters*, p. 112.

183 'I am obliged to force': *Letters*, p. 118.

183 a litany of complaints: *Letters*, p. 108.

183 Rosina Wheeler . . . Edward Bulwer: Mitchell, *Bulwer Lytton*, p. 38.

183 Lady Caroline Lamb was particularly warned: Farmer, *A Regency Elopement*, p. 170.

184 cohabited informally: Frost, *Living in Sin*.

184 Mary Elizabeth Braddon: Carnell, *Literary Lives of Mary Elizabeth Braddon*.

185 strip-searched by a suspicious female customs officer: *AWJ*, vol. 3, p. 192.

185 'excess of feminine timidity': *AWJ*, vol. 4, p. 203.

185 'done all I could for the last three years': Whittington Landon to Jerdan, Bodleian Library, MSS. Eng. lett. d. 113–14.

186 penning comic epigrams: Jerdan, 1848 memoir, p. x.

186 'a character of no ordinary cast': *Autobiography of Anna Eliza Bray*, p. 236.

186 'I cannot get over my disappointment': *Letters*, p. 124.

186 where she had been christened: Matoff, *Conflicted Life*, p. 18.

186 She pointedly described: TNA, Class: HO107; Piece: 1679; Folio: 427; Page: 5.

187 a baptismal record: London Metropolitan Archives, Register of Baptisms for Parish of Walworth St Peter in the district of Southwark, 1834, p. 6.

187 dancers at the Strand Theatre: *LG*, 1834, p. 853.

187 in the 1841 census: Matoff refers to this record, *Conflicted Life*, p. 374, but is wrong to state that the eldest child, Marion, was not christened.

188 Stendhal's girl: Weis, *The Real Traviata*, pp. 51–52.

188 she eventually died: Matoff, *Conflicted Life*, p. 523.

189 'I have often been told that my writings are too melancholy': L.E.L., *Francesca Carrara*, vol. 3, p. 4.

189 'tender' friendship: Graves, *Goodbye to All That*, p. 28.

189 Letitia and Hemans: Morrison, 'Effusive Elegies or Catty Critic.'

190 'like that lost lyre': *Works of Mrs Hemans*, vol. 7, 'The Lyre and Flower,' p. 83.

190 'When I have the good luck or ill luck': *Letters*, p. 121.

190 'As for falling in love': *Letters*, p. 131.

190 'cruel slander was old': L.E.L. to Bulwer, Sypher, *A Biography*, Appendix 1, p. 273.

190 'two other nice girls': *Diaries of William Charles Macready*, vol. 1, p. 173.

191 'Jerdan was in the box': Ibid.

192 'Called on Forster': Ibid., p. 262.

CHAPTER 10 VILE LINKS

194 'set of coarse men': Chorley, *Autobiography*, vol. 1, p. 252.

195 'the personal scurrility' . . . 'the sausage': Cited in Mitchell, *Bulwer Lytton*, p. 110.

195 'hardly intelligible': Thomas Carlyle to Margaret A. Carlyle, June 25, 1833, *Carlyle Letters Online*.

197 The text snidely insinuated: *Fraser's*, vol. 1, June 1830, pp. 605–6.

197 In her *Fraser's* profile: *Fraser's*, vol. 8, October 1833, p. 433.

197 'pernicious' practical effects on 'the happiness of women': *Westminster Review*, vol. 7, January 1827, p. 66.

198 'And, whoever was out, and whoever was in': Mackenzie, *Miscellaneous Writings of the Late Dr Maginn*, vol. 5, p. cviii.

198 'I am refreshing my Tory principles': *Letters*, p. 127.

199 their political enemy Bulwer: Bulwer, *The Last Days of Pompeii*, vol. 1, pp. 75–76.

200 Comte d'Orsay quipped: Le Fèvre-Deumier, *Célébrités anglaises*, p. 307.

200 The first, now lost: Graves, *The Royal Academy of Arts*, vol. 4, p. 152.

200 asking for his permission: Matoff, *Conflicted Life*, p. 251.

200 puffed it in the *Gazette*: *LG*, no. 700, June 18, 1830, pp. 402–3.

200 quick-fire pen-and-ink drawing: Harry Ransom Research Center, University of Texas at Austin.

201 'short and ill-made': Quoted in Sypher, *A Biography*, p. 10.

202 'kitten-like *mignonnerie*': Quoted in Bates, *The Maclise Portrait Gallery*, p. 200.

202 'most women have no Characters at all': Alexander Pope, *Of the Characters of Women*, Epistle 2, line 2.

205 obtrude a review copy on *Blackwood's*: W. Jerdan to Messrs Blackwood, December 29, 1835, MS letter in National Library of Scotland, cited in Matoff, *Conflicted Life*, p. 312.

205 Jerdan failed to pay the ten guineas: Matoff, *Conflicted Life*, p. 312.

205 'a lady in distress': L.E.L., *The Vow of the Peacock*, introduction.

205 'We give it as London gossip': *Rural Repository*, March 25, 1837, vol. 13, p. 164.

206 'an extraordinary advertisement': *The Spectator*, August 5, 1837, p. 12.

207 Maginn first made his mark: Latané, *William Maginn and the British Press*, p. 28.

208 The one recorded instance: Ibid., p. 160.

208 'Papa and ma delighted that I'm getting on so well': 'Poets of the Day,' *Fraser's*, vol. 7, June 1833, p. 662.

208 'dark ladye': Latané, *William Maginn and the British Press*, p. 202.

209 'dearest William': Mackenzie, *Miscellaneous Writings of the Late Dr Maginn,* vol. 5, p. lxxxv.

209 'You must no longer call': Davies, *John Forster,* p. 76.

209 Letitia rebuts the idea of an 'attachment' with Maginn: *Letters,* p. 140.

210 Forster also received anonymous letters: Mackenzie, *Miscellaneous Writings of the Late Dr Maginn,* vol. 5, p. lxxxv.

211 she had gone on to alienate him: *Letters,* pp. 16–17.

211 A surviving drawing by Maclise: Witt Library, Courtauld Institute of Art.

211 'the principal fribble among the namby-pambies': Quoted in Latané, *William Maginn and the British Press,* p. 205.

211 'Temper': Watts, *Alaric Watts,* vol. 2, p. 77.

211 'pray, Alaric Attila, where do you find those fine names': Quoted in Latané, *William Maginn and the British Press,* p. 205.

211 'despicable treachery': Quoted ibid., p. 207.

212 'conniptions': Latané, *William Maginn and the British Press,* p. 208.

213 'gossiping of Mr Hall': L.E.L. to Bulwer, quoted in Sypher, *A Biography,* p. 273.

213 'the refutation which the evil report met': *LLR,* p. 128.

214 'all connection between myself and Mr Forster at an end': L.E.L. to Bulwer, quoted in Sypher, *A Biography,* p. 273.

214 Letitia's letter to him breaking off the engagement: *LLR,* p. 131.

215 to spare Letitia at his 'own cost': Quoted in Stephenson, *Letitia Landon,* p. 49.

216 'I have suffered for the last three days a degree of torture': *LLR,* p. 130.

216 'melancholia' . . . 'torpor of the liver': Mayo, *Elements of the Pathology of the Human Mind,* pp. 112–13.

216 'feverish illness': [Thomson], 'Memorials,' p. 182.

216 their second child, Matilda: According to Matilda's marriage record, she was twenty-one when she married Charles Bickley in 1858. Sourced from www.ancestry.co.uk.

216 'My 'fastidious master' has a pupil': *AWJ,* vol. 4, p. 318.

216 A private memo: TNA, CO 267/167.

217 ' "Have those horrible reports" ': Howitt, *Homes and Haunts,* vol. 2, p. 161.

218 'I found her, as I have said, variable in spirits': [Thomson], 'Memorials,' p. 186.

218 'The truth of Miss Landon's story': Chorley, *Autobiography,* vol. 1, p. 252.

218 'in the exquisite novel of "Violet" ': [Thomson], 'Memorials,' p. 187.

219 'isn't she painted *con amore*?': *Fraser's,* vol. 14, January 1836, p. 80.

219 'the virgin's melting kiss': Ibid., p. 94.

219 'begged to propose a toast': *Diaries of William Charles Macready,* vol. 1, p. 324.

219 De Quincey had briefly considered challenging: Russett, *De Quincey's Romanticism*, p. 132.

220 'no indelicacy in stating that Mr Grantley Berkeley's mother': 'Mr Grantley Berkeley and his novel,' *Fraser's*, vol. 14, August 1836, p. 243.

221 'sixteen guineas per sheet': Grant, *The Great Metropolis*, p. 322.

221 'a certain person': Berkeley, *My Life and Recollections*, vol. 2, pp. 47–48.

222 'what blight?': Ibid., vol. 3, p. 195.

222 she was presenting such a beautiful tableau in the candlelight: Ibid., vol. 2, p. 51.

222 slavishly in love with her: Croker, *A Walk from London to Fulham*, p. 35.

222 'I could not praise a work as I have done yours' . . . 'should be proud of her bard': Berkeley, *My Life and Recollections*, vol. 2, pp. 80–81.

222 If the Fraserians continued to mock her in print: In 1836, the Fraserian Francis Mahoney, a defrocked Jesuit from Cork, published *The Reliques of Father Prout*, with a preface by Maginn and pictures by Maclise. The volume is so unintelligible to those 'not of the craft' that the modern reader is likely to be left in a state of bemused boredom. However, the images include 'Meet me by Moonlight,' in which Maclise portrays himself kneeling at Letitia's feet in an attitude of exaggerated romantic devotion, hardly a tactful portrayal in the circumstances, and a poem that portrays L.E.L. as a fallen angel.

223 'I have been so gay lately': *Letters*, p. 144.

223 'The longer I live': Quoted in Eger and Peltz, *Brilliant Women*, p. 130.

CHAPTER 11   THE GOVERNOR

224 'promised . . . lasting happiness': Roberts, *A Memoir*, p. 30.

224 Katherine Thomson attested: [Thomson], 'Memorials,' p. 188.

224 'change her name': S. C. Hall, *A Book of Memories*, p. 274.

225 'annoyed and depressed by the inconveniences': Jerdan to Lady Blessington, January 5, 1839, BL, Add. MS 43688, ff. 64–65.

225 two young Ashanti 'princes': Metcalfe, *Maclean of the Gold Coast*, p. 204.

226 precursor companies of the modern Unilever: For example, Forster and Smith's Gambia-based peanut export business, run by Matthew's brother William between 1818 and his death in 1849, was incorporated in 1873 into the Bathurst Trading Co., which was itself then acquired by Lever Bros. in 1917: Brooks, *Western Africa and Capo Verde*, p. 133; Swindell and Jeng, *Migrants, Credit and Climate*, p. 16.

226 a fleet of at least fourteen: Sherwood, *After Abolition*, p. 65.

226 Matthew was, for example: Ibid., p. 66.

226 a late Victorian photograph: Shenai, *Finding the Bergheims of Belsize Court*.

226 eight live-in servants: Census Returns of England and Wales, 1851, Civil parish: Hampstead; Piece: 1492; Folio: 50; Page: 2.

226 he acquired a stake: Matoff, *Conflicted Life*, p. 308.

226 Forster and Smith decided to go it alone: Wright, *The World and a Very Small Place in Africa*, p. 128.

226 'deprecated' her engagement: Jerdan to Lady Blessington, January 5, 1839, BL, Add. MS 43688, ff. 64–65.

226 Maria's unpublished diaries: I am grateful to her descendant David Burgess for allowing me to see these.

227 thrust a sheaf of papers into her hand: Cruickshank, *Eighteen Years on the Gold Coast*, vol. 1, p. 216.

227 'If Miss Landon still retained' Roberts, *A Memoir*, p. 29.

228 'public-private partnership': St Clair, *The Grand Slave Emporium*, p. 54.

230 'heavy debt' it owed Africa 'for the crimes': Sherwood, *After Abolition*, p. 69.

230 'highly polished manners': Blessington, *The Idler in France*, vol. 1, p. 200.

231 'Thus is Cape Coast Castle': Quoted in Metcalfe, *Maclean of the Gold Coast*, p. 205.

231 had previously been court-martialed in Jamaica . . . captain of the guard: Metcalfe, *Maclean of the Gold Coast*, pp. 191ff.

231 'somewhat perfunctory inquest': Ibid., pp. 180–81.

232 The goods that Forster and Smith: Sherwood, *After Abolition*, p. 69.

232 openly manufactured for export in Birmingham: *British and Foreign Anti-Slavery Reporter*, no. 15, July 15, 1840, p. 161.

232 an official exchange rate: Thanks to Professor John Styles, who is researching a history of the international textile market, for this information.

232 'The origins of the Forster & Smith partnership': Lynn, *Commerce and Economic Change in West Africa*, p. 87.

232 estate in the West Indies: According to Valerie Glass (in Creighton, *North East Slavery and Abolition Newsletter*, no. 7, September 2009), a Matthew Forster (1730–1798)—either our Matthew's father or his uncle—was a commissary general to forces in the West Indies, and later owned an estate on St. Eustatius in the Caribbean, as well as being elected five times as mayor of Berwick, the constituency for which our Matthew was later returned to Parliament in 1841.

233 'chivalric energy': Roberts, *A Memoir*, p. 29.

233 after a failed earlier career: Metcalfe, *Maclean of the Gold Coast*, ch. 1.

234 centerpiece for Prince Albert: www.royalcollection.org.uk/collection/1570/centrepiece.

235 'time-honoured customs': Cruickshank, *Eighteen Years on the Gold Coast*, vol. 1, p. 184.

235 the *Dos Amigos:* Metcalfe, *Maclean of the Gold Coast*, pp. 245ff.

236 A young British naval officer: Ibid., p. 260.

236 were there for debt: Ibid., p. 265.

236 'to legalise the Slave Trade to a certain extent': Quoted in Sherwood, *After Abolition*, p. 73.

237 'There can be no doubt': Minute by James Stephen, 2/4/1840, CO 267/162; Metcalfe, *Maclean of the Gold Coast*, p. 250.

237 'dry, reserved, hard-headed Scotchman': Note by Bulwer, CO 96/44, quoted in Metcalfe, *Maclean of the Gold Coast*, p. vii.

237 'In her enthusiasm': [Thomson], *The Queens of Society*, p. 187.

237 'his dark-gray eyes were seldom raised': Ibid., p. 212.

237 'African habits, African horrors, and African wonders': *LLR*, vol. 1, p. 136.

238 'unaccustomed . . . to ladies': Quoted in Metcalfe, *Maclean of the Gold Coast*, p. 214.

238 'portraits of distinguished authors': *Letters*, p. 186.

238 'much struck by her appearance': [Thomson], *The Queens of Society*, p. 188.

238 'most unattractive': Vizetelly, *Glances Back Through Seventy Years*, vol. 1, p. 127.

239 'plainness of looks and diminutiveness of form': Madden, *Countess of Blessington*, vol. 2, p. 268.

239 The Liddiards invited Letitia and Maclean: Unpublished diary of Maria Liddiard.

239 proof of her unblemished position in society: *LLR*, vol. 1, p. 226.

239 'You are canvassing for us': *Letters*, p. 158.

240 inquiry into his suspected misappropriation of funds: BL, Loan 96, RLF 1/500/25a: 'Extracts from the proceedings of the Literary Fund with respect to an enquiry by Charles Wentworth Dilke into the conduct of William Jerdan 12 April–10 May 1837'; also 1/511/31a.

240 'It was, for both of us': Chorley, *Autobiography*, pp. 253–54.

240 'I believe she is very timid': Quoted in Latané, *William Maginn and the British Press*, p. 187.

240 'I shall never forget': *Letters*, p. 162.

240 Maria and Anne Liddiard had spent the day with her: Unpublished diary of Maria Liddiard.

CHAPTER 12   ENGAGEMENT

241 fantasized about making her own voyage to Africa: *Letters*, pp. 7–8.

241 'Mr Maclean had sought her hand in marriage': [Thomson], 'Memorials,' p. 188.

242 Two letters Maclean wrote to Matthew Forster: Texts quoted in Metcalfe, *Maclean of the Gold Coast,* pp. 212–14.

243 'Never shall I forget the anguish of my poor friend': [Thomson], 'Memorials,' p. 188.

244 'To those who [to] indulge in a small envy': *Letters,* pp. 164–65.

244 'her applying to *you*' . . . 'impudence in having written to her so kindly' . . . 'various reports': Quoted in Metcalfe, *Maclean of the Gold Coast,* pp. 212–13.

244 'country marriages': Priestley, *West African Trade and Coast Society,* passim; St Clair, *The Grand Slave Emporium,* p. 148.

245 1837 list of Cape Coast female traders: Letter to the Colonial Office from Burgoyne, December 22, 1837, CO 267/144.

245 increase the number of women involved in commerce: See Adu-Boahen, *Abolition, Economic Transition, Gender and Slavery.*

245 'of colour, of respectability, living in Accra': Madden, *Countess of Blessington,* vol. 2, p. 283.

245 James Bannerman: Priestley, *West African Trade and Coast Society,* vol. 2, p. 59.

245 Yaa Hom: Jones and Sebald, *An African Family Archive,* p. 131, note 98.

245 'The African': *Fisher's Drawing Room Scrap Book* (1832), p. 35.

246 'I can scarcely make even you understand': *Letters,* p. 192.

247 relying on the hospitality: Unpublished letter from L.E.L., author's collection, November 23, 1837, refers to her staying with the Thomsons; unpublished Liddiard family diary makes plain how frequently she stayed with them.

247 'large fortune': [Thomson], *The Queens of Society,* p. 187.

247 'only a long sum' . . . 'to write what will sell': L.E.L., *Ethel Churchill,* vol. 2, p. 12.

247 'a sort of Radical': Quoted in Sypher, *A Biography,* p. 180.

248 'Oh, what a waste of feeling and of thought': *LLR,* vol. 2, p. 277.

248 'Which was the true philosopher?': *LLR,* vol. 2, p. 261.

249 ' 'Tis a strange mystery, the power of words!': *LLR,* vol. 2, p. 295.

249 'Gossipping': *LLR,* vol. 2, p. 276.

249 'Self-blindness': *LLR,* vol. 2, p. 274.

249 'Life has dark secrets': *LLR,* vol. 2, p. 263.

249 'The Marriage Vow': *LLR,* vol. 2, p. 277.

249 'Death in the flower': *LLR,* vol. 2, p. 281.

249 'glass mask': L.E.L., *Ethel Churchill,* vol. 2, p. 327.

249 as the victim gasps for breath: Ibid., vol. 3, pp. 257–61.

249 an excited reader from Bedford: *The Times,* February 1, 1839, p. 3.

250 admired the novel's 'astonishing qualities': Quoted in Sypher, *A Biography*, p. 179.

250 translated into German*: Adele Churchill, oder, die zwei Bräute, von der Verfasserin der Improvisatorin* (Leipzig: Kirchner, 1838).

250 'I on honey-dews have fed': *Letters*, p. 176.

250 'I saw L.E.L. today': Madden, *Countess of Blessington*, vol. 2, p. 183.

250 In a letter to the Liddiards' daughter Maria: Liddiard family papers.

251 'sumptuous' all-male dinner: *London Evening Standard*, March 19, 1838.

251 Whittington attended: Liddiard family diaries.

251 'the moment of his return': Madden, *Countess of Blessington*, vol. 2, p. 71.

252 Letitia applied to Richard Bentley: *Letters*, p. 179.

252 *Castruccio Castracani:* Discussed in Baiesi, *Letitia Elizabeth Landon and Metrical Romance*, ch. 4, passim.

252 made vain efforts: L.E.L. to Bulwer, ?early 1838, Sypher, *A Biography*, p. 281.

252 should be presented at court: [Thomson], *Queens of Society*, p. 187.

252 'utterly different': *Letters*, p. 169.

253 'one huge serpent, and one only': L.E.L., 'The Poppy,' *Flowers of Loveliness* (unpaginated).

254 first came across William Jerdan: Blanche Sully to her mother, January 1, 1838, Papers of Thomas Sully, Joseph Downs Collection of Manuscripts and Printed Ephemera, Winterthur Library, Col. 164, Acc. 84x130, vol. 1, accessed online.

254 The first sitting he made of Letitia: A photocopy of the picture, labeled Letitia Landon, was placed in the Heinz Archive at the National Portrait Gallery shortly after its sale at Christie's London in 1974. In the 1974 sale catalog it was described as being a portrait of 'Miss Maclean,' probably an error for Mrs. Maclean. The same picture later appeared at Sotheby's New York in 2007 as a first sitting of 'Miss McLean.'

255 a small auction house: Chiswick Auctions. Contacted by me on September 8, 2014.

255 'Although the profile was not the happiest view of her face': *LLR*, p. 291.

255 '[I]t was all so sad': Martineau, *Autobiography*, pp. 422–23.

256 'two nearest relatives': George Maclean to Sir John Maclean, October 12, 1838, quoted in Metcalfe, *Maclean of the Gold Coast*, p. 215.

256 'very strange and out of spirits': Unpublished Liddiard diary, May 16, 1838.

257 'Papa' had 'a long confab': Unpublished Liddiard diary, June 10, 1838.

258 'Miss Landon told me what surprised me': Unpublished Liddiard diary, June 21, 1838.

258 '2 strange notes': Unpublished Liddiard diary, June 23, 1838.

258 honed into publishing shape by Letitia: *Oxford Dictionary of National Biography.*

258 'which she could not have so long': S. C. Hall, *Retrospect of a Long Life,* vol. 2, p. 160.

258 'If Mrs McLean [*sic*] has as many friends': S. C. Hall, *A Book of Memories,* p. 278.

258 'More disquietude about the party': Unpublished Liddiard diary, June 25, 1838.

258 Letitia watched the procession: [Thomson], *The Queens of Society,* p. 190.

259 volume of sermons: *A Series of Practical Discourses* by the Rev. James Maclean (London: Smith, Elder, 1838).

259 'I trust that Mr G. Maclean': Metcalfe, *Maclean of the Gold Coast,* p. 232.

259 Only at the 'eleventh hour': *Letters,* p. 194.

259 'sitting on a hassock' . . . 'as long as I could trace her figure against the sky': Whittington's letter is quoted in full in *LLR,* vol. 1, pp. 176–81.

260 'Never is there one moment's quiet': *Letters,* p. 184.

260 'The sky is filled with stars': *Letters,* p. 185.

261 'But thou hast sunk beneath the wave': *LLR,* vol. 1, p. 191.

261 ' 'Tis Night, and overhead the sky is gleaming': *LLR,* vol. 1, p. 191.

261 'Those who had, in some measure, compromised her': Chorley, *Autobiography,* vol. 1, p. 252.

261 'All I can say': *Letters,* p. 185.

262 'Cape Coast Castle!': *Letters,* p. 185.

CHAPTER 13   HEART OF DARKNESS

263 alerted by letter in advance: Hutchinson, *Impressions of Western Africa,* p. 60.

263 the locals were fond of receiving letters: L.E.L. to Bulwer from Cape Coast Castle, undated; quoted in Sypher, *A Biography,* appendix 1, p. 288.

263 the government inspector Richard Madden: Madden, *Countess of Blessington,* vol. 2, pp. 289–90.

263 having questioned the castle staff: Ibid., p. 283.

264 'as well as possible' . . . 'pretty even in England': L.E.L. to Mrs. Hall, *Letters,* p. 186. (The text of this letter was published in *The Morning Chronicle* and *The Gentleman's Magazine* in early 1839 when the news of Letitia's death reached London.)

264 'dressing-room': Cruickshank, *Eighteen Years on the Gold Coast,* vol. 1, p. 224.

264 'On three sides' . . . 'the band plays all the old popular airs' . . . 'housekeeping': L.E.L. to Mrs. Hall, *Letters,* p. 186. (The text of this letter was

published in *The Morning Chronicle* and *The Gentleman's Magazine* in early 1839 when the news of Letitia's death reached London.)

264   the castle staff remained loyal: Madden, *Countess of Blessington*, vol. 2, p. 298.

264   'I begin to see daylight': L.E.L. to Mrs. Hall, *Letters*, pp. 186–87.

264   black prisoners sluggishly scrubbing the floors: L.E.L. to Lady Stepney, *Letters*, p. 190.

265   'I am very well and happy': L.E.L. to Mrs. Hall, *Letters*, p. 187.

265   'without variation' . . . 'favourable impressions of the country': *LLR*, vol. 1, p. 195.

265   'The castle is a fine building. . . . I am very well': *Letters*, p. 191.

265   'I am very well and happy. The Castle is a fine building' . . . 'Arabian nights': *Letters*, p. 188.

265   'I am most uninterestingly well and happy': L.E.L. to Bulwer, quoted in Sypher, *A Biography*, Appendix 1, p. 288.

265   'I cannot tell you how much better': *Letters*, pp. 194–95.

265   'I never was in better health': *Letters*, p. 196.

265   'The castle is a fine building': *Letters*, p. 198.

265   Sarah Bowditch: On the insect life at Cape Coast Castle, see St Clair, *The Grand Slave Emporium*, p. 75.

266   'stone deaf': *Letters*, p. 191.

266   'the nights are so hot': *Letters*, p. 194.

266   'At first I thought it rather hard': L.E.L. to Bulwer, quoted in Sypher, *A Biography*, appendix 1, p. 288.

266   'The people appear very intelligent': Ibid., pp. 288–89.

267   'You may suppose what a resource writing is': *Letters*, p. 189.

267   'payment to poor L.E.L. for *her* 60 pages of verse': *Journal of Thomas Moore*, vol. 5, p. 2027.

267   'If my literary success does but continue': *Letters*, p. 189.

268   'My brother who has lately acquired the habit': L.E.L. to Bulwer, c. May 1838, quoted in Sypher, *A Biography*, p. 286.

268   'You cannot think the complete seclusion': *Letters*, p. 186.

268   'The solitude is absolute': *Letters*, p. 189.

268   'My solitude is absolute': L.E.L. to Bulwer, quoted in Sypher, *A Biography*, appendix 1, p. 288.

268   'At seven Mr Maclean comes': *Letters*, p. 193.

268   'The solitude, except an occasional dinner': *Letters*, p. 198.

269   'godsend': L.E.L. to Matthew Forster, October 12, 1838, quoted in Sypher, *A Biography*, appendix 1, p. 291.

269   'most civil, obliging person': *Letters*, p. 194.

269   Prussic, or hydrocyanic, acid: On the history of prussic acid, see Earles,

'The Introduction of Hydrocyanic Acid into Medicine.'

269　'no intention of suicide at present': P. B. Shelley to Edward Trelawny, June 18, 1822, Trelawny, *Recollections of the Last Days of Shelley and Byron*, p. 100.

270　self-slaughterer's drug of choice: Dickens, *Pickwick Papers*, p. 28.

270　suicide by prussic acid and laudanum: *The Times*, 'Coroner's Inquests,' December 23, 1839, p. 7.

270　'spasms and hysterical affections' . . . 'prescribed for her by her medical attendant in London': *LLR*, vol. 1, p. 213.

270　His enthusiastic experimental use of it: Granville, *Historical and Practical Treatise*, p. 388. (Thomson's full letter to Granville describing his use of prussic acid on patients is printed on pp. 371–90.)

271　'extremely useful as an external application': Ibid., p. 375.

271　'a remedy of great efficacy': Thomson, *The London Dispensatory*, pp. 657–58, 749.

271　had never completed his own medical studies: *DNB*.

271　'pompous in his phraseology': Clarke, *Autobiographical Recollections of the Medical Profession*, p. 305.

271　'if properly diluted and dispensed': Earles, 'The Introduction of Hydrocyanic Acid into Medicine,' p. 312.

271　'certainly is a very powerful sedative': Thomson, *The London Dispensatory*, p. 749.

272　'We all know': *The Times*, January 22, 1839, p. 5.

272　'the aid of narcotics and that violent spasms': Madden, *Countess of Blessington*, vol. 2, p. 70.

272　'stimulate her energies': Burton, *Wanderings in West Africa*, vol. 2, p. 81.

272　'there was no author or authoress': Hayter, 'The Laudanum Bottle Loomed Large,' p. 37.

273　'Love's Last Lesson': *The Golden Violet*, p. 299.

273　'Many fashionable women attempt': Thomson, *The London Dispensatory*, p. 472.

274　'The Almond Tree': *PLG*, p. 326.

275　'affected' . . . 'had the spasms rather badly' . . . 'medicine in the bottle': *LLR*, vol. 1, p. 212.

275　'No my dear Mr Forster': L.E.L. to Matthew Forster, October 12, 1838, quoted in Sypher, *A Biography*, appendix 1, p. 290.

276　'still with opiates': *Letters*, p. 194.

277　'poor Blanchard': *Diaries of William Charles Macready*, vol. 1, p. 486.

277　'Dear Lady Blessington': Laman Blanchard to Lady Blessington, Friday (January 4) 1839, BL, Add. MS. 43688, ff. 67–68.

278　'There are eleven or twelve chambers': *Letters*, p. 197.

279   'That poor Sun': *Letters,* p. 184.
279   'no wonder that a man': L.E.L. to Fanny Liddiard, undated but written from Cape Coast Castle, Liddiard papers.
279   Her own breakfast coffee: [Thomson], *The Queens of Society,* p. 221.
279   'I must have seen it, had she been so unhappy': *LLR,* vol. 1, p. 250.
280   'And yet this is she who *had* written': *LLR,* vol. 1, p. 249.
280   Edmund Bannerman: For Bannerman's story, see Green, *White Man's Grave,* p. 164.
281   'The true history of Mrs Maclean's death': Burton, *Wanderings in West Africa,* vol. 2, p. 80.
281   'I conclude from your letter': Jerrold, *Poetical Works of Laman Blanchard,* p. 61.
282   Balzac explained: Balzac, *Lost Illusions,* p. 633.

CHAPTER 14   COVER-UP

283   'a great blow has fallen on me': George Maclean to Sir John Maclean, manuscript letter quoted in Watt, *Poisoned Lives,* p. 198.
283   'My neighbour': Buxton, *The Africa Slave Trade and Its Remedy,* p. 225, note.
284   'complaint in which he charged': Note made on December 11, 1839, on back of a subsequent letter from Whittington Landon to Her Majesty's Secretary of State for the Colonies, CO 267/157.
284   'My darling Whittington': *Letters,* p. 193.
285   'medical comment': Whittington Landon to Her Majesty's Secretary of State for the Colonies, December 11, 1839, CO 267/157.
285   'most anxious': Whittington Landon to Her Majesty's Secretary of State for the Colonies, February 15, 1839, CO 267/157.
285   'of all men': George Maclean to Sir John Maclean, May 10, 1839, manuscript quoted in Watt, *Poisoned Lives,* p. 207.
285   'I do not hesitate to say': *LLR,* vol. 1, p. 239.
286   'little native boy': [Thomson], *The Queens of Society,* p. 196.
286   'malignant woman' . . . 'calumnies': Hutchinson, *Impressions of West Africa,* p. 60.
287   'offensive' . . . 'persons of distinction': *The Times,* December 25, 1840, p. 7.
287   'I hereby declare': *The Times,* January 1, 1841, p. 5.
288   the *Robert Heddle:* Metcalfe, *Maclean of the Gold Coast,* p. 263; Sherwood, *After Abolition,* p. 71.
289   'It was no part of Captain Groves' duty': Sherwood, *After Abolition,* p. 71.
289   Parliamentary Select Committee . . . press vilification: Ibid., pp. 70–71.
290   'it was painful to hear the twaddle': Ibid., p. 72.

290 the guest list: Sourced from 'A Charles Dickens Journal,' www.dickenslive .com.

291 Mrs. Leo Hunter: *The Pickwick Papers,* ch. 15.

291 the unpublished letter he wrote to Lady Blessington: BL, Add. 43688, ff. 64–65.

293 Laura Deacon . . . friends with Letitia: Mitchell, *Bulwer Lytton,* pp. 48, 52, 70, 233.

294 'freemasonry which exists among "gentlemen" ': Rosina Bulwer Lytton, *A Blighted Life,* pp. 4–5.

294 poetry collection: Blanchard, *Lyric Offerings,* p. 71.

295 how good-looking he was: *Letters,* p. 46.

295 'dark, handsome jewish features': Vizetelly, *Glances Back Through Seventy Years,* p. 143.

295 injured by flying fragments of glass: Patmore, *My Friends and Acquaintance,* vol. 3, p. 210.

295 'Do you, my dear Mr. Blanchard': *Letters,* pp. 147–48.

296 an unpublished letter of 1832: Hertfordshire Archives and Local Studies, DE/K/C2/110. Bulwer's mention of Blanchard's poetry volume occurs in 'Retrospective Poetry,' *New Monthly Magazine,* May 1, 1832, p. 442.

296 Blanchard was, in Bulwer's view: Introductory memoir, *Sketches from the Life by the Late Laman Blanchard.*

296 'free lance': Bulwer's introduction, *Sketches from the Life by the Late Laman Blanchard,* p. vii.

296 'monstering': Patmore, *My Friends and Acquaintance,* vol. 3, p. 230.

297 'keep her memory as a pleasant odour': Letter from Blanchard quoted in S. C. Hall, *A Book of Memories,* p. 280.

297 'domestic fight this gallant little woman made': Jerrold, *Poetical Works of Laman Blanchard,* introductory memoir, p. 60.

297 'We have rarely opened a more painful or unsatisfactory book': *The Athenaeum,* May 29, 1841, p. 421.

297 he later moralized: Chorley, *Autobiography,* vol. 1, p. 252.

298 'passion' was 'pasteboard': *Letters of Elizabeth Barrett to Mary Russell Mitford, 1836–1854,* vol. 1, p. 252.

298 'into slander': Ibid., vol. 1, p. 170.

298 'If I have failed': S. C. Hall, *A Book of Memories,* p. 280.

298 'sudden attacks of tears': Bulwer's introduction, *Sketches from the Life by the Late Laman Blanchard,* pp. xxxii–xxxiii.

299 Bulwer believed: Ibid., p. vii.

299 'during a moment of temporary insanity': *Pictorial Times,* February 22, 1845.

299 'tasteful tribute': *Illustrated London News,* January 3, 1857.

299 'drifted away into London journalism': Ellis, *A Mid-Victorian Pepys,* p. 165, note.

299 'the angel in the house': Phrase coined by P. G. Patmore's son, the arch-Victorian poet Coventry Patmore.

300 'It is not the blood of my body': *The Times,* December 23, 1839, p. 7.

300 'I have heard too much calumny': Bulwer to Blanchard, January 6, 1839, introductory memoir, Jerrold, *Poetical Works of Laman Blanchard,* p. 61.

301 governess job: Matoff, *Conflicted Life,* p. 447.

301 'Sweet indeed is the bread': Hertfordshire Archives and Local Studies, DE/K/C24/26.

301 petty embezzlement: Cross, *The Royal Literary Fund,* p. 15.

301 'not worth having': L.E.L. to Bulwer, quoted in Sypher, *A Biography,* p. 279.

302 Whittington continued to bother the countess: Whittington Landon to Marguerite, Countess of Blessington, January 17, 1839; November 8, 1839; November 12, 1839; January 12, 1842: MSS: New York Public Library, Pforzheimer Collection, Blessington Papers, vol. 3, pp. 252–55.

302 lock of L.E.L.'s hair: BL Add. MS, 43688, hair originally contained in folded paper (folio 69a) with note in Lady Blessington's hand reading 'The Hair of poor dear L.E.L.'

302 Slebech: Pembrokeshire Archives and Local Studies.

302 he wrote to Bulwer: Hertfordshire Archives and Local Studies, DE/K/C24/26.

302 'united contributions of several old friends': Katherine Thomson to William Jerdan, undated, Bodleian, MSS. Eng. lett. d. 113–14.

302 buy from him the copyrights: Bodleian, MSS. Eng. lett. d. 113–14.

303 'When the lamp is flickering out': William Jerdan to Edward Bulwer Lytton, September 1, 1862, Hertfordshire Archives and Local Studies, DE/K/C11.

303 Their grandson married Nancy Mitford: information from WikiTree genealogical website.

304 £35,304: 'Stephen, Leslie,' *DNB,* 1887, vol. 11, pp. 254–55.

304 'an exacting husband': Davies, *John Forster: A Literary Life,* p. 181.

304 'entertained such a deep affection for her': Lady Blessington to Dr. Madden, December 19, 1840, Pforzheimer Collection, New York Public Library, Bless. 1.011 b.

304 'exonerated and demoted': Huzzey, *Freedom Burning,* p. 139.

305 Henry Hill: Metcalfe, *Maclean of the Gold Coast,* p. 305.

305 'guilty of bribery': Sherwood, *After Abolition*, p. 73.
305 butler at Belsize Villa was jailed: Ibid.
305 'the moral beauty of England': Metcalfe, *Maclean of the Gold Coast*, p. 270.
305 One of the men, Kwantabisa: Ibid., p. 274.

CHAPTER 15   HAUNTINGS

306 'ruin'd wall / Lies worn and rent' . . . 'flirtation' . . . 'feelings conjured up': Jerdan, 1848 memoir, p. xix.
307 'see how such a man': Hawthorne, *The English Notebooks*, p. 282.
307 'any truth in the scandalous rumours' . . . 'never yielded her virtue to him': Ibid., p. 283.
307 Bennoch knew about Fred: Matoff, *Conflicted Life*, pp. 488, 496.
308 'fatal facility': Lewes, *Rose, Blanche and Violet*, vol. 2, pp. 49–50.
309 'He gives no charming picture': *Letters of Charlotte Brontë*, vol. 2, p. 58.
310 Rose Ellen Hendricks: Salmon, *The Formation of the Victorian Literary Profession*, p. 178.
310 'for ever known' . . . 'celebrity': Robert Southey to Charlotte Brontë, March 12, 1837, *Letters of Charlotte Brontë*, vol. 1, p. 167.
311 John Chapman: Hughes, *George Eliot*, p. 103.
313 'L.E.L.'s Last Question': *Athenaeum*, January 26, 1839.
313 'I fancy it would have worked out better': *Letters of Elizabeth Barrett Browning to Mary Russell Mitford*, vol. 1, p. 235.
313 'an autobiography of a poetess': Cited in Salmon, *The Formation of the Victorian Literary Profession*, p. 176.
314 'The Old Stoic': *Emily Brontë: The Complete Poems*, p. 30.
315 'Yet saith a saint': *Poetical Works of Christina Georgina Rossetti*, p. 345.
316 hymn to Dolores: *Swinburne's Collected Poetical Works*, vol. 1, pp. 154–68.
316 'shame' . . . 'love that dare not speak its name': 'Two Loves,' by Lord Alfred Douglas, first published in *The Chameleon*, December 1894.
318 'the transitory, the fleeting, the contingent': Baudelaire, *The Painter of Modern Life*, 4, 'Modernity' (1859), p. 17.

Bibliography

WORKS BY LETITIA LANDON

L.E.L. was so preternaturally prolific that establishing her complete oeu-vre, including her every miscellaneous contribution to various magazines, annuals and anthologies, remains a work in progress. F. J. Sypher's *Letitia Elizabeth Landon: A Bibliography* (Ann Arbor, MI: Scholars' Facsimiles and Reprints, 2005) gives some idea of the sheer quantity of material and the number of editions, as does the online bibliography compiled by Glenn Dibert-Himes as part of Sheffield Hallam University's Corvey Project. They are invaluable resources but are not exhaustive.

Although little of Letitia Landon's work is today available in easily accessible or affordable modern editions, original nineteenth-century versions of many of her books have been digitally scanned and can be read online at www.archive.org.

1. Poems in periodicals

Poems from the Literary Gazette, ed. F. J. Sypher (Ann Arbor, MI: Scholars' Facsimiles and Reprints, 2003), collects all her contributions to that magazine, 1820–36.
Poems from the New Monthly Magazine, ed. F. J. Sypher (Ann Arbor, MI: Scholars' Facsimiles and Reprints, 2007), collects her contributions 1825–39.

However, L.E.L.'s poems also appeared in many other periodicals, including (among others) *The Examiner, The Gentleman's Magazine, The Court Journal,* and *Fraser's Magazine.*

2. Poetry collections

The Fate of Adelaide. London: John Warren, 1821.
The Improvisatrice and Other Poems. London: Hurst and Robinson, 1824.
The Troubadour: Catalogue of Pictures and Historical Sketches. London: Hurst and Robinson, 1824.
The Golden Violet: With Its Tales of Romance and Chivalry. London: Longman, Rees, Orme, Brown, and Green, 1827.
The Venetian Bracelet, The Lost Pleiad, A History of the Lyre, and Other Poems. London: Longman, Rees, Orme, Brown, and Green, 1829.
The Easter Gift: A Religious Offering. London: Fisher, Son & Co., 1832.
The Vow of the Peacock, and Other Poems. London: Saunders and Otley, 1835.
Flowers of Loveliness. London: Ackermann, 1838.

Posthumous editions, of which there were many, include:
Miss Landon's Complete Works. Boston: Phillips, Sampson and Co., 1854.
Poetical Works. London: George Routledge and Sons, 1873.

3. Novels

Romance and Reality, 3 vols. London: H. Colburn and R. Bentley, 1831. The one-volume 1848 reissue, published by Richard Bentley, includes an anonymous memoir by William Jerdan.
Francesca Carrara, 3 vols. London: Richard Bentley, 1834.
Ethel Churchill; or, The Two Brides. London: Henry Colburn, 1837.
Lady Anne Granard; or, Keeping Up Appearances. London: H. Colburn, 1842 (only part-written by L.E.L. and published posthumously).

Edited (possibly ghostwritten) by L.E.L.:
The Heir Presumptive by Lady Stepney. London: Richard Bentley, 1835.
Duty and Inclination, edited by Miss Landon. London: H. Colburn, 1838.

4. Annuals and gift books

Fisher's Drawing-Room Scrap Book for 1832, 1833, 1834, 1835, 1836, 1837, 1838.

L.E.L. also contributed material to many other annuals and anthologies, including *The Forget-Me-Not, Friendship's Offering, The Literary Souvenir, The Amulet, Death's Doings, The Pledge of Friendship, The Bijou, The Poetical Album and Register of Modern Fugitive Poetry, The Keepsake, The Juvenile*

Forget-Me-Not, Heath's Book of Beauty, Finden's Gallery of the Graces, Schloss's Bijou Almanac, and *The Pictorial Album.*

5. Criticism

It is hard to establish the extent of L.E.L.'s criticism given the culture of anonymous reviewing, but she regularly contributed reviews to the *Literary Gazette,* and to other magazines too. Some key works of criticism are collected in F. J. Sypher's *Critical Writings by Letitia Elizabeth Landon* (Delmar, NY: Scholars' Facsimiles and Reprints, 1996). Her essays on the female characters of Walter Scott are printed in Laman Blanchard's *Life and Literary Remains,* vol. 2.

6. Short fiction

Traits and Trials of Early Life. London: H. Colburn, 1836.

Other stories, which originally appeared in periodicals and gift books, are collected in S. J. Sypher, ed., *Tales and Sketches by Letitia Elizabeth Landon* (Delmar, NY: Scholars' Facsimiles and Reprints, 1999).

7. Drama

L.E.L. often wrote dramatic scenes and monologues, but her one play, never performed, was *Castruccio Castracani, or the triumph of Lucca: a tragedy,* printed in Laman Blanchard's *Life and Literary Remains of L.E.L.* (London: Colburn, 1841), vol. 2.

A NOTE ON MANUSCRIPT SOURCES

L.E.L. was a poet of print culture, and surprisingly few holograph manuscripts of her literary works have emerged. In contrast to, say, Emily Brontë, who wrote for herself and copied her poetry into treasured private notebooks, L.E.L. appears to have made no effort to preserve her originals. Given her dependence on Jerdan, and afterwards on Whittington, to 'correct' her manuscripts, it is possible that some of them arrived at the printer's in another's hand.

As a result, she is a literary figure who seems posthumously to rebuke the ideal of authenticity we tend to associate with the actual handwriting of poets on paper: the sense, not entirely misplaced, that the original manuscript is somehow infused with the aura of the writer, whose physical traces it bears, and can offer insights into the moment of literary production. The historical Letitia

Landon thus remains symbolically fugitive, the touch of her hand forever out of reach. Even the texts of many of Letitia Landon's most important private letters exist today only in their printed forms, as reproduced by memoirists such as Laman Blanchard and William Jerdan.

The Liddiard family papers, in the private collection of David Burgess, a descendant, include not only Maria Liddiard's diary, but two letters from Cape Coast Castle in Letitia's own hand and the manuscripts of her verse epigraphs to *Ethel Churchill*. Unpublished manuscripts by others consulted for this book include Jerdan's papers in the Bodleian Library (including letters to him from Letitia's mother, Whittington and the Thomsons), and the papers of Lady Blessington in the New York Public Library (including Whittington's pathetic requests for patronage). The British Library provides more Blessington papers (including the lock of L.E.L.'s hair), as well as the surviving accounts of the *Literary Gazette,* the papers of Thomas Hill, and those of the Royal Literary Fund. Edward Bulwer Lytton's papers at the Hertfordshire Archives and Local Studies, located in County Hall, Hertford, include the letters from Landon to Bulwer transcribed by F. J. Sypher in the appendix to his 2004 biography, but also many other unpublished letters, including some from Laman Blanchard, William Jerdan and Letitia's mother, Catherine Landon. The Colonial Office files relating to George Maclean and Cape Coast are housed in the National Archives in Kew. The letters of the artist Thomas Sully, housed at the Winterthur Museum in Delaware, are now available in transcription online.

One of the great paradoxes of Letitia Landon is that many of the facts of her private life are only accessible via public records, such as birth, marriage and death records, wills, and census returns. Lodged in the London Metropolitan Archives and the National Archives, these can now also be accessed online at www.ancestry.co.uk.

SELECT BIBLIOGRAPHY

This list excludes contemporary newspapers and magazines, such as *The Times* and *Blackwood's Edinburgh Magazine,* which are referred to in reference notes.

Adu-Boahen, Kwabena. 'Abolition, Economic Transition, Gender and Slavery: The Expansion of Women's Slaveholding in Ghana 1807–1874.' *Slavery and Abolition* 31, no. 1 (March 2010).

Alexander, Christine, and Jane Sellars. *The Art of the Brontës.* Cambridge, UK: Cambridge University Press, 1995.

Alphabetical List of the Officers of the Bengal Army. London: Longman, 1838.

Angeletti, Gioia. '"I feel the Improvisatore": Byron, Improvisation and Romantic

Poetics.' In *British Romanticism and Italian Literature: Translating, Reviewing, Rewriting*, ed. Laura Bandiera and Diego Salia. Amsterdam and New York: Editions Rodopi B.V., 2005.

Anon. *Andrew of Padua, the Improvisatore; a tale from the Italian of the Abbate Furbo.* London: Sir Richard Philips and Co., 1820.

Armstrong, Isabel, and Virginia Blain, eds. *Women's Poetry, Late Romantic to Late Victorian: Gender and Genre, 1830–1900.* New York: Palgrave Macmillan, 1999.

Austen, Jane. *Mansfield Park.* 1814; London: Penguin Classics, 2014.

Baiesi, Serena. *Letitia Landon and Metrical Romance: The Adventures of a Literary Genius.* Oxford: Peter Lang, 2009.

Balzac, Honoré de. *Lost Illusions.* Trans. Herbert J. Hunt. London: Penguin, 2004.

Barnard, John. 'First Fruits or 'First Blights': A New Account of the Publishing History of Keats's Poems (1817).' *Romanticism* 12, no. 2 (2006): 71–101.

Bates, William. *The Maclise Portrait-Gallery of Illustrious Literary Characters with Memoirs.* London: Chatto and Windus, 1898.

Baudelaire, Charles. *The Painter of Modern Life.* Trans. P. E. Charvet. London: Penguin, 2010.

Berkeley, Grantley. *My Life and Recollections.* 4 vols. London: Hurst and Blackett, 1865–66.

Berns, Ute, ed. *The Ashgate Research Companion to Thomas Lovell Beddoes.* Abingdon: Routledge, 2016.

Blanchard, Samuel Laman. *The Life and Literary Remains of L.E.L.* 2 vols. London: Henry Colburn, 1841.

———. *Lyric Offerings.* London: William Harrison Ainsworth, 1828.

———. *Sketches from the Life by the Late Laman Blanchard.* London: Henry Colburn, 1846.

Blessington (Countess of), Marguerite. *The Idler in France.* Philadelphia: Carey and Hart, 1841.

———. *The Magic Lantern: or, Sketches of Scenes in the Metropolis.* London, 1823.

Braudy, Leo. *The Frenzy of Renown: Fame and Its History.* Oxford: Oxford University Press, 1986.

British and Foreign Anti-Slavery Reporter.

Brontë, Charlotte. *The Letters of Charlotte Brontë.* Ed. Margaret Smith. 3 vols. Oxford: Oxford University Press, 1995–2004.

Brontë, Emily. *Emily Brontë: The Complete Poems.* Ed. Janet Gezari. London: Penguin, 1992.

Brontë, Patrick. *The Letters of the Reverend Patrick Brontë.* Ed. Dudley Green. Stroud: Nonsuch, 2005.

Brooks, George E. *Western Africa and Cabo Verde, 1790s–1830s: Symbiosis of Slave and Legitimate Trades*. Bloomington, IN: AuthorHouse, 2010.

Bulwer (afterward Lytton), Edward. *The Last Days of Pompeii*. London: Richard Bentley, 1834.

———. *Pelham: or the Adventures of a Gentleman*. Leipzig: Tauchnitz, 1842.

———. 'Romance and Reality. By L.E.L.' *New Monthly Magazine* 32, no. 132 (December 1831): 545–51.

———. *Sketches from the Life by the Late Laman Blanchard*. London: Henry Colburn, 1846 (introductory memoir).

Bulwer Lytton, Rosina. *A Blighted Life*. London, 1880.

———. *Unpublished Letters of Lady Bulwer Lytton to A.E. Chalon*. London: Everleigh Nash, 1914.

Burton, Richard. *Wanderings in West Africa, from Liverpool to Fernando Po.* 2 vols. London: Tinsley Brothers, 1863.

Buxton, T. F. *The Africa Slave Trade and Its Remedy*. London: John Murray, 1840.

Byron, Lord. *Poetical Works of Lord Byron*. Ed. Ernest Hartley Coleridge. London: John Murray, 1904.

Carlyle, Thomas. *The Carlyle Letters Online*. Ed. Brent E. Kinser. Durham, NC: Duke University Press, 2007. http://carlyleletters.dukeupress.edu/.

Carnell, Jennifer. *The Literary Lives of Mary Elizabeth Braddon*. Sensation Press, 2000.

Chapple, John. *Elizabeth Gaskell: The Early Years*. Manchester: Manchester University Press, 1997.

Chorley, H. F. *Autobiography, Memoir and Letters*. London: Richard Bentley, 1873.

Clarke, Eleanor. *Jibber Jabber and Giffle Gaffle: A Collection of Salacious Slang and Popular Profanities Through the Ages*. Chichester: Summersdale, 2013.

Clarke, James Fernandez. *Autobiographical Recollections of the Medical Profession*. London: J. & A. Churchill, 1874.

Coleridge, S. T. *Collected Letters of Samuel Taylor Coleridge*. Oxford: Oxford University Press, 1956–59.

Comet, Noah. 'Letitia Landon and Romantic Hellenism.' *Wordsworth Circle* 37, no. 2 (Spring 2006): 76–80.

Cook, Jon. *Hazlitt in Love*. London: Short Books, 2007.

Craciun, Adriana. ' "Life Has One Vast Stern Likeness in Its Gloom": Letitia Landon's Philosophy of Decomposition.' In *Fatal Women of Romanticism*. Cambridge, UK: Cambridge University Press, 2003), pp. 195–250.

———. 'Romantic Satanism and the Rise of Nineteenth-Century Women's Poetry.' *New Literary History* 34, no. 4 (Autumn 2003): 699–721.

Creighton, Sean, ed. *North East Slavery and Abolition Group*, no. 5, February

2009 (e-newsletter), www.tyneandweararchives.org.uk/pdf/NESAG-News letter_5.pdf.

Croker, Crofton. *A Walk from London to Fulham*. London: William Tegg, 1860.

Cross, Nigel. *The Royal Literary Fund, 1790–1918*. London: World Microfilms Publications, 1984.

Cruickshank, Brodie. *Eighteen Years on the Gold Coast of Africa*. 2 vols. London: Hurst and Blackett, 1853.

Dagley, Richard, ed. *Death's doings: consisting of numerous original compositions, in verse and prose, the friendly contributions of various writers; principally intended as illustrations of thirty copperplates, designed and etched by R. Dagley*. 2nd ed. London: J. Andrews, 1827.

Dart, Gregory. *Metropolitan Art and Literature, 1810–1840: Cockney Adventures*. Cambridge, UK: Cambridge University Press, 2012.

David, Deirdre. *Fanny Kemble: A Performed Life*. Philadelphia: University of Pennsylvania Press, 2007.

Davies, James A. *John Forster: A Literary Life*. Totowa, NJ: Barnes and Noble, 1983.

De Quincey, Thomas. *De Quincey's Works*. Boston: James R. Osgood and Co., 1873.

De Staël, Germaine. *Corinne; or Italy*. Original French version, 1807; English translation by Isabel Hill 'with metrical versions of the odes by L.E.L.' London: Richard Bentley, 1838.

Devey, Louisa. *Letters of the Late Edward Bulwer, Lord Lytton, to His Wife*. New York: G. W. Dillingham, 1889.

———. *Life of Rosina Lady Lytton, with Numerous Extracts from her M.S. Autobiography and Other Original Documents, Published in Vindication of her Memory*. London: Swann Sonnenschein, 1887.

Dibert-Himes, Glenn. *Introductory Essay to the Work of Letitia Elizabeth Landon*. Online at the Corvey Project, Sheffield Hallam University: extra.shu.ac.uk/corvey/database/authors/datal/landon/ghdessay.htm.

Dickens, Charles. *A Charles Dickens Journal*. www.dickenslive.com.

———. *The Pickwick Papers*. London: Penguin Classics, 2003.

Disraeli, Benjamin. *Letters*. Ed. J. A. W. Gunn et al. Vol. 1 (1815–1834). Toronto, 1982.

Douglass, Paul. *Lady Caroline Lamb: A Biography*. New York and Basingstoke: Palgrave Macmillan, 2004.

Dowden, Wilfred S., ed. *Journal of Thomas Moore*. Cranberry, NJ, London, and Ontario: Associated University Presses, 1988.

Du Plessix Grey, Francine. *Madame de Staël: The First Modern Woman*. New York and London: Atlas and Co., 2008.

Earles, Melvin P. 'The Introduction of Hydrocyanic Acid into Medicine.' *Medical History* 11, issue 3 (July 1967).

Eden, Emily. *Up the Country: Letters Written to Her Sister from the Upper Provinces of India.* 1867; London: Virago, 1983.

Eger, Elizabeth, and Lucy Peltz, eds. *Brilliant Women: Eighteenth-Century Bluestockings.* London: National Portrait Gallery, 2008.

Elfenbein, Andrew. *Byron and the Victorians.* Cambridge, UK: Cambridge University Press, 1995.

Eliot, George (Mary Ann Evans). *Middlemarch.* Ed. W. J. Harvey. London: Penguin Classics, 1988.

Ellis, S. M. *A Mid-Victorian Pepys: The Letters and Memoirs of Sir William Hardman.* New York: George H. Doran Company, 1923.

Enfield, D. E. *L.E.L.: A Mystery of the Thirties.* London: Hogarth Press, 1928.

Esterhammer, Angela. 'Improvisational Aesthetics: Byron, the Shelley Circle and Tommaso Sgricci.' *Romanticism on the Net,* no. 43 (August 2006).

———. 'The Scandal of Sincerity: Wordsworth, Byron, Landon.' In *Romanticism, Sincerity, and Authenticity,* ed. Tim Milnes and Kerry Sinanan. New York: Palgrave Macmillan, 2010.

Farmer, Hugh. *A Regency Elopement.* London: Michael Joseph, 1969.

Findlen, Paula, et al., eds. *Italy's Eighteenth Century: Gender and Culture in the Age of the Grand Tour.* Stanford, CA: Stanford University Press, 2009.

Frisch, Walter, ed. *Schubert: Critical and Analytical Studies.* Lincoln: University of Nebraska Press, 1996.

Frost, Ginger. *Living in Sin: Cohabiting as Husband and Wife in Nineteenth-Century England.* Manchester: Manchester University Press, 2008.

Garofolo, Daniela. *Women, Love and Commodity Culture in British Romanticism.* Farnham: Ashgate, 2012.

Gittings, Robert, ed. *Letters of John Keats: A Selection.* 1970; Oxford: Oxford University Press, 1982.

Godwin, William. *Memoirs of the Author of A Vindication of the Rights of Woman.* London: J. Johnson, 1798.

Gorman, Michael. *The Life and Murder of Letitia Landon, a Flower of Loveliness.* London: Olympia, 2008.

Gosse, Edmund, ed. *The Poetical Works of Thomas Lovell Beddoes.* London: J. M. Dent, 1890.

Gramsci, Antonio. *Selections from the Prison Notebooks.* Ed. and trans. Quintin Hoare and Geoffrey Nowell-Smith. London: Lawrence and Wishart, 1971.

Grant, James. *The Great Metropolis.* London: Saunders and Otley, 1836.

Granville, A. B. *Historical and Practical Treatise on the Internal Use of the Hydrocyanic (Prussic) Acid.* 2nd ed. London: Longman, 1820.

Graves, Algernon. *The Royal Academy of Arts: A Complete Dictionary of Contributors*. London: Henry Graves and Co., 1906.

Graves, Robert. *Goodbye to All That and Other Great War Writings*. Manchester: Carcanet, 2008.

Green, Lawrence G. *White Man's Grave: The Story of the West Africa Coast*. London: Stanley Paul and Co. Ltd., 1954.

Greer, Germaine. *Slip-Shod Sibyls: Recognition, Rejection and the Woman Poet*. London: Viking, 1995.

Hall, Anna Maria. 'The Portraits of L.E.L.' *The Art-Union: A Monthly Journal of the Fine Arts* 1, no. 1 (February 1839).

———. *A Woman's Story*. 3 vols. London: Hurst and Blackett, 1857.

Hall, Catherine. *Macaulay and Son: Architects of Imperial Britain*. New Haven, CT: Yale University Press, 2012.

Hall, Catherine, et al. *Legacies of British Slave-Ownership: Colonial Slavery and the Formation of Victorian Britain*. Cambridge, UK: Cambridge University Press, 2014.

Hall, Samuel Carter. *The Book of Gems: The Modern Poets and Artists of Great Britain*. London: Whittaker and Co., 1838.

———. 'Memories of Authors of the Age: A Series of Written Portraits (from Personal Acquaintance) of Great Men and Women of the Epoch: Miss Landon.' *The Art-Journal* 4, no. 39 (March 1865).

———. *Retrospect of a Long Life from 1815 to 1883*. 2 vols. London: Richard Bentley, 1883.

———. *A Book of Memories of Great Men and Women of the Age from Personal Acquaintance*. 1871; London: Virtue and Co., 1877.

Harris, Katherine D. *Forget Me Not: The Rise of the British Literary Annual, 1823–1835*. Athens: Ohio University Press, 2015.

Hawthorne, Julian. *Hawthorne and His Circle*. New York: Harper and Brothers, 1903.

Hawthorne, Nathaniel. *The English Notebooks by Nathaniel Hawthorne, Based on the Original Manuscripts in the Pierpont Morgan Library*. Ed. Randall Stewart. New York: Modern Language Association of America, 1941.

Hayter, Alethea. 'The Laudanum Bottle Loomed Large: Opium in the English Literary World in the Nineteenth Century.' *Ariel* 11, no. 4 (1980).

Hazlitt, William. *Complete Works*. Ed. P. P. Howe. London: Dent, 1831–34.

Heath, John. *The Heath Family Engravers*. London: Scolar Press, 1993.

Heine, Heinriche. *Heinrich Heines Sämtliche Werke*. Ed. Ernst Elster. 7 vols. Leipzig and Vienna: Bibliographisches Institut, 1892.

Hemans, Felicia. *Works of Mrs Hemans*. Edinburgh: Blackwood, 1839.

Higgins, David. ' "Isn't She Painted *Con Amore?*" *Fraser's Magazine* and the Spectacle of Female Genius.' *Romanticism on the Net*, no. 46 (May 2007).

———. *Romantic Genius and the Literary Magazine: Biography, Celebrity, Politics.* London and New York: Routledge, 2005.

Highfill, Philip, et al. *A Biographical Dictionary of Actors, Actresses, Musicians, Dancers, Managers, and Other Stage Personnel in London, 1660–1800.* Vol. 2. Carbondale: Southern Illinois University Press, 1973.

Hilton, Boyd. *A Mad, Bad and Dangerous People: England 1783–1846.* Oxford: Oxford University Press, 2006.

Hogg, James. *The Collected Letters of James Hogg.* Ed. Gillian Hughes. Edinburgh: Edinburgh University Press, 2006.

Howitt, Margaret, ed. *Mary Howitt: An Autobiography.* Boston and New York: Houghton Mifflin, 1889.

Howitt, William. *Homes and Haunts of the Most Eminent British Poets.* New York: Harper Bros., 1847.

Hughes, Kathryn. *George Eliot: The Last Victorian.* London: Fourth Estate, 1998.

Hutchinson, Thomas J. *Impressions of Western Africa, with Remarks on the Diseases of the Climate and a Report on the Peculiarities of Trade up the Rivers in the Bight of Biafra.* London: Longman et al., 1858.

Huzzey, Richard. *Freedom Burning: Anti-Slavery and Empire in Victorian Britain.* Ithaca, NY: Cornell University Press, 2012.

Jackson, T. V. 'British Incomes Circa 1800.' *Economic History Review* 52, no. 2 (1999): 257.

Jenson, Deborah. *Trauma and Its Representations: The Social Life of Mimesis in Post-Revolutionary France.* Baltimore: Johns Hopkins University Press, 2001.

[Jerdan, William.] 'Memoir of L.E.L.' Introduction to one-volume posthumous edition of *Romance and Reality.* London: Bentley, 1848.

Jerdan, William *The Autobiography of William Jerdan.* 4 vols. London: Arthur Hall, Virtue and Co., 1852–53.

———. 'The Sleepless Woman.' In *The Club-Book, being original tales by various authors.* London: Cochrane and Pickersgill, 1831.

Jerrold, Blanchard, ed. *The Poetical Works of Laman Blanchard.* London: Chatto and Windus, 1876.

Jones, Adam, and Peter Sebald, *An African Family Archive.* Oxford: Oxford University Press, 2005.

Jones, Colin. *The Smile Revolution in Eighteenth Century Paris.* Oxford: Oxford University Press, 2014.

Keats, John. *The Complete Poems.* Ed. John Barnard. London: Penguin Classics, 1988.

Kelly, Linda. *Ireland's Minstrel: A Life of Tom Moore, Poet, Patriot and Byron's friend.* London: I. B. Taurus, 2006.

Kenealy, E. V. 'William Maginn, LLD.' *Dublin University Magazine,* no. 23 (June 1844).

Knapp, Bettina. *Marie Dorval: France's Theatrical Wonder*. Amsterdam and New York: Editions Rodopi, 2007.

Knowles, Claire. 'Celebrity, Femininity and Masquerade: Reading Letitia Landon's Romance and Reality.' *European Romantic Review* 23, no. 2 (2012): pp. 247–63.

————. 'Poetry, Fame and Scandal: The Cases of Byron and Landon.' *Literature Compass*. 4, no. 4 (2007): 1109–21.

————. *Sensibility and Female Poetic Tradition, 1780–1860: The Legacy of Charlotte Smith*. Farnham: Ashgate, 2009.

Kramer, Lawrence. 'The Schubert Lied: Romantic Form and Romantic Consciousness.' In *Schubert: Critical and Analytical Studies*, ed. Walter Frisch. Lincoln: University of Nebraska Press, 1996.

Landon, Michael. 'The Death of L.E.L.: A Retrospective Inquest.' *Women's Writing: The Elizabethan to Victorian Period* 16, no. 3 (2009): 445–51.

Landon, Whittington. *Ten Sermons Preached in the Parish Church of Tavistock*. London: J. G. & F. Rivington, 1835.

Latané, David E. *William Maginn and the British Press: A Critical Biography*. Farnham: Ashgate, 2013.

Law, Robin, ed. *From Slave Trade to Legitimate Commerce: The Commercial Transition in Nineteenth-Century West Africa*. Cambridge, UK: Cambridge University Press, 1995.

Lawford, Cynthia. 'Diary.' *London Review of Books* 22, no. 18 (September 21, 2000): 36–37.

————. Review of F. J. Sypher's *Letitia Elizabeth Landon: A Biography*. *Women's Writing* 18, no. 3 (2011): 444–47.

————. ' "Thou Shalt Bid Thy Fair Hands Rove": L.E.L.'s Wooing of Sex, Pain, Death and the Editor.' *Romanticism on the Net*, no. 29–30 (February–May 2003).

Leary, Patrick. '*Fraser's Magazine* and the Literary Life, 1830–1847.' *Victorian Periodicals Review* 27, no. 2 (Summer 1994): 105–26.

Le Fèvre-Deumier, Jules. *Célébrités anglaises*. Paris, 1895.

Leighton, Angela. *Victorian Women Poets: Writing Against the Heart*. Charlottesville: University of Virginia Press, 1992.

Lennox, Lord. *Celebrities I Have Known*. London, 1876.

L'Estrange, A. G. K. *The Life of Mary Russell Mitford*. New York: Harper and Bros., 1870.

Lewes, G. H., *Rose, Blanche and Violet*. London: Smith, Elder, 1848.

Linkin, Harriet Kramer, and Stephen C. Behrendt. *Romanticism and Women Poets: Opening the Doors of Reception*. Lexington: University Press of Kentucky, 1999.

The Literary Jordan. BL, General Reference Collection 1865.c.3 (166).

Lokke, Kari E. 'Woman and Fame: Germaine de Stael and Regency Women Writers.' *Keats-Shelley Journal* 55: Women Writers of the British Regency Period (2006): 73–79.

Low, Dennis. *The Literary Protégées of the Lake Poets*. Hampshire: Ashgate, 2006.

Lutz, Deborah. *The Dangerous Lover: Gothic Villains, Byronism and Nineteenth-Century Seduction Narrative*. Columbus: Ohio State University Press, 2006.

Lynn, Martin. *Commerce and Economic Change in West Africa: The Palm Oil Trade in the Nineteenth Century*. Cambridge, UK: Cambridge University Press, 1997.

MacCarthy, Fiona. *Byron: Life and Legend*. London: John Murray, 2002.

Mackenzie, R. Shelton. *Miscellaneous Writings of the Late Dr Maginn*, vol. 5: *The Fraserian Papers with a Life of Dr Maginn*. New York: Redfield, 1857.

Macready, William. *The Diaries of William Charles Macready*. Ed. William Toynbee. London: Chapman and Hall, 1912.

Madden, R. R. *The Literary Life and Correspondence of the Countess of Blessington*. London: T. C. Newby, 1855; New York: Harper and Bros., 1855.

Mahoney, Francis. *The Reliques of Father Prout, collected and arranged by Oliver Yorke Esq*. 1836; London, 1889.

Mandel, Oscar. *The Theatre of Don Juan: A Collection of Plays and Views, 1630–1963*. Lincoln: University of Nebraska Press, 1963.

Marchand, Leslie A., ed. *Byron's Letters and Journals*. Cambridge, MA: Harvard University Press, 1974–82.

Marleyn, Roland. 'The Poetic Ideal in Schiller's *Über naïve und sentimentalische Dichtung*.' *German Life and Letters* 9, issue 4 (1956).

Martineau, Harriet. *Autobiography, with memorials by Maria Weston Chapman*. London: Smith, Elder, 1877.

Mason, Nicholas. *Literary Advertising and the Shaping of British Romanticism*. Baltimore: Johns Hopkins University Press, 2013.

Matoff, Susan. *Conflicted Life: William Jerdan, 1782–1869*. Eastbourne: Sussex Academic Press, 2011.

Mayo, Thomas. *Elements of the Pathology of the Human Mind*. London: John Murray, 1838.

McGann, Jerome, and Daniel Reiss. *Letitia Elizabeth Landon: Selected Writings*. Peterborough, ON: Broadview, 1997.

Mellor, Anne K. *Romanticism and Gender*. New York: Routledge, 1993.

Mende, Fritz. *Heinrich Heine: Chronik seines Lebens und Werkes*. Berlin: Akademie-Verlag, 1974.

Metcalfe, G. E. *Maclean of the Gold Coast: The Life and Times of George Maclean, 1801–1847*. London and Accra: Oxford University Press, 1962.

Miller, Lucasta. *The Brontë Myth*. London: Jonathan Cape, 2001.

———. 'The Brontës and the Periodicals of the 1820s and 1830s.' In *A Com-*

panion to the Brontës, ed. Diane Long Hoeveler and Deborah Denenholz Morse. Oxford: Blackwell, 2016.

Mitchell, Leslie. *Bulwer Lytton: The Rise and Fall of a Victorian Man of Letters.* London and New York: Hambledon Continuum, 2003.

Moers, Ellen. *The Dandy: Brummell to Beerbohm.* New York: Viking, 1960.

———. *Literary Women.* London: Women's Press, 1978.

Mole, Tom, ed. *Romanticism and Celebrity Culture, 1750–1850.* Cambridge, UK: Cambridge University Press, 2012.

Montgomery, Robert. *The Age Reviewed: A Satire in Two Parts.* London: William Carpenter, 1827.

Montwieler, Katherine. 'Letitia Elizabeth Landon (1802–1838): Whose Poetess?' In *Biographical Misrepresentations of British Women Writers,* ed. B. Ayres. Palgrave Studies in Life-writing, DOI 10.1007/978-3-319-56750-1_6.

Moore, Thomas. *Lalla Rookh: An Oriental Romance.* London: Longman et al., 1817.

More, Hannah. *Moral Sketches of Prevailing Opinions and Manners.* London: T. Cadell and W. Davies, 1819.

Morrison, Lucy. 'Effusive Elegies or Catty Critic: Letitia Landon on Felicia Hemans.' *Romanticism and Victorianism on the Net,* no. 45 (February 2007).

Mortimer, Thomas. *Hypocrisy and Other Poems.* London: Hunt and Clarke, n.d.

Nemoianu, Virgil. *The Taming of Romanticism.* Cambridge, MA: Harvard University Press, 1984.

Newton Crosland, Mrs. *Landmarks of a Literary Life.* London, 1893.

North, Julian. *The Domestication of Genius.* Oxford: Oxford University Press, 2010.

Page, William. *A History of the County of Hertford.* London, 1908.

Patmore, P. G. *My Friends and Acquaintance.* London: Saunders and Otley, 1854.

Peakman, Julie. *Lascivious Bodies: A Sexual History of the Eighteenth Century.* London: Atlantic Books, 2004.

Peterson, Linda H. 'The Brontës' Way into Print.' In *The Brontës in Context,* ed. Marianne Thormahlen. Cambridge, UK: Cambridge University Press, 2012.

———. 'Rewriting A History of the Lyre: Letitia Landon, Elizabeth Barrett Browning and the (Re)Construction of the Nineteenth-Century Woman Poet.' In *Women's Poetry, Late Romantic to Late Victorian: Gender and Genre, 1830–1900,* ed. Isabel Armstrong and Virginia Blain. New York: Palgrave Macmillan, 1999.

Planché, J. R. *The Recollections and Reflections of J. R. Planché: A Professional Autobiography.* London: Tinsley Bros., 1872.

Poe, Edgar Allan. 'Review of New Books.' *Graham's Lady's and Gentleman's Magazine* (Philadelphia) 19, no. 2 (August 1841): 90–93.

Priestley, Margaret. *West African Trade and Coast Society: A Family Study*. Oxford: Oxford University Press, 1969.

Rappaport, J. 'Buyer Beware: The Gift Poetics of Letitia Elizabeth Landon.' *Nineteenth-Century Literature* 58, no. 4 (2004): 441–73.

Raymond, Meredith B., and Mary Rose Sullivan, eds. *The Letters of Elizabeth Barrett Browning to Mary Russell Mitford 1836–1854*. 3 vols. Waco, TX: Armstrong Browning Library of Baylor University, 1983.

Read, William. *Rouge et Noir*. London: Ollier, 1821.

Reiman, Donald H., and Michael O'Neil. *Percy Bysshe Shelley: Fair-Copy Manuscripts of Shelley's Poems in European and American Libraries*. New York: Garland, 1997.

Reiss, Daniel. 'Letitia Landon and the Dawn of English Post-Romanticism.' *Studies in English Literature 1500–1900* 36, no. 4 (Autumn 1996): 807–27.

Reynolds, Frederic Mansel, ed. *The Keepsake*. London: Hurst, Chance, 1831.

Roberts, Emma. *The Zenana and minor poems of L.E.L. with a Memoir by Emma Roberts*. London: Fisher, 1839.

Roe, Nicholas. *John Keats: A New Life*. New Haven, CT, and London: Yale University Press, 2012.

Rollins, Hyder Edward, ed. *The Keats Circle*. Cambridge, MA: Harvard University Press, 1965.

Rossetti, Christina. *The Poetical Works of Christina Georgina Rossetti*. Ed. Michael Rossetti. London: Macmillan, 1904.

Rowden, Frances Arabella. *The Pleasures of Friendship: A Poem in Two Parts*. 3rd ed. London: G. and W. B. Whittaker, 1818.

Rowton, Frederic. *The Female Poets of Great Britain*. 1848; Philadelphia: Henry C. Baird, 1854.

Russett, Margaret. *De Quincey's Romanticism: Canonical Minority and the Forms of Transmission*. Cambridge, UK: Cambridge University Press, 1997.

Ryan, Richard. *Poetry and Poets: being a collection of the choicest anecdotes relative to the poets of every age and nation. Together with specimens of their works and sketches of their biography*. London: Sherwood, Gilbert and Piper, 1826.

S.S. [Sarah Sheppard]. *Characteristics of the Genius and Writings of L.E.L.* London: Longman, 1841.

Sadleir, Michael. *Blessington-d'Orsay: A Masquerade*. London: Constable, 1933.

———. *Bulwer and His Wife: A Panorama*. London: Constable, 1933.

St Clair, William. *The Godwins and the Shelleys*. London: Faber, 1989.

———. *The Grand Slave Emporium: Cape Coast Castle and the British Slave Trade*. London: Profile, 2006.

———. *The Reading Nation in the Romantic Period*. Cambridge, UK: Cambridge University Press, 2004.

Saintsbury, George, ed. *The Paris Sketch Book and Art Criticisms*. Oxford: Oxford University Press, 1908.

Salmon, Richard. *The Formation of the Victorian Literary Profession*. Cambridge, UK: Cambridge University Press, 2013.

Sampson, Fiona. *In Search of Mary Shelley: The Girl Who Wrote Frankenstein*. London: Profile, 2018.

Scott, W. B. Introduction to *The Poetical Works of L.E.L.* London: George Routledge and Sons, 1873.

Shelley, Percy Bysshe. *Selected Poems and Prose*. Ed. Jack Donovan and Cian Duffy. London: Penguin Classics, 2016.

Shenai, Mary. *Finding the Bergheims of Belsize Court*. London: Belsize Conservation Area Advisory Committee, 2007.

Sherwood, Marika. *After Abolition: Britain and the Slave Trade Since 1807*. London: I. B. Tauris, 2007.

Southey, Robert. *Letters from England: by Don Manuel Alvarez Espriella*. London, 1807.

———. *A Vision of Judgement*. London: Longman et al., 1821.

Stabler, Jane. *The Artistry of Exile: Romantic and Victorian Writers in Italy*. Oxford: Oxford University Press, 2013.

Stephenson, Glennis. *Letitia Landon: The Woman Behind L.E.L.* Manchester: Manchester University Press, 1995.

Stoddard, R. H., ed. *Personal Reminiscences by Chorley, Planché and Young*. New York: Scribner, 1874.

Suckling, Alfred. *The History and Antiquities of the County of Suffolk*. Ipswich: W. S. Crowell, 1846.

Swinburne, A. C. *Lesbia Brandon*. London: Falcon Press, 1952.

———. *Swinburne's Collected Poetical Works*. London: William Heinemann, 1924.

Swindell, Kenneth, and Alieu Jeng. *Migrants, Credit and Climate: The Gambian Groundnut Trade*. Leiden: Brill, 2006.

Sypher, F. J. *Letitia Elizabeth Landon: A Biography*. Ann Arbor, MI: Scholars' Facsimiles and Reprints, 2004.

———. 'The Occultation of Letitia Elizabeth Landon.' www.cosmosclub.org/journals/1999/sypher.html.

———. *The View from Rose Cottage in 1818: William Jerdan and Letitia Landon at Old Brompton*. New York: The Grolier Club, 2011.

Tastu, Amable [pseudonym of Sabine Tastu née Voïart]. 'Une jeune poète anglaise.' *Revue des deux mondes*, vol. 6, May 15, 1832, pp. 404–18.

Thackeray, William Makepeace. *The Paris Sketch Book*. 1840; London: Smith, Elder, 1870.

Thomson, A. T. *The London Dispensatory: A Practical Synopsis of Materia Medica, Pharmacy and Therapeutics.* 5th ed. London, 1830.

[Thomson, Katherine.] 'Memorials of the Departed Great, by a Middle-Aged Man.' Published anonymously. *Bentley's Magazine*, vol. 17 (1845).

[Thomson, Katherine, with John C. Thomson.] *The Queens of Society.* Published under the pseudonyms Grace and Philip Wharton. 1860; London: Routledge, 1872.

Thompson, William. *An Inquiry into the Principles of the Distribution of Wealth Most Conducive to Human Happiness.* London: Longman, 1824.

Thormählen, Marianne. *The Brontës in Context.* Cambridge, UK: Cambridge University Press, 2012.

Tomalin, Claire. *The Invisible Woman.* London: Viking, 1990.

Toynbee, William, ed. *The Diaries of William Charles Macready, 1833–1852.* New York: Putnam's Sons, 1912.

Traill, Henry Duff, ed. *Works of Thomas Carlyle.* London: Chapman and Hall, 1899.

Trelawny, E. J. *Recollections of the Last Days of Shelley and Byron.* London: Edward Moxon, 1858.

Uglow, Jenny. *Elizabeth Gaskell: A Habit of Stories.* London: Faber, 1993.

Vincent, E. R. *Ugo Foscolo: An Italian in Regency England.* Cambridge, UK: Cambridge University Press, 1953.

Vincent, Patrick H. 'Lucretia Davidson in Europe: Female Elegy, Literary Transmission and the Figure of the Romantic Poetess.' *Romanticism on the Net*, no. 29–30 (February–May 2003).

———. *The Romantic Poetess: European Cultures, Politics and Gender, 1820–1840.* Durham: University of New Hampshire Press, 2004.

Vizetelly, Henry. *Glances Back Through Seventy Years: Autobiographical and Other Reminiscences.* 2 vols. London: Kegan, Paul et al., 1893.

Wakefield, Edward Gibbon. *Popular Politics.* London: Charles Knight, 1837.

Watt, Julie. *Poisoned Lives: The Regency Poet Letitia Elizabeth Landon (L.E.L.) and British Gold Coast Administrator George Maclean.* Eastbourne: Sussex Academic Press, 2010.

Watts, Alaric Alfred. *Alaric Watts: A Narrative of His Life.* London: Richard Bentley and Son, 1884.

Waugh, Norah. *The Cut of Women's Clothes, 1600–1930.* London: Faber, 1968.

Weis, René. *The Real Traviata: The Song of Marie Duplessis.* Oxford: Oxford University Press, 2015.

Wellesley Index to Victorian Periodicals, 1824–1900. Ed. W. E. Houghton et al. Toronto: University of Toronto Press; London: Routledge, 1966–90.

Whitley, William T. *Art of England 1821–1837.* Cambridge, UK: Cambridge University Press, 1930.

Wilson, Frances, ed. *Byromania: Portraits of the Artist in Nineteenth- and Twentieth-Century Culture*. Basingstoke: Macmillan, 1999.

————. *The Courtesan's Revenge: Harriette Wilson, the Woman Who Blackmailed the King*. London: Faber, 2003.

Winslow, Forbes. *The Anatomy of Suicide*. London: Henry Renshaw, 1840.

Wollstonecraft, Mary. *A Vindication of the Rights of Woman*. 1792; London: Penguin, 1986.

Woolf, Virginia. *Letters of Virginia Woolf*. Ed. Nigel Nicolson. London: Hogarth, 1978.

————. *Orlando: A Biography*. 1928; London: Penguin, 1963.

Wright, Donald R. *The World and a Very Small Place in Africa: A History of Globalisation in Niumi, the Gambia*. Abingdon: Routledge, 2015.

Wu, Duncan, ed. *A Companion to Romanticism*. Chichester: Wiley-Blackwell, 1999.

Young, G. M. *Victorian England: Portrait of an Age*. Oxford: Oxford University Press, 1936.

Index

Page numbers in *italics* refer to illustrations.

Text Illustrations

Insert Illustrations

7 bottom   Fiftieth Wedding Anniversary card for Mr and Mrs Samuel Carter Hall, 1874. © National Portrait Gallery, London

8   Letitia Landon, portrait by Daniel Maclise, 1833. © The Trustees of the British Museum

9 top left   John Forster, portrait by Daniel Maclise, 1830. © Victoria and Albert Museum, London

9 top right   Letitia Landon in equestrian dress, portrait by Daniel Maclise, undated. © Victoria and Albert Museum, London

9 bottom left   Self-portrait by Daniel Maclise, after 1829. Sotheby's, London

9 bottom right   William Maginn, portrait by Daniel Maclise, 1830. © National Portrait Gallery, London

10 top   *The Disenchantment of Bottom,* by Daniel Maclise, 1832. Wadsworth Atheneum, Hartford, Connecticut/Roy Miles Fine Paintings/Bridgeman Images

10 bottom   Henrietta Sykes and her family in medieval dress, portrait by Daniel Maclise, 1837. By courtesy of Sir John Sykes, BT

11 left   Governor George Maclean, portrait by an unknown artist, c. 1836–38. Private collection. Photo: Nick McGowan-Lowe

11 right   Silver centrepiece by Garrard's, commissioned for Governor Maclean, 1836. Private collection. Photo: Nick McGowan-Lowe

11 bottom   Cape Coast Castle, Ghana. Courtesy of the author

12 top   Letitia Landon, unfinished portrait by Thomas Sully, 1838. Private collection

12 bottom   Letitia Landon, plaster medallion by Henry Weekes. Private collection